CONSUMER CULTURE THEORY

RESEARCH IN CONSUMER BEHAVIOR

Series Editor: Russell W. Belk

Vols 1–10: Research in Consumer Behavior

RESEARCH IN CONSUMER BEHAVIOR VOLUME 11

CONSUMER CULTURE THEORY

EDITED BY

RUSSELL W. BELK
York University, Ontario, Canada

JOHN F. SHERRY, Jr.
University of Notre Dame, Indiana, USA

ELSEVIER
JAI

Amsterdam – Boston – Heidelberg – London – New York – Oxford
Paris – San Diego – San Francisco – Singapore – Sydney – Tokyo

JAI Press is an imprint of Elsevier

JAI Press is an imprint of Elsevier
Linacre House, Jordan Hill, Oxford OX2 8DP, UK
Radarweg 29, PO Box 211, 1000 AE Amsterdam, The Netherlands
525 B Street, Suite 1900, San Diego, CA 92101-4495, USA

First edition 2007

British Library Cataloguing in Publication Data
A catalogue record for this book is available from the British Library

ISBN: 978-0-7623-1446-1
ISSN: 0885-2111 (Series)

For information on all JAI Press publications
visit our website at books.elsevier.com

Printed and bound in the United Kingdom

07 08 09 10 11 10 9 8 7 6 5 4 3 2 1

CONTENTS

FESTIVITY

GLOBALITY

IDENTITY

ARTISTRY

COMMUNITY

POETRY

LIST OF CONTRIBUTORS

Anat Toder Alon	Boston University School of Management, Boston, MA, USA
Eric Arnould	Norton School of Family and Consumer Sciences, University of Arizona, Tucson, AZ, USA
Russell W. Belk	Schulich School of Business, York University, North York, Ontario M3J 1P3, Canada
Shona Bettany	University of Bradford School of Management, Bradford, UK
John D. Branch	Stephen M. Ross School of Business, University of Michigan, Ann Arbor, MI, USA
Kevin Browne	InterSource Research and Consulting, LLC, Cambridge, WI, USA
Frédéric F. Brunel	Boston University School of Management, Boston, MA, USA
Carolyn Costley	Waikato Management School, Department of Marketing, Hamilton, New Zealand
Carl Ebbers	Waikato Management School, Department of Marketing, Hamilton, New Zealand
A. Fuat Fırat	University of Texas-Pan American, Edinburg, TX, USA
Eileen Fischer	Schulich School of Business, York University, North York, Ontario, Canada

Lorraine Friend	Waikato Management School, Department of Marketing, Hamilton, New Zealand
Eugene Halton	Department of Sociology and Program in American Studies, University of Notre Dame, Notre Dame, IN, USA
Elizabeth C. Hirschman	School of Business, Rutgers University, New Brunswick, NJ, USA
Ann T. Jordan	College of Public Affairs and Community Service, University of North Texas, Denton, TX, USA
Robert V. Kozinets	Schulich School of Business, York University, North York, Ontario, Canada
Clinton D. Lanier, Jr.	Department of Marketing, College of Business Administration, University of Nebraska-Lincoln, NE, USA
Emily Meese	Waikato Management School, Department of Marketing, Hamilton, New Zealand
Jenny Mish	University of Utah, David Eccles School of Business, Salt Lake City, UT, USA
Cele C. Otnes	Department of Business Administration, University of Illinois at Urbana-Champaign, Champaign, IL 61820, USA
Nil Ozcaglar-Toulouse	Université de Lille 2, GERME research center, Lille, France
Donald Panther-Yates	DNA Consulting, Santa Fe, NM, USA
Marie-Agnès Parmentier	Schulich School of Business, York University, North York, Ontario, Canada
Joseph D. Rumbo	Department of Sociology and Anthropology, James Madison University, Harrisonburg, VA, USA

Hope Jensen Schau	Eller College of Management, The University of Arizona, Tucson, AZ, USA
John Schouten	Pamplin School of Business, University of Portland, Portland, OR, USA
Eliana N. Shapiro	Department of Advertising, University of Illinois at Urbana-Champaign, Urbana, IL, USA
John F. Sherry, Jr.	Department of Marketing, Mendoza School of Business, University of Notre Dame, Notre Dame, IN, USA
Katherine Sredl	Institute of Communications Research, Department of Advertising, University of Illinois at Urbana-Champaign, Urbana, IL, USA
Craig Thompson	University of Wisconsin, Madison, WI, USA
Kelly Tian	Department of Marketing, College of Business, New Mexico State University, Las Cruces, NM, USA
Li-Jen Wang	Waikato Management School, Department of Marketing, Hamilton, New Zealand
E. Taçlı Yazıcıoğlu	Istanbul Technical University, Maçka Istanbul, Turkey
Geroge Zinkhan	University of Georgia, Athens, GA, USA
Mohammadali Zolfagharian	Prior to August 2007 Department of Marketing and Logistics, University of North Texas, Denton, TX, USA From August 2007 Department of Management, Marketing and International Business College of Business Administration, University of Texas-Pan American, Edinburg, TX, USA

INTRODUCTION

This volume includes a selection from the papers, poems, and photo essays presented at the inaugural Conference on Consumer Culture Theory held in August 2006 on the campus of Notre Dame University. What we had hoped might become a regular conference to be held every two years, proved to be so popular that it is becoming an annual event. The second conference will take place in May 2007 at York University.

Consumer Culture Theory (CCT) is an interdisciplinary field that comprises macro, interpretive, and critical approaches to and perspectives on consumer behavior. Relative to its maturity and diffusion as a sphere of interest in the discipline of marketing, it has accounted for a disproportionate number of the prize-winning articles published in the flagship *Journal of Consumer Research*, and is increasingly represented in other top venues including the *Journal of Marketing*, the *Journal of Marketing Research*, and the *Journal of Retailing*. The number of social scientists outside of marketing who conduct CCT research is large and growing. These researchers may publish books in their home disciplines, and claim the pages not only of their own flagship journals but also in such specialized venues as the *Journal of Consumer Culture*, *Journal of Material Culture*, and *Consumption, Markets and Culture*. The enterprise is flourishing, and has reached the point where a regular research conference has become inevitable.

Several years ago, (and after innumerable corridor conversations at sister conferences) a strategy session with many of the thought leaders in the CCT area of marketing and consumer research was held at the University of Wisconsin, to help provoke the field's next stage of development. The group determined that one prudent course of action would be to launch an alternating series of meetings – one devoted exclusively to training, the other exclusively to research presentations – that would provide the impetus to future growth. With sponsorship from a number of sources (including the Marketing Science Institute and the Association for Consumer Research), the first Workshop on Qualitative Data Analysis was conducted at the University of Nebraska in 2005, under the able direction of Eric Arnould. This conference was devoted entirely to training doctoral students and junior faculty in the methods and analytics of CCT. The cognate conference held in August 2006 at Notre Dame was a celebration of substantive research by a multinational, multidisciplinary, multigenerational group of scholars and practitioners that seeks to contribute to theory.

Presenters at this conference hailed from over 40 universities, 12 countries, several corporations, and numerous disciplines. Forty-eight papers and four videos received spirited discussion that consistently ran overtime and spilled into the hallways, lunches, and dinners of the conference. Poetry was posted and a series of videos were shown continuously as well. Several communal meals provided a less formal opportunity to talk shop and plot more gatherings. From the feedback we received, participants were stimulated by some interesting new knowledge, some productive new ideas for future research, some solid new options for collaborative work, and an even greater enthusiasm for the prospects of our collective enterprise.

We are grateful to the more than 80 reviewers of the 100 submissions to the conference. We especially appreciate the service of Sandra Palmer, Administrative Assistant at Notre Dame, as well as Robert Drevs, Phillip Corporon, Caitlin Schaefer, and Corrine Palmer. For their support, financially and otherwise, we give thanks to Dean Carolyn Woo (Mendoza College of Business, University of Notre Dame) and Dean Jack Brittain and Bill Moore (David Eccles School of Business, University of Utah).

Russell W. Belk
John F. Sherry, Jr.
Editors

THEORY/AGENCY

CONSUMER CULTURE THEORY (AND WE REALLY MEAN *THEORETICS*): DILEMMAS AND OPPORTUNITIES POSED BY AN ACADEMIC BRANDING STRATEGY

Eric Arnould and Craig Thompson

The aim of this paper is to clarify and extend theoretical and institutional debates raised in Arnould and Thompson (2005) and subsequent discussions of consumer culture theory (CCT) in scholarly venues. Approximately two years ago, we published a synthesizing essay on the interdisciplinary stream of research that had followed in the 20 year wake of consumer research's interpretive turn (Sherry, 1991). Our review article pursued three not so hidden agendas. First, we wanted to provide a heuristic framework for mapping out this diverse body of research in terms of recurrent core theoretical concerns. We felt that this framework could be particularly helpful for Ph.D. students, who based on our experience, seemed to struggle with the contextual and topical diversity presented by this research tradition and to loose sight of the proverbial theoretical forest for the manifold particularities of context rich research. Second, we wanted to confront and refute a number of misconceptions that we felt held considerable sway in the broader marketing field, particularly among those not trained in this sphere

Consumer Culture Theory
Research in Consumer Behavior, Volume 11, 3–22

ISSN: 0885-2111/doi:10.1016/S0885-2111(06)11001-7

of cultural inquiry. Some of the most notable of these misconceptions included the idea that this research stream is defined by the use of qualitative methods; that its findings are context-bound and a-theoretical; and that it only investigates entertaining esoterica (i.e., the wild and wacky worlds of consumer oddballs) that lack practical relevance. Third, we (thinking as marketers) hoped to create an accessible brand name for this research tradition; one that rhetorically countered these misconceptions while circumventing some of the semantic dilemmas posed by other commonly employed classifications, such as interpretivist (all research is), qualitative (much of CCT is not), or postmodern (conceptual black hole).

We may recount some success on agenda items one and three, less on item two. We have been amazed at how quickly and widely this CCT framework has diffused through the consumer research and marketing fields. We have been gratified by the number of doctoral students (again one of our primary target audiences) who have told us how this paper and its heuristic framework have helped them to make sense of this research tradition and to position their own research. An unanticipated benefit reported by doctoral students is that the CCT framework proves useful in justifying their proposed dissertations topics and methods to skeptical faculty members. We have even heard from a number of researchers in other traditions that the CCT framework has instilled a greater appreciation and understanding of the intellectual contributions generated by this research stream. In more pragmatic terms, CCT is gaining disciplinary traction. The first annual CCT conference held on the University of Notre Dame campus (and co-chaired by Russ Belk and John Sherry) was a success in numbers and range of presentations; the CCT brand has become the institutional category used by the Association of Consumer Research (ACR) for tracking its doctoral symposium and conference program. More broadly, CCT has quickly become a recognized institutional category that represents one of the three major pillars of consumer research, along with information processing/BDT (behavioral decision theory) and econometric modeling (see Kahn, 2006).

As Foucault (1983) reminds, however, solutions to specific institutional dilemmas are never resolutions but rather reconfigurations that pose new problems and dangers. And so what are the dangers of and to the CCT brand? When we took CCT public at the 2004 North American and 2005 European Association for Consumer Research (EACR) conferences, many of our colleagues provided constructive feedback (and pushback) that pointed to some potential areas of concern. In this essay, we use these concerns as a rhetorical vehicle for elaborating (and hopefully) improving upon our initial framework and then to discuss some dilemmas related to the social reproduction of CCT within the American marketing academy.

ELABORATING ON CCT

Totalizing Narrative versus Pragmatic Compromise

At both ACR 2004 and EACR 2005, Richard Elliott and Fuat Firat queried the need for CCT, and the thrust of their concerns seemed to be concerns with imposing CCT as a totalizing narrative. The major instigator of this totalizing concern is probably the singularizing semantics of CCT we adopted, which can be read – despite our original emphasis on the internal diversity of its constituent research traditions – as a call for a unified body of theory that is grounded in a vernacular of normal science and its epistemic goal of making incremental contributions to a system of verified propositions (Kuhn, 1962). It is worth noting that, for better or worse, this normal science orientation and its quest for a unified theory is taken as a normative goal (not a threat) by consumer researchers who work outside the CCT tradition. CCT, however, has emerged in the liberatory glow of the sociology of scientific knowledge (LaTour, 1988), reflexive critiques of power relations that are encoded in scientific narratives hailing from feminist, poststructural, and postcolonial critiques (see Bristor & Fischer, 1993; Haraway, 1994; Rosaldo, 1993; Thompson, Stern, & Arnould, 1998), and marketing's positivist–relativist debates (Anderson, 1986; Hudson & Ozanne, 1988). All have significantly problematized conventional notions of objectivity and the modernist project of totalizing theorizations.

While our CCT framework embraces this poststructural epistemology, we also see a troubling parallel between the hyper-reflexive dialogues that occur in the CCT tradition and the political left that fragmented into an array of identity-politics factions after 1968. As Gitlin (1996) discusses, while these political factions debated among themselves and between themselves about whether they were sufficiently radical, the conservative movement (which had no qualms about acting on totalizing narratives) accomplished a significant power grab. In the context of consumer research and marketing, we feel that the CCT tradition faces an ongoing danger of institutional marginalization by virtue of its two-fold commitment to scientific reflexivity and questioning of the boundaries of scientific practice on the one hand (Belk & Kozinets, 2005; Sherry & Schouten, 2002), and its epistemological reticence to argue that its constituent studies are not just discrete, contextually bounded investigations but that they pursue and develop common theoretical threads that transcend contextual nuance, on the other.

Thus, one of our primary aims in choosing the CCT moniker was to call attention to these common theoretical concerns and, to explicitly create a semantic disruption to the "no theory" jeremiad that maintains currency in many other disciplinary quarters, despite a preponderance of published evidence to the contrary (see, e.g., Lehmann, 1999; Simonson, Carmon, Dhar, Drolet, & Nowlis, 2001).[1] Also, we sought a term that would communicate rather than obfuscate, particularly for those who are looking at this research tradition from an outsider perspective. In this vein, we are sensitive to the unremitting institutional condition (and *realpolitik* complexities) that many CCT researchers (with particular concerns for Ph.D. students and new assistant professors) seek jobs and tenure in marketing departments. Thus, social reproduction in the field necessitated that these marginalizing misperceptions be redressed and the disciplinary identity of the tradition seemed like a reasonable leverage point. We opted for the straightforward term CCT, which traded poststructural percipience for communicative clarity and inter-tribal accessibility.

At the time, we saw very little risk in this rhetorical move. We felt that those who read the article and/or had working knowledge of the research tradition that the "theory" was being used in a way that was inherently polysemic and in keeping with Richard Rorty's (1979) notion of theory as a conversational vernacular rather than a cumulative body of verified truths. In contrast, for those in the marketing field who rested content to judge CCT on the basis of peripheral cues, potentially triggering a misconception that CCT is a cumulative theoretical corpus (i.e., Big T theory) would constitute a pragmatic improvement over the prevailing misapprehensions.

One unfortunate consequence of our pragmatic branding strategy is a rash of papers, typically written by those fairly new to the research game, that position their respective studies as making a contribution to CCT. From our standpoint, CCT cannot be regarded as a unified system of theoretical propositions. Accordingly, one cannot make a global advance to the different domains of theoretical interests that organize this internally diversified literature, anymore than one could make a global advance in BDT. Our framework for mapping this diversity into four clusters of theoretical interest should be used as an orienting device and nothing more. For example, it can help a researcher to identify a subset of CCT research questions and findings that have the most relevance for his/her given study or reciprocally, to discern important questions, identify boundary conditions, re-think research contexts as venues for programmatic theoretical contribution rather than ends-in-themselves, and more broadly, to identify domains of theoretical concern that have not been addressed by prior CCT studies.

In hindsight, a more epistemologically appropriate term would have been consumer culture theoretics. This label would have better represented the theoretical, ontological, and epistemological heterogeneity that has contributed to this research stream; an eclecticism that is itself a unique byproduct of the contested and rather circuitous way that "alternative" research perspectives gain a foothold in the psychologically dominated field of consumer research. It might have signaled to international colleagues that North American researchers are sensitive to issues of scientific cultural imperialism. However, it would also have had the likely drawback of striking most readers in the marketing field, "who often adopt the anti-intellect pose of being the proverbial working class kid from Cincinnati," as yet another cryptic and self-marginalizing entry into the "postmodernist's" lingua obscura.

Exclusionary Categories versus a Dynamic Conceptual Map

Another concern is that this CCT framework could place limits on the scope of culturally oriented consumer research and exclude topics and theoretical orientations that do not fit into one of the four categories. As a practical matter, we think the odds of such a reified application becoming widespread are slim to null but it might be worth explaining the circumstances and constraints under which we developed these four domains of theoretical interest.[2]

In developing this framework, we applied the iterative interpretive process so common to cultural research to the task of essentially thematizing the CCT literature. Our classification framework is predominantly inductive and hence reflecting characteristics of CCT research to date. Each of the four categories highlights a recurrent theoretical motif that cuts across research context and particularistic research questions, creating conceptual family resemblances among different studies. For example, studies of brand communities (Muniz & O'Guinn, 2001) and subcultures of consumption (Schouten & McAlexander, 1995) both address the ways in which marketplace resources and shared consumer affinities organize collective meanings systems and identities while also respectively elaborating on different research questions: the creation of community in post-industrial society (Muniz & O'Guinn, 2001; Muniz & Schau, 2005) and the volitional construction of identity and the postmodern phenomenon of identity play and the emancipatory uses of consumption (Firat & Venkatesh, 1995; Schouten & McAlexander, 1995). Of course, studies of brand communities may now be deployed to examine issues of co-production and value creation in which brand communities become moderating or mediating elements rather than theoretical ends-in-themselves.

Our synthesizing approach was also informed by broader theoretical concerns that motivate consumption research in other branches of the social sciences. We wanted the CCT framework to facilitate interdisciplinary conversations and this necessitated that our mapping highlight points of common ground and theoretical tangencies between CCT studies – which reflect historical ties to the marketing field to varying degrees (e.g., brand communities, brand relationships, consumer preferences, servicescapes, lifestyle, advertising meanings, experience economy dynamics) – and consumption research where marketing constructs and vernacular are not germane to the discourse. The *sociohistoric patterning of consumption* aligns CCT with burgeoning sociological and historical research on the role of class, gender, and ethnicity as structural influences on marketplace behaviors (Cohen, 2003; Dávila, 2001; Fine & Leopold, 1993); *consumer identity projects* aligns CCT with the cultural studies focus on identity work and the negotiation of cultural contradictions (Giddens, 1991) through the marketplace (Illouz, 1997) and the commodification of cultural rituals and emotions (Schmidt, 1997); *marketplace cultures* aligns CCT with anthropological studies on material culture and the role of everyday rituals in creating social and familial solidarity (Miller, 1998, 2001); and *mass-mediated ideologies and consumers interpretive strategies* aligns CCT with critical theory tradition and more contemporary media studies research on the active and creative media user (see Fiske, 1994; Jenkins, 2006; Willis, 1990).

Poaching from Wilk (1995), we (re)characterize our CCT framework as a heuristic mapping of the *common structures of theoretical interest* that systematically link together studies that manifest diversity in terms of methodological orientations (i.e., ethnography, phenomenology, multiple schools of textual analyses, historical methods, web-based methods), theoretical traditions (variously drawing from sociology, anthropology, literary criticism, critical theory, and feminist studies to name a few) and, of course, substantive issues emanating from the particular research context.

While our thematic organization of the CCT literature has reasonable textual and theoretical grounding, it remains one of many other possible classification schemes and it is by no means meant to be definitive or exhaustive. In terms of the exclusion concern, however, we also note that these four domains of theoretical interest are, by design, broad and can be applied in a very flexible way that should be able to encompass a wide spectrum of theoretical questions and concerns. The key to this flexibility is that this mapping framework is not geared to any specific listing of topical concerns or methodological orientations. Thus, no topic or method is excluded nor is any one method or topic given a privileged point of inclusion.

Arnould and Thompson (2005) proposed that these four structures of common theoretical interest were interrelated and mutually implicative rather than being independent factors. As we noted in the original article, a given CCT study can potentially tap into all four of these domains (e.g., Holt, 1997) though more typically, one of perhaps two of these domains will be the primary focus with the other remaining background or tacit considerations. For example, Crockett and Wallendorf (2004) investigated the role that normative political ideologies play in shaping African–American consumers responses to attenuated grocery store access in their urban neighborhoods. Their analysis and theoretical explications were primarily directed toward questions related to *mass-mediated marketplace ideologies and consumers' interpretive strategies* and *the socio-historic patterning of consumption* (via socialization in class-based and racial histories). Yet, implications for consumer identity projects and marketplace cultures could easily be derived from their ethnographic insights but, given the theoretical framing of the study, these implications remain tacit.

Our original account could have better explained and represented these holistic connections among our four proposed structures of common theoretical interest. Toward that end, we offer Fig. 1 to redress this shortcoming. Arnould and Thompson (2005) discussed in reasonable detail the nexus of issues that are listed within each structural category but not interstitial linkages. Accordingly, our elaboration of this figure will focus on the theoretical concerns that are associated with the connecting arrows beginning at the bottom and working through it counterclockwise.

Ideological Shaping of Consumer Identity Goals and Desires

One defining characteristics of CCT research, particularly over the past 10 years, has been a dialogical view (Bakhtin, 1982) of the relationships between ideology and consumer agency. In other words, a number of studies have been able to jettison the stale polemic which on one side portrays consumer culture as a domain of ideological indoctrination and consumers as passive dupes of the capitalist culture industry and, on the other side, libertarian celebrations of consumer culture as a sphere of

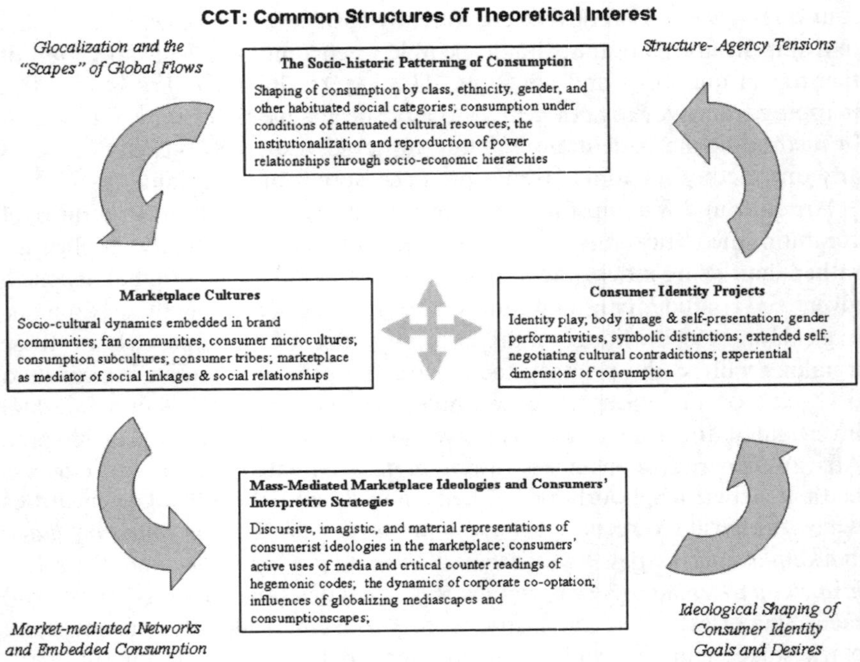

Fig. 1. CCT – Common Structures of Theoretical Interest.

symbolic choices that enables unfettered identity play and modes of self-creation. Rather, studies have interrogated a more complex and ambivalent dynamic in which consumers exert agency and pursue identity goals through a dialogue (both practical and narrative) with the cultural frames imposed by dominant ideologies (Askegaard, Arnould, & Kjeldgaard, 2005; Belk, Ger, & Askegaard, 2003; Crockett & Wallendorf, 2004; Holt, 2002; Kozinets, 2002; Peñaloza, 2001; Thompson, 2004). From this standpoint, one form of consumer agency is enacted through practices of re-scripting in which countervailing ideologies are leveraged to create an identity position that refuses a dominant institutional prescription, such as when the discourses and healing practices of holistic medicine are employed by consumers to contest their degenerative or pathologized medical identities (Thompson, 2004, 2005). In such case, agency is not an unconstrained expression of freedom from the logic of the marketplace, but an often contingent choice among competing ideological systems (and discourses of power).

Structure–Agency Tensions

This interstitial relation refers to issues of social reproduction and identity transformation. In other words, can individuals use consumer culture to transcend the internalized or habituated orientations that emanate from their socialization in class, gender, ethnicity, and other dimensions of social structuring? In parallel to the prior discussion of ideology and market-based emancipation, CCT research is seeking to push beyond the dichotomous opposition between sociological determinism and existential autonomy/authenticity (Sartre, 1956) or models of consumer which entail untenable and or culturally naïve models of sociological agency (Fuchs, 2001; Meyer & Jepperson, 2000; Swidler, 1986), in favor of more nuanced discussions of social reproduction.

These studies are not exploring reproduction in the sense of mechanical reproduction or genetic cloning (which would replicate exact copies of prevailing social conditions) but more in the sense of biological reproduction where genetic (i.e., contextual) fusions occur that create new and distinct identities that nonetheless bear family resemblances to their structural progenitors. Some of these studies highlight the creation of new hybrid identities, which still have to cope with vestiges of entrenched social and racial hierarchies (Kates, 2002; Peñaloza, 1994) while others highlight the ways in which consumers' conscious efforts to attain upward mobility and reconstruct their identities are subtly hindered and undermined by habituated (and institutionalized) class and gender stratifications (Allen, 2002; Üstuner & Holt, in press).

Glocalization and the "Scapes" of Global Flows

Glocalization refers to the interpenetration of globalizing structures, linked to the institutions of the global economy (such as the global diffusion of entertainment media and the marketing actions of transnational corporations), and local cultures and economies: intersections which tend to create heterogeneity rather the homogeneity (Robertson, 1992; Wilk, 1995). Appadurai (1990) has conceptualized these glocalizing dynamics as operating through a series of flows which are channeled through five dimensions – ethnoscapes, mediascapes, technoscapes, financscapes, and ideoscapes – and to which Ger and Belk (1996) have added a sixth integrative dimension: the consumptionscape which refers to localized patterns of consumption and their organizing systems of (emic) meanings.

Research on the dynamics of glocalization (which can be distinguished from cross-cultural research) has been gaining momentum in the CCT tradition and these new generation of studies has begun to explore much more specific tensions between local and global meanings systems and institutions. For example, Kjeldgaard and Askegaard (2006) investigate the ways in the glocalization of Greenlandic youth culture involves negotiations over not only the appropriation of global flows through the mediascape but also their marginalized ethnic identity in the Scandinavian region and their postcolonial relationships to Danish culture. Cayla and Peñaloza (n.d.) investigate the way in which learning cultural knowledge through narrative practices and within the constraints imposed by transnational organizational cultures impacts the ways in which managers socially construct local consumers.

Market-Mediated Networks and Embedded Consumption

This fourth interstitial linkage is one that has been intrinsic to a number of CCT studies but, only in recent years, have its implications become a primary point of concern as two important conceptual arguments gained currency within the CCT community: (1) a culture is best conceptualized as a dynamic network of boundary spanning connectivities (See Hannerz, 1992; Wilk, 2006) and (2) social actions are embedded in institutional structures and hence, social actors' rational calculations, emotional responses, reasoned preferences and choices, and performative scripts are fundamentally shaped by localized institutional influences (Granovetter, 1985).

In the vernacular of CCT studies, these twin conceptualizations translate into analyses that investigate the ways in which exchange networks mediate social relationships, performative identities, social practices, and consumer experiences. In these studies, exchanges (material, symbolic, instrumental, and agapic) are reconfigured in rhizomatic terms (Delueze & Guattari, 1987) that explode conventional notions of reciprocity and dyadic relationships.

Arnould (1989) is a harbinger of this network approach in his ethnography of preference formation and the diffusion of novel goods in Hausa village communities and their embeddedness in localized systems of status which were further embedded in the (postcolonial) structures both mythic and economic of center to periphery economic power relationships. More recently, Holt (2004) investigates the embeddedness of brand meanings, and more or less successful brand strategies, in what he refers to as myth markets: that is, constellations of icons and mythic stories that emerge around prominent cultural contradictions and that are still further embedded in broader national ideologies.

The emergence of this theoretical viewpoint in the CCT literature has been greatly facilitated by the digital revolution and the integration of the World Wide Web into everyday life. This now commonplace technology provides a potent praxeomorphic (Bauman, 2000) metaphor for conceptualizing a system of endless linkages and embedded structures. Not surprisingly, the web has provided a fertile context for studying consumption as an embedded phenomenon (Miller & Slater, 2000). Research on brand communities (Muniz & O'Guinn, 2001; Muniz & Schau, 2005) highlights the way in which technology and market structures facilitate new forms of communal organization and rituals of solidarity. Giesler (2006) provides an innovative re-conceptualization of gift giving practices that are embedded in the rhizomatic networks of cyberspace and that evinces a degree of plurality, geographic dispersion, and polyadic complexity that could not exist without the technological infrastructure of the digital age.

CCT AND THE COMPLEXITIES OF LEGITIMACY

Anyone who has attended any of the specialized conferences that have a high representation of CCT research has probably been in a session or conversation where a rather resigned and melancholy discourse takes hold lamenting CCTs marginalized status in the academic marketing field.[3] Not too long after these sentiments are expressed, however, other more optimistic members of the community will counter with a "stop feeling sorry for yourself" admonition and point out that CCT is now well-established in two of the four designated A-level marketing publications (the *Journal of Consumer Research* and the *Journal of Marketing*), plays a prominent role in the national conferences, and that many of its community members have chairs, sit on editorial boards, and otherwise hold positions of institutional authority.

This very debate arose in the opening "big picture session" of the first CCT conference, which provided the papers for this volume as the pessimistic and panglossian members recited their expected lines. In this recurrent dramatic enactment, a few important considerations tend be glossed over. First and foremost, institutional legitimacy is a multi-faceted and institutionally complex status game. Just as the achieved social status of a select subset of an ethnic minority does not refute the realities of institutionalized racism, the institutional success of some members of the CCT community does not necessarily mean that CCT researchers no longer have to grapple with marginalization problems. Another very important consideration is that success on certain institutional dimensions, namely publication in leading journals does not necessarily translate into forms of capital that can be exchanged for other kinds of institutional goods, such as job placements for new Ph.D.'s with CCT-oriented dissertations and envisioned research streams.

Straight to the point, we see this problem of initial placement as the most serious institutional problem confronting those in the CCT community. In the current market environment (and we believe these conditions have been in play for many years), CCT students have much less room for error in their market positioning than students working in more institutionally dominant arenas and their accomplishments need to be comparatively higher than their institutionally legitimated counterparts just to get into the consideration sets of many hiring institutions. This overcompensating model is a common economic survival strategy among marginalized social groups that assures if nothing else its brightest, hardest working, and importantly most adaptable and socially facile members will manage to in some sense get ahead. However, in recent years, there seems to have been some retrenchment in the American marketing academy that is undercutting even this tried and true survival strategy.

As a rough benchmarking exercise, we undertook an informal (and by no means definitive) survey of the representation of CCT-oriented and CCT-friendly faculty at the top 20 US marketing departments, as ranked by research productivity. CCT-oriented faculty refer to tenure track or tenured faculty whose primary research stream falls in the CCT tradition and who would professionally self-identify with this disciplinary area (though not necessarily embracing the "CCT" brand). Our tabulation also includes CCT-friendly faculty, whom we define as researchers who do not self-identify as CCT researchers but have demonstrable affinities for this research tradition and/or have collaborated with CCT researchers in joint projects. This category includes scholars such as Susan Douglas (New York University), Aric Rindfleisch (University of Wisconsin), Richard Late (University of Florida) and Debbie MacInnis (University of South Carolina). These CCT-friendly faculty have been scored as a 0.5 faculty representation in Table 1.

Based on our approximations, the CCT-oriented and CCT-friendly faculty constitute less than four percent of the total faculty at the top 20 US marketing departments where the mean number is less than one and the mode is 0. Given shifts in faculty and the prospect of our own inadvertent errors of omission or inclusion, we emphasize that our count is imprecise. Give or take a few faculty members our primary point remains: CCT researchers are a tiny minority at upper tier research schools. We also note that this problem of representation is particularly pointed at opinion leading and trend setting upper tier private schools. In the private school set, Morris Holbrook of

Table 1. CCT-Friendly Faculty in Top 20 US Research-Active Marketing Departments.

Institution	CCT-Oriented and CCT-Friendly Faculty	Total Tenured and Tenure Track Marketing Faculty	%
1. University of Pennsylvania	1.0*	26	3.85
2. University of Texas-Austin	0.0	16	0.00
3. Columbia University	1.0	16	6.25
4. Northwestern University	1.0	37	2.70
5. University of Florida	0.5	17	0.03
6. University of Wisconsin-Madison	2.5	12	20.83
7. New York University	0.5	23	2.17
8. University of Michigan	1.0	20	5.00
9. University of Minnesota	0.0	18	0.00
10. University of Southern California	0.5	19	2.63
11. UCLA	0.0	17	0.00
12. University of Chicago	0.0	21	0.00
13. Duke University	0.5	20	2.50
14. Indiana University	0.0	27	0.00
15. University of South Carolina	3.0	10	30.00
16. Texas A & M University	0.0	22	0.00
17. Stanford University	0.0	9	0.00
18. Arizona State University	1.0*	21	4.76
19. Penn State University	0.0	15	0.00
20. University of Arizona	3.0	14	21.40
Total	15.05	380	4.07
Mean	0.75	19	3.95
Mode	0		

*Cases where the department has no CCT-oriented faculty but it does have more than one CCT-friendly researcher.

Columbia and Kent Grayson of Northwestern are currently the only faculty members to have a research stream with a prominent CCT thread. The University of Pennsylvania's Wharton School has two faculty members who we classify as CCT-friendly (i.e., Americus Reed via co-authorship with David Wooten and Dawn Iacobucci who developed a cultural account of sacredness based on a hermeneutic reading of biblical text (Iacobucci, 2001). In terms of social reproduction, research profile, doctoral training, and intellectual culture, however, two friendly faculties offer less representation of the CCT tradition than would one dedicated member. We also note that the times have been different and better in the private school sector. Northwestern's Kellogg school has had noteworthy tradition of CCT-oriented faculty, including Sidney Levy, John Sherry, Robert Kozinets, and Kal Applbaum. Though not included in our Table 1, the Harvard Business School until recently has had a cadre of CCT-oriented researchers, including Susan Fournier, Grant McCracken, and Douglas Holt. However, these two private school clusters have, at least temporarily, fallen by the wayside as its key members have moved on to other institutions.[4]

Top notch students will understandably shy away from research areas that offer inherently constrained career opportunities and, over time, this institutionally conditioned brain drain will only reinforce biases against hiring. Even before this longer term consequence kicks in, the paucity of CCT faculty at leading institutions is creating immediate problems. These upper tier institutions are the opinion leaders and taste makers for much of the field and their students tend to flow to other upper tier institutions.

If this next generation of thought leaders has no direct exposure to CCT research, it becomes very easy for them to retain a provincial view of what counts as legitimate consumer research and, hence, perpetuates the hiring biases against CCT research into the indefinite future. Even if a given faculty collectively holds a fairly pluralistic view of consumer research, there is still likely to be a clannish or tribal aspect to hiring decisions. In other words, a group of econometric modelers or BDT researchers will simply feel stronger affinities for someone who shares common paradigmatic interests and training, and quite literally speaks their language. For CCT researchers to be placed at leading institutions, they also have to bridge a significant tribal chasm and a vast array of subtle judgments and biases that as Malcolm Gladwell (2005) notes happen unconsciously and in the blink of an eye.

To date, the CCT community has tried to redress and overcome these institutional barriers through contributions to social science knowledge and by showing how cultural perspectives can significantly advance core marketing concerns such as branding (Brown, Kozinets, & Sherry, 2003; Fournier, 1998; Holt, 2002; Kates, 2004; McAlexander, Schouten, & Koenig, 2002; Muniz & O'Guinn, 2001; Thompson, Rindfleisch, & Arsel, 2006) and customer satisfaction (Arnould & Price, 1993; Fournier & Mick, 1999). Unquestionably, CCT research has been impactful, garnering numerous awards, high citation rates, and crossing disciplinary boundaries. Yet, this academic push has not been able to "turn the dial" on institutional hiring preferences.

At the CCT conference, a number of potential strategies were suggested for changing this set of circumstances. Rob Kozinets suggested that it is time for CCT researchers to start thinking outside the academy, noting the burgeoning industry demand for anthropologically-oriented market research.

John Sherry noted that many academic opportunities lie outside the confines of business schools in marketing related areas such as consumer sciences and advertising departments. Eileen Fischer emphasized the need for students who are on the job market to position themselves around their substantive research areas rather than method or even the CCT brand. In other words, it is better to be classified as a person who studies brand relationships rather than someone who does "ethnography." Doug Holt has, in other forums, promoted the strategy of in effect doing an end run around congealed department structures: by taking cultural insights to industry and business leaders, market forces (i.e., corporate demand) will pressure Deans and thus departments to have more CCT representation in their faculty make-up. Research in transformative consumer research provides an opportunity for CCT scholars with a policy agenda like Ron Paul Hill and Julie Ozanne and their colleagues to link up with scholars from more traditional branches of the public policy area. Eric Arnould (this volume) proposes an alliance between CCT and strategy-oriented marketing scholars working with the emerging Service–Dominant Logic (S-D Logic) (Vargo & Lusch, 2004). The topic of co-participation and co-production of value is central to S-D Logic and a topic about which CCT has already produced significant insights.

Each of these proposed solutions to this social reproduction problem has merit and they point to a need for a multi-faceted strategy. It is the network model once again rearing its postmodern, googlelized head. We know from the biogeosphere that linkages are power and CCT researchers need to aggressively work on building greater and more diversified connections to industry, to other branches of the social science, to the marketing mainstream and social marketing networks. Our informal observation from more academic conferences than we care to remember is that paradigmatic groups do tend to socially cluster together. At ACR conferences, for example, distinct clans tend to move from the sessions that target their specific interests, to the coffee breaks and receptions (where the real intellectual and social work of conferencing occurs) to the evening festivities and late night socially lubricated conversations. This clannish homogeneity may be periodically punctured by interlopers from other groups but these are transitory disruptions.

Though communities are widely heralded, they also create boundaries and exclusion. The CCT community is tightly knit, as are the other paradigmatic communities in the consumer research field. Each of these communities provides emotional support, camaraderie, intellectual stimulation, and all forms of pragmatic benefits to their respective members. Each of us values these professional friendship networks and conferences are prime setting where these social connections can be renewed and deepened. On the other hand, these same bonding activities also create social distance between paradigmatic camps that are an impediment to creating a more pluralistic field.

We acknowledge that the extent of this communal/tribal segregation is not quite as stark as we portray it. However, we do feel that building strong linkages between CCT and other communities of researchers (as they exist in the marketing field) is an important strategy for improving placement prospects for our students. Borrowing from Bourdieu (1990), the CCT community has relied almost exclusively on culture capital, via publications, to make institutional inroads. Circumstances now dictate that we spend more time building our social capital within the field of marketing. This strategy, like all those listed above, bear the mark of institutional marginalization; in other words, those who are not benefiting from the dominant power structures are the ones who have to adapt and mobilize to change these aversive conditions. Some of our colleagues may see this stance as a form of self-marginalization but we believe it is more an acknowledgement of *realpolitik* institutional circumstances.

CONCLUSION

Our aims for this paper have been modest. First, we hoped to benchmark the brief recent history of the CCT initiative, marking success and remaining challenges. Second, we hope to offer both a theoretical and institutional clarification concerning the value of the CCT framework as an orienting heuristic for ongoing research. Finally, we sought to address concerns about the institutional reproduction of the family of CCT theoretical projects and the theorists themselves, and offer some suggestions for how this may be fostered in the coming years.

NOTES

1. In their otherwise pluralistic assessment of the state of consumer research, for example, Simonson et al. (2001) found it necessary to exclude "postmodern consumer" research from their continuum of theory development to theory application on the grounds that this research stream eschews explanation and managerial relevance in favor of poetic modes of representation, subjective relations to qualitative data, and an interest in unusual topics. While these conclusions are completely at odds with the revealed orientations of actual CCT studies, they do reflect some enduring disciplinary perceptions that were formed in the early and heated days of

the paradigm struggles of the mid to late 1980s. While the CCT tradition has advanced considerably since these formative struggles, broader disciplinary perceptions have remained wedded to these memorable moments of paradigmatic contestation.

2. Another aspect of this exclusionary concern lies in the fact that original review focused on research published in the *Journal of Consume Research*, which was an editorially imposed constraint we had to work under. Though we acknowledge that the published scope of CCT research extended well beyond the pages of JCR, the fact remains that our account did not specifically highlight the merits and contributions of studies appearing in other forums. On the other hand, our review suggested our orienting framework did effectively encompass the theoretical concerns advanced by this body of work. We suspect, however, that the *realpolitik* concern being expressed has to do with the relative lack of authors from non-US institutions that are published in the American marketing journals and certain understandable frustrations over the imperialist domination of the American institutions and publishing standards in the global field of academic marketing. The pitfalls of this Americanization to marketing thought and the CCT tradition are important matters that warrant further consideration.

3. Some of these conferences include the Bi-Annual Association for Consumer Research Conference on Gender, Marketing, and Consumer Behavior, the annual HCR event that precedes the ACR American and European/Pacific conferences, and now the annual CCT conference.

4. Outside of the United States, however, the representation of CCT researchers among marketing faculties is similar. Oxford (The Said Business School), The University of Southern Denmark, Bilkent University, The University of Exeter, York University, Bocconi School of Management, and ESCP-EAP are some of the schools that are developing culturally oriented marketing research and academic curriculum.

REFERENCES

Allen, D. (2002). Toward a theory of consumer choice as sociohistorically shaped practical experience: The Fits-Like-a-Glove (FLAG) framework. *Journal of Consumer Research*, *28*(March), 515–532.

Anderson, P. F. (1986). On method in consumer research: A critical relativist perspective. *Journal of Consumer Research*, *13*(September), 155–173.

Appadurai, A. (1990). Disjuncture and difference in the global cultural economy. *Theory, Culture and Society*, *7*, 295–310.

Arnould, E. J. (1989). Toward a broadened theory of preference formation and the diffusion of innovations: Cases from Zinder Province, Niger Republic. *Journal of Consumer Research*, *16*(September), 239–267.

Arnould, E. J., & Price, L. L. (1993). River magic: Extraordinary experience and the extended service encounter. *Journal of Consumer Research*, *20*(June), 24–45.

Arnould, E. J., & Thompson, C. J. (2005). Consumer culture theory (CCT): Twenty years of research. *Journal of Consumer Research*, *31*(March), 868–882.

Askegaard, S., Arnould, E. J., & Kjeldgaard, D. (2005). Post-assimilationist ethnic consumer research: Qualifications and extensions. *Journal of Consumer Research*, *31*(June), 160–171.

Bakhtin, M. M. (1982). *The dialogic imagination: Four essays*. Austin, TX: University of Texas Press Slavic Series.
Bauman, Z. (2000). *Liquid modernity*. New York: Polity.
Belk, R. W., Ger, G., & Askegaard, S. (2003). The fire of desire: A multi-site inquiry into consumer passion. *Journal of Consumer Research, 30*(December), 326–352.
Belk, R. W., & Kozinets, R. V. (2005). Videography in marketing and consumer research. *Qualitative Market Research: An International Journal, 8*(February), 128–141.
Bourdieu, P. (1990). *In other words: Essays toward a reflexive sociology*. Stanford, CA: Stanford University Press.
Bristor, J. M., & Fischer, E. (1993). Feminist thought: Implications for consumer research. *Journal of Consumer Research, 19*(March), 518–553.
Brown, S., Kozinets, R. V., & Sherry, J. F., Jr. (2003). Teaching old brands new tricks: Retro branding and the revival of brand meaning. *Journal of Marketing, 67*(July), 19–33.
Cayla, J., & Peñaloza, L. (n.d.). *Cross-cultural market learning*. Working paper. Sydney, AU: Australian Graduate School of Management.
Cohen, L. (2003). *A consumer's republic: The politics of mass consumption in postwar America*. New York: Knopf.
Crockett, D. X., & Wallendorf, M. (2004). The role of normative political ideology in consumer behavior. *Journal of Consumer Research, 31*(December), 511–528.
Dávila, A. (2001). *Latinos, Inc.: The marketing and making of a people*. Berkeley: University of California Press.
Delueze, G., & Guattari, F. (1987). *A thousand plateaus: Capitalism and schizophrenia*. Minneapolis, MN: University of Minnesota Press.
Fine, B., & Leopold, E. (1993). *The world of consumption*. London and New York: Routledge.
Firat, A. F., & Venkatesh, A. (1995). Liberatory postmodernism and the reenchantment of consumption. *Journal of Consumer Research, 22*(December), 239–267.
Fiske, J. (1994). *Media matters: Everyday culture and political change*. Minneapolis, MN: University of Minnesota Press.
Foucault, M. (1983). On the genealogy of ethics: An overview of work in progress. In: M. Foucault (Ed.), *Beyond structuralism and hermeneutics* (pp. 229–252). Chicago, IL: University of Chicago Press.
Fournier, S. (1998). Consumers and their brands: Developing relationship theory in consumer research. *Journal of Consumer Research, 24*(March), 343–373.
Fournier, S., & Mick, D. G. (1999). Rediscovering satisfaction. *Journal of Marketing, 63* (October), 5–23.
Fuchs, S. (2001). Beyond agency. *Sociological Theory, 19*, 24–40.
Ger, G., & Belk, R. W. (1996). I'd like to buy the world a coke: Consumptionscapes of the 'Less Affluent World'. *Journal of Consumer Policy, 19*(3), 271–304.
Giddens, A. (1991). *Modernity and self-identity: Self and society in the late modern age*. Stanford, CA: Stanford University Press.
Giesler, M. (2006). Consumer gift systems. *Journal of Consumer Research, 33*(September), 283–290.
Gitlin, T. (1996). *The twilight of common dreams: Why America is wracked by culture wars*. New York: Owl Press.
Gladwell, M. (2005). *Blink: The power of thinking without thinking*. New York: Little, Brown, & Company.

Granovetter, M. (1985). Economic action and social structure: The problem of embeddedness. *American Journal of Sociology*, *91*(November), 481–510.

Hannerz, U. (1992). *Cultural complexity*. New York: University of Columbia Press.

Haraway, D. (1994). A manifesto for cyborgs: Science, technology, and socialist feminism in the 1980's. In: S. Seidman (Ed.), *The postmodern turn: New perspectives on social theory* (pp. 82–115). New York, NY: Cambridge University Press.

Holt, D. B. (1997). Poststructuralist lifestyle analysis: Conceptualizing the social patterning of consumption. *Journal of Consumer Research*, *23*(March), 326–350.

Holt, D. B. (2002). Why do brands cause trouble? A dialectical theory of consumer culture and branding. *Journal of Consumer Research*, *29*(June), 70–90.

Holt, D. B. (2004). *How brands become icons: The principles of cultural branding*. Boston, MA: Harvard Business School Press.

Hudson, L. A., & Ozanne, J. L. (1988). Alternative ways of seeking knowledge in consumer research. *Journal of Consumer Research*, *14*(March), 508–521.

Iacobucci, D. (2001). Commonalities between research methods for consumer science and biblical scholarship. *Marketing Theory*, *1*(1), 109–133.

Illouz, E. (1997). *Consuming the romantic utopia: The love and the cultural contradictions of capitalism*. Berkeley, CA: University of California Press.

Jenkins, H. (2006). *Convergence culture*. New York, NY: New York University Press.

Kahn, B. (2006). Moving the needle: Can ACR help increase our research productivity. Association for Consumer Research Presidential Address, Orlando, FL. Retrieved from http://www.acrwebsite.org/topic.asp?artid = 378

Kates, S. (2004). The dynamics of brand legitimacy: An interpretive study in the gay men's community. *Journal of Consumer Research*, *31*(September), 455–464.

Kates, S. M. (2002). The protean quality of subcultural consumption: An ethnographic account of gay consumers. *Journal of Consumer Research*, *29*(December), 383–399.

Kjeldgaard, D., & Askegaard, S. (2006). The glocalization of youth culture: The global youth segment as structures of common difference. *Journal of Consumer Research*, *33* (September), 231–247.

Kozinets, R. V. (2002). Can consumers escape the market?: Emancipatory illuminations from burning man. *Journal of Consumer Research*, *29*(June), 20–38.

Kuhn, T. (1962). *The structure of scientific revolutions*. Chicago, IL: University of Chicago Press.

LaTour, B. (1988). *Science in action: How to follow scientists and engineers through society*. Cambridge, MA: Harvard University Press.

Lehmann, D. R. (1999). Introduction: Consumer behavior and Y2K. *Journal of Marketing*, *63*(Special Issue), 14–18.

McAlexander, J. H., Schouten, J. W., & Koenig, H. F. (2002). Building brand community. *Journal of Marketing*, *66*(January), 38–54.

Meyer, J. W., & Jepperson, R. L. (2000). The 'Actors' of modern society: The cultural construction of social agency. *Sociological Theory*, *181*(March), 100–120.

Miller, D. (1998). *A theory of shopping*. Ithaca: Cornell University Press.

Miller, D. (Ed.) (2001). *Car cultures*. Oxford: Berg.

Miller, D., & Slater, D. (2000). *The Internet: An ethnographic approach*. Oxford: Berg.

Muniz, A., & O'Guinn, T. C. (2001). Brand communities. *Journal of Consumer Research*, *27*(March), 412–432.

Muniz, A. M., & Schau, H. J. (2005). Religiosity in the abandoned apple Newton brand community. *Journal of Consumer Research, 31*(March), 737–747.
Peñaloza, L. (1994). Atravesando fronteras/Border crossings: A critical ethnographic study of the consumer acculturation of Mexican immigrants. *Journal of Consumer Research, 21*(June), 32–53.
Peñaloza, L. (2001). Consuming the American west: Animating cultural meaning at a stock show and rodeo. *Journal of Consumer Research, 28*(December), 369–398.
Robertson, R. (1992). *Globalization: Social theory and global culture*. London: Sage.
Rorty, R. (1979). *Philosophy and the mirror of nature*. Princeton, NJ: Princeton University Press.
Rosaldo, R. (1993). *Culture & truth: The remaking of social analysis*. Boston, MA: Beacon.
Sartre, J. P. (1956). *Being and nothingness*. New York: Washington Square Press.
Schmidt, L. E. (1997). *Consumer rites: The buying and selling of American holidays*. Princeton, NJ: Princeton University Press.
Schouten, J., & McAlexander, J. H. (1995). Subcultures of consumption: An ethnography of the new bikers. *Journal of Consumer Research, 22*(June), 43–61.
Sherry, J. (1991). Postmodern alternatives: The interpretive turn in consumer research. In: T. S. Robertson & H. H. Kassarjian (Eds), *Handbook of consumer research* (pp. 548–591). Englewood Cliffs, NJ: Prentice Hall.
Sherry, J. F., Jr., & Schouten, J. W. (2002). A role for poetry in consumer research. *Journal of Consumer Research, 29*(September), 218–234.
Simonson, I., Carmon, Z., Dhar, R., Drolet, A., & Nowlis, S. M. (2001). Consumer research: In search of identity. In: S. T. Fiske, D. L. Schacter & C. Zahn-Waxler (Eds), *Annual review of psychology*, (Vol. 52, pp. 249–275). Palo Alto, CA: Annual Reviews.
Swidler, A. (1986). Culture in action: Symbols and strategies. *American Sociological Review, 51*(2), 273–286.
Thompson, C. J. (2004). Marketplace mythologies and discourses of power. *Journal of Consumer Research, 31*(June), 162–180.
Thompson, C. J. (2005). Consumer risk perceptions in a community of reflexive doubt. *Journal of Consumer Research, 32*(September), 235–248.
Thompson, C. J., Rindfleisch, A., & Arsel, Z. (2006). Emotional branding and the strategic value of the Doppelgänger brand image. *Journal of Marketing, 70*(January), 50–64.
Thompson, C. J., Stern, B., & Arnould, E. (1998). Writing the differences: Poststructural pluralism, retextualization, and the construction of reflexive ethnographic narratives in consumer research. *Consumption, Markets, and Culture, 2*(September), 105–160.
Üstuner, T., & Holt, D. B. (in press) Dominated consumer acculturation: The social construction of poor migrant women's consumer identity projects in a Turkish squatter. *Journal of Consumer Research, 34* (June).
Vargo, S. L., & Lusch, R. F. (2004). Evolving toward a new dominant logic for marketing. *Journal of Marketing, 68*(January), 1–17.
Willis, P. (1990). *Common culture: Symbolic work at play in the everyday cultures of the young*. Milton Keynes: Open University Press.
Wilk, R. (1995). Learning to be local in Belize: Global systems of common difference. In: D. Miller (Ed.), *Worlds apart: Modernity through the prism of the local* (pp. 110–131). London, UK: Routledge.
Wilk, R. (2006). *Home cooking in the global village: Caribbean food from buccaneers to ecotourists*. Oxford: Berg Publishers.

WORKING TO CONSUME THE MODEL LIFE: CONSUMER AGENCY UNDER SCARCITY

Marie-Agnès Parmentier and Eileen Fischer

ABSTRACT

Prior research on consumer agency has tended to focus on contexts where there are few restrictions on the type or number of people who can consume a desired object, provided they have adequate resources. This study develops theoretical insights into the modes of consumer agency adopted by consumers who desire a commodity that is in scarce supply, and to which access is restricted by powerful agents. Based on interviews and archival data from the fashion modeling industry, and drawing on Bourdieu's praxeology, this paper identifies distinct modes of consumer agency that are manifest in a context characterized by enforced scarcity. Depending in part upon initial human capital endowments, in part upon conditions in the field, and in part upon deliberate choices, models adopt different modes of agency in order to survive, thrive in a highly restricted aesthetic field and ultimately consume the coveted good, which we refer to as the "model life." This paper thus contributes not only to our understanding of consumer agency in an under-studied type of context, but also to our understanding of the seemingly burgeoning phenomena of the quest for fame, celebrity, and status.

Consumer Culture Theory
Research in Consumer Behavior, Volume 11, 23–39

ISSN: 0885-2111/doi:10.1016/S0885-2111(06)11002-9

INTRODUCTION

Consumer agency is a topic that has attracted considerable recent interest (Kozinets et al., 2004; Thompson, 2004, 2005). To date, however, little attention has been given to how consumers exert agency when they seek to attain a commodity that is in scarce supply and to which access is limited by powerful agents. This omission is significant since the modes of agency pursued by consumers in such markets are likely to be distinct from those observed in contexts where there is plenty of what consumers desire, and where the interests of marketers are served by having many people consume a good. Moreover, restricted access is characteristic of markets for some of those commodities most valued by consumers, such as educational opportunities, careers, and lifestyles.

In this paper, we follow Thompson's (2004) suggestion that we should study how power relationships operate and shift through institutional discourses and practices. We examine a context, the field of fashion modeling, that constitutes a setting where individuals pursue an extremely coveted outcome, the "model life," a term we coin to refer to becoming a member of a small, elite group of models whose bodies and personae are intensely sought after for their aesthetic singularity, and who reap culturally celebrated rewards such as money, luxurious goods, and celebrity status. The modes of agency that would-be models adopt in the face of restricted access to this coveted thing are the central focus of this research project.

This paper is organized as follows: after briefly reviewing relevant literature on consumer agency and our methodology, we describe the field of fashion modeling. We then report on our findings in regard to the different modes of consumer agency practiced by models. Finally, we discuss the implications of this research for theory regarding consumer agency.

CONSUMER AGENCY

Consumer agency has been theorized in contexts where resources are plentiful and access relatively easy. Most notably, Kozinets et al.'s (2004) study of ludic agency in a spectacularized retail setting shows how consumption is negotiated between consumers and producers when their respective interests are mutually served by agentic consumers. These insightful findings fit within the tradition of thought exemplified by Holt (2002) and others (e.g. Prahalad, 2004) that argues that markets thrive on nonconformist producerly consumption practices. Such thinking meshes well with what Vargo and

Lusch (2004) refer to as marketing's new "dominant logic." This logic venerates concepts such as co-creation and co-production: it emphasizes that (co) producerly consumers' input is crucial for market innovation and commercial success. An unexamined assumption can be discerned in this line of thought, however. It is that marketers flourish by accommodating the needs and wants of an ever-greater number of co-producing consumers, whose variety offers marketers new insights and learning opportunities.

In markets where individuals *compete* for the opportunity to co-produce commodities because the supply is restricted, the power dynamic between those who seek to consume that which they desire and those who control access to the desired commodity, may create a somewhat distinctive "logic." Positions in prestigious universities, elite sports teams, and haute monde fashion modeling are examples of consumption objects that are coveted but scarce. In each case, powerful agents determine who gains access, and have considerable influence over what constitutes effective co-production. Such social spaces are structured by rules that typically favor powerful agents and by struggles for control over economic, cultural, social and symbolic capital (Bourdieu, 1990a). In such contexts, barriers to becoming a consumer are complex, and maintaining agency whilst co-producing requires the navigation of a complex and shifting terrain.

The fashion modeling field proves to be an interesting setting for studying consumer agency under such conditions. In modeling, many are called, few are chosen, and even fewer end up consuming the model life they initially desired. We thus ask: How do consumers exhibit agency in contexts where there is controlled access to a scarce and coveted good? Is conforming to the rules of the game the only option? We now describe the methodology used to address these questions.

METHODOLOGY

Overview

Given that a chosen context of investigation must provide one or more conceptual contrasts with contexts in which extant theory has been built or tested (Price, Arnould, & Mosio, in press), our choice of the fashion modeling field rests first and foremost on the fact that, as argued above, it contrasts with other consumer agency research contexts. Our investigation of this phenomenon took the shape of a field analysis where: (1) we conducted, audio-taped, and transcribed 13 in-depth interviews (McCracken, 1988) with models and other figures such as photographers, agents, an advertising client, and a stylist; (2) we reviewed several sources of archival data (e.g., books and articles from magazines, newspapers, and academic journals, television footage, films, websites about the industry and/or models, as well as electronic archives of fashion magazines); and finally, (3) we took into account the experience of the first author who worked as model in her teenage years. This extensive data enabled us to map out the terrain quite thoroughly and ultimately contributed to our understanding of the rules of the game and of the power struggles. The appendix summarizes informants' characteristics.

Bourdieu's Praxeology and Data Analysis

The process of assessing the "fit" of existing consumer agency theory to the context under investigation led us to the insight that Bourdieu's (Bourdieu, 1984, 1993) praxeology offered a theoretical lens that would enhance our understanding of the phenomenon. It is likely that Bourdieu would have considered modeling a subset of a field of cultural production. By "field", Bourdieu meant a symbolic space, including a network of social relations, and a structured system of social positions within which there are struggles over resources, stakes, access, and above all power, symbolic as well as economic. For him, fields of cultural production could be characterized by the struggle between dominating and dominated actors, and new entrants, or *parvenus,* who do not possess much specific capital. The struggle for power between actors can restructure both, which counts as capital in the field, and "rules" that actors take for granted in terms of what is appropriate and inappropriate action. The structures of the field and the rules of the game remain stable only as long as all actors involved endorse and carry out the game and its rules.

The field of fashion modeling can be conceptualized as an element of the larger field of fashion. Fashion can be interpreted as a code that allows for social distinction and activates forces of differentiation in terms of taste, social identity, and cultural capital. In this sense, Finkelstein (1998, p. 80) notes that "fashion is an organization of knowledge based on restricted access to goods and services", and that the ability to recognize the fashionable reflects an actor's cultural capital. For instance, in a study of the male fashion modeling field Entwistle (2002) shows how modeling agents' abilities to distinguish a valued look (the model) within the field depends mostly on the agent's habitus and "aesthetic sensibilities and cultural capital, as well as the social, cultural, and institutional connections and relationships which sustain them" (p. 338). In this field, powerful actors strive to maintain their influence over tastes and over the means by which subordinate actors (models) take advantage of their aesthetic capital. Informed by Bourdieu's theoretical insights regarding the dynamics of fields of cultural production, the next section presents our overview of the modeling field.

THE FIELD OF FASHION MODELING

The contemporary fashion modeling field is comprised of an international network of relationships between various mutually dependent, but unequally powerful, sets of actors. Relative to the models themselves, among the most powerful actors in the field are: modeling agencies; fashion designers; photographers and their clients; and the fashion press. Typically less powerful players include the hair, makeup, and clothing stylists/artists employed for the various photo shoots and fashion shows. In the following paragraphs, a brief account of the more powerful actors is provided.

The most prestigious *modeling agencies* are based in fashion capitals of the world, i.e. New York, Paris, London, and Milan. These agencies have branches in various influential cities around the world (e.g., Tokyo, Berlin, Montreal), and there are many regional "feeder" agencies in these centers as well. Agents help to provide the industry with a constant supply of fresh faces, sending scouts to seek talent both in formal venues and informal hunting grounds ranging from schools to shopping malls.

Most models are represented by a "mother agency" that helps them to get work in certain geographic markets and provides them with a connection to allied agencies in other geographical markets. In general, agencies, in exchange for a percentage of the model's earnings, help models to build up a portfolio of images and gain editorial and/or commercial contracts. The distinction between commercial and editorial work is crucial. Commercial refers to modeling for catalogs, department stores, and to promote products ranging from detergent to chewing gum; it can be very lucrative but is not considered prestigious by those within the field. Editorial refers to being featured on the cover of or inside the fashion pages of high fashion magazines including *Elle*, *Vogue*, and *Harper's Bazaar*. It also refers to modeling for couturiers' and designers' fashion shows and being featured in their campaigns. Editorial work is considered extremely prestigious but is not necessarily very lucrative in itself. Posing for the cover of *Vogue* earns about

$400US while being featured in a luxurious designer product can bring in several thousands of dollars.

Designers have been among the most influential actors within the field of modeling since its inception. Designers' tastes have dictated who was and who was not an acceptable potential model. For example, aesthetic preferences were profoundly altered in the 1940s by Christian Dior when he launched "The New Look" in his Paris *salon*. His style was immediately identified with wealth and distinction, and required elegant looking woman in their mid-30s. Soon, all the top models looked like Dior's standard type: haughty eyebrows and glossy groomed hair. In the late 1950s, as the ready-to-wear industry was becoming important, and the middle class woman became the target, Dior's sense of the ideal image changed. He hired a dark, petite and inexperienced model called Victoire. Dior established Victoire's body as the aesthetic symbol of the times. This process continues into the present. As recently as the mid-1990s, designers switched from choosing tall, blond "Amazonian" models, to feature their fashions, to short, darker, more gamine, or boyish looking models (Singer, 2004).

Photographers are a third group, which had and has profound influence in the field of modeling. Photographers not only influence which models are given the opportunity to compete for lucrative opportunities with commercial clients, but also contribute to the creation of the model's aesthetic impact. The artistry of the photographer contributes immeasurably to the ways models are perceived by designers, agents, clients, and the fashion press. Celebrity photographers, such as Peter Lindbergh and later Steven Meisel, are regarded as the "emperors" of fashion image making (The Fashion Book, 2004).

The *fashion press* itself constitutes another group with considerable power in the field under consideration. While much influenced by photographers, it is they who choose which faces will grace the covers and the editorial pages of the most prominent fashion magazines. The fashion press, which must ensure that their magazines are attractive to the middle class buyers of their advertisers' products, exercise aesthetic judgments that may coincide with or differ from those of the designers of haute couture; their tastes too matter to which models are considered to have the right look at any given point in time. For example, in the 1960s, younger and younger women – girls – were considered by the fashion press to embody the less aloof and sophisticated, more relaxed and friendly images thought to appeal to the middle class. Fashion magazines such as *Vogue* responded to these influences by featuring ever-younger faces on their front covers.

Strategic decisions taken by the fashion press have also helped models as a group to gain, and later lose, power in the field. For example, during the 1960s, editors began to feature models' faces, rather than designers' clothes, on the front pages of their magazines. This gave models as a group, and the models who were favored by fashion editors in particular, a level of public visibility hitherto unprecedented. Further, during the same period, a war for exclusivity of faces began between the two New York powerhouse magazines: American *Vogue* and *Harper's Bazaar.* With fashion magazines competing for exclusivity, models were able to command significantly greater fees (Bailey, 1998). Much more recently, fashion editors have taken decisions that may ultimately reduce the power of models in the field. Specifically, for approximately the last five years, fashion editors in North America have frequently chosen to feature actresses rather than models' faces on their front covers. Doubtlessly, a decision motivated by the fashion editors' desires to gain sales, this move has reduced one important opportunity for models to gain the attention of the wider public, and may thus impact the fees they can command.

In fashion modeling, as in other fields, positions occupied by actors are in fact positions of possibilities as they are unstable and reflect the ongoing struggles for power. Actors occupy positions in the field according to the overall volume and relative combinations of capital available to them, and they can only distinguish themselves according to the distinction principle (Bourdieu, 1990b) or, in other words, in relation to other actors. At the same time, powerful actors struggle to maintain control over the distinctions that are valued. It is in this context that individual women pursue their goals of achieving "the model life." Two principle modes of agency that models enact are outlined below.

MODES OF AGENCY

In the modeling industry, unlike other high visibility industries, the aim is not to produce celebrities with individuated personae. Instead, the ideal model (from the point of view of actors such as designers and the fashion press) should be nothing more than a blank slate, a commodity that is intended to be just slightly ahead of the cultural curve; a trend promoter, but not a trend setter. For most new models however, modeling is about consuming the dream of the model life rather than about becoming a more or less anonymous clothes hanger.

Our analysis suggests that two different modes of agency are adopted by models in reaction to other players' attempts to control their trajectory and restrict their ability to consume the model life. These differences exist mainly because of aesthetic judgments in regard to the "looks" possessed by the models. Agents, designers, photographers, and models themselves make aesthetic judgments that some women are viable primarily for commercial niches while others have the potential to be editorial models. This categorization between "commercial" and "editorial" sits at the very heart of the modeling field and basically allows or restricts a model's ability to gain full access to the model life. The greater prestige accorded to editorial versus commercial work within the field makes it difficult to envision that a model classified as commercial could ever consume the model life. Our findings suggest, however, that some models find means of exerting agency and consuming the model life despite their potential for being relegated to the lesser status of commercial models.

The first mode of agency presented in the following paragraphs is more aligned with the rules of the field but nonetheless enables models with a certain degree of control over the extent to which they gain access to model life. The second mode seems to clearly challenge the rules of the field and even makes it possible for a model to transcend them almost altogether.

Mode of Agency 1: Resist Commercial Categorization

Entwistle (2002) observes that in any aesthetic economy, preferred aesthetic content constantly changes, as the history of art or design illustrates. However, aesthetic values do not come from nowhere; they are generated internally in the field of production itself and may be influenced by concurrent developments in other aesthetic fields. Editorial models may not be beautiful by standards outside the field, but they will have what insiders refer to as the "it" or "in" look of the moment. Julie reflects on the look of the moment as follows: "You always have an 'in' girl. Right now, she has red hair, a round face, is scrawny looking, and looks like a fifteen year old. … Before that, you had the androgynous look." More broadly, AA, an agent, states: "Editorial [models are] of a rarer breed. You take a look at her, and you're not sure she is beautiful but you know she has an interesting face."

Our analysis suggests that the models who seek to gain access to the fame and fortune they desire by exploiting (or attaining) the "look of the moment" do not succeed simply by developing and maintaining a purely editorial profile. Instead, they succeed by avoiding a *categorization* as commercial.

Thus we observe that virtually all models who begin their careers in the editorial pages of fashion magazines do some commercial work as well. Some begin soon after their editorial debut, while others solidify their editorial status before seeking commercial contracts, but none who remain in the industry for more than a few years refrain completely from commercial contracts. The key is to be able to seek the status of an editorial model by being invisible as a commercial one.

Seek the Status of an Aesthetic Object

For a model aspiring to avoid commercial categorization, it is imperative to become thought of as a valued aesthetic object – almost a work of art. In order to achieve such status, models must gain the attention and assistance of tastemakers in the field. Typically, these will be photographers, fashion editors, and designers.

Editorial models seeking to gain editorial exposure are encouraged by their agents to seek the attention of photographers to gain aesthetic standing and to win access to other tastemakers. As Marianne explains, attracting attention is no simple matter.

> It's true that you can meet the top photographers during casting periods, but it's tough to stand out when you're in the middle of literally hundreds of beautiful girls. And they're all beautiful. So, quite often, the agencies will tell you that it's a good idea to go to night clubs, parties... Quite often, he [the photographer] is the one who makes the decision.

As in other fields, networking that later translates into social capital is important in the modeling context. For those adopting the agentic mode of resisting commercial categorization, effective networking may yield both social and aesthetic capital. That is, models who attract the attention of influential photographers can benefit twice over. First, they may gain access to someone whose tastes are respected and influential, and who can recommend them to fashion editors, designers, and commercial clients. Second, they may create the opportunity to work with a set of actors in the field who collectively can help to create images of them that will help them be perceived as differentiated, desirable aesthetic products.

Steadily Innovate: Be a Chameleon

Models who successfully adopt this agentic mode do not endeavor to build one single enduring image. Instead, they seek constantly to re-invent themselves as aesthetic products. A model who embodied this approach is Kate

Moss. Our informant Ariane, summarizing much of what the popular press reports on her, states:

> Kate Moss, you don't realize it but she changes all the time. One season she is trashy, another one she is a beautiful femme fatale. Well that's how she reinvents herself. With the PR that she does and the way she dresses everyday, her personal style, she gives ideas to the designers. She shows them that she can be all sorts of styles. She will go to a party with diamonds all over her, and then, she will be booked for a jewelry company that's going to make her tons of money. ...Why? Because she was able to reinvent herself.

As Ariane's quotation indicates, models adopting this agentic mode would lose their "of the moment" image if they rested on their laurels. Constant image innovation is essential for those who resist commercial categorization.

Avoid Overexposure

Another challenge for the model who wishes to resist categorization is to gain visibility while avoiding the impression of being too ubiquitous. As Marianne puts it: "The dividing line between too much exposure, and not enough, is really thin, if you don't want people to get tired of you. You must keep a certain want, a certain reserve." Creating the perception of rareness or scarcity is a tactic long associated with luxury goods. It appears that in the modeling field, models who wish to achieve the status of aesthetic objects must balance the need to be seen in the right venues with the need to maintain some mystique. Overexposure, particularly at too early a stage, can also create a tarnish that may push the model toward commercial categorization.

Seek Recognition versus Renown

Ultimately, models who seek the model life by avoiding commercial categorization must attain extremely high visibility among their peers within the fashion field. However, they avoid a wider renown among the general public and commercial clients. Margaret, an informant who is currently gaining a strong editorial reputation, states: "In general, success is when you're known by your peers." This statement indicates that for those pursuing the agentic mode of avoiding commercial categorization, the ideal type of visibility is recognition within the field. Lang and Lang (1988) in their study of another aesthetic field, graphic etching, noted that peer recognition was of less importance than renown beyond one's peers in determining whether an individual etcher would be remembered. In the context of fashion, our research suggests that models who achieve peer recognition but not renown beyond their field may be tacitly or explicitly conforming to the rules that have evolved within the field in recent years. It appears that a trend among powerful actors, including both fashion editors and designers, is to prefer models' visibility to be contained within the modeling field. American *Vogue* contributor Sally Field states: "It's cooler to walk down the street and have only the people who *should* know you. It makes you part of this super-cool club." (Singer, 2004, p. 748). She means that models should not be celebrities, except to others in the field.

In summary, this agentic mode rests on gaining the endorsement of those with the power to shape what will count as aesthetically preferable among dominant figures in the field, and in keeping an image sufficiently fluid that it can evolve as rapidly as tastes in the field. It is the importance of novelty – indeed of *inconsistency* – that distinguishes this agentic mode. Resisting categorization and steadily re-inventing imply an underlying uncertainty or lack of predictably which may be uniquely valued by the tastemakers in an aesthetic economy.

Mode of Agency 2: Become A Brand

> I understand that CINDY CRAWFORD is a brand. When I hire people, as assistants or whatever, I always say: "Look, we all work for CINDY CRAWFORD, myself included." (Crawford, 2000, p. 182).

The agentic mode of becoming a brand has been successfully pursued by a relatively small number of models, most of whom began their careers between 1970 and 1995. Prior to this period, only a small number of models were known to those beyond the field. During the 70s, several models sought and achieved fame beyond the modeling field. Some did so by striving to be both models and actresses (e.g., Lauren Hutton, Cybil Shepherd). Others simply courted constant media attention: they became "famous consumption objects" (Veronica Webb quoted in Soley-Beltran, 2004, p. 314). Particularly from the 1980s onward, a number of them built upon the familiarity and appeal of their images, licensing their names to clothing, television shows, exercise videos, and beauty products. And as the public awareness of and attachment to the most recognizable models grew, many were able to command fees hitherto unimaginable (Quick, 1997).

In the early 1990s, the recession hit the fashion industry hard, and designers turned to the brand-name models to gain publicity. Versace may have initiated the practice, reputedly paying multiple-branded models nearly $10,000 each for modeling his Milan collection (Bailey, 1998). Chanel and others followed suit, and as designers competed for the brand-name models, their fame and their ability to command fees grew ever greater. As the power of the models relative to the designers increased, designers grew dissatisfied with the branded model. In 1991, Valentino stated, "I like them but I hate the stardom created around them … I ask them not to be stars but Valentino women" (Quick, 1997, p. 155). Designers complained bitterly of the fees the branded models could demand, and fed stories to the media which delighted in characterizing models as over-privileged children who "won't get out of bed for less than $10,000 a day" (Quick, 1997, p. 155). As early as 1993 the *Daily News* christened such models: "the coat hangers from Hell." (Quick, 1997, p. 155). Since the mid 1990s, the trend among fashion designers who influence which models obtain editorial work has been to patronize and celebrate those who avoid becoming brands in their own right with the potential to distract attention from the fashions and other products they are hired to promote (Marsh, 2003).

Notwithstanding the apparent backlash against branded models, the brand-building agentic mode is worth distinguishing from the first one as some branded models who might have retired by now given the field's veneration of youth, continue to reap rewards from the mode they pursued (e.g., Cindy Crawford and Tyra Banks) and as it appears that certain contemporary models (e.g., Heidi Klum and Gisele Bündchen) are adopting the branding mode with considerable success.

Seek Categorization as an Idealized Type

Models who become brands are, typically, beautiful in more conventional ways that those considered by the tastemakers in the field to embody its aesthetic ideals. In regard to their raw human capital – their faces and bodies – models who become brands tend to be more similar to those who have commercial potential than to those with the highest editorial potential.

Models who pursue a branding mode of agency seek categorization as an idealized type by becoming associated with some culturally valorized category or idea, or some cultural tension (Holt, 2004). They differentiate themselves from others who are "pretty faces" (e.g., commercial models) by selectively emphasizing how they embody this cultural notion. For example, Cindy Crawford has worked to become the ideal "all American Girl," and this is reflected in how she talks about herself as a brand. She emphasizes that she is "approachable, not too elitist" and that she doesn't come across as "unattainable" (Crawford, 2000, p. 231).

Adopt the Brand Association Logic

Building upon and maintaining the consistency of their image appears to be a key to embodying an idealized type. Unlike those who resist commercial categorization and adopt a more chameleon-like approach, those who wish to be branded must reinforce their positioning just as marketers reinforce the images of their branded products (Keller, 2003). Susan, an informant who adopted the first agentic mode, emphasized that as a model she constantly and consciously re-invented herself. She compares her situation with others "like Claudia Schiffer or Cindy Crawford [who] never changed their looks… They answer the North American woman's desire to look like them and look healthy."

Crawford (2000) herself reinforces this approach, saying that "Fashion is evolutionary; it's about constant change. [But] I haven't changed… I'm always Cindy. I think that's helped make me commercially successful" (p. 182). She is careful to ensure consistency in the contracts that she accepts, as the associations of the products could detract from her positioning. She states, "It wouldn't make sense, for example, for CINDY CRAWFORD to do a cigarette campaign" (p. 182). Interestingly, consistency appears more important than status when it comes to building a brand. Crawford's early work with Sears and K-mart did not forever tarnish her reputation. Indeed, it may have helped her build or reinforce the all-American, down to earth positioning that she has carved for herself.

Seek Exposure Within and Beyond the Modeling Field

Quite unlike models who avoid commercial categorization, those who seek brand status must work to become "renowned" (Lang & Lang, 1988) or known to a public well beyond the circle of their peers. In particular, models pursuing a branding agentic mode require visibility among those who might be expected to purchase the products or services that are consistent with their image. For Cindy Crawford, this has meant gaining exposure to the middle class American women who might buy her line of skin care products or her brand of home furnishings. For some of the newer branded models, such as Gisele Bündchen, it entails obtaining steady media coverage among young women in her native Brazil where she sells a line of footwear.

Strive for Steady Exposure

Given that the success of a branding agentic mode rests in building a strong, attractive, and consistent image, a sustained lapse in exposure could lead to target audiences losing interest in or attraction towards the model. Worse, it might lead to the perception that the model is a "has been" and no longer au courant. It is apparent that models who are successful in pursuing a brand agentic mode take little time out from the marketplace. Instead, they try to remain rather steadily in the public eye. Their brand equity is at risk of eroding quickly if they fail to do so. Thus, while the branded models gain agency within the field and potentially transcend the rules of the modeling game, they are nonetheless subject to the rules of the wider marketplace.

In summary, models pursuing a branding mode of agency are successful in gaining access to the model life only if they can associate themselves with meanings that resonate with a particular group or groups, just as brands in other categories do (Holt, 2004). In regard to audience, whereas models adopting the first mode need to convince only a subset of field insiders of their worth and capital, models adopting the second mode must convince field insiders as well as the consuming public in the marketplace, not just that they are beautiful, but that they signify some culturally attractive identity or category. Models pursuing a branding agentic mode must build their image in the eyes of a wider public so that, when they endorse someone else's product or when they launch a product line of their own, the set of meanings that they embody can be transferred to the product by association (McCracken, 1989).

DISCUSSION AND CONCLUSION

We are living at a point in time where the urge to be unique can supposedly be answered by the marketplace where merchants of dreams offer an extremely wide range of consumption avenues designed to answer that very need. But while we may long to be unique individuals, free agents, Bourdieu would argue that we are, to a considerable extent, shaped by structures, our *habitus*, and by the rules of the field(s) we operate within. And yet, fields are not static entities but dynamic, as they are shaped in return by their actors' interactions and struggles.

Thus, our findings suggest that while models who adopt the first agentic mode seem to conform more to the rules and structures of the field, they nonetheless resist total control over their access to the coveted good, the model life. They do so by adopting strategies that enable them to be viewed by dominant figures as aesthetically deserving of a place within the fashion field. The model life, like the academic life or the life of a professional team athlete is not something that can be purchased or handed down; it requires a tacit recognition of the rules of the game, an endowment of initial capital to pursue success, and a combination of skill and luck to play by or work around the rules of the field. Dominant figures in highly restricted fields pick and choose the new entrants, judging that they know how these will contribute to both their own status and social reproduction. Even as they enter, however, these newcomers *may* gain a measure of power within the field or even challenge some of the rules of the game, effectively reducing the influence of those who were once dominant. Struggles and power relations thus function as the motor of the field – without it, the field would simply stagnate, and possibly lose its relevance within the broader culture.

Viewed in this light, models who pursue the branding mode while breaking "rules" and defying norms (as did Cindy Crawford, who violated the norm that models should avoid low status commercial contracts if they want to obtain editorial exposure) also contribute to the field's vitality and relevance in a consumer society and a celebrity culture. Indeed, while modeling long suffered from a reputation not much better than prostitution, today it is viewed as a highly glamorous career where one can actually make a name for oneself and gain all types of rewards. Cindy Crawford, Tyra Banks, Gisèle, and other "model brands" are themselves consumed by fans and aspiring models who ardently seek the model life, and consequently feed the modeling field.

More broadly, this analysis suggests that in order to fully understand consumer agency, it is useful to diversify the contexts examined and to take into account those with restricted access to coveted commodities. Though the agentic modes identified in the aestheticized field of fashion modeling may differ from those adopted in other such contexts, this analysis reinforces Bourdieu's insights regarding the pivotal roles played by actors other than would-be consumers in such settings. Moreover, the dynamic "rules" in such contexts are critical to take into account, as their evolving nature will shape and be shaped by the agentic tactics adopted by striving consumers. Whereas in other settings, consumer agency may well be regarded as co-production, in contexts such as the one here examined, consumer agency may sometimes resemble an almost entrepreneurial type of creative destruction.

ACKNOWLEDGMENTS

The authors wish to thank the participants at the first Consumer Culture Theory Conference and the reviewers for their helpful comments.

REFERENCES

Bailey, D. (1998). *Models close-up*. London: Macmillan.

Bourdieu, P. (1984). Haute couture et haute culture. *Questions de sociologie* (pp.132–139). Paris: Minuit.

Bourdieu, P. (1990a). Social space and symbolic power. *In other words: Essays towards a reflexive sociology* (trans. M. Adamson, 122–140). Stanford, CA: Stanford University Press.

Bourdieu, P. (1990b). Structures, *habitus*, practices. *The logic of practice* (trans. R. Nice, 52–66). Stanford, CA: Stanford University Press.

Bourdieu, P. (1993). *The field of cultural production*. New York: Columbia University Press.

Crawford, C. (2000). Faces to remember. *Vogue*(June), 177–183.

Entwistle, J. (2002). The aesthetic economy: The production of value in the field of fashion modeling. *Journal of Consumer Culture, 2*(3), 317–339.

Finkelstein, J. (1998). *Fashion: An introduction*. New York: New York University Press.

Holt, D. B. (2002). Why do brands cause troubles? A dialectical theory of consumer culture and branding. *Journal of Consumer Research, 29*(June), 70–90.

Holt, D. B. (2004). *How brands become icons: The principle of cultural branding*. Boston, MA: Harvard Business School Press.

Keller, K. L. (2003). Brand synthesis: The multidimensionality of brand knowledge. *Journal of Consumer Research, 29*(4), 595–601.

Kozinets, R. V., Sherry, J. F., Jr., Storm, D., Duhachek, A., Nuttavuthisit, K., & DeBerry-Spence, B. (2004). Ludic agency and retail spectacle. *Journal of Consumer Research, 31*(3), 658–672.

Lang, G. E., & Lang, K. (1988). Recognition and renown: The survival of artistic reputation. *The American Journal of Sociology, 94*(1), 79–109.

Marsh, L. (2003). *The house of klein: Fashion, controversy and a business obsession*. New Jersey: John Wiley & Sons Inc.

McCracken, G. (1988). *The long interview*. Thousand Oaks, CA: Sage.

McCracken, G. (1989). Who is the celebrity endorser? *Journal of Consumer Research, 16*(3), 310–321.

Prahalad, C. K. (2004). The concept of co-creation. *Strategic Direction, 20*(11), 25–27.

Price, L. L., Arnould, E. J., & Mosio, R. (in press). Making contexts matter: Selecting research contexts for theoretical insight. *Handbook of qualitative research in marketing*. London: Sage Publication.

Quick, H. (1997). *Catwalking: A history of the fashion model*. New Jersey: Wellfleet Press.

Singer, S. (2004). Model and supermodel. *Vogue* (September).

Soley-Beltran, P. (2004). Modeling femininity. *European Journal of Women's Studies, 11*(3), 309–326.

The Fashion Book (2004). New York, NY: Phaidon Press.

Thompson, C. J. (2004). Marketplace mythologies and discourses of power. *Journal of Consumer Research, 31*(June), 162–180.

Thompson, C. J. (2005). Consumer risk perceptions in a community of reflexive doubt. *Journal of Consumer Research, 32*(September), 235–248.

Vargo, S. L., & Lusch, R. F. (2004). Evolving to a new dominant logic for marketing. *Journal of Marketing, 68*(1), 1–17.

APPENDIX: LIST OF INFORMANTS

Pseudonym	Nationality/Race	Year/Age of Entrance in the Field	Type of Modeling Work	Longevity	Current Occupation
Models					
Marianne	Canadian/white	1992/ 15 y-o	E/C	13 years	Model/Grad Student
Caroline	Canadian/white	1995/ 19 y-o	E/C	10 years	Model's agent
Helene	Canadian/white	1998/ 21 y-o	C	4 years	Administrative assistant
Ariane	Ethiopian-Canadian/black	1989/ 15 y-o	E/C	16 years	Model/Fashion stylist
Julie	Canadian/white	1999/ 16 y-o	E/C	6 years	Model/Student
Susan	Canadian/white	1985/15 y-o	C	10 years	Photographers' Agency Owner
Margaret	Canadian/white	1997/ 16 y-o	E/C	8 years	Model
Jane	Canadian/white	1985/ 21 y-o	E/C	20 years	Model/Mother
Other actors					
AA	Canadian/white	2003/ 24 y-o	–	2 years	Model's Agent
Megan	Canadian/white	1995/20 y-o	–	10 years	Model's Agent
Rick	Canadian/black	1993/19 y-o	–	12 years	Photographer
Molly	Canadian/white	1996/19 y	–	9 years	Photographer
Christy	Canadian/white	1999/23 y	–	6 years	Advertising client

Note: E, editorial; C, commercial.

THE MATERIAL SEMIOTICS OF CONSUMPTION OR WHERE (AND WHAT) ARE THE OBJECTS IN CONSUMER CULTURE THEORY?

Shona Bettany

ABSTRACT

This article presents an analysis of a seemingly mundane consumption object, the Mars Coat King, a manual grooming device employed within Afghan hound breeding and exhibition cultures, to develop current conceptualizations of the consumption object in consumer culture theory (CCT). In doing so it extends theory of the ontology of, and relation between, subject and object into the realms of the post-humanist. The chapter illustrates how by employing post-humanist theory, the consumption object can be conceptualized as a mutable, contradictory and active entity within complex consumption cultures and when conceptualized as such, can enrich understanding of consumption objects within consumer research.

INTRODUCTION

In the article used as the basis for this conference (Arnould & Thompson, 2005) the authors provide a synthesis of 'the sociocultural, experiential,

Consumer Culture Theory
Research in Consumer Behavior, Volume 11, 41–56

ISSN: 0885-2111/doi:10.1016/S0885-2111(06)11003-0

symbolic and ideological aspects of consumption' into four thematic domains of interests and as such develop the 'disciplinary brand' of consumer culture theory (CCT). In assessing the contribution and potentials of the CCT brand, they provide novel theorizations of these four domains of interest. This outlines that CCT is underpinned by a family of allied theoretical perspectives that orient towards the study of 'cultural complexity' and more specifically to 'the dynamic relationships between consumer action, the marketplace and cultural meanings'. The article documents a laudable shift in consumer culture theory away from traditional 'economic' analysis, which is overdetermined by the essential characteristics of the consumption object. As Holt argues, this type of analysis produces research in which consumption is structured by the properties of consumption objects conceptualized as 'vessels of meaning that signify similarly across all consumers' (Holt, 1995, p. 1). CCT, on the other hand, comprises an analytical focus on consumer meaning, consumer action and consumer processes with culture being conceptualized, following Geertz (1973) as fragmented, heterogeneous, multiple and overlapping circulations of experience, meaning and action. This shift has had two linked consequences for the theory base and empirical output of work deemed to be within the parameters of CCT. First, the focus on meaning and experience as a basis for knowledge construction about consumer culture has shifted the ontological basis for CCT from the object to the subject side of the subject–object binary which has had the consequence; second, of essentializing the consumption object in CCT as something which is acted on, and a 'thing in itself' about which consumers make meaning. In CCT, the consumption object is seen as something that 'groups use' to construct 'practices, identities and meanings – to make collective sense of their environments and to orient their members' experiences and lives' (Arnould & Thompson, 2005, p. 869). This has the effect of shifting from a position of overdetermination of the object, to under determination of the object both of which essentialize the object and neither of which provides a theoretical rendering of the part the consumption object plays in consumer culture, which is commensurate with contemporary theories of cultural materiality. In contemporary cultural studies of science and technology (Latour, 1999; Law, 2000) and feminist cultural theory (Haraway, 2005) among others, an attempt has been made to 'recover the object' in analyses, to subvert the dominant Cartesian dualism of subject and object and to develop theoretical tools to examine the entangled co-production and ontological indeterminacy of subject and object in cultural processes and action. These analyses view 'the object' as multiple, ambiguous, ambivalent and mutable and co-emergent as such, in material–semiotic relations within heterogeneous, multiple and overlapping human and non-human cultural formations. This work provides an illustration of such an analysis stimulated by these approaches to understand a consumption object, the 'Mars Coat King©' as mutably and multiply emergent within the trans-national, highly networked exhibition Afghan hound community.

RECOVERING THE OBJECT

Emphasis on the symbolic properties of objects (Belk, 1976; Joy, 2001; Mick & De Moss, 1990) and ideological issues (Murray, 2002; Thompson & Hirschman, 1995), how material objects symbolize social and cultural relationships and become part of identity construction at the group (Mehta & Belk, 1991) and individual level (Belk, 1988; Holt, 2002; Ozanne, 1992), our emotional relationships with things (Holbrook, 1993) and 'how' we consume (Holt, 1995) have traditionally been the focus of consumer research when considering the consumption object. In short, consumer research has focused upon consumer meaning and usage in considering the consumption object theoretically. Dant (1999) argues that in studies of material culture and consumption in the social sciences and anthropology (Campbell, 1989; Douglas & Isherwood, 1979; Millar, 1987; Slater, 1997) it is no longer sufficient to explore the cultural and symbolic meanings we imbue to the material objects that help make up our cultural worlds. This is part of a development in cultural theory towards theories that can account for the 'sociality of things', not just in terms of the meanings we imbue them with or the myriad ways in which we use them but in terms of bringing into the analysis the radical indeterminacy of the material object within its multiple arrays of cultural relations. This has been both a theoretical shift in ontology from 'social construction' formulations (i.e. the object is socially constructed by the human and subjective relations around it) and an epistemological/empirical shift away from a focus upon what and how things mean and/or how they are used (i.e. an instrumentalist approach). This shift has underpinned the development of theory, which does not begin with an ontologically primitive object upon which multiple meanings are ascribed, with which multiple practices are engaged in and from which multiple experiences are derived. Instead they seek to understand how the objects and their boundaries co-emerge with other human and non-human entities, are ontologically mutable, active and embedded in relations of emergent and entangled meaning and materiality.

There has been a significant tranche of research developing these approaches. First, the Actor Network Theory (ANT) tradition in cultural studies of science and technology (Latour, 1992). This approach is used to consider the 'missing masses' (material objects) which 'knock at the door of sociology requesting a place in the accounts of society as stubbornly as the humans masses did in the 19th century'. Latour, drawing upon the post-structuralist semiotics of Greimas, presents an ontology of 'relational materiality', in which all human and non-human participants in the analysis are treated equally as active participants. In this 'radical constructivism', Latour argues that 'purposeful action and intentionality may not be properties of objects, but they are also not properties of human either. They are properties of … collectives of human and non-humans' (Latour, 2000, p. 192). That is, agency is seen, following Greimas (Perron & Collins, 1989) as attributed in terms of formations of meaning and materiality in which objects, bodies and other heterogeneous entities are embedded and not as a property of human actors. ANT is therefore a theory of 'relational materiality', what is taken as the material object emerges in relation as effects of those relations. Of course, this also means that objects are seen as ontologically mutable and indeterminate, they might 'be' more than one thing, their boundaries are not fixed, but take shape through the relations in which they emerge. In feminist cultural theory, Haraway (1989) has developed a similar ontological approach, although it has a very different political basis. Rather than Latour's material relationality, she describes her ontology as 'material–semiotic'. That is, she views objects as material–semiotic generative nodes, their boundaries, which are not to be seen as pre-existing, materialize in social interaction among humans and non-humans. These emergent 'hybrid' (Haraway, 1997, p. 126) objects 'act' within cultural groupings in ways which are not robustly theoretically or empirically rendered in analyses which emphasize human meaning and action.

The ontological assumptions of these approaches are what provide the point of departure from the types of approaches outlined in the CCT paper. In CCT, meaning is ascribed to objects by subjects, practices are engaged in by subjects 'using' objects, and subjects' experiences, identities, and so on are derived from objects. My interpretation of the ontological shift of CCT is therefore that it has exchanged one deterministic analysis for another, in earlier consumer work, overdetermined by the object, the object determined the social and in current CCT the opposite is true, the object is underdetermined, that is the social (largely) determines the object. CCT with its commitments to post-structuralist and post-modern analyses allows for, and appropriately theorizes, the radical indeterminacy of the subject. However, the approaches outlined above are based on the radical indeterminacy of both 'subject' and 'object'. Using approaches like those mentioned above which begin from the assumption of an emergent ontology with bodies, objects and meaning entangled, co-constituted, fragile and often ambivalent can avoid overdetermination of either subject or object and provide a novel way to theorize consumer culture and consumer-object relations. In these approaches what might have been called subject and object collapse into complex analyses of meaning and materiality, and things that 'matter' (i.e. that both 'materialize' and 'mean' borrowing Judith Butler's (1996) telling play on words) multiply co-emerge in inherently fragile, non-literal and ambivalent co-constitution, hybridity, impurity and complexity from within specific cultural milieu.

METHOD

This paper was developed as part of an extensive three-year multi-site ethnography (MSE) of, and personal involvement with, the transnational exhibition and breed Afghan hound community. The paper detailing this ethnography in full (Bettany & Daly, 2007) provides the empirical excerpt presented here to illustrate the theoretical point being made. MSE (Marcus, 1995, 1998) was developed following the 'writing culture' critique of the 1980s (Clifford & Marcus, 1986). This critique intervened in the traditional ethnographic 'geographical location = culture' trope in response to the deterritorialization of culture in the post-modern contemporary distributed and highly networked world. MSE is about defining an object of study that cannot be accounted for in terms of its geographical location but in terms of the circulation, flow and process of cultural meanings, objects and identities in diffuse time-space (Hannerz, 2003; Hage, 2005). This method is highly relevant for the context considered here. In Afghan hound cultures, I engage in highly networked, distributed and heterogeneous domains of cultural meanings, objects and bodies, from the multiple virtual engagements of web fora and discussion groups, social meetings and gatherings, through glossy magazines, periodical journals and year books, to the intense physicality of the dog shows themselves. To cope with such a complex field, MSE is designed around 'chains, paths, threads, conjunctions or juxtapositions of location in which the ethnographer establishes some form of literal presence with an explicit, posited logic of association or connection among sites' (Marcus, 1998, p. 90). The way to establish this literal presence is obviously less straightforward than traditional ethnographic research. Tracking strategies, following an object, metaphor, plot, story or allegory have emerged as a mode of engagement, defining the field as an ongoing confrontation between that conceptual/material tracking and the researcher (Martin, 1994). What sutures fieldwork together as ethnography is the researchers own logics of association. For me as ethnographer and participant within this logic the tracking strategy became one of the obduracy and resilience of formations that were encountered as a new exhibitor. Recognizing how, when and why I was coming 'to matter' within this heterogeneous milieu, sometimes even despite my resistance, became the loci from which I then 'analyzed outward' to explore the heterogeneous formations that were 'producing' me, my hounds and my practices within this culture.

THE CONSUMING CULTURE OF THE EXHIBITION AFGHAN HOUND

In the transnational, highly networked cultures of the exhibition Afghan hound community, as with many pedigree breed cultures, interesting cultural formations co-exist in complex and multi layered strata of cultural meanings and materialities. The Afghan hound itself and its owners come 'to matter', within multiple formations of overlapping and sometimes contradictory material–semiotic entanglements of stories, bodies and objects. Of concern to the paper here, are two such contradictory formations which figure large in this complex cultural milieu; the first concerns 'preservation and authenticity' and the second 'progress and adaptation'.

Preservation, Authenticity and the 'Really Real'

The Afghan hound emerges in Afghan hound exhibition and breeding cultures as an entity to be preserved in its authenticity. Pedigree breed communities commonly detail their complex histories as embedded within master narratives of natural history, collection and preservation of the breed (Clutton-Brock, 1994). These histories and origin stories in Afghan hound culture are complex with specific human and canine bodies being worked up in the discourse as material–semiotic nodes of contestation which configure present day relationalities and practices.

One such body is the dog 'Zardin' who is displayed within this culture as the material–semiotic evidence of the status of the Afghan hound as something authentic to be preserved and protected. In 1907, Zardin was important by the British Captain John Banff as a trophy of the British Afghan war. Zardin caused frenzied excitement in the British pedigree breeds community and was even displayed at Buckingham Palace. However, in 1921, Miss Jean Manson and Major and Mrs. Bell-Murray imported twelve Afghan hounds to their kennels in Scotland, establishing the Bell-Murray type of Afghan hound (Harrison, 1971). This Afghan hound type was quite different to Zardin; rangy, lean, sparsely coated and from the desert regions. Following this development, in 1925, Major and Mrs. Amps returned from their Ghazni kennels in Kabul with their own Ghazni type hounds, these hounds were 'mountain' type, more compact and with heavy coats to withstand the freezing conditions, and quite similar to Zardin. Mrs. Amps began to publicly hint that the Bell Murray type were not in fact pure Afghan but a result of outcrosses to Saluki dogs and inevitably this led to direct and open confrontation between these two factions. This dispute over what constituted (and who controlled) the 'real' Afghan hound was conducted through heated and aggressive exchanges in the breed newspaper, 'Our Dogs' until in 1946, a breed standard allowing room for interpretation was forged (Niblock, 1980, p. 62). This ensured that the question of what constituted the authentic Afghan hound was, as a consequence never settled and today there is a plethora of different types of Afghan hounds accepted in the show ring. However, debates about who owns and breeds the 'really real' Afghan hounds among this myriad of types still rage on as part of the common discourse.

These debates and the quest for authenticity can be read through an analysis of breeders websites.[1] Breeders' websites present a public display of personal histories, past and present hounds and document the successes, achievements and aspirations of the breeder. In many breeders' web sites, constellations of material–semiotic evidence are presented to convince the audience of the endurance of the kennel brand. Websites show photographic evidence of involvement with the breed from the earliest possible date. These aged photographs of long dead Afghan hounds are presented, bearing now defunct affix names spoken of reverently; woven with narratives of association entangling the old with the new. Mission statements and histories of involvement read like the genre of ethnographic 'arrival stories'. They locate the kennel brand as 'being there' (Geertz, 1973) and 'in the action' long before others were. The narratives, mission statements, bodies of dogs and breeders now passed, photographic evidence and stories of times and achievements past, produce the breeder as a true natural historian and custodian of the real and authentic Afghan hound and their kennel name or affix, a 'brand' to be taken seriously.

PROGRESS AND ADAPTATION

The corollary of the story of preservation and authenticity is the story of progress and adaptation. The tension within these stories is common in the dog fancy. Darwin (1859), for example, cited pedigree dogs in his origin of the species manifesto, as nowhere could descent with adaptation be more clearly and popularly seen than in the burgeoning breed proliferation of the 19th Century pedigree dog fancy (Ritvo, 1987). Yet, as seen above, stories of authenticity and preservation proliferate within pedigree breed cultures. However, at the same time as stories of preservation and authenticity proliferate, so do adaptive practices. To illustrate this tension, the story of how Afghan hound culture responded to the issue of the cloning of dogs can be used. The issue of cloning in Afghan hound cultures became a 'hot topic' during the time that the infamous cloned Afghan hound puppy, Snuppy emerged as a breaking news story. The predominant reaction from all breed communities in the UK was horror at the health implications for the dog and this was obviously of paramount concern. However, more interesting concerns emerged; the UK Kennel Club issued a statement that, 'Canine cloning runs contrary to the Kennel Club's objective to promote in every way the general improvement of dogs. Cloning cannot be used to make improvements because the technique simply produces genetic replicas of existing dogs'. For the authenticity and preservation obsessed Afghan hound enthusiast this would seem like nirvana, the preservation and genetic purity of the Afghan hound would be assured. However, even placing to one side the welfare concerns, the response to the potential of cloning was largely negative. During the discussions, some breeders elaborated upon their skills of breeding, garnered from many years involvement, citing the thrill of producing 'the one', that is the dog that stood above all other dogs of its generation and that would become part of breed history. More experienced breeders argued that their skill was measured not just in terms of producing one good dog, but in producing 'strength in depth', that is to produce litters of consistent type and quality. Within the discourses of puppy production, the aim of improvement of the breed, of producing 'something better', is often cited as part of the breeders' rationale. Folk knowledge of the repercussions of using and mixing particular bloodlines is privileged in this culture, and therefore ability to produce litters of good quality puppies time and time again is also evidence of the value of the kennel brand. Simply put, breeders who have been involved longer know more and have more skill and, concomitantly, cloning through technology and genetic manipulation leaves skilled breeders de-skilled. Using cloning technology, presumably anyone could replicate a winning dog with lack of ability and little or no in-depth knowledge of the breed being no obstacle to their success.

MANAGING AMBIVALENCE IN AFGHAN HOUND PRACTICES: THE COAT KING

The analysis above presents a story of a culture displaying a core tension between authenticity/preservation and progress/adaptation within its own rationale of its activities. The trope of authenticity provides breeders and exhibitors with the important rationale that their activities are for a greater purpose than the simple ego enhancement benefits of winning prizes. In doing so, this trope provides an important distinction between the Afghan hound culture of fanciers and other breed fancies that have these more trivial concerns. On the other hand, breeders have demonstrated that their concerns and skills, like other breed fancies, are directed towards improvement of the breed and change, in other words, progress and adaptation. This has the effect of enacting distinctions between Afghan hounds for the benefit of competition purposes.

This part of the analysis progresses from the complex and ambivalent material–semiotic cultural formations above towards a specific analysis of a consumption object that 'matters' and 'acts' in both of these formations. This will be used to illustrate the contribution of this work in terms of providing a new way to analyze and understand subject/object relations in consumer cultures. When we talk about subject/object relations using the language in CCT, it has a particular effect on the implicit ontology of CCT regarding the subject/object binary, as explained earlier in this chapter. That is, the consumption object is seen as something that 'groups use' to construct 'practices, identities and meanings – to make collective sense of their environments and to orient their members experiences and lives' (Arnould & Thompson, 2005, p. 869) and meaning is 'ascribed' to objects by subjects, practices are engaged in by subjects 'using' objects, and subjects' experiences, identities, and so on are derived from objects. This has the effect of conceptualizing objects as inert entities that are used in particular ways and for particular purposes by human actors. Within this conceptualization, distinctions are drawn between subject and object and the analytical attention is focused upon how the consumer uses, or consumes, the object. This not only preserves and reiterates the Cartesian subject/object binary, but maintains a humanist notion of human agency. Latour (1999) suggests that instead of this notion of human agency, agency should be seen instead as the property of ontologically heterogeneous collectives, made up of human and non-human entities. The objects within this ontology 'act' within cultures but not in the sense that they are animate entities, action is instead seen as a product or products of the collective, and not in terms of the capacity of any one object or subject. Latour (1994) uses the example of the gun as a metaphor to explain this ontology (see also Borgerson, 2005). Latour discusses the controversy over gun control using the slogans mobilized on both sides of the argument, 'Guns kill people' and 'Guns do not kill people, people kill people' as two examples of the same ontology that maintains the subject/object binary. He concludes that neither guns nor people act alone to kill people, but that the gun/person hybrid within its various collectives of action define what the action and its consequences are,

> you are a different person with the gun in your hand…if I define you by what you have (the gun) and by the series of associations that you enter into when you use what you have (fire the gun) then you are modified by the gun-more so or less so depending upon the weight of other associations that you carry. This translation is wholly symmetrical. You are different with a gun in your hand, the gun is different with you holding it, you are another subject because you hold the gun-the gun is another object because it has entered into a relationship with you.

The gun/person hybrid within its various collectives can 'be' very different entities and act very differently according to the series of associations within which they are embedded. These relational entities and the actions that result are mutable and often difficult to simply predict and explain. This results in a highly complex rendering of the object as embedded within potentially infinite, hybrid collectives that are very difficult to completely analyze, and often 'act' in ways certainly not intended or predicted by the original producer. This renders the object ontologically indeterminate; it emerges as 'what it is' only within its collective of relations, and that emergence is neither simplistic, one-dimensional, coherent nor wholly predictable. Moreover, it emerges in such a way as it helps to configure the emergence of other human and non-human ontologies within (and indeed without) the collective.

This part of the analysis will examine how a specific, and seemingly mundane, consumption object can emerge with an indeterminate and mutable ontology across these different cultural formations and also how that object and 'myself as exhibitor' acted in two completely different and seemingly incompatible ways within this culture. In this way the object is re-conceptualized as ontologically indeterminate, but also as a generative entity, not just how it 'matters' but how it 'matters others' within different cultural formations. The consumption object used for this analysis, The Mars Coat King©' available in several sizes and grades, is a non-electronic manual coat raking device. The Mars Coat King, has emerged within these contradictory stories in ways which seem to manage their inevitable conflict by performing as 'both/and at the same time', a tool of preservation/authenticity and progress/adaptation. Analyzing how this consumption object mutates (and helped me to mutate) within this culture in relation to the material-relationalities within which we are embedded can be used to illustrate how conceptualizing the consumption object as radically indeterminate and as a mutable actor can enhance analyses of consumption behavior.

Coat King as Actor for Authenticity: Coat King as Plucking Tool

The Coat King has become a consumption object steeped in Afghan hound folk lore and native techniques. The first time I saw the Coat King I was struck by the artisanal quality of it. It reminded me of the strange and wonderful implements I saw in my grandfather's forge as a child. I never worked out what those were for either! Needless to say, this odd-looking device comes with no instructions. The Coat King feels heavy in the hand, it is not altogether clear how to use it, what one should do. When I first used it and was faced with my precious puppy and this heavy metal device I was struck by the fact that one does not just need a coat king to perform Afghan hound grooming regimes, one requires an assemblage of objects, people, stories and embodied skills.

Within the authenticity narratives and practices of Afghan hound culture, there is a requirement to present the Afghan as 'nature intended'. That is, no artificial means such as cutting or clipping with blades can be used to prepare the show exhibit. The breed standard of points states clearly that the 'coat must be allowed to develop naturally'. As illustrated by the stories above, the melding of the two distinct types of Afghan hound has resulted in a coat that is like neither one or the other, as such this coat requires management by the exhibitor in order to deal with this 'man made' anomaly within a culture configured strongly by the trope of authenticity and the quest for the 'really real' Afghan hound. The explanatory myth emerging from this culture is that coats are heavier because the Afghan no longer has to negotiate terrain that would naturally remove the excess coat and the Afghan hound no longer lives within packs that would nibble and pluck the coat from each other as a natural coat management process. Following this, the coat management practice emerging as the only legitimate way to remove excess coat is plucking with the hands to approximate the plucking action of trees, rocks and the hound pack. The Coat King is an important consumption object because it can be argued that it does not use 'artificial' means to sculpt the dog, it does not have sharp blades or moving parts but resembles a claw or a row of blunt teeth. It could easily approximate the action of branches of a bush or the teeth of a fellow pack member because it does not cut the coat but helps to pluck the hair out by the roots with a skilled action of the groomer's wrist and hand. However, the Coat King speeds up the plucking process and is easier on the hands than the strict hand plucking regime. In acting as a tool that plucks or nibbles, the coat king helps to produce the 'user' in a particular way. The Afghan hound exhibitor + Coat King as plucking tool hybrid produces the human subject within that hybrid as a (quasi) natural historian and, concomitantly, the breed community itself emerges within its associations of other breed fancies as a formation concerned with the safety and preservation of the authentic, original and natural Afghan hound rather than as a breed fancy concerned predominantly with winning prizes and ego enhancement. Using the Coat King, I become a subject within the cultural formation of preservation and authenticity. The Coat King as part of this material semiotic formation produces me as a 'guardian of the authentic', someone who has higher concerns than 'winning' and as someone who is 'doing it properly'.

Coat King as Actor for Adaptation: Coat King as Cutting Tool

Within this culture, as one becomes more entangled and embedded, the Coat King emerges as a very different tool. As has been explained above, the Coat King is intended to mimic the natural plucking of the other pack members, removing extraneous long hair only from certain areas of the areas of the coat to expose the shape of the dog for exhibition purposes. Stories emerge, however, which locate the Coat King very differently, as an agent for artifice and adaptation. The Coat King can be used to sculpt streamlined shapes to thin out the long coat, lifting areas of long coat to remove coat from underneath so as to not give away this artifice. Using such means, heavy shoulders can be made to appear more streamlined and shallow hocks more angulated. The Coat King can be used to naturalize areas of the long coat cut by scissors. On the body, the long silky coat hangs from the frame of the dog, showing how the frame is constructed. I was made aware of the practice of cutting the ends of the long body coat to give the impression of a well-constructed frame. If the Coat King is then raked along the cut edges this naturalizes the edges so that they look as if the coat is falling to that length from the frame due to natural growth. The scissor cut ends, thus treated, do not give away the artifice that has been employed. As has been explained, as an exhibitor within this culture, cutting of coat is highly frowned upon and contravenes the breed standard of points regulations. This is not simply an action intended to expose conformation, this action is intended to deceive the judge and approximate correct conformation through tricking the eye. In these material semiotic formations the Coat King emerges as a tool of contrivance, it produces the user as an agent of artifice. The Afghan hound exhibitor + Coat King as cutting/disguising tool hybrid, produces me as more concerned with show ring success, and with little scruples about how to achieve this. However, winning is the currency of exhibition and breeding, and success in the show ring allows the exhibitor to carry on breeding safe in the knowledge that the stock that is produced will be more easily sold. Unsuccessful dogs (and their owners) drop out of the cultural gene pool and become entities that do not 'matter' within Afghan hound culture. The ability to win has literal consequences of existence for dogs and owners within this culture. Unsuccessful hounds soon drop out and become pets rather than exhibition specimens and a succession of failures in the show ring also renders the exhibitor (literally) a 'non-entity'.

Managing the practice of grooming the Afghan hound using the coat king has become a juggling act within which the Coat King emerges as an ontologically ambivalent consumption object located within both (and at the same time) the natural and the contrived. The mutability of the Coat King helps to maintain the important performance of both presenting the dog as near to the ideal shape as possible (thus being a tool of artifice and adaptation) and as if it has not been intervened with by artificial grooming practices (thus being a tool of authenticity and preservation). As has been argued, the Coat King therefore acts to produce the exhibitor as a natural historian of the Afghan breed, with higher concerns that mere prize winning, but at the same time it acts to produce the exhibitor as one who is more likely to win prizes and thus become part of the history of the breed, to develop the necessary longevity of association with the breed through multiple successes in the show ring and concomitant maintenance and establishment of the breeders bloodlines.

CONCLUSION

This work has developed a story of a consumption object, the 'Mars Coat King' which illustrates the fluid boundaries and ambivalent ontologies of seemingly stable consumption objects. The Mars Coat king emerges and acts as a tool for preservation of the authentic, a basic implement requiring learned skill and dexterity to mimic the plucking of the Afghan hound pack. At the same time it acts as a tool of artifice and the contrived, to trick the eye into seeing shapes that don't exist in specific Afghan hounds and to disguise the cutting activities of exhibitors. As such this 'consumption object' is 'worked up' by this consumer culture as ontologically 'both/and at the same time'. Within the overlapping cultural formations illustrated above the Coat King loses its form and integrity as an essential object, it become indeterminate and as such cannot be seen as an ontological primitive. Its form/s emerge only in heterogeneous relationalities. Further to this, the Coat King becomes an important actor in the formation of others, for example, the ongoing performance of the Afghan hound culture as a successful exhibition and breeding culture as seen within its broader milieu and at the same time as an important collective of quasi natural historians, preserving the authenticity of the Afghan hound beyond the trivial matters of show success.

In the paper stimulating this conference the writers state that, 'CCT is infused by a spirit of critical self-reflection and paradigmatic reinvention and a corresponding antipathy towards the idea of settling into a comfortable but intellectually stultifying orthodoxy' (Arnould & Thompson, 2005, p. 870). As a development of this laudable statement they ask, 'what are the new frontiers for CCT?'(2005, p. 876). I would argue that, in response to this, examining and theorizing the complex and ambivalent co-emergence of meaning and materiality as has been illustrated here can add a new dimension to CCT work where the tendency has been to reduce objects to things that have meanings projected onto them or objects that are simply rendered as (for example) mundane or meaningful, sacred or profane, complex or simple. In this illustrative example, the Coat King, a seemingly mundane grooming device, emerges as both/and at the same time, a sacred and a profane object, complex and simple and as mundane and meaningful. Unpicking the different worlds from which it emerges as such, examining how it acts within these different worlds and how the complex contradictions between these worlds are managed provides an interesting new area of understanding for consumer research. There is a requirement, I would argue, to enhance existing CCT analyses with a requirement to not only look at consumer culture in terms of how 'consumers consume', but also at how objects 'object', where 'object' is taken as a verb rather than a noun. In this way, CCT can attend to our own 'missing masses' by conceptualizing consumption objects as ontologically mutable and active participants in the ontological entanglements of emergent meaning and materiality that characterizes complex consumer cultures.

NOTE

1. Links to worldwide breeders websites can be found here http://www.affieloverbreedclubs.co.uk/links.htm

REFERENCES

Arnould, E. J., & Thompson, C. (2005). Consumer culture theory: Twenty years of research. *Journal of Consumer Research*, *31*(4), 868–893.

Belk, R. W. (1976). It's the thought that counts: A signed diagraph analysis of gift giving. *Journal of Consumer Research*, *3*(December), 155–162.

Belk, R. W. (1988). Possessions and the extended self. *Journal of Consumer Research*, *15*(September), 139–168.

Bettany, S., & Daly, R. (2007). Figuring companion species consumption: A multi-site ethnography of the post-canine Afghan hound. *Journal of Business Research*, *60*.

Borgerson, J. (2005). Materiality, agency, and the constitution of consuming subjects: Insights for consumer research. In: G. Menon & A. R. Rao (Eds), *Advances in consumer research*, (Vol. 32, pp. 439–443). Duluth, MN: Association for Consumer Research.

Butler, J. (1996). *Bodies that matter*. London: Blackwell.

Campbell, C. (1989). *The Romantic ethic and the spirit of modern capitalism*. Oxford: Blackwell.

Clifford, J., & Marcus, G. E. (1986). *Writing culture: The poetics and politics of ethnography*. London: University of California Press.

Clutton-Brock, J. (1994). The unnatural world: Behavioral aspects of humans and animals in the process of domestication. In: A. Manning & J. Serpell (Eds), *Animals and human society: Changing perspectives* (pp. 36–38). London: Routledge.

Dant, T. (1999). *Material culture in the social world*. Buckingham: Open University Press.

Darwin, C. (1859). *The Origin of Species by Means of Natural Selection* (1st ed.). London: John Murray.

Douglas, M., & Isherwood, B. (1979). *The world of goods: Towards an anthropology of consumption*. London: Routledge.

Geertz, C. (1973). *The interpretation of cultures*. New York: Basic.

Hage, G. (2005). A not so mult-sited ethnography of a not so imagined community. *Anthropological Theory*, *5*, 463–475.

Hannerz, U. (2003). Being there and there and there. *Ethnography*, *4*(2), 210–216.

Haraway, D. J. (1989). Teddy bear patriarchy: Taxidermy in the Garden of Eden, New York City, 1908–1936. *Primate visions: Gender, race, and nature in the world of modern science* (pp. 26–58). New York: Routledge.

Haraway, D. J. (1997). Modest Witness_Second_Millennium.FemaleMan©_Meets_OncoMouse^{TM}. Routledge: New York.

Haraway, D. (2005). *Live theory (Schneider)*. London: Continuum Press.

Harrison, C. (1971). *The Afghan Hound*. Arco Pub: UK.

Holbrook, M. B. (1993). Nostalgia and consumption preferences: Some emerging patterns of consumer tastes. *Journal of Consumer Research*, *20*(2), 245–256.

Holt, D. (1995). How consumers consume: A typology of consumption practices. *Journal of Consumer Research*, *22*(June), 1–16.

Holt, D. (2002). Why do brands cause trouble? A dialectical theory of consumer culture and branding. *Journal of Consumer Research*, *29*(June), 70–90.

Joy, A. S. (2001). Gift giving in Hong Kong and the continuum of social ties. *Journal of Consumer Research*, *28*(September), 239–256.

Latour, B. (1992). Where are the missing masses? The sociology of a few mundane artifacts. In: W. Bijker & J. Law (Eds), *Shaping technology/building society studies in sociotechnical change*. USA: MIT Press.

Latour, B. (1994). On technical mediation: Philosophy, sociology, genealogy. *Common Knowledge*, *5*(1), 29–64.

Latour, B. (1999). On recalling ANT. In: J. Law & J. Hassard (Eds), *Actor network theory and after*. Oxford: Blackwell.

Latour, B. (2000). When things strike back: A possible contribution of science studies to the social sciences. *British Journal of Sociology*, *51*(1), 107–123.

Law, J. (2000). *Objects, spaces, others (draft)*. Centre for Science Studies and the Department of Sociology Working Papers, Lancaster University.

Marcus, G. E. (1998). Contemporary problems of ethnography in the modern world system. In: J. Clifford & G. E. Marcus (Eds), *Writing Culture* (pp. 165–193). Berkeley: University of California Press.

Marcus, G. E. (1995). Ethnography in/of the world system: The emergence of multi-sited ethnography. *Annual review of anthropology*, *24*, 95–117.

Martin, E. (1994). *Flexible bodies: Tracing immunity in American culture from the days of polio to the age of AIDS*. Boston: Beacon.

Mehta, R., & Belk, R. W. (1991). Artifacts, identity and transition: Favorite possessions of Indians and Indian immigrants to the US. *Journal of Consumer Research*, *17*(March), 391–411.

Mick, D. G., & De Moss, M. (1990). Self gifts: Phenomenological insights from four contexts. *Journal of Consumer Research*, *17*(December), 322–332.

Millar, D. (1987). *Material culture and mass consumption*. Oxford: Blackwell.

Murray, J. (2002). The politics of consumption: A reinquiry on Thompson and Haytko's speaking of fashion. *Journal of Consumer Research*, *29*(December), 427–440.

Niblock, M. (1980). *The Afghan hound: A definitive study*. New York: Arco Publishing.

Ozanne, J. L. (1992). The role of consumption and disposition during classic rites of passage: The journey of birth initiation and death. In: J. F. Sherry & B. P. Stenthal (Eds.), *Advances in consumer research* (Vol. 19, pp. 396–403). UT: ACR.

Perron, P., & Collins, F. (Eds) (1989). *Paris school Semiotics. 1. Theory*. Amsterdam: J. Benjamins.

Ritvo, H. (1987). *The animal estate: The English and other creatures in the Victorian age*. Harvard: Cambridge.

Slater, D. (1997). *Consumer culture and modernity*. Cambridge: Polity.

Thompson, C. J., & Hirschman, E. C. (1995). Understanding the socialised body: A poststructuralist analysis of consumers self conceptions, body images and self care practices. *Journal of Consumer Research*, *22*(September), 139–153.

SERVICE-DOMINANT LOGIC AND CONSUMER CULTURE THEORY: NATURAL ALLIES IN AN EMERGING PARADIGM

Eric J. Arnould

ABSTRACT

The aim of this paper is to suggest some potential linkages between Consumer Culture Theory (CCT hereafter) and the evolving Service-Dominant logic (S-D hereafter) propounded by Vargo and Lusch in a series of publications (Vargo & Lusch, 2004, 2006a, 2006b). I begin by discussing why this alliance makes sense. To do this, I review the CCT roots of several foundational propositions for the S-D logic Vargo and Lusch (2004) offer. Then I offer a suggestion for rethinking the notion of consumer itself. And finally, I discuss some potential changes in preferred constructs that I believe are necessary to fulfill the theoretical promise of the CCT perspective, and follow on from embracing a CCT/S-D perspective.

The aim of this paper is to suggest some potential linkages between Consumer Culture Theory (CCT hereafter) and the evolving Service-Dominant logic in marketing strategy (S-D hereafter) propounded by Vargo and Lusch

Consumer Culture Theory
Research in Consumer Behavior, Volume 11, 57–76

ISSN: 0885-2111/doi:10.1016/S0885-2111(06)11025-X

in a series of publications (Vargo & Lusch, 2004, 2006a, 2006b). I begin by discussing why this alliance makes sense. Then I offer some suggestions and a rationale for rethinking the notion of consumer itself. And finally, I discuss some potential changes in preferred terminology that follow on from embracing a CCT/S-D perspective and moving CCT in the direction of theoretical coherence (not hegemony, I hasten to add).

WHY AN S-D/CCT ALLIANCE?

Vargo and Lusch (2006b) acknowledge that one source of inspiration for their S-D logic proposal derives from the services scholarship that grew out of the pioneering vision of Gummesson, Shostak, Lovelock, Langeard and Eiglier, and Bitner and others. And they argue that in some ways, the S-D proposal simply works through the logical consequences of the insights services scholarship provides.

I will argue that some of the propositions outlined in Vargo and Lusch (2004) are ideas that researchers associated with the CCT tradition have pioneered (Arnould & Thompson, 2005). Typical of the strategy area in marketing in general, however, this tradition is unacknowledged (even unknown) terrain in Vargo and Lusch's work. Some CCT theorists may not share S-D theorists' strategic interests. Nevertheless, the parallelism makes CCT a natural resource for theorists seeking to elaborate Vargo and Lusch's (2006a) foundational premises.

A second rationale for exploring possible S-D/CCT synergies has to do with the future institutional legitimacy of CCT. The founding strokes in the emergence of the cultural perspective on consumer behavior in the business disciplines were struck to wean consumer research away from a narrow focus on managerial issues. The reason for this departure was in part the belief that developing consumer behavior theory would be best served by a broadened social science perspective on the full range of consumer behaviors rather than a narrow one grounded in economics and psychology and dedicated to understanding and predicting purchase decisions (Belk, 1987; Holbrook, 1987). There is little doubt that this was a prescient call at the time, given subsequent developments in consumer research that have brought anthropological, historical, and sociological perspectives to bear on consumption phenomena (Arnould & Thompson, 2005; Miller, 1995a). Currently, the downside of this is a deepening schism between consumer research and managerial marketing in the academy (Holbrook, 2005; McAlister, 2005).

I would argue that scholars working in the CCT tradition should bring evolving trends in theory, practice, and method together. This is not to deny that some scholars are doing this, but a more self-conscious more intentional effort is desirable. Why? On the one hand, concerned that without theoretical grounding, the potential of ethnographic methods is constrained, some prominent practitioners have argued for more attention to the guiding role of theory in applied cultural research (Denny, 2007) and to the theoretical grounding of ethnographic practitioners themselves (McCracken, 2006). On the other, without stronger theoretical development *and* the institutional legitimacy afforded CCT by grounding in managerial practice, already embattled, CCT's future in the business academy is in grave peril. An alliance with an emergent strategic paradigm makes both tactical and theoretical sense. Alternatively one may pursue a heroic quest to make business schools more hospitable to pure social science (Holbrook, 2005), but this seems a quest not merely quixotic but Herculean in scope.

CCT FOUNDATIONS FOR S-D PREMISES

Let me discuss the CCT foundations for a few of the S-D premises, since the conceptual linkage is a key to the alliance rationale. These premises do not dovetail neatly with the four-fold classification of research initiatives described by Arnould and Thompson (2005), nevertheless there is a clear overlap that suggests a basis for fruitful collaboration. For example, Vargo and Lusch (2004) articulate foundational premise three, "Goods are Distribution Mechanisms for Service Provision". Note that service in the S-D framework refers to behavioral manifestations of the application of specialized knowledge or competences. In this framework of understanding, tangible goods may embody tacit or domain-specific explicit knowledge; they may also be seen as "appliances" (e.g., a drug) for the performance of (e.g., medical) services; and platforms for performances that people encode as experiences, which in turn, represent valued states of acting or being (Vargo & Lusch, 2004).

For those of us in CCT, premise three evokes Sid Levy's (1959) "Symbols for Sale". I submit this is the Ur-text of CCT; one in which Levy asserted the now uncontroversial point that people buy things for what they mean; or in S-D terms, things provide the service of identity provision and communication. This point is central to the work of anthropologist Mary Douglas (1992) who is largely responsible for the development of interest in consumption in that discipline, as well as Grant McCracken (1988). More fundamentally, following Miller (1987, 2005), consumption behaviors employing consumer goods are existential acts of appropriation whereby humans define, bound, and recognize themselves in the material world. In fact, access to the means of consumption is a crucial act of resistance to the abstraction and alienation entailed in the capitalist separation of production from consumption.

In its concern with identity, CCT has been developing and using frameworks to understand how market offerings provide "symbolic services" – that is, how market offerings provide the service of symbolizing things to self and others (for a comprehensive review, see Mick, Burroughs, Hetzel, & Brannen, 2004). Moreover, CCT researchers emphasize researching consumers in context, and as a result, we are better able to understand how consumers perform identity service with firm-provided offerings. A good example among many is Ritson and Elliott's (1999) demonstration that teenage affinity groups use advertisements' tropes and lingo to communicate knowledge of self and others, and thereby create the ads' value for this "network". Work of this type that draws inspiration not only from anthropology and sociology generally but also from sources like the Birmingham school of cultural studies (e.g., Agger, 1992; Hebdige, 1996; Willis, Jones, Canaan, & Hurd, 1990) and reader response theory in literary criticism (Hirschman, Scott, & Wells, 1998; Scott, 1994b), thus provide a foundation for understanding how advertising language moves from the sphere of marketing communications to broader linguistic and cultural communities.

This foundational premise as well as Vargo and Lusch's definition of service (Vargo & Lusch, 2004, p. 2), "as the application of specialized competences (knowledge and skills) through deeds, processes, and performances for the benefit of another entity or the entity itself" also recalls a relatively unexploited text in CCT. In this paper, Deighton (1992) contends that people do not buy objects but instead buy performances or the inputs that allow them to produce them. Deighton (1992) proposed a four-fold classification in terms of customer roles and performance realism. Focusing just on the former, performances can be differentiated in a couple of ways. First, performances might be differentiated by the degree to which the consumers' performative operant resources (that is, skills and knowledge), is constrained or liberated by the deployment of firm-provided operant and operand resources. Thus, the Mall of the Americas and the West Edmonton Mall offer customers the opportunity to play relatively flexible coproductive roles by making use of the plethora of resources being offered. And some authors argue that these malls provide settings for relatively fantastical, that is festive performances (Andrieu, Badot, & Macé, 2004; Hetzel, 1998). In contrast, the furniture retailer IKEA controls and channels its customers' in-store purchase performance, although creative postpurchase do-it-yourself identity performances emerge through which consumers create new value (Ritson, Elliott, & Eccles, 1996).

Performances also can be differentiated by the degree to which retailers' deployment of resources places outcomes in doubt, tests values, or introduces tension or uncertainty into customer experience. In Deighton's terms, these would fall under the heading of thrill performances. For example, the Boston department store Filene's Basements sales famously challenged shoppers' skills and endurance (Schindler, 1989); consequently, customers' operant resources were at a premium in value extracting performances in this retail context. Gift stores, flea markets, garage sales, and festival malls also lean toward the uncertainty, skill-demanding end of this performative continuum (Herrmann, 2004; Maclaran & Brown, 2005; Sherry & McGrath, 1989; Sherry, 1990). Other retail venues deploy resources in such a way that consumers' operant resources are likely to be deployed in more ritualistic or predictable ways; that is, they tend to affirm rather than test values (Arnold, Kozinets, & Handelman, 2001; Badot, 2005). Successful mainstream retailers and mundane brand purchases may fall toward this end of the performative continuum as Miller (1998a) argues in his theory of mundane shopping as a sacrificial act. Some authors have initiated research into consumers' role performances (Coupland, 2005; Grove, Fisk, & Dorsch, 1998; Kiecker & Hartman, 1993; McCracken, 1986; McGrath & Otnes, 1995), but the area invites further theorization (e.g., Moisio & Arnould, 2005). Research could further systematize performance types and their connections to consumers' use of operant resources and traditional marketing outcome variables. Some further research suggestions are offered in the discussion section below.

How do consumers make firm-supplied operant resources perform? One way might be through deploying narrative frames (Deighton, 1992; Thompson, 2004) that reimagine marketers' value propositions in terms of significant consumer projects aimed at identity formation or community building. For example, market mavens enact coupon usage games in which coupons become more than a mere vehicle to deliver the implicit contracted performance, namely, a price rebate (Price, Feick, & Guskey-Federouch, 1988) but as a competitive game in which consumers deploy operant resources to exert mastery. Supermarket shoppers can reframe these contracted performances as treats (Miller, 1998a) or self-gifts (Mick & De Moss, 1990).

Similarly, thrift shoppers might reframe the contractual bargain of shopping performance so that it becomes a dramatic hunt for treasure (Bardhi & Arnould, 2005); while garage sale participants may reframe price negotiations as gender performances (Herrmann, 2004).

Narrative reframing introduces active consumer agency into the firm-supplied resource by associating the consumer's self, life project, and goals with the firm-provided resources, such as appliances, the shopping process, and habitats. As noted, some authors have proposed framing typologies (Deighton, 1992; Holt, 1995; Stern, 1995), and some empirical research has explored them (Stamps & Arnould, 1998; Peñaloza, 2001). But researchers need to know a lot more about the different types of consumer frames, the ways in which these different types facilitate value-adding performances by firm-provided operant resources, and how product and retail servicescapes may cue consumer-framing practices.

In the CCT tradition, Venkatesh, Sherry, and Firat (1993) anticipated foundational premise four, "Knowledge is the Fundamental Source of Competitive Advantage". Indeed, their article includes a table and discussion outlining shifts in the nature of valued knowledge in postmodernity. For instance consistent with Bourdieuan theory, they stress that sophisticated semiotic knowledge is a central resource to operate effectively in a postmodern marketing context, a theme some of the authors return to in a commentary on Vargo and Lusch (Venkatesh, Peñaloza, & Firat, 2006).

More fundamentally, in its concern with ideology and reproduction, CCT research has developed a foundation for understanding the nature and effects of consumption knowledge. Because of CCT research inspired by phenomenological and literary critical perspectives, we know that knowledge is not veridical "information," but is instead culturally situated understandings of "what things mean" and "how things work" (Scott, 1994a; Stern, 1988) in particular contexts and from particular subjects' standpoints (Dobscha & Ozanne, 2001; Thompson & Troester, 2002). Further, we know that knowledge is embodied practice (Thompson & Hirschman, 1995; Thompson & Haytko, 1997; Murray, 2002). Thus by deploying narrative frames while actively touring of sites and museums at the Gettysburg battlefield, participants perform moral lessons that link sacrifices of the past to contemporary sacrifice (e.g., 9/11) and reinforce Lincoln's post-Civil War message enshrined in the Gettysburg address (Chronis, Arnould, & Hampton, n.d.).

Hopefully, CCT researchers may be forgiven a wry response to foundational premise six, "The Customer is always a Co-Producer". Particularly in its work on consumer cultures, CCT provided an empirical basis for conceptualizing the cocreative role of consumers well before strategic marketing consultants' advanced their somewhat more arid model (e.g., Firat & Venkatesh, 1993, p. 235; cf. Prahalad & Ramaswamy, 2000). Much of the work on brand and consumption communities develops these ideas in particular contexts, but more formal synthetic models of consumer coproduction could still be developed, perhaps by developing deCerteauan ideas such as the notion that coproductive practices embody a kind of vernacular theorizing with the operant resources put into play by firms and consumer groups (McLaughlin, 1996). Finally, CCT can be an ally to research and practice in relation to this foundational premise because CCT research illuminates the consumption cycle, that is, the full range of consumers' pre- and postacquisition behaviors through which value is engendered from the integration of marketer- and consumer-provided resources (Arnould & Thompson, 2005).

Foundational premise eight, "A Service-Oriented View is Customer-Oriented and Relational" is perhaps the least well developed in Vargo and Lusch (2004). CCT can be an ally to research and practice in relation to this foundational premise for the following reasons. CCT researchers working on market place cultures and the socio-historical patterning of consumption have developed frameworks to account both for the fact that marketing involves more than one-off exchanges and also that individuals exchange as part of institutionalized social relationships. Work on class, brand and consumption communities emphasizes that part of what companies end-up selling is access to like-minded consumers. Indeed, Cova (1997; Cova & Cova, 2002) stresses that one of the core services provided by market offerings is precisely implicit or explicit social links to groupings that are themselves products of the development of a market-mediated society. Relationships in marketing are not just repeated exchanges over time between firms and consumers as in the customer lifetime value framework (Rust, Lemon, & Zeithaml, 2004), or even merely localized social networks (Muniz & Schau, 2005), but evolve out of the interaction between marketer-provided resources, deeply rooted norms and cultural templates for behavior (McAlexander, Schouten, & Koening, 2002) and in some cases embodied social categories like class and ethnicity (Holt, 1998; Crockett & Wallendorf, 2004). Moreover, the gift-giving literature in which CCT's contribution is foundational (Sherry, 1983; Otnes & Beltramini, 1996), and the limited work on disposition (Curasi, Price, & Arnould, 2004) both emphasize how relationships constrain what service gets exchanged and how value is derived from it.

In some recent empirical work, we have found that consumers adopt a host of partnering strategies with firms through which they capture value from firm-provided resources. The most obvious of these is outsourcing. Households outsource tutoring their children to firms like Sylvan Learning Centers and meal preparation to firms like Dream Dinners. And of course they outsource certain aspects of childcare to day care centers and live-in nannies. A more subtle strategy we identify in this work is integration, a strategy that enables families to service multiple conflicting interpersonal loyalties simultaneously by drawing on the services firms provide. Prominent in our data was recourse to franchised family restaurants to provide a venue for "family meals", although the choice was often a compromise preferred by none but acceptable to all. Olive Garden adopts this strategy explicitly in its "we are family" themed marketing communications. Another strategy we call segmentation in which consumers use the so-called "lifestyle" brands to create boundaries around activated or segregated selves. Thus, when wearing Brand X, the consumer becomes a surfer, runner, diver, etc. This parallels some of Cova and Cova's (2002) findings. These three strategies do not exhaust the catalogue of partnering strategies we find that consumers adopt with regard to firm-provided resources but they suggest fruitful avenues for future research into the relational aspects of coproduction.

In summary, I have tried to argue that there are significant conceptual overlaps between ongoing work in CCT and the premises on which S-D would like to ground a new approach to marketing strategy. These overlaps provide a basis for fruitful future collaborations that could provide practitioners with useful theoretical tools, CCT academics with greater institutional legitimacy, and S-D with more robust models of service, knowledge, relationships, and coproduction from a consumer-centric perspective. I now turn to a conceptual challenge that the work so far done now confronts both S-D and CCT.

TOWARD A POSTCONSUMER

The term "consumer" poses some theoretical and practical problems for an evolving S-D logic (Vargo & Lusch, 2006b, p. 9). This is because S-D increasingly imagines firm exchange partners as coproducers of firm offerings (Prahalad & Ramaswamy, 2000, 2004). This relatively egalitarian model of coproduction may be summarized in Fig. 1. However, what I have said above also allows us to expand the consumer side of the model as shown in Fig. 2 and discuss elsewhere (Price, Arnould, & Malshe, 2006). Fig. 2 fleshes out the consumer side of the partnership in terms of the range

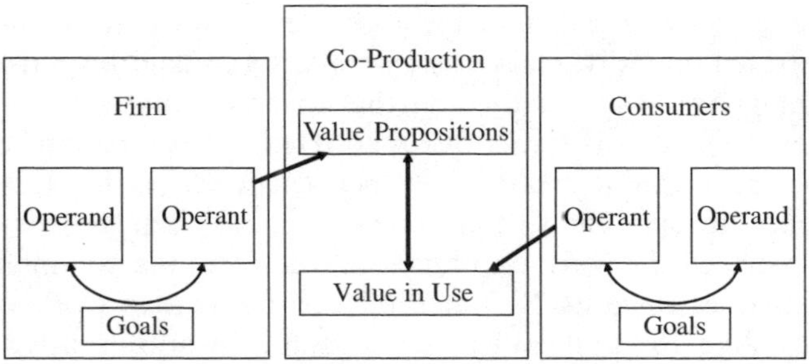

Fig. 1. Firm and Consumer Resource Interaction.

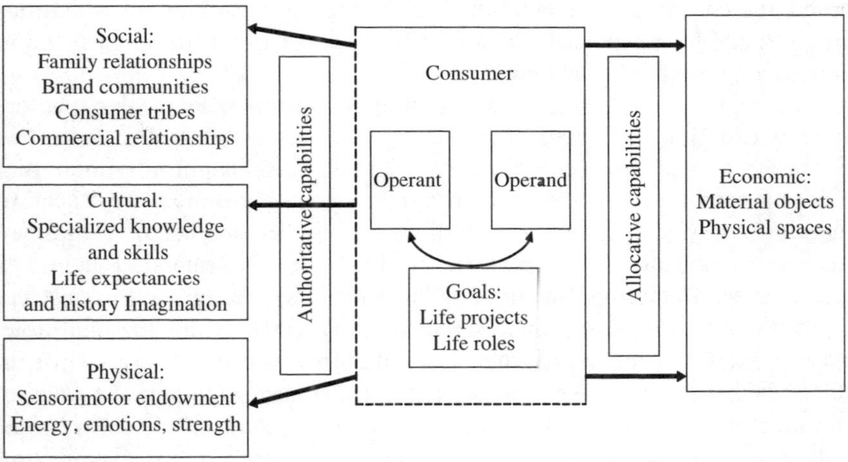

Fig. 2. The Consumer's "Operant" and "Operand" Resources. *Source:* Price, Arnould, and Malshe (2006).

of culturally embedded resources consumers may bring to their exchanges with marketers.

However both the S-D model and CCT lack a well-developed conception of firm's cocreative exchange partners. I would argue that the term "consumer" is as problematic for CCT researchers as for S-D Logic, but also that the evolving body of work in CCT should provide an appropriate source of ideas with which to develop conceptions of a postconsumer. CCT should be in the forefront of this theoretical and pragmatic effort.

Thus, a further point of departure for an alliance between S-D logic and CCT may lie in CCT's shift from an essentialist to a postessentialist logic of consumption. It's a truism that most consumer research in marketing is narrowly fixated on individual decision makers and their responses to marketing stimuli. And it is equally clear that this mechanical hobbyhorse has carried the mail about as far as it can go. Hence, CCT researchers should embrace socialized value creators, partners, networks, collectives, couples, families, peer groups, clubs, and communities as their primary units of analysis, as indeed the work on brand and consumption communities, and experiential tribes suggests. So much of recent empirical work shows that whether questing for authenticity or engaging in authoritative performances, whether gift giving, or acquiring things, consumers do this as aspirants to or members of a host of collectivities. Indeed, how could it be otherwise for primates such as us? And instead of accepting the idea that brand and consumption communities and other more situational affiliations are marginal to consumer behavior, we should insist that they are central to an understanding of consumption.

At a minimum we should stop thinking of consumers as passive reactors and instead think of them as proactive partners in cocreative acts. For instance, services research generally acknowledges Deighton's point that service is something performed, and in many cases consumers are crucial to successful service performance (Williams & Anderson, 2005). Hence are such persons full-fledged performers and not consumers? Further, a bricoleur who employs free-floating firm provided resources to construct an avatar like on-line persona (Schau & Gilly, 2003) is not the malleable, mass market consumer imagined by mid-20th century managers (Cohen, 2003; Packard, 1957). Neither are those prosumers who remake and remanufacture firm-provided resources (Muniz & Schau, 2005). More radically, if a person willingly transforms him or herself through the acquisition of commercially available technological, biological, or biotechnological prostheses is s/he a consumer or a cyborg? (Schroeder, 1994; Warwick, 2003; Wood, 1998). And if the latter, what are the roots to cyborgization, and how should we rethink materiality (Miller, 2005) and consumption on this terrain (Mitchell, 2003)? Consequently, by understanding these dynamics as manifest in shifts in our conceptualization of consumers, consumption, marketing, and the rest, the overall shift in our conceptualization of marketing logic can be brought into clearer relief.

To the extent this shift drives insight into empirical processes, we might make the case that such processes and conceptual shifts accelerate the reorientation from the Goods-Dominant to the Service-Dominant logic. Underlying both shifts are consumer practice-driven modifications and implosions of taken-for-granted distinctions between firm and customer, all of which are the focus of CCT. Thus, the "operant resource" CCT provides to S-D is research that focalizes, thematizes, explores, and problematizes the firm-customer dialectic. And such study in turn should inform our understanding of what the social science construct "consumer" is and what "consumer" does.

TOWARD A CCT/S-D FRIENDLY LEXICON

In recent comments, Hanssens (2006) contended that part of the success of the finance discipline both in academia and popular business thought is its development of a distinctive and evocative vocabulary, and encouraged proponents of CCT to follow suit. In this vein, Vargo and Lusch (2006b) outline in tabular form some conceptual reorientations entailed by the S-D logic they think necessary to unlock its conceptual potential. This move, like the relatively rapid adoption of CCT as a label for a distinctive family of research programs illustrates the liberatory potential of useful concepts. Thus, a table with some key conceptual reorientations implied by Arnould and Thompson's conception of CCT and the discussion above for rethinking the exchange partners within a general S-D logic may be outlined.

G-D Logic-Derived Concepts	CCT-Derived Concepts
Subjects, consumers	Actants, bricoleurs, prosumers, cyborgs, performers, partners, networks, collectivities
Needs, wants, motivations	Intentions, life projects, and desires
Involvement	Engagement, commitment
Personality (to be acted on)	Identity (to be constructed)
Stable demographic and psychographic segments	Temporary emotional and interpretive groupings, brand and experience focused networks and communities
Get inside the consumer's head	Participate in consumers' life worlds; unpack consumption "fields" within social space
Purchase decisions	Acquisition, consumption and disposition strategies and tactics (e.g., gift giving)

G-D Logic-Derived Concepts	CCT-Derived Concepts
Benefit-deriving	Value creating, Meaning-making, coproducing, aesthetics
Ownership	Experience, access, participation, guardianship
Materiality/Objects	Images, knowledge goods, cyberspace
Possessions	Epistemic objects, experiences, appropriations

Let me discuss just a few of these proposals for terminological changes in addition to encouraging critical reassessment of the construct of consumer. Each merits more thorough debate than space here allows. For example, I claim that the construct of intentions should replace motivations as a preferred term for CCT. The latter term takes researchers to the domain of psychological universals, psychological equilibrium models, negative psychology, and even to reductionism, as Holt (1997) has argued. In this frame consumer behavior is linked to a hydraulic model of the psyche. Rather like the oil in a car, consumers' need states get activated when the "lubricant" gets too low and a figurative red light flashes in the brain. Note that motivation research is linked to psychologists' interests in developing universal typologies to dimensionalize the evident psychic unity of the human species. Schwarz, and his five factors, and Hofstede and his four (or is it five?) cultural binaries are the heirs of Maslow and Murray in this respect. Such models also resurface in the work of consulting star Clotaire Rapaille (2006). While a worthy project these high-level abstractions do not take us very far in developing culturally situated understandings of behavior in a coproductive model. CCT shows over and over that much consumer behavior is linked to a positive, and proactive quest for meaning, identity, self-expression, community, authenticity, and so on, and that it is fundamentally creative and tactical in orientation, not redressive. And yet we are a far from a theory of such things.

Most consumer research in marketing, and much applied consumer research including that which adopts qualitative data collection and interpretive analytic strategies, clearly aims "to get inside the head of the consumer". The recent fad for neurological approaches to consumption merely accentuates a long-standing trend in management thinking that one could argue has its origins in post-War economics (Mirowski, 2002). CCT research by contrast should aim to get inside the life world of the consumer. But we should also go beyond this fundamental injunction of phenomenological approaches that aim for emic understanding. For we should come to a more analytic understanding of the entire domain of consumption itself, recognizing that it is partitioned into partially autonomous fields in the Bourdieuan sense in which consumers allocate resources for advantages in various games of taste and taste-making. Thus, architecture, especially evident in trends such as gentrification or do-it-yourself; shopping as in Big Box estates, themed urban places and arts districts; or tourism as differentiated into mass, eco, extreme, Lonely Planet, and other segments, create contested consumption spaces for taste-making (Fürsich, 2002; Miller, 1998b; West & Carrier, 2004; Zukin, 1990). And of course we should recognize that the organization of some such consumption fields, as demonstrated with regard to education (Allen, 2002) or tourism (Kirtsoglou & Theodossopoulos, 2004), allow for class-related domination, and structured advantages and disadvantages with regard to consumption and access to cultural resources more generally to be created and reproduced. In short, we need an ecology of consumption practice.

While objects and ownership are not unimportant, these ideas are fundamentally bound up with the purchase behavior focus of modernist consumer research. Instead, it would be useful to move away from conceptions of consumers and their object relationships. Instead we should move toward a more service-oriented view that both problematizes subject–object relationships through such concepts as communication, participation, and guardianship (Schiffer, 1999; Ludicke, 2006; Curasi et al., 2004; Zwick & Dholakia, 2006) and the object itself through a serious interrogation of materiality (Miller, 2005), that is the coconstituting relationship between culture-bearing agents and the material world, including its immaterial dimension. Transcending the purchase decision context, we should also focus on the array of service extraction practices and performances through which consumers engage with the object world some of which are fundamentally semiotic, and others presemiotic, performative, or constitutive in a phenomenological sense.

I wish neither to overstate nor understate the value of terminological changes for CCT. But like the emerging S-D logic, CCT's analyses are often steeped in the constructs and interpretive positions they seek to overcome. As much as CCT has succeeded in contesting some of the theoretical assumptions weaving a conceptual cage called the consumer or consumption, those foundational to the Enlightenment scientific project still operate (representationalism, essentialism, dualism, etc.) and indeed seem to be entrenched in some quarters. Operationally, we seem to proceed with a conceptual vocabulary that is little more than an accretion of textbook topics derived from managerial marketing and consumer studies whose ontological status goes largely unquestioned. In this regard, it is worth paraphrasing Richard Rorty[1] to the effect that it is no truer that consumers are what they are because we researchers employ the term "consumer" as we do than that we use the term "consumer" as we do because consumers are as they are. The foundational premises of the emerging S-D logic just as the emerging tropes in CCT may lead to a new postconsumer, new theory, and new practice but they should no more become shibboleths than elements of the old Goods-Dominant vocabulary or constructs associated with economic man or the psychological subject of modernist consumer research.

PROSPECT

In this paper, I have suggested how and why an alliance between two emerging perspectives that of S-D and CCT seems logical and desirable. I have reviewed some common conceptual ground, some shared conceptual concerns, and some directions for changes in preferred conceptual vocabulary. On a theoretical level, to realize its promise, CCT should be building on foundational thought in the social sciences (Arnould & Thompson, 2005) toward developing and making explicit the theoretical foundations of the schools of thought guiding future research. Adhocracy is not an option. More specifically, research on consumer identity work needs a theory of intentionality; a self-reflexive critique of identity; bricolage; and the consumer construct itself. Research on consumer cultures needs a Bourdieuan systematization of fields, resources, coproduction, and games. Research on the socio-historic patterning of consumption needs a much more vigorous investigation of past and alternate consumption regimes whether those attached to the ancient Silk Road, the Ottoman empire, the trans-Saharan caravan trade, the Triangle trade (Mintz, 1985; Wilk, 2006), or what have you, and the way such regimes are linked to the basic organizing categories of society. Research on ideology and reproduction would be well served by a reappropriation of the idea of "lay theory" from psychology (Dweck, 1996; Mukhopadhyay & Johar, 2005) and its integration with the notion of "vernacular theorizing" from deCerteauan thought into better understanding of folk models of consumption (McLaughlin, 1996); a fundamental reflection on materiality; attention to local challenges to the hegemonic Euro-American construction of the consumer good life; and a vigorous rethinking of the psycho-economic folk theory that organizes too much of our scholarly thinking.

On a pragmatic level, CCT researchers should think pragmatically. They are in a position to develop answers to three compelling questions of managerial importance. First, how do marketers manage to create "value" consumers recognize as such? And, where does "value" come from and what makes that "value" worth coproducing? CCT research on cultural theories of branding and retailing, myth, and consumer meaning more generally point us in the right direction, but much remains to be done (Holt, 2004; Holt & Thompson, 2004; Johar, Holbrook, & Stern, 2001; Schroeder & Salzer-Mörling, 2006; Scott, 1994b; Stern, 1995; Thompson, 2004).

Second, how and under what conditions do consumers extract the managerially desired types of "value" from firm provided resources or "twist" (Aubert-Gamet, 1997) those values to their own socially and culturally embedded ends? CCT work inspired by Goffman and de Certeau on everyday consumption practices (Deighton, 1992; Moisio & Arnould, 2005; Zwick & Dholakia, 2006) and work on secular consumption rituals (Miller, 1995b, 1998a) including gift giving points in the right direction, but again much remains to do.

Third, at the end of the day, in a broader existential sense what is the social life of things? In other words, how do consumers make use of the "value" derived through service performance from firm-produced resources? Here work on "object biography", (Kopytoff, 1986), post-Bourdieuan doing of consumption (Holt, 1995, 1997), and materiality (Miller, 2005) points in the right direction, but the mortar of foundational theory is barely dry.

NOTE

1. A very big thanks to Markus Geisler for this pithy aphoristic insertion!

ACKNOWLEDGMENTS

The author gratefully acknowledges the conceptual contributions of Maia Beruchashvili, Doulgas Brownlie, Markus Geisler, Kent Grayson, Risto Moisio, and Craig Thompson. While these original thinkers provided "operant resources", the author is responsible for the resulting integration.

REFERENCES

Agger, B. (1992). *Cultural studies as critical theory*. London: Falmer Press.

Allen, D. E. (2002). Toward a theory of consumer choice as sociohistorically shaped practical experience: The fits-like-a-glove (FLAG) framework. *Journal of Consumer Research*, *28*(March), 515–532.

Andrieu, F., Badot, O., & Macé, S. (2004). Le West Edmonton Mall: Un Échafaudage Sensoriel Au Service d'une Cosmogonie Populaire? *Revue Française du Marketing*, *196*(February), 53–67.

Arnold, S. J., Kozinets, R. V., & Handelman, J. M. (2001). Hometown ideology and retailer legitimation: The institutional semiotics of Wal-Mart flyers. *Journal of Retailing*, *77*(2), 243–271.

Arnould, E. J., & Thompson, C. J. (2005). Consumer culture theory (CCT): Twenty years of research. *Journal of Consumer Research*, *31*(March), 868–883.

Aubert-Gamet, V. (1997). Twisting servicescapes: Diversion of the physical environment in a re-appropriation process. *International Journal of Service Industry Management*, *8*(1), 26–41.

Badot, O. (2005). L'Autre Raison du Succès de Wal-Mart: Une Rhétorique de L'Infra-Ordinaire. *Revue Française du Marketing*, *197*(July), 97–108.

Bardhi, F., & Arnould, E. J. (2005). Thrift shopping: Combining utilitarian thrift and hedonic treat benefits. *Journal of Consumer Behaviour*, *4*(June), 223–233.

Belk, R. W. (1987). A modest proposal for creating verisimilitude in consumer information processing models and some suggestions for establishing a discipline to study consumer behavior. In: R. Bagozzi, N. Dholakia & A. F. Firat (Eds), *Philosophical and radical thought in marketing* (pp. 361–372). Lexington, MA: Lexington Press.

Chronis, A., Arnould, E. J., & Hampton, R. D. (n.d.). *Gettysburg re-imagined: The role of narrative imagination in consumption experience*. Unpublished manuscript, California State University Stanislaus.

Cohen, L. (2003). *A consumer's republic: The politics of mass consumption in postwar America*. New York: Knopf.

Coupland, J. C. (2005). Invisible brands: An ethnography of households and the brands in their kitchen pantries. *Journal of Consumer Research*, *32*(June), 106–119.

Cova, B. (1997). Community and consumption: Towards a definition of the "linking value" of product or services. *European Journal of Marketing*, *31*(3/4), 297–316.

Cova, B., & Cova, V. (2002). Tribal marketing: The tribalisation of society and its impact on the conduct of marketing. *European Journal of Marketing*, *36*(5/6), 595–620.

Crockett, D., & Wallendorf, M. (2004). The role of normative political ideology in consumer behavior. *Journal of Consumer Research*, *31*(December), 511–529.

Curasi, C. F., Price, L. L., & Arnould, E. J. (2004). How individuals' cherished possessions become families' inalienable wealth. *Journal of Consumer Research*, *31*(December), 609–623.

Deighton, J. (1992). The consumption of performance. *Journal of Consumer Research*, *19* (December), 362–373.

Denny, R. (2007). Pushing the boundaries of ethnography in the practice of market research. In: R. W. Belk (Ed.), *Handbook of qualitative research methods in marketing*. Armonk, NY: Edward Elgar.

Dobscha, S., & Ozanne, J. L. (2001). An ecofeminist analysis of environmentally sensitive women using qualitative methodology: The emancipatory potential of an ecological life. *Journal of Public Policy & Marketing*, *20*(Fall), 201–214.

Douglas, M. (1992). Why do people want goods? In: S. Hargreaves & A. Ross (Eds), *Understanding the enterprise culture* (pp. 19–31). Edinburgh: Edinburgh University Press.

Dweck, C. S. (1996). Implicit theories as organizers of goals and behavior. In: P. M. Gollwitzer & J. A. Bargh (Eds), *The psychology of action: Linking cognition and motivation to behavior* (pp. 69–90). New York: Guilford Press.

Firat, A. F., & Venkatesh, A. (1993). Postmodernity: The age of marketing. *International Journal of Research in Marketing*, *10*(3), 227–250.

Fürsich, E. (2002). Packaging culture: The potential and limitations of travel programs on global television. *Communication Quarterly*, *50*(Spring), 204–226.

Grove, S. J., Fisk, R. P., & Dorsch, M. J. (1998). Assessing the theoretical components of the service encounter: A cluster analysis examination. *The Service Industries Journal*, *18*(3), 116–593.

Hanssens, D. (2006). Concluding comments. Marketing Science Institute Conference, Business Insights from Consumer Culture, Toronto, Canada, 3–5 May.

Hebdige, D. (1996). *Hiding in the light: On images and things*. London: Routledge.

Herrmann, G. M. (2004). Haggling spoken here: Gender, class, and style in US garage sale bargaining. *Journal of Popular Culture*, *38*(August), 55–81.

Hetzel, P. (1998). When hyperreality, reality, fiction and non-reality are brought together: A fragmented vision of the mall of America through personal interpretation. In: B. G. Englis, & A. Olofsson (Eds), *European advances in consumer research* (Vol. 3, pp. 261–266). Provo, UT: Association for Consumer Research.

Hirschman, E. C., Scott, L., & Wells, W. B. (1998). A model of product discourse: Linking consumer practice to cultural texts. *Journal of Advertising*, *27*(Spring), 33–50.

Holbrook, M. B. (1987). What is consumer research? *Journal of Consumer Research*, *14*(June), 128–133.

Holbrook, M. B. (2005). Marketing education as bad medicine for society: The gorilla dances. *Journal of Public Policy & Marketing*, *24*(Spring), 143–145.

Holt, D. B. (1995). How consumers consume: A typology of consumption practices. *Journal of Consumer Research*, *22*(June), 1–16.

Holt, D. B. (1997). Poststructuralist lifestyle analysis: Conceptualizing the social patterning of consumption in postmodernity. *Journal of Consumer Research*, *23*(March), 326–351.

Holt, D. B. (1998). Does cultural capital structure American consumption? *Journal of Consumer Research*, *25*(June), 1–25.

Holt, D. B. (2004). *How brands become icons: The principles of cultural branding*. Boston: Harvard Business School Press.

Holt, D. B., & Thompson, C. J. (2004). Man-of-action heroes: The pursuit of heroic masculinity in everyday consumption. *Journal of Consumer Research*, *31*(December), 425–441.

Johar, G. V., Holbrook, M. B., & Stern, B. B. (2001). The role of myth in creative advertising design: Theory, process and outcome. *Journal of Advertising*, *30*(Summer), 1–25.

Kiecker, P., & Hartman, C. L. (1993). Purchase Pal use: Why others choose to shop with others. In: R. Varadarajan & B. Jaworski (Eds), *Marketing theory and applications* (pp. 78–384). Chicago, IL: American Marketing Association.

Kirtsoglou, E., & Theodossopoulos, D. (2004). They are taking our culture away. *Critique of Anthropology*, *24*(June), 135–157.

Kopytoff, I. (1986). The cultural biography of things: Commoditization as process. In: A. Appadurai (Ed.), *The social life of things: Commodities in cultural perspective* (pp. 64–91). New York: Cambridge University Press.

Levy, S. J. (1959). Symbols for sale. *Harvard Business Review*, *37*(July–August), 117–124.
Ludicke, M. (2006). *A theory of marketing*. Doctoral thesis, St. Gallen, St. Gallen University, Switzerland.
Maclaran, P., & Brown, S. (2005). The centre cannot hold: consuming the Utopian marketplace. *Journal of Consumer Research*, *32*(June), 311–323.
McAlexander, J. H., Schouten, J. W., & Koening, H. F. (2002). Building brand community. *Journal of Marketing*, *66*(1), 38–55.
McAlister, L. M. (2005). Toward insight and relevance. *Journal of Public Policy & Marketing*, *24*(Spring), 131–132.
McCracken, G. (1986). Culture and consumption: A theoretical account of the structure and movement of the cultural meaning of consumer goods. *Journal of Consumer Research*, *13*(June), 71–84.
McCracken, G. (2006). Ethnography: pros and cons. Presentation at conference on Business Insights from Consumer Culture, Marketing Science Institute, Toronto, CA, 3–5 May.
McGrath, M. A., & Otnes, C. (1995). Unacquainted influencers: When strangers interact in the retail setting. *Journal of Business Research*, *32*(March), 261–264.
McLaughlin, T. (1996). *Street smarts and critical theory: Listening to the vernacular*. Madison, Wisconsin: University of Wisconsin Press.
Mick, D. G., Burroughs, J. E., Hetzel, P., & Brannen, M. Y. (2004). Pursuing the meaning of meaning in the commercial world: An international review of marketing and consumer research founded on semiotics. *Semiotica*, *152*(1/4), 1–74.
Mick, D. G., & De Moss, M. (1990). Self-gifts: Phenomenological insights from four contexts. *Journal of Consumer Research*, *17*(December), 322–332.
Miller, D. (Ed.) (1995a). *Acknowledging consumption*. London: Routledge.
Miller, D. (Ed.) (1995b). *Unwrapping Christmas*. Oxford: Clarendon Press.
Miller, D. (1998a). *A theory of shopping*. Ithaca: Cornell University Press.
Miller, D. (Ed.) (1998b). *The dialectics of shopping*. Chicago: University of Chicago Press.
Miller, D. (Ed.) (2005). *Materiality*. Durham, NC: Duke University Press.
Mintz, S. (1985). *Sweetness and power: The place of sugar in modern history*. New York: Penguin.
Mirowski, P. (2002). *Machine dreams: Economics becomes a cyborg science*. New York: Cambridge University Press.
Mitchell, W. J. (2003). *Me++ The cyborg, self and the networked city*. Cambridge: MIT Press.
Moisio, R., & Arnould, E. J. (2005). Extending the dramaturgical framework in marketing: The role of drama structure, drama content, and drama interaction in shopping performances. *Journal of Consumer Behaviour*, *4*(4), 246–256.
Mukhopadhyay, A., & Johar, G. V. (2005). Where there is a will, is there a way? Effects of lay theories of self-control on setting and keeping resolutions. *Journal of Consumer Research*, *31*(March), 779–786.
Muniz, A. M., Jr., & Schau, H. J. (2005). Religiosity in the abandoned Apple Newton brand community. *Journal of Consumer Research*, *31*(March), 737–747.
Murray, J. B. (2002). The politics of consumption: A re-inquiry on Thompson and Haytko's (1997) "speaking of fashion". *Journal of Consumer Research*, *29*(December), 427–440.
Otnes, C., & Beltramini, R. F. (1996). *Gift giving: A research anthology*. Bowling Green, OH: Bowling Green State University Popular Press.
Packard, V. O. (1957). *The hidden persuaders*. New York: D. McKay Co.

Peñaloza, L. (2001). Consuming the American west: Animating cultural meaning and memory at a stock show and rodeo. *Journal of Consumer Research*, *28*(December), 369–399.

Prahalad, C. K., & Ramaswamy, V. (2000). Coopting customer competence. *Harvard Business Review*, *78*(January–February), 79–87.

Prahalad, C. K., & Ramaswamy, V. (2004). Co-creation experiences: The next practice in value creation. *Journal of Interactive Marketing*, *18*(Summer), 5–14.

Price, L. L., Arnould, E. J., & Malshe, A. (2006). Toward a cultural resource-based theory of the customer. In: Robert F. Lusch & Stephen L. Vargo (Eds), *The new dominant logic in marketing* (pp. 91–104). Armonk, NY: M. E. Sharpe.

Price, L. L., Feick, L. F., & Guskey-Federouch, A. (1988). Couponing behaviors of the market maven: Profile of a super couponer. In: M. J. Houston (Ed.), *Advances in consumer research* (Vol. 15, pp. 354–359). Provo, UT: Association for Consumer Research.

Rapaille, C. (2006). *The culture code: An ingenious way to understand why people around the world live and buy as they do*. New York: Broadway.

Ritson, M., & Elliott, R. (1999). The social uses of advertising: An ethnographic study of adolescent advertising audiences. *Journal of Consumer Research*, *26*(December), 260–278.

Ritson, M., Elliott, R., & Eccles, S. (1996). Reframing IKEA: Commodity-signs, consumer creativity and the social/self dialectic. In: K. P. Corfman & J. G. Lynch, Jr. (Eds), *Advances in consumer research* (Vol. 23, pp. 127–131). Provo, UT: Advances in Consumer Research.

Rust, R. T., Lemon, K. N., & Zeithaml, V. A. (2004). Return on marketing: Using customer equity to focus marketing strategy. *Journal of Marketing*, *68*(January), 109–127.

Schau, H. J., & Gilly, M. C. (2003). We are what we post? Self-presentation in personal web space. *Journal of Consumer Research*, *30*(December), 385–404.

Schiffer, M. B. (1999). *The material life of human beings*. New York: Routledge.

Schindler, R. M. (1989). The excitement of getting a bargain: Some hypotheses concerning the origins and effects of smart-shopper feelings. In: T. Srull (Ed.), *Advances in consumer research* (Vol. 15, pp. 396–402). Provo, UT: Association for Consumer Research.

Schroeder, J. E., & Salzer-Mörling, M. (Eds) (2006). *Brand culture*. London: Routledge.

Schroeder, R. (1994). Cyberculture, cyborg post-modernism and the sociology of virtual reality technologies. *Futures*, *26*(June), 519–529.

Scott, L. M. (1994a). Images in advertising: The need for a theory of visual rhetoric. *Journal of Consumer Research*, *21*(September), 252–274.

Scott, L. M. (1994b). The bridge from text to mind: Adapting reader-response theory to consumer research. *Journal of Consumer Research*, *21*(December), 461–481.

Sherry, J. F., Jr. (1983). Gift giving in anthropological perspective. *Journal of Consumer Research*, *10*(September), 157–169.

Sherry, J. F., Jr. (1990). A sociocultural analysis of a Midwestern American flea market. *Journal of Consumer Research*, *17*(June), 13–30.

Sherry, J. F., Jr., & McGrath, M. A. (1989). Unpacking the holiday presence: Ethnography of two gift stores. In: E. C. Hirschman (Ed.), *Interpretive consumer research* (pp. 158–167). Provo, UT: Association for Consumer Research.

Stamps, M. B., & Arnould, E. J. (1998). The Florida classic: Performing African American community. In: J. W. Alba & W. Hutchinson (Eds), *Advances in consumer research* (Vol. 25, pp. 578–584). Provo, UT: Association for Consumer Research.

Stern, B. B. (1988). Medieval allegory: Roots of advertising strategy for the mass market. *Journal of Marketing*, *52*(3), 84–94.

Stern, B. B. (1995). Consumer myths: Frye's taxonomy and the structural analysis of consumption text. *Journal of Consumer Research*, *22*(September), 165–186.

Thompson, C. J. (2004). Marketplace mythology and discourses of power. *Journal of Consumer Research*, *31*(June), 162–181.

Thompson, C. J., & Haytko, D. L. (1997). Speaking of fashion: Consumers' uses of fashion discourses and the appropriation of countervailing cultural meanings. *Journal of Consumer Research*, *24*(June), 15–43.

Thompson, C. J., & Hirschman, E. C. (1995). Understanding the socialized body: A poststructuralist analysis of consumers' self-conceptions, body images, and self-care practices. *Journal of Consumer Research*, *22*(September), 139–154.

Thompson, C. J., & Troester, M. (2002). Consumer value systems in the age of postmodern fragmentation: The case of the natural health microculture. *Journal of Consumer Research*, *28*(March), 550–572.

Vargo, S. L., & Lusch, R. F. (2004). Evolving to a new dominant logic for marketing. *Journal of Marketing*, *68*(January), 1–7.

Vargo, S. L., & Lusch, R. F. (Eds) (2006a). *The service-dominant logic of marketing: Dialog, debate, and directions*. Armonk, NY: ME Sharpe.

Vargo, S. L., & Lusch, R. F. (2006b). Service-dominant logic: Reactions, reflections, and refinements. *Marketing Theory*, *6*(September), 281–288.

Venkatesh, A., Peñaloza, L., & Firat, A. F. (2006). The market as a sign system and the logic of the market. In: S. L. Vargo & R. F. Lusch (Eds), *The service-dominant logic of marketing: Dialog, debate, and directions* (pp. 251–266). Armonk, NY: M. E. Sharpe.

Venkatesh, A., Sherry, J. F., Jr., & Firat, A. F. (1993). Postmodernism and the marketing imaginary. *International Journal of Research in Marketing*, *10*(3), 215–224.

Warwick, K. (2003). Cyborg morals, cyborg values, cyborg ethics. *Ethics and Information Technology*, *5*(3), 131–137.

West, P., & Carrier, J. G. (2004). Ecotourism and authenticity. *Current Anthropology*, *45*(August), 483–491.

Wilk, R. R. (2006). *Home cooking in the global village: Caribbean food from buccaneers to ecotourists*. New York: Berg.

Williams, J. A., & Anderson, H. H. (2005). Engaging customers in service creation: A theater perspective. *Journal of Services Marketing*, *19*(1), 13–23.

Willis, P., Jones, S., Canaan, J., & Hurd, G. (1990). *Common culture: Symbolic work at play in the everyday cultures of the young*. Milton Keynes: Open University Press.

Wood, M. (1998). Agency and organization: Toward a cyborg-consciousness. *Human Relations*, *51*(October), 1209–1227.

Zukin, S. (1990). Socio-spatial prototypes of a new organization of consumption: The role of real cultural capital. *Sociology*, *24*(February), 37–56.

Zwick, D., & Dholakia, N. (2006). The epistemic consumption object and postsocial consumption: expanding consumer object theory in consumer research. *Consumption Markets & Culture*, *9*(March), 17–44.

FESTIVITY

POSTMODERN CONSUMPTION AND THE HIGH-FIDELITY AUDIO MICROCULTURE

John D. Branch

INTRODUCTION

> As [Alexander Graham] Bell raced to perfect his telephone, he was also writing up specifications to be filed with the United States Patent Office in Washington. On March 7, 1876, he was issued patent number 174,465. Meanwhile, Bell had discovered that a wire vibrated by the voice while partially immersed in a conducting liquid, like mercury, could be made to vary its resistance and produce an undulating current. In other words, human speech could be transmitted over a wire. On March 10, 1876, as he and Mr. Watson set out to test this finding, Bell knocked over what they were using as a transmitting liquid – battery acid. Reacting to the spilled acid, Mr. Bell is alleged to have shouted, "Mr. Watson, come here. I want you!" (PBS, 2003)

It is a matter of debate among historians if such an event ever transpired. And likewise, many have dismissed Bell's now famous words as mere folklore. But the impact which the telephone has had on society cannot be denied. Indeed, with respect to audio technology more broadly, the advent of the telephone spawned a human fascination with the mechanical and electronic reproduction of sound, and nurtured a corresponding entrepreneurial drive to develop new and ever more complex equipment for this reproduction.

Consumer Culture Theory
Research in Consumer Behavior, Volume 11, 79–99

ISSN: 0885-2111/doi:10.1016/S0885-2111(06)11004-2

One manifestation of this human fascination and corresponding entrepreneurial drive is the high-fidelity audio microculture. Discussed in the marketing literature under various terms including consumption tribes (Maffesoli, 1996; Ross, 1994), social collectivities (Holt, 1997), brand communities (Muniz & O'Guinn, 2001), fan communities (O'Guinn, 2000), consumption worlds (Holt, 1994), cultures of consumption (Kozinets, 1997, 2001), and localized interpretive communities (Thompson & Haytko, 1997), consumer microcultures (Sirsi, Ward, & Reingen, 1996) recognize the structural fragmentation of consumer culture (Firat & Venkatesh, 1995) and "how its variegated subsystems of meaning cut across the master sociological categories such as gender, class, ethnicity, and age cohort" (Thompson & Troester, 2002, p. 557). Unlike traditional sociological subcultures, therefore, in which membership depends on ascribed socio-demographic variables (See Hebdige, 1979, for example.), consumer microcultures are based on membership which is volitional (Kozinets, 2001; Maffesoli, 1996; Muniz & O'Guinn, 2001; Schouten & McAlexander, 1995). Consequently, they reflect distinct patterns of meanings of their members (Thompson & Troester, 2002).

This article focuses on the distinct pattern of meanings of the members of the high-fidelity audio microculture. The article is based on one phase of a larger study, which explored the phenomenon of consumer values, in the high-fidelity audio microculture. It begins by briefly summarizing this study. The history of high-fidelity audio is then traced and the high-fidelity audio market is characterized. The distinct pattern of meanings of the members of the high-fidelity audio microculture is outlined. Finally, these meanings are discussed vis-à-vis postmodern consumption.

A PHENOMENOLOGY OF CONSUMER VALUES IN THE HIGH-FIDELITY AUDIO MICROCULTURE

The concept of consumer values has been accorded a position of great importance by marketers and marketing scientists alike, and consequently, an extensive consumer values literature has emerged in the discipline of marketing. A critique of this literature, however, concluded that the importance which the concept of consumer values has been accorded has, to a large extent, failed to materialize. One specific conceptualization of consumer values – that of Rokeach – has come to dominate the discipline of marketing. Rokeach's conceptualization of values, however, suffers from several weaknesses, the consequence of which is a limited understanding of the phenomenon of consumer values. Indeed, basic questions about consumer values, including if, how, why, and in which ways consumers value, remain largely unanswered.

I suggested, therefore, that in order to re-ignite the concept of consumer values, a new conceptualization of consumer values which improves our understanding of the phenomenon of consumer values is needed. The purpose of the research, therefore, was to develop a new conceptualization of consumer values. In order to do so, the research aimed to address the weaknesses of Rokeach's conceptualization of values. It was both exploratory and descriptive in nature. It took a decidedly phenomenological perspective, and drew heavily on axiology – the philosophy of value. It adopted the postmodern notion of consumer microcultures. And it followed hermeneutic data analysis procedures.

Specifically, the research explored the phenomenon of consumer values, in the high-fidelity audio microculture. Eleven members of the high-fidelity audio microculture were interviewed several times during the period July 1998 to February 1999. The interviews followed the phenomenological interviewing method and allowed each research participant to articulate the meanings of high-fidelity audio, in the context of his lifeworld. During the interviews, observations of the research participants, of their audio equipment, and of their other belongings were made. Photographs of the research participants' audio equipment and other belongings were also taken. Additionally, audio magazines, audio equipment catalogs, and other audio-related documents were collected. Verbatim transcriptions of the interviews, the notes, the photographs, and the other documents were entered into a computer-aided qualitative data analysis software package.

Analysis of the interview transcripts and other data occurred in three separate but interrelated phases. First, individual level – or emic – analyses of the interview transcripts were performed in order to understand the meanings of high-fidelity audio for each of the research participants, in the contexts of their lifeworlds. The second phase moved up to the microcultural level. Its goal was to understand the distinct pattern of meanings of the members of the high-fidelity audio microculture. And in the third phase, the analysis explored the phenomenon of consumer values among the research participants, and aimed to develop a new conceptualization of consumer values.

HIGH-FIDELITY AUDIO

According to Thompson, Pollio, and Locander (1990), the distinct patterns of meanings of the members of a consumer microculture are analogous to a melody. The notes of a melody can be transposed into different keys; the melody, however, remains the same. In the same vein, although the life-worlds of the members of a consumer microculture differ, the way in which an object is experienced meaningfully remains the same. The object in this instance was high-fidelity audio.

It is within the context of the high-fidelity audio market, however, that this consumer microculture developed. And as such, the high-fidelity audio microculture cannot be understood without considering the historical development of high-fidelity audio, and the nature of the high-fidelity audio market. This section, therefore, traces the history of high-fidelity audio and characterizes the high-fidelity audio market.

It was less than two years after Bell's supposed utterance that Thomas Edison patented his tin foil phonograph, thereby solidifying his position as the "Wizard of Menlo Park" (Morton, 2000). Edison's demonstration of his machine at the offices of *Scientific American* magazine was met with huge fanfare, and convinced the public of the phonograph's unlimited potential as a mechanical stenographer for businessmen, a talking book for the blind, an elocution instructor, a music box, a family album, a speaking toy, an announcing clock, a historical chronicler, a student's note-taker, and even a telephone recorder (Edison, 1989). Ironically, several years passed before Edison made any attempts to commercialize it, and even then, the company which he formed in pursuit of this end focused primarily on the production and sales of dictation machines (Rosenberg, 1994).

Competition from other inventors in the 1890s, however, spurred improvements in sound reproduction technology, and resulted in numerous competing machines and recording media. The most notable of these machines was the gramophone, which was conceived by Emile Berliner. Unlike Edison's tin foil phonograph, which used a cylinder as its recording medium, the gramophone was based on a flat disc of hard plastic which Berliner could stamp quickly and easily from a master disc. As Edison continued his quest to perfect his cylindrical medium, the gramophone captured the consumer's interest, and Berliner set out to satisfy that which he perceived was an enormous untapped market for pressed musical records (Read, 1976). The company which he formed in order to do so was the now famous Victor Talking Machine Company. And home entertainment was born.

The sound quality of this early audio equipment, however, could hardly be called good. Indeed, even into the late 1920s, the limited sonic range and high levels of noise and distortion which were associated with the gramophone (and with early radio receivers) meant that the words and music were sometimes barely recognizable. Fortunately, listeners "often knew the words to popular songs already, or could recognize the melody of even a badly recorded song. Then as now, it was not usually necessary for the recording of a song to be perfectly free of scratches, hissing, or distortion for it to be thoroughly enjoyable" (Morton, 2000, p. 17).

In the early 1930s, when the demand for gramophones and radio receivers waned, manufacturers started producing and promoting audio equipment with much better sound quality. The manufacturers gave the products a new name – high-fidelity. The term captured perfectly the notion of "realistic and uncolored reproduction of music" (Morton, 2000, p. 15) which had been the quest of Edison and the countless other inventors and sound engineers who followed him, including those at the British Broadcasting Corporation (AV International Limited, 2003).

High-fidelity audio, however, was a commercial disaster. Access to it was limited in the general population, and most people remained wedded to their gramophones and radio receivers. Consequently, high-fidelity audio became the province of the elite – a small group of relatively wealthy consumers who looked on it as their exclusive hobby. These audiophiles, as they became known, invariably used high culture as a point of reference, and high-fidelity became synonymous with high-brow. As summarized by Morton (2000), "the cult of high-fidelity recording and listening in America was completely devoted to classical, orchestral, or operatic forms of music, pieces that could be preformed live in a concert hall and which were generally agreed to represent the best possible sound" (p. 15).

With the invention of the transistor in the 1940s, however, came a process of democratization of sound quality. The transistor reduced both the price and size of audio equipment, thereby making it less expensive and more "livable" for consumers. More importantly, the transistor improved the sound quality of audio equipment so dramatically that the masses flocked to new transistorized equipment. By the 1970s, home entertainment had become the third major household purchase after the house and the family vehicle (Ominous Valve, 2003).

The better sound quality which was made possible by the transistor, however, only raised the bar for high-fidelity audio. Indeed, in democratizing sound quality, the transistor had given the public "good" ... but audiophiles wanted more. Consequently, they continued in their pursuit of realistic and uncolored reproduction of music. And high-fidelity continued to be viewed as both élitist and a black art – derided by those on the outside and considered a religion for those within (AV International Limited, 2003).

The development of digital audio technology in the 1980s – principally the compact disc and its associated player – brought another dramatic change to sound quality which thrilled the general public. The improvement in sound quality was not just somewhat noticeable, but infinitely better. Consumers raced to replace their scratchy vinyl records and old stretched cassette tapes. For audiophiles, however, the purity and transparency of the digital medium only revealed the limitations of studio and concert hall recording equipment, and, closer to home, emphasized the weaknesses in the individual components of their downstream home entertainment systems. Consequently, more attention was directed toward the upgrade of their preamplifiers, their amplifiers, and their speakers, for example, not to mention their connecting cables and their speaker wires.

As for today? Today, home entertainment continues to evolve. It has become even bigger business – part of a much broader consumer electronics industry which, in addition to audio equipment, also includes televisions, telephones, electronic games, and computers, and which is expected to reach nearly $160 billion in sales by 2008 (Consumer Electronics Association, 2006). It is a consumer-driven industry, with technological innovation geared towards consumers, and product successes and failures dictated solely by consumers. As summarized by the Consumer Electronics Association, it "continues to evolve in order to keep up with changing consumer preferences and add the latest performance-enhancing technologies" (Consumer Electronics Association, 2003a).

Evidence of this evolution, and of the consumer- and technology-driven nature of the consumer electronics industry, is the growth of home theater in a box (HTiB) systems. Indeed, as of January 2003, 30% of all American households had a home theater set up (Consumer Electronics Association, 2003b). With respect to audio, all-in-one systems which, in contrast to a system which is composed of individual components, combine audio/visual components in one unit, have become the norm. And the past few years alone have witnessed the introduction of several new digital audio formats, including DVD-audio, HDCD, mini-disc, MP3, and SACD, each of which is competing to be the "next best thing."

The high-fidelity audio market specifically, represents a relatively small portion of the broader consumer electronics industry – less than 1% of overall industry sales (Consumer Electronics Association, 2003c). The high-fidelity audio market, however, despite its small size, is unique. In some ways it mirrors the dominant consumer electronics industry. Indeed, it is both consumer- and technology-driven. However, it is characterized by its own peculiar philosophy, practices, consumer stances, and vernacular, which are intertwined with both the historical development of high-fidelity audio, and the nature of the high-fidelity audio market.

To begin, high-fidelity, philosophically, adheres steadfastly to Edison's original quest for realistic and uncolored reproduction of music. Indeed, it is guided by the assumption that an audiophile wants "his recordings to sound clearer, less tiring to listen to and more like the real thing. Freed of the distortion that exists in normal commercial Hi-Fi, he can listen longer with less effort and get even more pleasure from his collection" (AV International Limited, 2003).

This philosophy, however, creates the tension between high-fidelity and mass-produced consumer electronics. Globalization has resulted in the ubiquity of inexpensive Chinese-manufactured equipment, which is mass-marketed around the world. In purchasing this equipment, the average consumer eschews faithful sound reproduction in favor of any number of other purchase decision factors, including price, convenience, design, portability, and functionality. Essentially, high-fidelity is "simply not on everyone's shipping list. A good mid system or multi-channel surround system will satisfy the requirements of the substantial majority" (AV International Limited, 2003).

This tension is matched by a certain amount of snobbishness by audiophiles. Indeed, the mass-produced audio equipment is chided for being the lowest common denominator in sound reproduction, which barely provides even a toe-tapping experience. Snobbishness turns to contempt when the subject switches to video and home theater. Indeed, "[m]odern, dumb-downed TV is something from which they wish to escape" (AV International Limited, 2003), and other than watching television or a movie as an occasional diversion, sound remains the holy grail of sensory experience.

The philosophy of high-fidelity is also mirrored in a variety of high-fidelity practices. There is an on-going debate, for example, between vacuum tube amplification and transistor amplification. The precision and clarity of the compact disc is always compared to the "warmth" of analog turntables. And a discussion of loudspeakers will invariably compare the advantages and disadvantages of electrostatic panels, electromagnetic drivers, ribbons, and piezo elements.

These different practices also reveal different consumer stances on high-fidelity. There are the do-it-yourselfers, for example – the tinkerers – whose quest for realistic and uncolored reproduction of sound is achieved through their own active participation of the building, configuring, and tweaking of the system. There are also the golden ears (Ominous Valve, 2003) who, on the contrary, are more passive, treating high-fidelity as wine snobs would treat wine – by describing the nuances of the sound of different audio equipment with an equally nuanced vocabulary.

Finally, digital versus analog, tinkerer or golden ears, the high-fidelity is cloaked in its own specialized terminology which refers to very specific things, and which is used in conjunction with both the description and assessment of audio equipment. A compact disc player, for example, is no longer simply a compact disc player; its performance is never judged as simply poor or good or even excellent. Instead, it is described by its 24 bit 96 kHz Burr Brown DAC, or by its Vishay-Telefunken SF4007 1A 1000 V Epitaxial Diode array; its performance is measured in terms of the number of dB in its signal to noise ratio, or of the level of total harmonic distortion (THD) in its output stage. This specialized terminology has served to perpetuate the élitism, which was first associated with high-fidelity, and it amplifies the tension between high-fidelity and mass-produced consumer electronics.

THE HIGH-FIDELITY AUDIO MICROCULTURE

The previous section, in tracing the history of high-fidelity audio and characterizing the high-fidelity audio market, hinted at that which high-fidelity audio might mean to members of the high-fidelity audio microculture. This section presents the results of the microcultural analysis phase of the larger study on the phenomenon of consumer values, by outlining the distinct pattern of meanings of the members of the high-fidelity audio microculture. This distinct pattern of meanings is organized in a model à la Thompson and Troester (2002), which situates the meanings in the context of postmodernism consumption (see Fig. 1.). Specifically, the meanings are regarded as mirroring the inflections of the five conditions of postmodern consumption which were defined by Firat and Venkatesh (1995): hyperreality, fragmentation, reversal of production and consumption, decentered self, and juxtaposition of opposites.

Hyperreality

Modernity was transfixed by science, as evidenced by the effects of the industrial revolution in the 19th century (Milner, 1994). With postmodernity, however, came the proliferation of technologies which enabled the replication of products, texts, information, etc. (Eco, 1986). According to

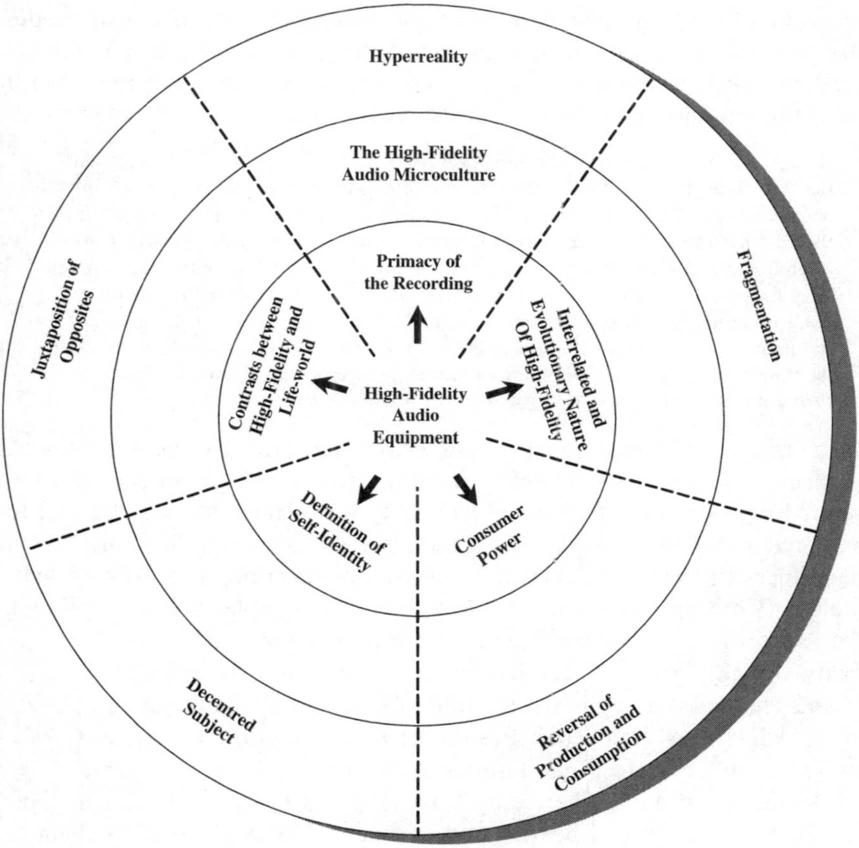

Fig. 1. A Model of the High-Fidelity Audio Microculture.

Gottdiener (1995), therefore, contemporary life became dismantled and re-produced in facsimile form – re-constituted as simulations which can be purchased and consumed. When one of these simulations is adopted "by a community, its members begin to behave in ways that authenticate the simulation so that it becomes the social reality of the community" (Firat & Venkatesh, 1995, p. 252). In other words, postmodernity has led to manufactured experiences which are more real than reality itself – that which Baudrillard called the hyperreal (Connor, 1989).

This hyperreal condition of postmodern consumption is most pronounced among the research participants in terms of the primacy which they give the recording. For them, the recording of the performance, in effect, supersedes the performance itself. Indeed, the performance is neglected; it is the recording which is the main focus of consumption. The following excerpt from the interview with Robert illustrates this theme.

> Because I'm much more conscious of disturbances and disruptions ... it's not like ... that I ... I dislike the nature of the occasion. But I, I, I'm sure that it's because my life has become progressively busier and busier in terms of my time. So I may resent the fact that I, I have to spend ... If I go to London, effectively I'm six hours on something, whereas I can effectively do the same thing in an hour and a half sitting in my home. Very lazy isn't it? Tells me something about me. Umm, the basis for for doing it. I, I don't think it's economically driven ... umm ... though that once you've invested substantially in something, you, you're going to use that ... aah ... an alternative to taking the train or driving down to London or indeed going to a performance in Cambridge in such a fine auditorium as the music school at the university.

This primacy of the recording is matched by the emphasis that the research participants place on high-fidelity audio and the quest for realistic and uncolored reproduction of music. High-fidelity is explained not with respect to how well it re-plays the real performance, but with respect to how faithfully it reproduces the recording. This faithfulness was described variously as "naturality" (Christian), the "illusion" (Morris), a "holographic image" (Andrew), the "suspension of disbelief" (Jon), "neutral and genuine" (Fraser), "invisibility" (Nick), "truthful" (Phil), and "accurate" (Bill), for example.

This emphasis on high-fidelity audio also ties in to the theme of "perfect pitch" which was discovered. Postmodernism, according to Milner (1994), caused a shift in perceptual abilities as technology became capable of reproducing sense data. The research participants possess (at least in their minds) an acute sense of hearing and a sonic memory, which allow them to evaluate sound reproduction in seemingly objective terms. This excerpt from the interview with Christian, for example, demonstrates this theme.

> I, I chose that that set ... I can tell you that, aah ... I definitely went through a lot of listening. And not just 5 min at a time – 20 min or more. And really wanted to compare the performance in terms of naturality of sound and ... aah ... yeah, balanced sound. I knew what sound ... aah ... I was after. So ... aah ... I listened to them with ... naturality as the goal. Yeah. Definitely it 〈points to system〉 was the best I was listening to. That's why I bought it finally.

Fragmentation

Modernity, as suggested previously, was based on highly specific and structurally-organized forms of social differentiation and division. Postmodernity, on the contrary, is marked by a breaking down of structure, or, perhaps more accurately, an absence of structure – by fragmentation. According to postmodernism, culture has displaced structure and its determinations, yielding a world with a new set of cultural ideals: fluidity, adaptability, agility, systemic interconnectedness, and symbiotic relations (Thompson & Troester, 2002). The postmodern consumer, therefore, rather than being part of some grandiose or unifying theory, is considered in terms of habitus (Bourdieu, 1990) or, as Fiske (1992) called it, the culture of everyday life (Firat & Venkatesh, 1995).

The fragmentation of postmodern consumption in the high-fidelity audio microculture is evident in the interrelated nature of high-fidelity. The research participants acknowledge that the reproduction of music relies on the contributions of many disparate variables, from the quality of the engineer's microphones, through the transparency of the speaker baffles, and even to the sensitivity of the ears. They underline, however, that these variables work together in a single whole. The following excerpt from the interview with Colin reinforces this theme.

> Umm, yes. I, I mean the, the d, the move from vinyl discs to CD was really quite a spectacular improvement. After that, umm, the developments that have been made in DACs I think have been really quite significant. Umm, the next thing is development in speakers and the, the research and science that's gone into the cabinets that the driver units are put into. I think that's important. Then after that, I, I've taken it to the stage further where I think the room is important. So, I've gone to some lengths as I'll show you to … aah … set up a listening room. Most fortunate to be able to do that. I realise that, you know, the bigger marketplace wouldn't be able to, to do that sort of thing because, the normal domestic dwelling perhaps wouldn't allow it. Umm, but those are the sort of the stages. The, the source of the signal, that is, the CD disc or wherever it's going, sorting card or, or whatever. Umm, then the, the processing of that signal and the, the, aah, driver units and the cabinets all coming together. Umm, and finally the, the environment in which the equipment is used. It's very, very difficult to achieve perfection. Umm, I'm lucky that … aah … we have a separate area where we can use it, but in a family situation of course, not everybody likes classical music. Umm, so it interferes. There's an intrusion in other people's lives with hi-fi, isn't there? Aah, and, we're mostly double-glazed, but there's an awful lot of racket comes in from outside wherever you are: aeroplanes and whatever, you know. Aah, and cars and motorbikes and, and so on. And aah, you know, that sort of … from about half past ten in the evening till half past eleven, there's a sort of lull when everything is ⟨motion of stillness with hands⟩ and so between movements there's perfect silence, absolute stillness, you know it's just ⟨emphasizes silence, then smiles and chuckles⟩.

That there are so many disparate variables, and that perfection, as suggested by Colin, is difficult to achieve, means that evolution is an inevitable and accepted part of high-fidelity. Indeed, the interrelated system is always in a state of tentativeness, serving the purpose at that moment in time, but evolving with each new life event, with technological advancements, with changes in taste, and even with new financial states. This theme of evolution comes through in the following excerpt from the interview with Jon.

> Aah … well, okay there's mostly QUAD. There's a power amp and controller and radio tuner. Umm, I bought all those at the same time to replace earlier QUAD power amp, controller unit because the older ones were noisy. They were made with electronics which were, fairly soon after I got them, wasn't as good as they could be in terms of how much thermal noise it produces out the output. Umm, and I got QUAD because it's fairly, umm, unobtrusive and is also quite accurate. I'm not particularly interested in having lots of knobs to turn and flashing lights or anything. Aah, there's a pair of QUAD ESL63 electrostatic speakers which I got to replace an earlier pair of the the … umm … QUAD Electrostatics – the original ones. And I got them because the original ones can't handle full symphony orchestra. Aah … there's a Meridian CD player which I sort of didn't intend to get. The only reason for getting it was I bought a CD player which was a Philips – I can't remember the number, something like CDP101 – which was essentially chosen because it was the first one that cost less than the … umm … record deck I would have got if I hadn't decided to get a CD player. When CD players first came on the market they were quite expensive – not particularly good – and I decided that I'd get one when it was good enough and cheap enough compared to a a decent turntable. But the snag with that was that it had … umm … only sixteen … you could only select select from the first 16 tracks. Umm … if you wanted to listen to any tracks after that, you just had to let it continue. And with classical music, it's very often a number of distinct pieces and you have three tracks that constitute one piece and typically you want to listen to one piece and not just let it run into the rest of them. So that if you've got tracks after track fifteen or so on which are all supposed to be one and then you want to start it there. So that was the motivation for getting a new one.

Reversal of Production and Consumption

In modernity, cultural activity was subordinate to economic activity, with everything grounded on the notion of production. Indeed, modernism suggested that "what underlies every social and economic system, what forms its secret identity-principle, [was] its 'mode of production,' what products get produced, by whom and how" (Connor, 1989, p. 51). Postmodernity, however, is marked by its consumer-driven capitalism – production has given way to consumption. As summarized by Thomas and Walsh (1998), in postmodernism there is now …

> a destructuring of the market in favor of its enculturation in which mass production based on mechanical means of production for a mass-market is replaced by flexible and niche production based on media, communication, and informational technologies and systems using intensive advertising and focused to maintain a continuous and innovatory relation with and response to consumer tastes and demands (p. 379).

This condition of postmodern consumption is certainly realized in the high-fidelity audio microculture. Indeed, the research participants exercise their consumer power at all times. Their purchases are not driven by materialistic endeavors, and are always calculated and planned. They are incredibly wary of manufacturers' claims, and equally suspicious of magazine reviews and sales pitches. They expend a tremendous amount of time and energy researching equipment before purchasing. And they demand specific product characteristics, such as durability, design, and, ultimately, improvement of sound reproduction. The following dialogue from an interview with Andrew demonstrates this consumer power.

Andrew: I'm not a regular buyer of hi-fi magazines at all. Aah … it's, it's cases like "Well, I know what I want to change next." And … aah … it's a case of what you can afford. At any rate, the market will have changed by the time you can afford it … not that I read enough magazines anyway. 'Cause I went to a listening session for a hi-fi magazine once and the volume that they reviewed everything at was just incredible. I thought, "If you review everything at this volume. …"

Interviewer: Loud or soft?

Andrew: Oh very loud, very loud. How can you possibly relate to what this is going to sound in the average living room at the average listening level?

Interviewer: Mmm-hmm.

Andrew: I thought, "You guys are crazy!" And … aah … any review I've read when I've actually listened to it it bore no resemblance to … aah … what I actually hear. And also the whole concept of reviewing things within a system in a listening room seems like nonsense to me. You know it's, it's that you can't say that, "Well, the hi-fi system is the hi-fi system (the electronics) and the room." I don't think you can separate the two.

Interviewer: Okay.

Andrew: Well, as I have already discovered to my own ⟨laughs⟩ as I have experiences and it's going to cost me money.

Interviewer: Do you bring the kit home before you buy it? Try it out here?

Andrew: Umm … I do. There's a particular shop I buy a lot of my stuff from and they're quite happy to let me bring it back.

Interviewer: In town?

Andrew: Aah, no, down in Kent.

Interviewer: Right.

Andrew: They're all … they don't do good deals.

Interviewer: Umm, yeah.

Decentered Subject

Modernity was dependent on the Cartesian conception of humans in which the self was governed by consciousness, free will, and rationality which yielded a centered, goal-directed, and purposive self-identity (Firat & Venkatesh, 1995). In a postmodern culture of consumption, however, consumerism has "now itself become the basis of the self as people use or are seduced into constructing their identities in terms of the consumption of codes, images, media, and information" (Thomas & Walsh, 1998, p. 387). Self-identity, therefore, is dependent on a mutually reinforcing process which links material consumption and symbolic processes (Gottdiener, 1995).

This condition of the decentered self was obvious among the research participants, whose self-identities were developed in part through perceived contrasts to others outside the high-fidelity audio microculture. Indeed, their sense of "who-I-am" is constantly defined and redefined through a comparison between high-fidelity audio and mass-produced consumer electronics. Most generally, the research participants hold a wide disregard for the mass-produced consumer electronics which predominate the audio main-stream. Indeed, they associate this equipment symbolically with "cheap" (Nick), "noisy" (Jon), "unnatural" (Morris), "colored" (Andrew), "distorted" (Bill), and "artificial" (Robert), for example.

The research participants, however, also underscore, more precisely, the idea that music, like fine art, ought to be savored. For many, art is considered nothing more than mere wall decoration. And likewise, according to the research participants, for many, music is considered nothing more than a melodious backdrop – the muzak of life. For the research participants, however, music is life. Nick's description of himself highlight's this perceived contrast.

> There's no question in my mind … aah. I'm a second movement man, I tell people. The second movement of a lot of piece, pieces of music, is absolutely stupendous. You know? And beautiful, really beautiful. Aah … not all music is beautiful. Some of it is exciting, stirring, terribly sad. But there's a lot of it that is just truly beautiful. The sound that … I mean in Mahler's third. If you listen to the post horn solo, just on your own quietly, it's not too difficult to have the odd tear rolling down your cheek. You know. It's phenomenal.

This idea that music ought to be savored is linked to the hedonic nature of music. Whereas mass-produced consumer electronics allow listeners some level of enjoyment, the research participants believe that high-fidelity audio equipment is necessary for the most pleasurable experience. Phil's holiday listening captures this hedonic nature.

> I've just been on holiday with a ghetto blaster in the caravan. It's quite a nice one, and it sounds okay. You plug earphones in; it's really quite acceptable. But after awhile you get tired … sooner. You get tired sooner with poor quality music, with poor quality sound. I think anyone would – not knowing about hi-fi – anybody would find themselves drifting off and getting tired sooner. But if you're involved with hi-fi equipment and so on and so forth, it affects you sooner. But people who go in and buy a good kit off the shelf and come home and the recordings are bad or whatever else, will unknowingly say, you know, tire and drift off quicker.

The pleasurable experiences which can be had by listening to music on high-fidelity audio equipment, according to the research participants, can lead to Nirvana-like effects, which could otherwise not be realized. For Robert, for example, it has the ability to remove stress, clear the mind, and refresh the spirit. For Christian, it takes him to an even higher level in which his self-identity can be freed from social constraints.

> [l]et us say every act that … aah … helps me to … umm … detach myself from the general concept that I should behave with certain contexts – aah … In particular, what I perceive others to think of me when I do certain things – work in particular, and the working environment, or in private when I meet people, or … So … aah … this … aah … this sense of possibly feeling silly about doing things and then refraining from doing them because I don't want to make a fool of myself. That is one of the worst kinds of the restricting on … I am putting much too often on, on … aah … my own self, and I think I can reach beyond these boundaries as soon as I do something like that. It just … I mean, even if I'm here on my own dancing around I always around in my head the concept "Oh this looks silly. If someone would be watching me, they would probably … aah … laugh their heads off." Aah … but I really cherish the, the not only the opportunity, but the, the, the, the experience to be able to do that by just to say "Yeah, so what?" I'm really laughing at myself at that point and saying "It doesn't matter." Then I do make a fool of myself. So … And that definitely helps me to free myself from these bonds and although it may seem a completely different situation … aah … the effect, at least on a certain level, it has – in terms of connecting to what, to what I perceive to be the roots of my true self – aah … that's the same thing that happens, for example, when I go to the Lake District and, and sit in front of a blooming daffodil field or something like that. I mean on top of that, the profound impact that music can have … aah … I mean, to sit down here and, for example, starting to cry because I just take in the beauty of it … aah, aah … that can happen to me when I listen to pieces.

And the research participants define themselves as active consumers. First, when they listen to music, they listen actively. Whereas, most people have music playing passively in the background, the research participants engage themselves in the music; they do not just hear the music, they listen to it. Second, they are bricoleurs of sound. They construct and configure their systems, thereby playing an active role in the consumption of the music. The following dialogue with Morris illustrates his active consumption.

> **Morris:** It's a it's a mish-mash of things ... umm ⟨pause⟩ I built the power amplifiers myself. Umm ... the speakers I bought second hand ... aah ... because they were passive speakers. ATCs are normally active. They were the only pair of passive ATC speakers I could find.
>
> **Interviewer:** Mmm-hmm.
>
> **Morris:** And I particularly wanted to drive, use my own power amplification. Umm ... the preamplifier at the moment is an old Rogers valve ... umm ... 1/2 of the Rogers Master Mk II system which was built in about 196, what 65ish, I would have thought that was built. I used to have an AVi solid state preamp but I gave that to my son. Umm, when CDs came out about what 10, 12, 14 years ago ... umm ... I thought I'd wait until ⟨pause⟩ the, the, if you like, the umm ... the medium had settled down some. Sort of standard ... aah ... at the time, I was using analogue thorens turntable with a hancock arm and a very old ortofon cartridge. And then a friend upgraded his hi-fi and gave me a, a old Philips CD player on semi-permanent loan. At that time, that was a very good CD player and that £400, with the 10, 15 years ago, which was a fair amount to pay for a CD player then. And then I finally decided that perhaps I should get one of my own and ... umm ... I looked around and the Meridian 500 was very well thought of at the time. And so I got (Forgive me smiling.), I got somebody from University Audio in Cambridge to bring out a 500 transport. I'd bought an old 200 series DAC second hand from a friend. And ... aah ... person from University Audio, who's a very old campaigner – very experienced man – brought out the 500 series transport to plug into the system and ... aah ... to test it. And I got the feeling that when he came he was just a little bit dismissive of my ... Then, I had a pair of Spendor loudspeakers. These are a more recent acquisition. And he was a bit dismissive of my speakers and the home-made power amplification that went with it until we played the first CD. And then his attitude changed very abruptly. Anyway ... so it's a mixture of things, part of which I got myself. I get a lot of pleasure out of building things that work well. Umm, sort of it, the, the, the Rogers preamplifier was in fact my 21st birthday present for me. The power amp is still in the roof in the loft which still works very well. And that really is a brief history. The Thorens turntable I still have. I bought that in 1967 for 25 pounds brand new without an arm or cartridge. That was a lot of money to spend then. And it still works very well. I don't know. I just get a lot of gratification out of building something which works very well and is as sensibly good as can be. I mean, I'd have to ... I don't know, but I'd have to spend an awful lot of money on top of the line amplification to better the power amplifiers that I built.

Juxtaposition of Opposites

Finally, modernity, with its highly specific structurally-organized forms, created opposites which were invariably viewed as a superior/inferior couplet (Thomas & Walsh, 1998). Fragmentation, however, rather than unification, is the basis of postmodernity. Consumer experiences, therefore, are not meant to reconcile differences and paradoxes, but to allow them to exist freely (Firat & Venkatesh, 1995). And the decentering of the subject in postmodernism means that opposites can be mutually represented and even juxtaposed at all times (Gottdiener, 1995). Pastiche, therefore, is a condition of postmodern consumption.

Juxtaposition is evident in the high-fidelity audio microculture. Indeed, the research participants displayed a number of juxtapositions between high-fidelity and their lifeworlds. There was an obvious dynamic, for example, between sound and vision. Although the research participants had an aural fixation, there was a simultaneous existence of video equipment. The following excerpt from an interview with Bill supports this theme.

> My daughters both like listening to music, either on the main stereo which is right around the corner, or we have a mini one in the kitchen. We've also just got a ... uh ... we just got a new television with surround sound on which they enjoy as well, especially the elder daughter who likes watching the ... we've got a DVD player, so she likes that. She's getting into the quality of things as well – appreciates the difference. So we tend to use the ... we don't sit down quite so often now just simply to sit down and relax and listen to music. It's more of a background thing now. I find rather than, you know, you have it on in the background while you're doing something else. Just occasionally you sit down and listen and relax. But that's more to do with the change in lifestyle rather than not appreciating the music as much.

The theme of "system and space" which was discovered is also indicative of the juxtapositions in the high-fidelity audio microculture. Indeed, the research participants support the intrusion of their systems. Similarly, the research participants accept the technological look and feel of high-fidelity audio equipment, despite (even because of, in some instances) its contrast with their living environments. In the following excerpt, for example, Fraser describes this juxtaposition.

> They don't look out of place in a home. I've got a lot of old furniture in this room, there 〈points to television〉 very modern modern television, but sort of 300 400 old furniture. And here is a 200 year old furniture. And so on it all seems to match in fairly well.

And there is the conspicuous contrast between the beauty of the music and the homeliness of high-fidelity audio equipment. This juxtaposition is seen very clearly in the following dialogue with Andrew.

> **Interviewer:** Is it furniture to you?
>
> **Andrew:** No, 'cause it's ugly.

Interviewer: So when you're buying a piece of equipment does, does the beauty of the thing come in? You said that the sound reality, significant sound reality, does play? Does the actual physical beauty of it do anything for you?

Andrew: Not really.

Interviewer: No?

Andrew: Not really. It's … I'd rather have it in a nice bit of wood than a bit of ship board or a bit of plastic yes. But beyond that I'm under no illusion that it's pretty.

Interviewer: Mmm.

Andrew: 'Cause it's not! ⟨laughs⟩ It's not pretty. It's imposing … aah … It gets in the way. But … aah … So it's, it's all a bit too masculine as well. 'Cause that's who it's designed for, isn't it?

Interviewer: I suppose, yeah. Would rather have it hidden away than in view?

Andrew: Umm … only if it didn't compromise. That's the only reason this … There's flat speakers and all that. Listened to some of those in shows. I know it's difficult to judge these things at show but there's no comparison. They sound cheap and nasty and somehow flat. They sound flat – the sound stage is flat. And that's important. I mean if they came out with something smart enough, something good enough which sounded as good, then I'd be very happy to hide them away. I mean look at the cable nightmare around here.

DISCUSSION

The previous section presented the results of the microcultural analysis phase of the larger study on the phenomenon of consumer values, by outlining the distinct pattern of meanings of the members of the high-fidelity audio microculture. The results continue the discourse on postmodernism in the discipline of marketing, lending support to the basic tenets of postmodern consumption which have been adopted by marketing scientists.

To begin, postmodernism asserts that the consumer is not someone who attempts to assuage needs which are dictated by his/her psychological make-up, but instead is someone who is active in the on-going production of meaning. That is, the products which people consume are not for consumption but for production – for the purpose of producing something: self-image, lifestyle, or attractive personality, for example. As summarized by Firat and Venkatesh (1995), the consumer is "a participant in an on-going, never-ending process of construction that includes a multiplicity of moments where things (most importantly as symbols) are consumed, produced, signified, represented, allocated, distributed, and circulated" (259).

The research results support this postmodernist assertion. Indeed, as outlined previously, the research participants are active not only in building and configuring their systems, but in the construction of meaning. They (literally and figuratively) construct their equipment into meaning. This construction occurs continually; their systems, the meaning of high-fidelity, and the meaning of high-fidelity audio equipment are always in a state of tentativeness. And the consumption of their high-fidelity audio equipment is central to their self-identities. The research participants' sense of "who-I-am" is a meaningful construction.

Postmodernism also claims that, with the power of the market forces, consumers can only escape the hegemony of society by constructing ideographic meanings in opposition to society. That is, only by adopting a postmodern fragmentation and decenteredness can consumers create "emancipated spaces" which free them from the dominance of the "totalitizing logic of the market" (Firat & Venkatesh, 1995).

The research results also support this postmodernist claim. Indeed, for the research participants, high-fidelity stands in stark contrast to the meanings of mass-produced consumer electronics. The distinct pattern of meanings of the members of the high-fidelity audio microculture is fundamental to the construction of their self-identities. The research results point, however, to a far less hermetic and discontinuous notion of market fragmentation and decenteredness, as theorized by both Holt (1997) and Thompson and Troester (2002). Indeed, the microcultural analysis revealed a network of broader historical and cultural continuities which are manifest in the distinct pattern of meanings of the members of the high-fidelity audio microculture.

An important insight from the broader research, which ought to be mentioned here is that the meanings which the research participants' ascribe to their high-fidelity audio equipment also include value. The deeply rooted self-identities and the emancipating high-fidelity audio microculture are reflected in the value of their high-fidelity audio equipment. That is, value is how they are substantiated. In other words, the research participants create their own oasis – their own territory – in society, through their consumption. It is the value of the high-fidelity audio equipment which facilitates this oasis, reinforcing the notion of postmodern anarchy which, in this microculture, high-fidelity audio both induces and affords.

Finally, the distinct pattern of meanings of the members of the high-fidelity audio microculture suggests some interesting avenues for future research. The first revolves around the postmodern condition of hyperreality, which was so pronounced among the research participants. This condition is especially intriguing when you consider the current spate of so-called reality television programming, or the popularity of hobbies such as scrapbooking. Another links to high-fidelity itself, and how it facilitates an élitism among the research participants, supports the construction of their self-identities, and forwards their transcendence of societal mundanity. Do other products perform similar microcultural functions? Could something as seemingly boring as philately do the same for its members? And a third avenue for future research stems from the theme of "perfect pitch" which was discovered. It does not seem far-fetched to think of members of the cigar aficionado microculture placing a similar emphasis on the "perfect smoke."

REFERENCES

AV International Limited. (2003). Hi-Fi: Why is it so important? Retrieved from http://www.avihifi.co.uk/Why%20bother/Why%20bother.html

Bourdieu, P. (1990). *The logic of practice*. Cambridge, England: Polity Press.

Connor, S. (1989). *Postmodernist culture: An introduction to theories of the contemporary*. Oxford, England: Blackwell Publishers.

Consumer Electronics Association. (2003a). Overview. Retrieved from http://www.ce.org/publications/books_references/digital_america/audio/default.asp

Consumer Electronics Association. (2003b). Surround sound music: DVD-audio, SACD. Retrieved from http://www.ce.org/publications/books_references/digital_america/audio/surround_sound.asp

Consumer Electronics Association. (2003c). Traditional audio components. Retrieved from http://www.ce.org/publications/book_references/digital_america/audio/audio_components.asp

Consumer Electronics Association. (2006). Industry statistics. Retrieved from http://www.ce.org/Research/Sales_Stats/275.asp

Eco, U. (1986). *Faith in fakes: Travels in hyperreality*. London, England: Minerva.

Edison, T. (1989). *Works: The papers of Thomas A. Edison*. Baltimore, MD: Johns Hopkins University Press.

Firat, F., & Venkatesh, A. (1995). Liberatory postmodernism and the reenchantment of consumption. *Journal of Consumer Research*, *22*(December), 239–267.

Fiske, J. (1992). Cultural studies and the culture of everyday life. In: L. Grossberg, C. Nelson, P. Treichler, L. Baughman & J. Wise (Eds), *Cultural studies* (pp. 38–55). New York: Routledge.

Gottdiener, M. (1995). *Postmodern semiotics: Material culture and the forms of postmodern life*. Oxford, England: Blackwell Publishers.

Hebdige, D. (1979). *Subculture: The meaning of style*. New York: Methuen.

Holt, D. (1994). Consumers' cultural differences as local systems of tastes: A critique of the personality/values approach and an alternative framework. In: J. Cole & S. M. Long (Eds), *Asia Pacific advances in consumer research*, (Vol. 1, pp. 178–184). Provo, UT: Association for Consumer Research.

Holt, D. (1997). Poststructuralist lifestyle analysis: Conceptualizing the social patterning of consumption in postmodernism. *Journal of Consumer Research*, *23*(March), 326–350.

Kozinets, R. (1997). I want to believe: A netnography of the X-philes' subculture of consumption. In: M. Brucks & D. MacInnis (Eds), *Advances in consumer research*, (Vol. 24, pp. 470–475). Provo, UT: Association for Consumer Research.

Kozinets, R. (2001). Utopian enterprise: Articulating the meanings of Star Trek's culture of consumption. *Journal of Consumer Research*, *28*(June), 67–88.

Maffesoli, M. (1996). *The time of tribes: The decline of individualism in mass society*. London, England: Sage Publications.

Milner, A. (1994). *Contemporary cultural theory: An introduction*. London, England: University College London Press.

Morton, D. (2000). *Off the record: The technology and culture of sound recording in America*. Piscataway, NJ: Rutgers University Press.

Muniz, A., & O'Guinn, T. (2001). Brand community. *Journal of Consumer Research*, *27*(March), 412–432.

O'Guinn, T. (2000). Touching greatness: The central Midwest Barry Manilow Fan Club. In: J. Schor & D. Holt (Eds), *The consumer society reader* (pp. 155–168). New York: New Press.

Ominous Valve. (2003). Tube hi-fi: An anthropological view. Retrieved from http://www.ominous-valve.com/hifi.html

PBS. (2003). More about Bell. Retrieved from http://www.pbs.org/wgbh/amex/telephone/peopleevents/mabell.html

Read, W. (1976). *America's mass media merchants*. Baltimore, MD: Johns Hopkins University Press.

Rosenberg, N. (1994). *Exploring the black box: Technology, economics, and history*. Cambridge, England: Cambridge University Press.

Ross, A. (1994). Triablism in effect. In: S. Benstock & S. Ferris (Eds), *On fashion* (pp. 284–300). New Brunswick, NJ: Rutgers University Press.

Schouten, J., & McAlexander, J. (1995). Subcultures of consumption: An ethnography of the new bikers. *Journal of Consumer Research*, *22*(June), 43–61.

Sirsi, A., Ward, J., & Reingen, P. (1996). Microcultural analysis of variation in sharing of causal reasoning about behavior. *Journal of Consumer Research*, *22*(March), 345–372.

Thomas, H., & Walsh, D. (1998). Modernity/Postmodernity. In: C. Jenks (Ed.), *Core sociological dichotomies* (pp. 363–390). London, England: Sage Publications.

Thompson, C., & Haytko, D. (1997). Speaking of fashion: Consumers' uses of fashion discourses and the appropriation of countervailing cultural meanings. *Journal of Consumer Research*, *24*(June), 15–42.

Thompson, C., Pollio, H., & Locander, W. (1994). The spoken and the unspoken: A hermeneutic approach to understanding the cultural viewpoints that underlie consumers' expressed meanings. *Journal of Consumer Research*, *21*(December), 432–452.

Thompson, C., & Troester, M. (2002). Consumer value systems in the age of postmodern fragmentation: The case of the natural health microculture. *Journal of Consumer Research*, *28*(March), 550–571.

GLOCAL ROCK FESTIVALS AS MIRRORS INTO THE FUTURE OF CULTURE(S)

E. Taçlı Yazıcıoğlu and A. Fuat Fırat

ABSTRACT

Rock festivals, as a part of global rock culture, disclose a domain of consumption that allows a multiplicity of activities and practices in Turkey, where modernity is entrenched, but not fully hegemonic. This provides the possibility of illuminating the conditions of being a contemporary consumer as well as the potentials for the future. This paper presents some preliminary findings from research at two major rock festivals in Turkey. Ideology emerges as an important factor in consumption of these festivals and illustrates possible grounds to interpret cultural production. These practices suggest aspirations for experiencing different modes of being in the world and provide signs of the future of culture(s).

INTRODUCTION

It has been argued that we may be experiencing a period of potential epochal cultural transformation(s) (Featherstone, 1991; Fırat & Venkatesh, 1993; Jameson, 1984; Ross, 1988). Under this condition, it is necessary to

Consumer Culture Theory
Research in Consumer Behavior, Volume 11, 101–117

ISSN: 0885-2111/doi:10.1016/S0885-2111(06)11005-4

consider where we might encounter contexts that might provide the richest insights of where these transformations may take us. Contexts where one trend is not singularly dominant, but where several are competing and contesting, may be the most informative. Specifically in such contexts the potentials and possibilities may be best observed, because no vying alternative is easily crushed by an order that is hegemonic. With this in mind, the study reported here was conducted in such a context, Turkey, where modernity is well present, but not fully hegemonic, and the specific content selected was rock festivals where consumption activities represent a richly textured variety.

Consumption of music, specifically, rock music, has not attracted much attention by consumer researchers as a commodity. Rock music is not an ordinary commodity; it started and has evolved as an ideological project. Since Bob Dylan's battle hymn, "Blowing in the Wind," from the 1960s, rock music has accompanied developments in social movements.

Ideology, an understudied topic in consumer research, appeared as a significant factor in choices for consuming rock festivals in Turkey. Furthermore, rock music, in rock festivals, was found to be utilized as an ideological consumption commodity, in advancing a political social movement. We develop some initial insights into the meanings and future implications of findings from these rock festivals. It seems clear that particular consumption practices are developing in a world where capabilities of having access to music genres and their consumption from different regions and cultures of the globe allow hybridization as well as possibilities of experiencing of different modes of being in the world, modes that both (re)present and cross the traditional, the modern, and the postmodern.

AN IDEOLOGICAL GENRE: ROCK MUSIC

"Rock" has always been a mass-produced music genre, which embodies a critique of its own means of production; it is a mass-consumed music that constructs its own "authentic" audience. Behind rock music stands not only a complex web of contexts of use, but also a context of reflection mediated in political and ideological terms, i.e., "rock is a weapon in cultural revolution" (Wicke, 1995). Such discourses gave rock a political ambience made up of protest, revolution, and progressive claims as well as a mission to improve the world. Keightley (2001, p. 109) argues that rock culture has also been defined historically by its process of exclusion. Although the idea of rock rejects mass-consumed or mass-produced music (i.e., the worthless pop), millions of rock music CDs, cassettes, LPs, or concert DVDs are still sold and are believed to produce feelings of freedom, rebellion, oppositionality, authenticity, and uniqueness.

Evolution of rock in Turkey began almost two decades earlier and has been different from those in other non-Western countries. It was never banned nor did it emerge as a counterculture, as in the cases of China (Steen, 1996) or Russia (Cushman, 1995), nor has it become subservient, as in the cases of Mexico and Quebec in the early 1960s (Straw, 1993), nor was it a blatant imitation of its Anglo-American counterparts.

To briefly introduce the context, Turkey has an almost five decades old rock music tradition, given the first rock concert was in 1957. Interestingly, despite the long tradition of rock music in the country, which was limited to a practice of listening at concerts and bars, as well as on records and CDs, a rock boom (in production and consumption) started only in the last decade and recognizable rock festivals started to emerge in the last six years, as many academics, columnists, and producers agree.

In Turkey, the 1980s have characteristics that parallel the rest of the world – e.g., Thatcherism era in the UK. One of the most recognizable outcomes was the depolitization of the youth, who have always been the main consumers of rock (Frith, 1981). Today, it is estimated that there are between 1,000 and 1,500 rock bands in the country. Contests are held each year by different group and organizations. Following the arrival of the Internet, rockers from various cities get together on the Internet (e.g., anatolian-rock.com has more than 330,000 subscribers). The share of the rock music market currently varies between 15 and 20%. Extensions of rock music, such as rock festivals, provide us with the richness that allows a deciphering of the ideology of consumption.

METHOD

Several methods were used in data collection to provide insights into the meanings of consumption of music in a context where modes of consumption and experiences of music are contested. These included participant observations at two rock festivals in 2004 and 2005, *Rock'n Coke* and *Rock for Peace*, visual data (mostly photography) from both festivals, and interviews and conversations with participants at the festivals. Discourses on online forums were also analyzed (Kozinets, 2002a). This paper contains analyses from *eksisozluk,* a publicly influential political online discussion group, where each entry has to be written as a dictionary entry (pretending to serve as a de facto encyclopedia, as the entries reflect completely subjective views). In *eksisozluk*, 572 "definitions" of the two rock festivals were analyzed. Following the festivals, interviews with promoters, people who participated in the festivals, activists, rock bands, and intellectuals and academics who study related topics were also conducted. Two hundred sixty-six photographs were used in interviews with academics to incite semiotic analyses. The texts so created were, then, analyzed using semiotic and narrative textual analyses (Barthes, 1973; Patton, 2002). A discussion of some of the preliminary findings from this research follows.

IDEOLOGIES IN ROCK FESTIVALS

The rock festival (in Western practice) symbolizes the state of contemporary music: fans and musicians gather hoping for the unexpected and/or the realization of a dream of experience. There are potential threats of drugs, alcohol, and anarchy, while the only real threat is the weather. Frith (2001) argues that the festival is symbolic of the industry that is concerned with the rational organization of irrational forces – talent and taste – while celebrating itself as piracy. In fact, festivals, carnivals (DaMatta, 1991; Kozinets, 2002b; Stallybrass & White, 1986), and even country fairs can provide microcosms of the world around them, and serve as a laboratory for social scientists.

In 1993, the first Western rock band to give a concert in Turkey was Metallica. In 1994, MTV started broadcasting. From Rolling Stones to Eric Clapton, Robert Plant, and Jimmi Page of Led Zeppelin have given concerts in stadiums or big concert halls in Turkey since the 1990s. Rock bars are popular in major cities in Turkey, but rock concerts are held in a wider area. The "Rock Festival" is a relatively new, but equally long-expected "event" in Turkey, given the stories of the legendary Woodstock. The concert or show contexts have been converted into a rock festival format in the last few years. This started with H2000 İstanbul in 2000. Opening a new "Rock Festivals" era, the major leap occurred with *Rock'n Coke* and its rival *Rock for Peace* festivals (see appendix). Differences in the nature of these two festivals are informative about the divisions among rock communities, and, furthermore, regarding the local hybrid forms of rock culture.

Rock'n Coke (Fig. 1) was first held in 2003 as part of the *Coca Cola* Company's Soundwave Project in Europe It was a year after *Coca Cola* hired sociologists to conduct fieldwork in different regions of Turkey. Not everybody liked the idea of this festival. Firstly, "real rockers" in the public,

Fig. 1. Rock'n Coke.

including several serious columnists, criticized the use of "Rock" and "Coke" together in the same sentence. Leftists and Islamists described it as a cover-up operation disguised to make people forget what the *Coca Cola* Company had perpetrated in the less affluent world – backing a fascist coup in Guatemala in 1954; supporting Israel against Palestine; being one of the major agents of globalization and cultural imperialism; exploitation of workers, were among those mentioned. They also related it to the war in Iraq and accused *Coca Cola* for attempting to help the US Government convince citizens of the Republic of Turkey against their Iraqi neighbors. In fact, no one liked Saddam and his regime, but, arguments went, fighting against neighbors should not have been a mission of the Republic of Turkey. The National Assembly's vote in 2003 to deny help to the US army in invading Iraq had encouraged anti-US fans. Equating *Coke* with the US, this festival was interpreted by some as a PR attempt to make Turkey and the US allies again. Above all, rock represented rebellion and Coke was one of the symbols of globalization, which contradicted the rebellious spirit of rock music. Consequently, the most popular rock band, Mor ve Ötesi, stated a change of mind about performing at *Rock'n Coke* and was forced to pay a fine to the Coca Cola Company. Erkin Koray, the "father of Turkish rock," performed at the festival. He was criticized severely by rock communities and felt forced to state an apology after the Festival. More than 30,000 people attended the festival for two days (some of them stayed overnight in camps paying extra money for the privilege).

In 2004, the second year of the festival, the featured group was 50 Cent, the best-selling American hip-hopper of the year. There was criticism, as some felt that hip-hop had nothing to do with rock. In 2005, the featured group – The Cure – was more than satisfactory. To many rockers, seeing them live on stage had been a fantasy. The festival had an intense marketing campaign using billboards and newspapers. Columnists did not comment on the mismatch of "*Coke* and *Rock*" this time after the massive advertisement budget spent on the newspapers while "the real rockers" kept on protesting it. According to rumors, *Coca Cola* Company spent around $8–10 million. There were approximately 60,000 people at the festival from all around Turkey, mainly from Istanbul, a theme park, yoga, tattooing, "Rock'n Shop" stands, and various food choices from McDonald's to local fast-food restaurants. The beverages available were *Coke* and beer (in *Coke* cups), and less frequently *Jack Daniels*, which also organized a rock music contest (JD Music Rock Contest) in 2006.

Pros of *Rock'n Coke* associate the festival in the *eksisozluk* with Coke consumption and its relationship with rock as well as produce some hedonist remarks:

> An event which can sponsor Radiohead simply with the number of *Coke*s I drank so far (bruthuss, posted on ⟨*eksisozluk*⟩ in June 27, 2003).

> A festival which provides nice scenes thanks to female participants' way of clothing (heart shaped box, posted on ⟨*eksisozluk*⟩ in September 7, 2003).

Cons are fierce in their critiques and emphasize how *Coca Cola* is not related to the rebellious and "anti-capitalist" rock culture:

> An event which is better called "Pop'n Coke" (the last hard man, posted on ⟨*eksisozluk*⟩ in July 2, 2003).

> An event to which people who live in countries where they are fed up with festivals and who are wise would never go to… (neriman koksal, posted on ⟨*eksisozluk*⟩ in August 27, 2003).

> A festival that needs a name change urgently (bigette, August 20, 2004).

The most apparent reaction to *Rock'n Coke* has been another rock festival, *Rock for Peace: Counter Festival* (*Barışa Rock: Karşı Festival*). This rival festival was held on the same weekend as *Rock'n Coke* in 2003 with the slogan "Rock can't exist in a bottle," in 2004 with the slogan "World is Our Home," and in 2005 with the slogan "Our Songs are for the Skies." The organizing committee consisted of activists and rock musicians. The festival participants were able to stay overnight just as in *Rock'n Coke. Coca Cola*

Fig. 2. Rock for Peace.

was protested all through these festivals. In 2005, *Rock for Peace* was free while *Rock'n Coke* cost around $45–60 for both days (camping overnight was an additional cost), not an easy-to-afford amount for most university students in Turkey. The participants at *Rock for Peace* were mainly university students and activists (Fig. 2). Festival place served as an amalgam to gather activists with others.

> It is also because of this: we're young, we got so many dreams; we are inflamed by even the smallest things, but calmed down with the smallest things as well. Apart from all of these, we are dreaming of the same classless, borderless world where there is no exploitation. If we want to talk about the most basic things here [Rock for Peace], we can say that if these people want to unite, [we can] under the dream of an unoccupied society in peace (Activist, F, 26).

A significant event at *Rock for Peace* in 2005 was the participation of *Coca Cola* workers who were laid off for attempting to unionize. Stands were allowed only for the representatives of some political groups or the press. There was beer and branded soft drinks except *Coke*, and chess tournaments to emphasize the theme of the festival, which was peace. *Rock for Peace* is described, cynically, in the ⟨*eksisozluk*⟩:

> An event that was organized by those of who have never consumed Coca Cola, Pepsi, Fanta, Nike, Adidas, Puma, Reebok, HP, BP, Levi's, Tommy Hillfiger, Benetton, Diesel, Compaq, Nokia, Ericsson, etc., etc. It's a fact that none of us is innocent (coffeenicotine, posted on ⟨*eksisozluk*⟩, in August 8, 2003).

> A totally "loser" activity (mysterious, posted on ⟨*eksisozluk*⟩, in August 25, 2003).
>
> It's not only a music festival, with speeches, stands, theatres, it's a culture festival as well. Although it's been positioned against *Rock'n Coke*, an organization which now stands on its own feet (tuonela, posted on ⟨*eksisozluk*⟩, in August 28, 2005).

Following these two festivals, new festivals (such as, *Rock'n Dark* Festival, *Kent Rock Fest* Festival, *University Rock* Festival) were launched. Further festivals are expected. Participants of the two festivals in focus are "consumers" of the events. Promoters are either multinational giants, such as *Coca Cola*, or activists and rock bands. Therefore, each can be studied separately, although they meet on the same grounds: rock music and rock music festival.

CONSUMPTION MEANINGS IN THE ROCK FESTIVALS

The analyses of the data collected reveal several insights. One is the ideological nature of (rock music festivals) consumption.

Consumption and Ideology

The role of ideology in consumption has been largely absent in studies of consumers and consumption, which may mostly be because in everyday consumption practices ideology is present but hidden; a matter of social structure and discourse (Eagleton, 1991). In a world of conflicts, the importance of ideology becomes more apparent. In the context of music festivals in a context where meanings of rock music itself and, specifically, its links to a brand name such as *Coca Cola* are contested, this hidden dimension of consumption becomes especially visible.

Choices made to attend either festival, or both, are informed by ideological considerations, mostly because ideology is inescapably called to act by those who are for or against these festivals. While the "festival," specifically the "mainstream" rock festival, *Rock'n Coke*, is, at one level, an event to *enjoy* and *experience*, there is this nagging question/doubt of "should you/I be here?" At the least, given the history of rock music, there is, still, the trace of an implication that rebellion is at hand. Then, there is the whiff of the mystery of (un)expected rough play. Finally, in the context of the politics reflected on/by *Coke* is the question of betrayal, to a cause, to humanity, to those who are oppressed. Thus, an ideological position is, has to be, taken; there is no escape. The most mainstream ideological position is: "C'mon, after all this is only a music festival, I am coming here to listen to music I love; and isn't this music a rejection of mainstream values and culture?"

> To get there or not can push someone into categories with sharp exclusions. By saying politization, I meant that. How many of them are aware of this? How many of them know what they are saying by "It doesn't matter, I can go to any of them [Rock festivals]"? (Academic, M, 39).

The ideological position in participating in the counter festival, *Rock for Peace*, seems much clearer among the participants: "We are on the side and supporting the cause of the oppressed, in all senses of the word. This music we come to hear is uniting us against world dominance by corporate interests and imperialism, but it also is local rock that cannot globally achieve the status of rock music that is coming from "the outside" and that is integrated with commercial, corporate hegemony." Yet, the music is rock, one that has its roots in cultures that represent that which is hegemonic, imperialistic, and despite its appropriated tones and context "foreign!"

In the end, participants in both festivals are influenced by the ideological discourses of the rock music culture, which is actually a subset of global consumer values as depicted in the diagram in Fig. 3 with photographs from the festivals.

The insight from studying the texts compiled in this research is that no consumption, however singularly (ideologically) unambiguous or straightforward it seems at first, is devoid of (ideological) contradiction and tension. There are interesting implications of this, some of which we explore briefly below.

Rebellion and/through Conformity

The themes of rebellion and conformity seem constantly present in ideological discourses of consumption. Yet, there is no resolution to this opposition; there is no safe point where the consumptive act can be identified purely as rebellion or as conformity. There is an inescapable unity of the two seemingly opposite ends. At *Rock'n Coke*, where conformity – to the hegemonic rock culture, to the commercial marketing efforts of global corporatism, to consumerism – may at first glance reign, many undercurrents of rebellion persist – of the youth against mainstream values of "proper"

Fig. 3. Ideological Discourse of Rock Music and Global Values of Consumer Culture.

behavior, of attire readily visible in the flamboyant colors and styles of clothing. Yet, this rebellion is expressed in conformity to worldwide rock'n'roll mythology. There is the desire to be like the "rock legends," to have the experiences that idols of rockers have as the quest of being different is pursued. Do participants become *real* rockers only after such an experience; as if fulfilling a task or another cliché of the rock myth (becoming authentic rockers/rock musicians) can show this off to others: Been there, done that?

Rebellion at *Rock for Peace* – against consumer culture represented by the global corporate system that oppresses – is declared and evident. Yet, the forms through which this rebellion is sought to be acted conform to those of a "rock festival." There is the stage with the bands, the "audience" on the ground, activities of eating and drinking and socializing that parallel the other festival – to indicate that there is community and experience of liveliness and fun in rebellion; a satisfaction out of having "done the deed:" "We have accomplished what we were supposed to do, now let the others fix it." While the consumption culture represented by *Coke* is confronted, other brands of beverages, Nike shoes, Marlboro cigarette packs are present (See Fig. 3). It is rebellion through conformity and conformity through rebellion.

Ideology of rock is the *leitmotiv* in the consumption practices as described in Fig. 3. Participants and activists frequently utilize rock music to justify things. *Rock'n Coke* (RC) participants think that they have the right to go to the festival where they can listen to the real rock music (i.e., the worldwide known bands), and activists in *Rock for Peace* (RP) put the blame on *Coke* for ruining the name of rock.

Activists at *Rock for Peace* frequently emphasized two notions, sincerity and insincerity, to describe both the political attitude of rock bands and *ideal* nature of a festival. By sincerity, they aim to deify the rock music as a means to stress its contrast with Coke.

> But rock music is noble and rebellious, it has an attitude. It shouldn't be bought or sold [as a commodity], and capped [mentioning the cap of a *Coke* bottle]. Rock music is rebellion, and a roar. Here, people are shouting, money is not hegemonic here, cooperation is hegemonic here. But there [*RC*] is *Cardrock* [a designated festival credit card for shopping], "ticket" or payment for tents. Leave [the notion of] festival aside, it is a festival for exploitation. They are both advertising and exploiting the kids out there. It is something insincere, I mean (RP, Activist, M, 23).

> They [*RC* participants] only listen to music, with no message inside. (RP, Activist, M, 33).

> We think that *Coca Cola* is making fake music that you'd call as rock monkeys (RP, Activist, M, 23).

On the other hand, *Rock'n Coke* participants approach *worldly* activities (i.e., going to a rock festival, drinking Coke) more pragmatically.

> Researcher: What do you think about rock and Coke match?
>
> I don't worry about such stuff anymore, because there is nowhere you can't find any *Coke* (RC, Backstage Planner, F, 25).

Cause and/through Fun

Thus, most apparent at *Rock for Peace*, but present in both festivals, is the question: "Are we here for a cause or for fun? Is fun allowed if a cause is to be advanced? If we have fun, can we still be advancing a cause?" There are shameless calls to enjoyment and entertainment at *Rock'n Coke*. This is part of the cause; the dominant commercial culture, one built on Protestant Ethics, calls to reason, detachment from emotion, "be rational and frugal!" The rebellion, the cause, is to say "life is more than following "proper" rules; there is a need to engage in and "feel," "taste" "life." (They are not free of charge naturally, but it's the rule of the game. Not everybody can afford *Rock'n Coke* anyway. Experiencing rock festivals like Woodstock is (has always been) a privilege. It shouldn't be for free). Questioning limit(ation)s, sampling possibilities provides meaning to life. This questioning is, however, vague at *Rock'n Coke*; there is no clear target that is questioned.

The target, the questions are clear at *Rock for Peace*, but this clarity threatens texture and textuality, especially if the cause (i.e., peace, anti-globalization, imperialism) is a serious matter, and fun is not. How do we sustain interest, maintain involvement? Activities are planned, games like chess or origami are created in the vicinity of the stage to infuse fun and engagement. Not everybody is dancing, especially in the daytime. So, then, why are people here? For the cause or for the fun? For some of them it is clearly fun:

> Veni, vidi, I had fun, vici (prefect, posted on ⟨*eksisozluk*⟩, in August 22, 2004).

Hybridization and/through Difference/Similarity

It seems that in hybridization, different forms merge and become one, and yet this hybrid construction is impossible to regress to any of its roots; it is unique and different, it is itself. Thus, rock music defies clear definition and each of its "genres" defies persistent identification. The hybrid is an independent experience. There is a different tone, style, and personality to each festival. Each festival provides a mode of ideology, mood, and being to experience. In the end, this experience may be what draws the participant from a context where there exist different cultures that compete and beckon, yet each is replete with contradiction, oppositions, and tensions. The festival, then, presents the possibility of another culture that can be sampled, experienced, and learned from; a key lesson being that oppositions are not to be resolved but to be explored and playfully, critically engaged.

There are many "others" between and within the festivals reflecting these oppositions. The tensions that arise from the image of the "other" reveal the competing and contrasting ideas and the unshakable idealism on the activists' side:

> They were aware of it when I asked them [consumer elites in the beauty salon] about *Rock'n Coke*, but not about *Rock for Peace*. They'd either go to Reina or Laila [trendy clubs], but I don't think that they'd deal with activism in the woods. They might think that it is primitive (RP, Beauty Salon Worker, F, 29).

> When I think of *Rock for Peace*...an image like people who weren't able to enter any university was evoked, the ones still with black jeans and black shirts (RC, Backstage Planner, F, 26).

> Everything you spent for a *Coca Cola* product is probably converted into a bullet to kill a child. But since these people [at *Rock'n Coke*] were brought up in a different way, they spend a lot money, they jump and hop and try to entertain themselves, there is no such world. This is the real life, we are making something different here, we are against war, we demand peace (RP, Activist, M, 23).

> As I said, if we'd reached those world famous [rock] bands, they could have thought that, their place is here (RP, Activist, M, 33).

> *Rock'n Coke* is only one example...It's an active movement to go to that festival, that's why I wouldn't want to be there, because of the things it symbolizes, capitalism, et cetera. Because of this I wouldn't want, but I don't object. I act like them in the end.

> Researcher: Acting like them? How do you act? What does "to act like them" mean?

> Acceptance... Accepting the bad things that we live in (RP, Student, M, 23).

Consumer as Producer

Consumers of rock music from different backgrounds, experiencing rock music in different spheres, in rock bars, on the e-groups, at school, or on television, position themselves at festivals, each contributing his/her culture and ideological position. This yields a hybrid culture that consists of different signs from local and global rock myths. In fact, there is a double contextualization: Rock music consumer constructs the festival collectively and the experience in the festival makes the consumer another being (i.e., different from the ones at, say, a rock bar, and similar to the mythical ones at the nostalgic Woodstock). As such, consumers are not under the hegemony of any ideology, they are rather, as a community, producers of their experience, which is a product of their ideological choice.

> In a place like this, there is an opportunity to absorb rock music, I mean it's really nice to be in nature. It's a lot more different than a normal concert place, it's really a festival, although it lasts short, a festival atmosphere is really nice (RP, Interpreter, F, 25).

> We saw that cleaning people couldn't resist [the music] and jumped and hopped [in RC]. It was a lovely scene (wounded walker, posted on ⟨*eksisozluk*⟩ in September 8, 2003).

> A festival that a friend of mine has exaggerated and had a special tent made for himself to stay [at *Rock'n Coke*] (sellme, posted on ⟨*eksisozluk*⟩ in June 5, 2004).

In other words, consumers experience the product of their ideologies that is a hybrid culture under the rock *leitmotiv*, and become producers of their own framework to be consumed as a festival. Hence, consumption choices through ideologies become productive processes (Fırat, Venkatesh, & Dholakia, 1995). They are not simply reproducing the images of the festival as imagined by the festival's promoters; they are 'producing' the festival in the act of creating, and participating in, the activities.

Multiplicity of Cultures

Another finding is that as cultures of styles, ideologies, and music coexist, presenting themselves to be sampled as they compete against and contest each other, so do the cultures of humanity's epochs (traditional, modern, postmodern) coexist, compete and contest, rather than replace each other. Elements of the traditional, the modern, and the postmodern are present in the experiences and the cultures at rock festivals. The traditional exists in the stratification, the status rankings, the search for community, and unity. The modern exists in the 'business' of the festival, in the urge to instill an order into the event and make it a (commercial) success by making sure that the behaviors that will fulfill this project are performed by the participants. The postmodern exists in that, despite all the efforts on the part of the promoters, there is the 'undetermined' – the excess (Bataille, 1985) – the unexpected, the 'on the spot' production and performance.

The multiplicity of cultures contradicts the idea that we should find a *single order*, that is usually suggested to be out there – possibly because modern thought has conditioned us to seek it, and we may be forcing this observation on to what in fact exists. Most interestingly, the observations from the rock festival in a context where what is dominant today is contested may be giving us a peek into the future; that is, if we do not resist it.

CONCLUSION

Observations at two competing rock festivals discussed above begin to provide us with insights about the conditions of contemporary consumption. One relates to the inescapability of ideology in consumption. Every consumption decision and experience is infused with ideology, whether it be overtly expressed, internally debated, or remain unnoticed. In contemporary cultures, where not only ideologies clash, but cultures are sought to be experienced, contested, and constructed, this struggle with ideology seems to come to play in terms of certain tensions between contrary positions that in modern sensibility were considered to be exclusive; either one or the other position was (to be) taken, and both could not coexist. This condition of segregation of positions, states of being, and/or existence can no longer be assumed to exist. Each position seems to embrace its 'opposite' or the 'other' to exist. This condition, then, tends to provide fertile ground for multiplicity, play, and creative engagement with potential cultures through the formation of 'theaters' or 'communities' of performative acts.

We wish to suggest that understanding contemporary consumption and possible future trends, therefore, will be enriched by finding contexts that are made complex by the existence of multiple, competing, and contested cultures and 'orders', and through further investigating the interplay of tensions along an increasing array of dimensions created by contrary yet coexisting (cultural/ideological) positions.

ACKNOWLEDGMENTS

The authors wish to thank the organizing committee of *Rock for Peace*, and the interviewees.

REFERENCES

Barthes, R. (1973). *Elements of semiology*. New York: Hill and Wang.

Bataille, G. (1985). *Visions of excess: Selected writings, 1927–1939*. Minneapolis, MN: University of Minnesota Press.

Cushman, T. (1995). *Notes from underground, rock music counterculture in Russia*. New York: SUNY Press.

DaMatta, R. (1991). *Carnivals, rogues and heroes, an interpretation of the Brazilian dilemma*. Notre Dame: University of Notre Dame Press.

Eagleton, T. (1991). *Ideology, an introduction*. London: Verso.

Featherstone, M. (1991). *Consumer culture and postmodernism*. London: Sage.

Fırat, A. F., & Venkatesh, A. (1993). Postmodernity: The age of marketing. *International Journal of Research in Marketing*, *10*(4), 227–249.

Fırat, A. F., Venkatesh, A., & Dholakia, N. (1995). Marketing in a postmodern world. *European Journal of Marketing*, *29*(1), 40–56.

Frith, S. (1981). *Sound effects: Youth, leisure, and the politics of rock'n'roll*. New York: Pantheon Books.

Frith, S. (2001). The popular music industry. In: S. Frith, W. Straw & J. Street (Eds), *The Cambridge companion to pop and rock* (pp. 26–52). Cambridge: Cambridge University Press.

Jameson, F. (1984). Postmodernism, or the cultural logic of late capitalism. *New Left Review*, *146*(July–August), 59–72.

Keightley, K. (2001). Reconsidering rock. In: S. Frith, W. Straw & J. Street (Eds), *The Cambridge companion to pop and rock* (pp. 109–142). Cambridge: Cambridge University Press.

Kozinets, R. V. (2002a). The field behind the screen: Using netnography for marketing research in online communities. *Journal of Marketing Research*, *39*(February), 61–72.

Kozinets, R. V. (2002b). Can consumers escape from the market? Emancipatory illuminations from Burning Man. *Journal of Consumer Research*, *29*(June), 20–38.

Patton, M. Q. (2002). *Qualitative research & evaluation methods* (3rd ed.). London: Sage.

Ross, A. (Ed.) (1998). *Universal abandon?* Minneapolis, MN: University of Minnesota Press.

Stallybrass, P., & White, A. (1986). *The politics and poetics of transgression*. New York: Cornell University Press.

Steen, A. (1996). Der Lange Marsch des Rock'n'Roll: Pop- und Rockmusik in der Volksrepublik China [The long march of rock'n'roll: Pop and rock music in the People's Republic of China], *Berline China-Studien, 32*. LIT Hamburg: Verlag.

Straw, W. (1993). The English Canadian recording industry since 1970. In: T. Bennet, S. Frith, L. Grossberg, J. Shepherd & G. Turner (Eds), *Rock and popular music* (pp. 52–65). New York: Routledge.

Wicke, P. (1995). *Rock music: Culture, aesthetics and sociology*. Cambridge: Cambridge University Press.

APPENDIX: IDEOLOGIES IN THE ROCK FESTIVALS

Ideology	Rock for Peace: "Counter Festival"	Rock'n Coke Festival
Slogan	"Rock Can't Exist in a Bottle" in 2003, "World is Our Home" in 2004, "Our Songs are for the Skies" in 2005	No specific slogan, advertising stresses out the joy and fun through good music
Promoters	Activists and Local Rock Bands	*Coca Cola* (Soundwave Project)
Consumption setting	Public place for picnics	A designated place in the suburb (an unused airport)
Performing bands	Local Rock Bands	Local Bands/Worldwide known bands (not necessarily rock bands)
Participants	Students/Activists/Rockers/Socializers/Woodstock Nostalgia Seekers	Anybody/Rockers/Companies (for product promotion)/Woodstock Nostalgia Seekers
Social setting	Communal	Individualistic/Entrepreneurial/Hedonistic
Political mode	Social activism/Left/Unspecific	Unspecific
Dress code	Black (for rockers)/Traditional/Anything	Trendy/Fashionable/Sexy/Anything
Social responsibility	Improving consciousness for anti-globalization and peace /Supporting Laid-off Coca Cola Workers	Life + Youth Project to promote funds for 10 sustainable projects (with Youth for Habitat International Network and UNDP)
Cause	Activism & Entertainment	Entertainment
Leisure activities	Chess, origami, workshops for ecological problems, anti-globalization, anti-brands, playing silent movie	Themed Park/Tattoo/Yoga/Hikingand Shopping
No. of participants	1,000–1,500	30–40,000
Budget	$100–200 thousand	$8–10 million
Cost	Free ($8–10 in the last 2 years)	$45–60
Time	2 days (3 Nights for campers)	2 days (3 Nights for campers)

COMEDY OF THE COMMONS: NOMADIC SPIRITUALITY AND THE BURNING MAN FESTIVAL

John F. Sherry, Jr. and Robert V. Kozinets

ABSTRACT

In this account of our long-term ethnographic investigation of the Burning Man Project, we examine the emergence of nomadic spirituality among the citizens of Black Rock City, Nevada. We describe this emergence as a reaction to consumers' increasing dissatisfaction both with conventional religious denominations and with consumption as an existential ground of meaning. We provide an emic view of the pilgrimage experience at Black Rock City, from the perspective of participants in and organizers of the event. We propose a theory of the comedy of the commons to interpret the surface structure of the moment, and embed our deep structural interpretation of the nomadic spirituality of the phenomenon within the context of new religious movements (NRMs). In so doing, we shed new light on the topic of the sacred and profane in consumer experience.

INTRODUCTION

Religious affiliation in contemporary North America has been aptly described as a spiritual marketplace, fueled in part by a loss of faith both in

Consumer Culture Theory
Research in Consumer Behavior, Volume 11, 119–147

ISSN: 0885-2111/doi:10.1016/S0885-2111(06)11006-6

conventional denominational orthodoxy and in secular alternatives, sustained by a questing mood and resulting in the proliferation of religions of the self (Roof, 1999; Taylor, 2001; Csordas, 1997). With the spread of the "culture of authenticity," the rise of "expressive individualism," and the flourishing of the therapeutic ethos – each coinciding with, if not originating in, the consumption ethic of late capitalism – a "reflexive spirituality" of "lived religion" has attracted legions of converts in the past few decades (Taylor, 2001, pp. 83, 88; Roof, 1999, pp. 41, 75). Religious semiosis has migrated from temples to other "architectonic" spaces of "mutual display" such as festivals (Pike, 2001a; Fernandez, 1982; Taylor, 2001), and this movement has generated spiritual genres that are characterized as dynamic, decentralized fluid networks (Roof, 1999; Pike, 2004).

Such evolution from denominational doctrinal orthodoxy to personalized, experiential religious forms unfolds within a long American tradition of alternative worship reaching back to 19th century evangelical camp meetings (Pike, 2001b). The emergence of new spiritual forms, deliberately constructed by bricoleurs of the sacred who have sifted traditions in cross-cultural and cross-temporal perspective to create genres of relevance to contemporary seekers – generating as much criticism as acclaim in the bargain (Wallis, 2003) – affords researchers a compelling opportunity for re-examining the sacred and profane in consumer experience (Belk, Wallendorf, & Sherry, 1989; Belk, 2004; Sherry, 2004).

Among these new or disestablishment religious forms are genres broadly labeled "New Age" or "Neopagan" (or "Neoshamanic"), an eclectic mélange of syncretic expressions that converge upon the goals of personal experience and insight, and for whom ritual is the touchstone of identity and community (Pike, 2004, p. 22). In his meditation on James' (1982) opus, Taylor accepts experience over cognition as the real locus of religion, but disputes the diagnosticity of individual experience, maintaining that certain emotions arise only in solidarity, and that experience mutates when shared (2001, p. 28). Via such sharing, these groups seek to harmonize humans with nature, sacralize the carnal, cauterize intolerance, and socialize within communities. To do so, they may travel to transformative spiritual frontiers, seeking to experience immanence. The festivals at which they convene often culminate in a sacrificial fire (Pike, 2001a). We articulate the nature of lived religion in just such a communal context, in the present ethnographic study of nomadic spirituality at Burning Man.

As anthropologists sympathetic to Graebner's (2004, p. 105) call to "make common cause" with the anarchists, and as consumer researchers aware of the need to position our work within a relevant theoretical niche, we have adopted a compromise strategy in our interpretation of the phenomenon. Burning Man is perhaps most cogently described by borrowing Naipaul's (1990) metaphor: "a million mutinies now." It is a subculturally diverse congeries of campers, anarchists, ravers, digerati, artists, spiritual seekers, tourists, urban planners, visionaries, and, increasingly, researchers and media reporters. The event has evolved rapidly and distinctively over the past two decades, in dynamic response to intraorganizational politics, popular appropriation, and the clash of personalities across stakeholder camps (Doherty, 2004). In order to capture different aspects of the phenomenon's complexity, we have parsed our interpretation over many outlets and theories. Our present effort is devoted to a particular dimension of the event's appeal – its spiritual cast – that articulates with an important consumer research issue: the interplay of sacred and profane in contemporary life. Recently, Belk (2004) has offered a retrospective account of this issue, noting especially some areas in need of illumination and extension: landscapes and cyberscapes, violence and the gift, the "cool," festivals, and transgressive desires. In this article, we explore the ways in which many of Belk's frontier concerns are implicated in a remarkable consumption ritual.

THE FESTIVAL

Captured in the character of its own aesthetic charter, Black Rock City might be described as a pastiche of paintings. Begin with a shifting landscape of scenes from Dali's "Archeological Reminiscence of Millet's Angelus," "The First Days of Spring," and "Enchanted Beach with Three Fluid Graces." Imagine the surreal setting crawling with figures from Brueghel's "The Feast of Fools," "The Battle Between Carnival and Lent," and "The Flemish Fair." Finally, anchor the vision on the center panel of Hieronymous Bosch's "The Garden of Earthly Delights" (allowing the water to evaporate in the mind's eye), and permit the gaze to dart from the left wing of "Paradise" to the right wing of "Hell," as the shutters close to enfold the painting in a depiction of "The Creation of the World." Give this vision a kaleidoscopic spin, dub in a soundtrack that runs the aural gamut from simple percussion to synthesized techno, let the thermostat range from 110 to 40 degrees Fahrenheit over the course of your viewing, and, just when you think you're too tired to concentrate any longer, set the whole thing on fire. If you can step outside of yourself while embodying the flame, and cheer as it both consumes you and fuses you with surrounding viewers, you have visited Black Rock City. You have entered the realm of Burning Man. It is a "psychedelic vision made visceral," its art meant to be "touched, then torched" (Pinchbeck, 2002, pp. 81, 91).

Chronicled in many places (Doherty, 2004; Kozinets, 2002, 2003; Gilmore & van Proyen, 2005; http://www.burningman.com/), the evolution of the Burning Man Project can be summarily charted. Launched on a whim in 1986 by Larry Harvey and a few friends who gathered on Baker Beach in San Francisco to burn an 8 ft effigy of a man, apochryphally to mark the break up of a relationship, the gathering drew increasing numbers of interested passersby on each successive annual outing. As the event became publicized among Bay area culture jammers, its numbers overwhelmed the venue, prompting a move to the Black Rock Desert in Nevada, a terrestrial Mare Imbrium that permitted the kind of countercultural sprawl the moment was demanding. The event unfolds the week prior to Labor Day. Over time, the Man grew larger, and was augmented with other art installations, many destined for the same fiery destruction. Performance art grew to surround the installations, and throngs of participants from around the globe swelled a week-long festival, directed by an arts organization coordinating the voluntary labor of thousands. (It is not uncommon to hear informants wonder aloud about the similarity to the building of the Egyptian pyramids.) Harvey has remained the genus locus of the festival, his Man an intentionally underspecified polysemic projective vessel his concelebrants adore as the beacon guiding their pilgrimage to the place they call Black Rock City. Imagistic depictions of the site are being published with increasing frequency (Brill & Bee, 2003; Kreuter, 2002; Pinchbeck, 2003; Sherry, 2003; Sherry & Kozinets, 2003; Traub, Plunkett, Brown, & Wieners, 1997; http://www.burningman.com/).

Our account is based on an intensive multi-year ethnographic and netnographic inquiry into the Burning Man Project, conducted with participants drawn from all quarters of the event. Hundreds of hours of physical and virtual immersion in the sites were complemented with interviews of hundreds of informants. Data were recorded manually in fieldnotes, and electronically in photographs and both audio- and videotape. Informants assisted in member checks, and provided insightful feedback on our interpretations. As befits a long-term investigation, our findings are reported in a variety of outlets in addition to the present article (e.g., Kozinets & Sherry, 2003, 2005). In the balance of the text, emic language is placed in quotation marks, and informants identified mostly by "playa names."

THE GREETING

After the long and frequently arduous journey to reach the Black Rock Desert, one of the first salutations a pilgrim receives from a "Greeter" at the gates of this emerging city of art, and one that she will hear repeated often in the coming week during her wanderings through the city's theme camps, is a heartfelt "Welcome home." This greeting is extended especially to first-time "newbies" as well as returning "burners" (a label loathed by the festival's organizers but beloved by the citizenry of Black Rock City); neither is the benediction denied to the despised "yahoos" who enter the festival late and leave early, behaving rudely like voyeuristic revelers. This hailing is not merely a cordial offer of hospitality. Rather, it is an invocation, an invitation, and an induction.

The nomad is incorporated into the fold, his apparent status as visitor soon transformed to host. Prodigal pursuits in the commercial world of formal institutions are checked at the gate, as the pilgrim is (re-)initiated into the antistructural world of the postmodern paraprimitive technoshamanic vision quest. Dropping out of time and space for a manic burst of creative destruction that will celebrate an evanescent retroscape and mark the passing of a noetic oasis, each nomad receives the greeting as a blessing and a challenge.

The greeting is a gift, the promise of religion in its ancient etymological sense: a binding back to the source. Pilgrims have flocked to Black Rock City to recover a primal experience of immanence and transcendence, and some to take that spark back with them to the "world," in hopes of infusing their everyday lived experience with grace and the possibility of renewal.

BEFORE THE BURN

Over the course of the week, upon a geomantic infrastructure designed by Project directors and laid down by a first wave of nomad volunteers, pilgrims, who will eventually number over 30,000 strong, labor to create Black Rock City. From a barren Pleistocene lake bed ringed by mountains erupts a luminous city of art, with a Wild West ethos, a retrofuturistic architecture, a dense cacophonous soundscape, and a New Age vibe. As quickly as it achieves fluorescence, it evaporates in a swirl of dust, only to re-appear a year hence. It is a tangible mirage.

The city, comprised of theme camps and villages dedicated to aesthetic production, is arrayed in medieval hub and spoke fashion around the axis mundi of the Man, a 50 ft effigy on a multistory pedestal set out on the playa amid a host of mega-installations of art. The Esplanade divides the playa proper from the encampment, which radiates from the center camp

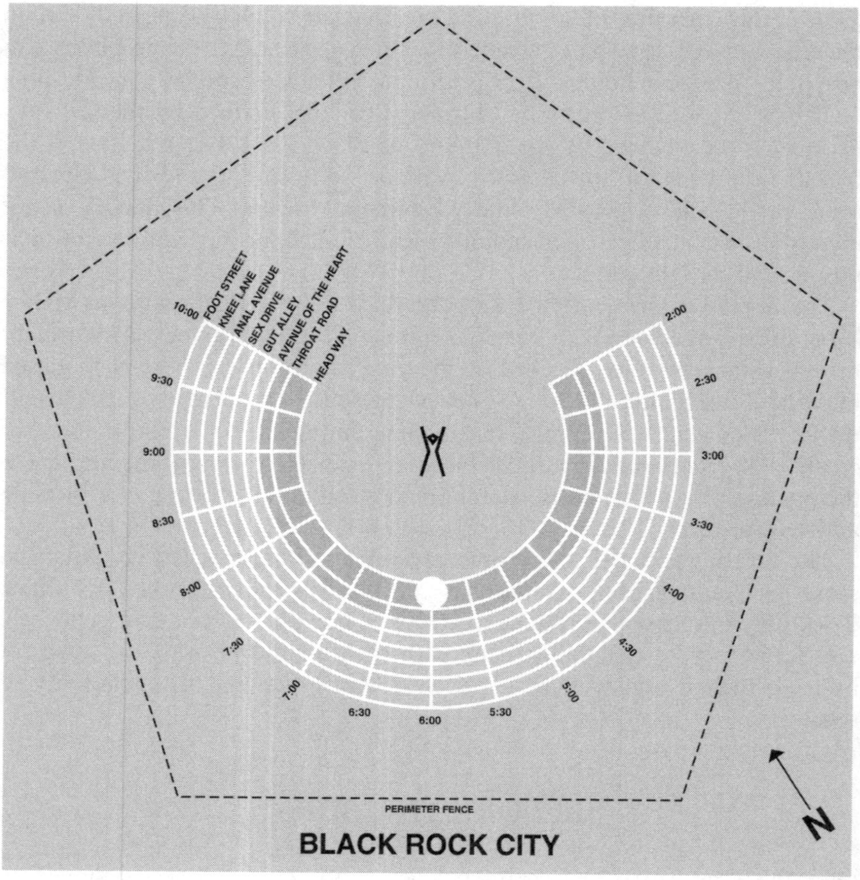

Fig. 1. City Plan

communal café nearly to encircle the playa. Fig. 1 is an artist's depiction of a common plan for Black Rock City. At any given moment, the arteries are choked with pedestrian, bicycle and art car traffic whose predictability in terms of speed, direction, and interaction moves lower as it flows onto the playa; desert darkness drops predictability close to zero.

Interaction ritual among citizens is governed by the festival's twin ideological pillars: radical self-expression and no spectators. Pilgrims are expected to participate actively in the construction of community that, like a chrysalis, will facilitate the emergence of a transformed and renewed self. "This is who I really am" is a commonly asserted affirmation of the playa self that a pilgrim comes to discover in a week of aesthetically mediated leveling and bonding rituals that draw her into intimate association with her fellow travelers. Through a communally enforced gift economy (commerce is banned, save for the sale, by volunteers, of coffee, tea, chai, and ice in Center Camp, the proceeds of which serve only to help defray festival costs and support the nearest local high school), presentations of food and drink, goods, and services, circulate alongside the endless exchange of the aestheticized self. Pilgrims are present for one another most hours of the day, sharing cordial facework, labor, performances, epiphanies, and, most often, simple immediacy. The anomie of the "world" is banished in the building of this organic community, or exorcised in public forums should it arise during the week.

Playgrounds of diminutive and gigantic scale are scattered throughout Black Rock City. Nomads are constantly encouraged to play, to regress to childhood. Trampolines, swing sets, life-sized interactive board games, toy boxes, and sports equipments are offered by nomads to one another. One theme camp makes components of dolls available to visitors, who are invited to combine the parts in novel and creative ways. The costumes worn by nomads as gifts to one another are effective masks, allowing multiple personae to emerge from the multiphrenic self, harnessing play in the service of self-discovery and self-disclosure.

Sexuality and gender are publicly problematized and communally celebrated. Many participants are on permanent naked walkabout. Ambulatory and automotive genitalia are on constant parade in costumed amplification. Transvestism teems. Public displays of hetero- and homosexual affection abound. Transsexual pilgrims in various stages of gender reassignment have a physical presence, while confounding costumery causes other pilgrims to contemplate the conundrum of hermaphroditism. "Sacred sexuality" is preached and practiced in some of the theme camps. Weddings (and the renewal of vows) are a common event in Black Rock City, performed by a variety of intermediaries and witnessed by close friends and spontaneous gatherings of strangers.

Sacred clowns pervade the festival, and shamans (in the guise of witch doctors, magicians, soothsayers, ecstatic drummers, clerics, and the like) meander the midways. Devils, angels, and interesting hybrids populate the playa. Both Pan and the Green Man are popular festival costumes. Jesters may seek to provoke response from the complacent and the jaded. For example, a performance artist misanthrope may harangue pilgrims with a steady stream of expletives. "Fuck you! Fuck you and your 'no spectating.' Fuck your 'experience.' And fuck you!" may dupe an unwitting nomad into a public debate of festival premises. Another pilgrim, naked save for satanic and nazi symbolism painted on his body, may preach love and tolerance, enjoining his interlocutors to "Have a nice day!" This same pilgrim, re-painted the next day with flowers and smiley faces, will hurl an aggressive "Fuck you!" at admirers of his gentle images. A Dust Devil, dressed as a visual pun of the natural phenomenon, may run a vacuum over the playa surface, complaining of the ceaseless futility of his task. Reversals, parodies, and lampoons of many of the institutions of the "world" are enacted in Black Rock City. Trickster (Hyde, 1998) must surely be among the genius loci of this desert encampment.

Therapeutic practice and ritual relief of all manner are available to pilgrims. Mother Bear conducts healing ceremonies and informational seminars at the Women's Temple. Practitioners of "revirgination" and "rehymenation" offer to renew pilgrims' sexual energy. Massage is widely offered throughout the encampment. Yoga and meditation sessions abound. A variety of exorcisms and baptisms are on offer. Extropians discuss the eventual and inevitable liberation of consciousness from the body, while extollers of entheogens help pilgrims to out-of-body experiences through chemical means. Fortunetellers are abundant. A cursory check of the theme camp manifest suggests no metaphysical ailment or curiosity need go untreated during the pilgrim's sojourn.

Black Rock City can be imagined as a New Age/Neopagan mirror image of the spiritual supermarket its residents have encountered in the "world." The city is a bazaar of beliefs, a hive of heterodoxy, a convocation of callings. The event is as sacral as the Run for the Wall (Dubisch, 2004), and as festal a mountain man rendezvous (Belk & Costa, 1998). The aesthetic medium in which these theologies thrive over the week serves also as a lingua franca for the nomads.

While the theme camps that are the city's residential unit busy themselves with the aesthetic production – substantive and processual – that becomes their gift to the gathering, individual artists and their helpmates erect distinctive installations on the playa. Playa artwork is often colossal in scope, to suit the seemingly trackless expanse of the outdoor gallery and to match the monumental majesty of the Man in apprehension. Strolling nomads might pass by an enormous shattered chandelier, apparently fallen to earth from the hall of Norse gods, or see a gigantic rubber duckie housing a nightclub, or watch a Janus-faced bronze sculpture weep fiery tears, or encounter a prodigious lingam and yoni vibrating to the touch of passersby, or marvel as megaton slabs of granite dangle from chains, swaying as pilgrims dance upon them overhead, or laugh at a larger-than-life scatological rendition of the Merrill Lynch logo.

Often this artwork incorporates ingenious technology, such that stationary sculptures of swimmers stroke to life under the influence of stroboscopes, or musical tones emanate from invisible lyre strings as pilgrims move their hands through empty space, or laser beams trace out the shape of the Man overhead, for the amusement of any watchers from the sky. Humble works are present as well, from elegant postings of poetry, through terra cotta warrior-type battalions of statuettes, to the occasional nonfunctional phone booth or drinking fountain.

Most strikingly, the playa is rife with artwork that is sacred, if not overtly religious (and quite frequently blasphemous), in character, whether allusive or allegorical, literal or ironic, approving or critical. Religious referents across time and space are incorporated into much of the art, whether built or found. Allusions to fire worship, and attendant sacrifice by immolation, are endemic. Constant exposure to the sky draws reference to its divinity as well. Altars abound. Ancient mythological deities are evoked in sculpture, song, and dance. Replicas of the Buddha, both monumental and diminutive, are pervasive, as are Hindu icons and imagery. A pilgrim playing a didgeridoo as he methodically wends his way around the Man – whose base is frequently constructed by design to resemble an altar, and is so designated by burners – may respond to the ethnographer's inquiry into his activity with textbook Eliade (1954) precision, "I'm creating sacred space." In 2003, the altar (in fact, a pyramid) was built to accommodate 16 alcoves or grottoes, in which performance artists assumed the roles of demigods, forming tableaux vivants of spiritual devotion in their embedded niches; that they also bore a parodic resemblance to department store window dressings was not lost on informants. A row of crucifixes may invite DIY simulated crucifixion. Chapel installations with simulated stained glass may beckon pilgrims to leaf by candle light through a book that chronicles the exploits of abusive clergy. Sacred iconography from Marian tradition may appear in panel murals in the café in Center Camp, or in extravagant abundance (and in combination with profane images harnessed in the service of goddess worship) on the mobile Church of the Chocolate Martini. Ecstatic trances induced by repetitive drumming, dancing, and/or chemical ingestion can be observed. Theme camp services may deliver a therapeutic cleansing effect to patrons, via channels such as yoga, bodywork, healing rituals, and even self help groups.

Whether aestheticized spiritual seekers, cultural transvestites, eclectic syncretists, or hardy partiers, the focus of the pilgrims' attention throughout their physical and metaphysical journeys of the week, is the burning of the Man that occurs on Saturday night. As the effigy is assembled early in the week, trimmed with neon lighting and installed as a devotional shrine for the pilgrims who will traverse its structure often in the balance of the week, the talk turns inevitably to the coming burn, to the transience of the creative process, and to the renewal of the world.

THE BURN

In the gathering darkness, pilgrims stream down the dusty avenues, across the Esplanade and fan out over the playa, staking out their places around the neon-lighted Man. Dressed in full regalia, armed with glow sticks and el-wire, bearing musical instruments and cameras, pilgrims banter with each other and the rehearsing performers. The surrounding throng is boisterous and rowdy as the momentum of the previous week achieves its peak. Rangers urge the crowd to sit, to ensure maximum visibility for the greatest number. Fire dancers on foot, on stilts, and in wheelchairs parade around the Man, inciting the crowd with the promise of imminent conflagration. As the ceremonial dancing concludes, Rangers instruct the closest ring of pilgrims in the etiquette of "rushing" the burn, seeking to minimize the danger to life as pilgrims invariably mob the fire raging around the collapsed man.

As pyrotechnics begin to explode, and early flames begin to lick the pedestal, the Man raises his arms (or arm, or not, in the event of a commonly occurring engineering snafu), as if to signal "Touchdown!" or to exhort the crowd to its feet. Pilgrims leap at this command, cheering lustily as the flames devour the Man. Nomads are enraptured by the blaze, some laughing hysterically, others weeping, still others marveling aloud about all the effort going up in smoke. The awe expressed in the face of the burn feels most like adrenalized joy and wonderment, a profoundly playful combustion of the id, releasing pilgrims from any pretext of restraint.

As the Man collapses upon itself, the crowd rushes the enormous bonfire, sometimes under a hail of burning debris raining from the sky. Pilgrims often hurl artifacts into the flames, taking literally the most-asked question of the previous week: "What did you bring to burn?" Sometimes the sacrifice is a carefully planned or hastily prepared document of deep personal significance to the pilgrim; it may be a photograph or other memento. It may be a piece of art. One year, we witnessed the immolation of a Christmas tree, passed hand over hand above the heads of the crowd, as one of the revelers barked out, "Merry Christmas! Merry fuckin' Christmas!" The rush gradually assumes the shape of an enormous conga line, as pilgrims, braving the incredibly intense heat, dance for hours around the massive perimeter of the bonfire. The physical feel of the fire accompanies a symbolic stripping of the self, as the dancers enact their purification ritual (Pike, 2001a, p. 165). Musicians in the crowd add their efforts to this free-form dancing, helping to keep the circle turning until the fire begins to subside.

Eventually, pilgrims desert the dance, disoriented not merely from the bacchanal, but more profoundly from the loss of the Man as their axis mundi. All week the Man has been the lodestar by which they have navigated the emerging city, and its absence robs many of their sense of direction. Before eyes adjust to the darkness, pilgrims may stumble inadvertently upon passionate lovers on the desert floor, as if they had wandered onto the set of *The Wicker Man* (a burner favorite). Small islands of nomads congregate in the dark, some reliving the rapture or slowly coming down, and some regrouping with friends to continue a night of unbridled partying. Drum circles reconvene around fire barrels closer to the Esplanade, beckoning returning pilgrims with their smaller home fires. Still other nomads drift to installations farther out on the playa, to commune with art and the solitude of the deeper desert night.

AFTER THE BURN

Backlit by the gibbous moon, the smoldering remains of the Man and his "altar" become the staging ground for ritual activity far into the morning hours. Some pilgrims, hands folded and heads bowed, perform a devotional walk around the perimeter of the area. Others walk barefoot across the glowing embers, some making slow repeated crossings, some dancing out quickly as the heat becomes unbearable and the pain too intense. A pilgrim may rub his face with the ashes of the Man, in ritual recognition of corporeal transience and acknowledgment of metaphysical transcendence. The Man is widely compared to "the phoenix," and some pilgrims are not content to wait an entire year for him to rise from his ashes.

Squatters tend small campfires about the site, conversing in low tones about the personal significance of "the burn," stoking their high with infernal husbandry and conversation. This high is sometimes amplified or modulated with mind-altering substances, often accompanied by the ingestion of the charred remains of the Man himself. Musicians drift to these communal fires, jamming, and riffing at volumes suited to each gathering's mood. Dancers, drawn to the music, match their movements to these rhythms. Drum circles arise, and trance dancing may result.

Some pilgrims may be moved to song. In a moment of what may fairly be described as cosmic, let alone postmodern, irony (and which invites comparison with Kubrick's singing manchild warriors in *Full Metal Jacket*), we observed a young woman with a trained voice begin a haunting solo a cappella rendition of the Disney anthem, *"When You Wish Upon a Star."* As she completed the first verse, other pilgrims, pulled into the orbit of her spell, drew close to her and added their voices to the balance of the song. A wandering flautist began his accompaniment midway through the impromptu performance. At song's end, after quietly thanking and reverently complementing the lead singer, and exchanging hugs, the pilgrims dispersed, each to her own destination, with no commentary on this apparently striking juxtaposition of sacred and profane, of TAZ with theme park.

Individual onlookers may use these tableaux, or any of the myriad of scattered embers still glowing, as objects of contemplation. These pilgrims become suspended, in meditative pause, for long minutes on end. Then, they resume their journeys, stepping off into the darkness and steering by the distant lights of Black Rock City's festive precincts, to be replaced by other nomads at ground zero, until dawn dampens ardor.

THE MORNING AFTER

In the early morning light, dozens of pilgrims converge upon the burn site, sifting the scorched surface of the playa and culling the detritus of last night's conflagration. Looking for all the world like a post-apocalyptic version of Millet's *Les Glaneuses*, these gleaners industriously amass the bricolage of the afterburn – carpenter's nails, fused glass, wire, cinders – bundling away the treasure like so many pieces of the true cross. Ashes from the Man are packed tightly into empty coffee cans, Mason jars, plastic bags, and other containers near to hand. (A similar collection of ash occurs after the "Temple burn" a day hence.) These relics are destined for a variety of ends. Some entrepreneurial pilgrims fashion jewelry, keychains, and other artifacts from the gleanings, creating auratic art that both keeps the gift circulating and tangibilizes (and sometimes commodifies) the process of creativity that the Burning Man Project celebrates. These pieces may become trade goods at subsequent burns. Some of the relics end up as objects of contemplation on shelves and in corners of the permanent homes of pilgrims, retired from circulation. Some pilgrims believe the relics to have healing properties for both physical and spiritual ailments, and so bring their bounty back to friends and relatives unable to make the pilgrimage, in the hope of effecting mitigation and cure.

On the morning after the burn of 2003, gleaners were greeted by an apparition arising from the ashes, in the form of an exquisitely curated replica of the original Burning Man, erected by Project directors. The 8 ft tall figure, quite humble in appearance when compared to its present incarnation, quickly became an altar upon which gleaners and other pilgrims installed a variety of offerings (in the fashion of a spirit house) and inscribed a host of sentiments directly upon the wood. Votaries treated the little man as they did the Temple, its accessibility inviting sacrifice in a way the current Man does not. Offertory activity accelerated as word spread that the figure was to be burned that very night. Adjacent to the figure, a laminated legend presented the history of "Early Man," from its origin in 1986, and included photographs of the "First Man" prior to and during the original figure's burning. This playful confounding of anthropological and biblical meanings by the curators resonated with comments such as "He is risen" and "It's the phoenix rising from the ashes" voiced by some of the gleaners.

THE TEMPLE BURN

Gradually, many pilgrims have felt a shift in the "energy" or "soul" of the festival away from the burning of the Man and toward the burning of the Temple. The "Temple" is the cover term used by informants to describe the project of artist David Best that has unfolded over the past four years. As the concept has evolved, its contrast with the festival's traditional culmination has become more marked, and more remarked upon by pilgrims. "Screw the Man, the Temple is where it's at" is the voice one informant gives to an increasingly popular sentiment. Her statement is not as dismissive or hyperbolic as it sounds. Rather, it reflects many pilgrims' nascent dissatisfaction with spectacle in the face of a more sacral alternative. The citizenry at large of Black Rock City seems gratified to have a second cynosure whose ethos complements or balances the main event.

David Best, a bricoleur of the first order and a master of lateral cycling, installed his first playa temple (the Temple of the Mind) in 2000, and in subsequent years has erected temples of Tears, Joy, and Honor. Each temple has also been designated a "mausoleum," as each is a house of memory for those who make the pilgrimage. The airy structures have grown increasingly monumental with time, from 20 feet to three stories in height. Early efforts were constructed of the wooden filigree discards that are the byproduct of manufacturing model toy dinosaurs, and have had a Southeast Asian Buddhist gingerbread hybrid pagoda-wat kind of feel. The latest temple was fabricated from piñata components, and sported turrets, minarets, and huge garlic bulb domes that invited comparison with middle eastern Islamic mosques and the Kremlin. The surfaces of this latest temple were covered in allegorical iconography from the middle ages.

The overtly spiritual architecture of the temples facilitates a correspondingly reverent demeanor among the normally rowdy nomads of Black Rock City. Bicycles are parked a respectful distance away from the site, and pilgrims complete the journey quietly on foot. Art cars that blare music of almost unbearable decibels mute their speakers in passing. Pilgrims speak in hushed tones, and wandering musicians play quietly, if at all, in the Temple precincts. Dwellers feel a palpable sense of quietude at the site. Pilgrims are encouraged to divest themselves of toxic emotions, to express grief, to commemorate or venerate significant others, and otherwise express themselves in a way that leads to enhanced self-acceptance, by inscribing their thoughts on the monument itself, by leaving an artifactual representation of their intention (e.g., a photograph or document), by listening to the artist periodically meditate aloud about his purpose (and engaging him in dialogue), and by participating in rituals (e.g., mourning) that are convened at the site. Behavior at the Temple contrasts strikingly with the festive comportment that characterizes the festival at large.

The Temple burn is a correspondingly solemn occasion. A smaller gathering than saw off the Man, a host of partied-out pilgrims, anticipating postpartum blues, converges upon the site. The raucous revelry of the previous night's burn is replaced by a contemplative calm. The pyre is ignited, cheers are baffled by decorum, and the blaze is witnessed rather than encouraged. Unlike the Dionysian dancing around the consumed Man, an Apollonian procession attends the remains of the Temple. A disorientation similar to the one produced by the extinction of the lodestar Man afflicts the departing pilgrims, who are deprived of the last beacon on the playa, and must dead reckon their dark return home.

Several factors account for the Temple burn's ascendant exaltation. The Temple is a personal labor of love, designed and largely executed by a "people's" artist. It is widely viewed as the single most heartfelt gift given to the entire community. The artist has designed the Temple to be a projective vehicle, an intimately interactive work that pilgrims believe demands their participation (if not outright appropriation) to be fully realized. The structure invites deep inscription and evokes empathic, cathartic, therapeutic response in its dwellers. It convenes community in the heart of community, and harnesses communitas in the service of mindfulness or soulfulness. The site is regarded as holy, and as a respite or sanctuary from the sensory overload of Black Rock City proper. It is the wake that counterbalances the party (Pinchbeck, 2002, p. 104). The progress of its erection, on a lonely stretch of playa, is closely monitored throughout the week, and attended by a growing sense of reverential awe. Finally, much like an ancient scapegoat or sin eater, the Temple holocaust becomes a communal sacrifice that purifies its attendants, as pilgrims' personal baggage heads skyward in a blaze of stunning intensity.

STAYING-WHILE-LEAVING

The caravan departing Black Rock City begins early the morning after the burn, and pulses again the morning after the Temple burn. Each nomad who has pulled up stakes wears a mantle of playa dust, and will continue finding traces of the desert in his belongings months after his decamping. Many bear contraband containers of the dust, making just this one exception to the ethics of eco-propriety, to have a sensual remembrance of this dwelling when the comfort of the permanent residence palls. (This despite a common fear that their precious cargo will be mistaken for anthrax by airport security.) Soot from the Man and from the Temple clings to their skin as well.

This dusty hejira is a nonconscious, paradoxical inversion of the pilgrims' leave-no-trace adoption of Mary Douglas' deep structural understanding of dirt as "matter out of place" (or "MOOP" in playa-speak): place into matter is the rule of the road, this second skin the desert's handsel to the dwellers it releases to the world. It is as well the re-enactment of the mythic theft of fire, as the nomads carry the antistructural spark of the liminoid back with them to their distant homes, there to be fanned at regional gatherings, through the ether, and in their everyday lives, in the coming year. Staying connected and spreading the word are important maintenance rituals for burners making the countdown to the next "Happy New Day."

The expatriates of Black Rock City dwell in the state of *staying-while-leaving*, if an analogy with Weiner's (1992) keeping-while-giving is entertained. In this state, an erehwon of the mind, the sedentary burner retains a stake in the liminoid oasis from which she has emigrated physically, but where she still resides in reverie. Insomuch as the kingdom of the Man is within you, the nomad bears the TAZ on every journey undertaken from the source.

The Internet, which Neopagans pioneered (Pike, 2004) and which burners have always used to grow and orchestrate their event (Pinchbeck, 2002), provides a heterotopic limbo in which the pilgrims will dwell in the year between visits to the desert. Web rings, bulletin boards, and chat rooms will thrum with the activity of image posting and reminiscence, anticipation and planning, and, most of all, community building born of constant chatter. The telenomadic technopresence of the pilgrims in each other's lives betwixt and between their sojourns in the desert, is sprinkled, like so much pixel dust, in the eyes of every fellow traveler. Each is reminded of her reclamation and reconversion of the postmodern spectacle – the material reconstruction of religious illusion that replaces participating with spectating, pace Debord (1967/1975) – in the service of re-enchanting the world, at once exalting individual and tribal identity, and decommodifying spirituality.

FOUNDER'S PERSPECTIVE

In a depth interview conducted in situ with Larry Harvey, the founding father and general steward of the Burning Man Project, we elicited a number of insights into the festival's origins and intended orientation, as they bear upon our core interest in spiritual consumption. As a key informant, Harvey (Larry, hereafter, in keeping with his iconic status in Black Rock City) is uniquely qualified to comment on all things physical and metaphysical pertaining to the festival.

The psychodynamic origins of Burning Man are especially intriguing, and the break up that catalyzed the Baker Beach burn seems simply the surface structure of emergence. Larry recalls a lifelong fascination, beginning in childhood, with "sacred architecture," and found MesoAmerican structures particularly compelling. His father (a carpenter) instilled a passionate love of nature in Larry, and reinforced this love on camping trips taken with Larry and Larry's brother. Larry came to believe that "nature was charged with the numinous." He also envied the "holistic" or organic solidarity of the so-called "first civilizations," to which he attributed a seamless interfacing of sacred and secular realms.

His father was an autodidact (a pattern Larry subsequently emulated) and belonged to a Masonic lodge, whose rituals and fraternity Larry found laudable, although he himself did not prove to be "Mason material." An adopted child, Larry felt his family to be isolated from the local community. Over time, in his consultation with theologians, and in his wide reading of the humanities and social sciences (William James and Heinz Kohut being important influences), he laid the intellectual foundation for the "conversion experience" that resulted from his "dark night of the soul."

Claiming to be "messianic" rather than "charismatic," and resonating with Kohut's (2000) theory of the good parent, Larry couches his own interpretation of the Man in a kind of apotheosis of parenthood. The Man (and, by extension or incorporation, Larry himself), is symbolic of the good parent, delivering the two-fold gift that children most desire: "Pick me up!" and "Watch me!" He speculates that Burning Man is an attempt in part to change his own past, to revise his childhood in more self-enhancing ways. The Man might best be understood at core as the symbolic cosmic continuity of fatherhood.

While Larry steadfastly refuses to reduce the Man to a single interpretation, he is alternately amused and touched by the readings of his fellow pilgrims. He's been told countless times that the Man is "Larry," or "Larry's father," or "Larry's son." He's heard the figure christened "Old Man Gloom." When asked for his interpretation, Larry prefers to remain "cagey," for fear of dictating meaning that would ultimately subvert the goal of the festival. Larry refuses to give the pilgrims a "pill" that will absolve them of their own semiotic obligation, as such pill dispensing characterizes the passive dependency of the "world" from which the pilgrims are currently fleeing.

He staunchly maintains that the Man is not "God," but that it is "God-like." He sees the figure as the "transcendent" focal point of the gaze, and speaks of its "sacred" nature (even likening the annual city-building process to Genesis). He tells pilgrims that the Man is "yours" and reminds them constantly that "you built the thing." He sees the Man as a projective vehicle of "merged selves," producing a "conversion experience" that can lead pilgrims to a "connection with the oversoul." It is a theologically "immediate" emblem of "being" that radiates among the pilgrims, "shedding light" as it "touches everything."

The scale of the Man is designed to "dwarf you," to "humble you," and to provide a conduit for the "great power" that emerges from and passes through the thronging pilgrims. Perhaps most perceptively, he understands the Man as not merely a "gift," but rather as a kind of gift "chimney," an engine of sacrifice that draws in vast amounts of economic and extra-economic "resources" and transmutes them to immanence. Veteran burners have sometimes castigated him for raising the Man on a pedestal, instead of leaving it directly on the ground in the immediate physical presence of the pilgrims: "We can't touch it! You took it away from us! You can't touch it! Your transcendence is fascist!" Putting the Man on a pedestal so that everyone might have a better, safer view was charged with unintended and unanticipated consequences.

Larry often emphasizes the importance of sacred festivity, and is discouraged when he hears some people think of the event as simply "the world's biggest party." If it were only a party, Larry feels his hard work would neither be justified nor rewarding. The ludic, festal impulse pervades the event and integrates it, but the party is a means to an end. Burning Man is a "spiritual movement far from the church," promoting a "sacred vision of unity" (in diversity). The event is a "vision quest," realized through mimesis, sacrifice, and the "holy medium" of fire.

Here is his own account of the vision or origin myth that raised Black Rock City from the desert floor:

> ... We started out on the beach before the broad Pacific, and though the figure was only eight feet tall, it was enough to feel transcendence .... Had it been backed by an eight storey building, I don't suppose it would seem so transcendent.... When we came out here, we had this great flat expanse, and by that time, the Man was four stories. And that was enough to induce awe, and enormous mystical resonance for me. I may be the only one that thought that, to tell you the truth. And that's what chiefly struck me. That's why I thought they'd come. I stood there, and I looked up, and I looked around, and I could imagine .... I saw great cyclones of dust generated by armies marching from the four quarters of the playa, and it looked to me like columns of dust generated by armies marching toward the center of the world. And this thing that looks cosmic in scale is part of it. It made sense to me.

Striving to create a "visionary void" where his "stagecraft" can facilitate visions for pilgrims, he encourages the development of rituals which will have "seizing" and "conversion" effects upon pilgrims, and result in a "change of life" experience for burners willing to accept that the "ultimate source of value" is not rationality, but, rather, faith.

Such faith is grounded in what Larry refers to as a "living philosophy of being." Convinced that religion has co-opted the sacred, and that consumer culture has trivialized it, he is eager to restore the sacred to everyday life. This is the restoration of "untraditional reality," achieved in part theatrically (as it was in the "mystery religions" for which he feels an affinity), and in part by his frequently stated "refusal to commodify belief." Burning Man has fewer "overt dogmas" than conventional religion, but the spiritual trappings of religion are ripe for syncretic borrowing. Larry's dogma resides in the immediacy of personal experience that opens the way for an oceanic merger of selves and nature. He espouses a holistic experience of "sacred unity," predicated on a "spiritual arc" that runs from "I am" through "You are" to "It is." Traversing this arc opens pilgrims to the possibility of being "pervaded by a god" and "reversing" the effects of living in the "world." He describes the alienation arising from consumer culture in several striking metaphors. Society is viewed as a "vending machine," dispensing materiel and predigested ideologies to passive recipients. The ethos of this world is characterized as "consumerism simony," the "unhallowed trafficking in sacred things."

Larry promotes a return to the "old world" or nomadic view of "reality," a re-embracing of "It is." Personal experience is sacred, and begets connection to others (a kind of Baker Beach spin on the Baker's Square mantra: Come for the party, stay for the tribe). "Ideology" grows out of "immediate experience," and canalizes "transcendence" in the service of community. Through mysticism, stagecraft, and encampment in a harsh environment (wherein Larry has "seen the hand of God"), the event creates the conditions that will allow animal alertness (Berman, 2000a) to (re-)appear.

"New ideas," emerging from the desert, have the power to "transform the world." Personal, social, and cultural transformation demands an "opening of the heart." Larry acknowledges that his "utopianism" has required the directors of the event to become "more worldly," both to protect the sanctity and viability of the annual event, and to export the reformation to the "world" at large. Some of this worldliness is pithily detailed in recent work by Doherty (2004).

Featuring himself a social planner, Larry desires to carry the lesson of his desert temporary autonomous zone (Bey, 1994) to the level of a cultural revitalization movement. His entrepreneurial outreach has broadened and intensified in recent years, as he has worked the lecture circuit at home and abroad, and stepped up the pace of his writing. Organizers of regional "burns" turn to him for advice and publicity. Consumer activists – such as the Rev. Billy and the Church of Stop Shopping – have formed alliances of convenience with the Burning Man Project. Larry extols the "social capital" in the "world" that helps facilitate the aims of his organization, burner "moles" who are able to use their professional offices of lawyer, lobbyist, architect, physician, and so forth, to provide the "gift" of free service that helps Burning Man flourish.

Larry recognizes and laments that the individual festival may not be "sustainable" because currently there is "not enough of a backbone to it," as the population grows exponentially while the number of infrastructure-providing volunteers remains constant or grows slowly. Even activist pilgrims who carry the "gift thing" home with them re-acclimate themselves to the "world" rather quickly, leaving much of the "beautiful good" created in the desert in the dust of their repatriation. Acquisition of a permanent site for the event looks to be a short-term solution to sustainability, but its impact on the liminoid character of the festival may prove harmful in the long run. Fission, fusion, and franchising of a sort may disseminate the vision and distribute it about the planet physically at the same time the

Internet fuels its virtual spread around the globe, such that a host of heterotopias – a nomadic diaspora of glocal proportion and influence – acts upon the world to transform it.

GNOSTALGIA, MONASTICISM AND THE BURNING MAN NETWORK

We interpret the Burning Man Project in the context of new religious movements (NRMs) that seek to counterbalance people's dissatisfactions with consumer culture and conventional religious institutions with an awakening, or, more properly, a re-awakening, that promises polysemy and heterodoxy (York, 1995). Burners enact a "deregulated" reality in a retro key, splitting "imaginal space" from the marketplace where it has come principally to be lodged, and reattaching it to the infrastructure of tribal travel (Davis, 1998, pp. 177, 225; Brown, 2001; Brown, Kozinets, & Sherry, 2003). They reclaim the liminoid from the liminate (Sherry, 2004), and follow the song lines (Chatwin, 1987) in the ether between sojourns in the desert.

As we have described it, Burning Man is not an overtly religious form of NRM. Henotheistic in matters of devotion and tolerance, it is a confederacy of spiritual orientations, a docking station for the heterodox. It partakes of a "popular Western cultural criticism expressed in terms of a secularized esotericism" (Hanegraaff, 1998, p. 521), where gnostic experience is privileged above reason and faith, the twin pillars of American cultural ideology. Gnosis is perhaps the most precise way to describe the experience to which burners aspire, as the Burning Man Project struggles to develop a "vocabulary" of "spirituality" stripped of religious connotation. This experience is gnostalgic in the sense that its technologies of the sacred are both archaic and futuristic. Pilgrims employ the cutting edge to return to the carved in stone.

In this article, we have continued to push the theorizing of sacred travel in the direction of kinetic ritual (Turner & Turner, 1978), emphasizing the interplay between the central shrine (Coleman & Eade, 2004), the prayerful/playful dynamic of serious tourism (Schramm, 2004) or post-tourism (Urry, 2002), and the telenomadic role of cyberspace in the prolongation of the TAZ. Pilgrimage is currently being "reframed" as a constellation of interrelated activities, featuring movement as performative action, as embodied action, as semantic field, and as metaphor (Coleman & Eade, 2004, pp. 16–17). Burning Man encapsulates each of these types of movement.

Among the options available for activists seeking to combat the "spiritual death" of the culture, for whom the "anodynes" of consumption provide no balm and the "vital kitsch" of co-opted social movements no consolation, Berman's (2000b, pp. 2, 129, 136) "guerrilla" monasticism – the spiritual nomadism that we detailed earlier and theorize more fully below – best captures the ethos of the Burning Man Project. This ethos is more precisely understood in terms of NRMs rather than New Social Movements (NSMs) because of this spiritual cast. While the nomad may be aware of the "historical irony" that works to convert corrective movements to oppressive orthodoxies (Berman, 2000b, p. 138; Doherty, 2004), the movement nature of the gnostic moment portends an interesting interaction of NSM and NRM dynamics, as the routinization of charisma and communitas proceeds apace.

The Burning Man Network, an emerging linkage of quasi-franchised regional affiliates, organized (despite the fears of corporate cultural imperialism of some participants) not only to keep the event from being "commodified" as a consequence of its "national cachet," but also to "co-opt" the forces of "consumerism" itself, is a "movement" designed to coordinate the effect the Burning Man "ethos" is projected to have upon "mainstream American life." Intended to be loosely coupled, with benign oversight and assistance from the Burning Man Project (which will provide affiliates with such outreach and development services as "Burning Man Film Festival in a Box"), the Burning Man Network appears to be the next phase of the organization's effort to revitalize the "world." This phase also includes the professionalization of formerly voluntary positions (Harvey, 2004). Regional affiliates must affirm and disseminate the principles of radical inclusion, gifting, decommodification, radical self-reliance, radical self-expression, communal effort, civic responsibility, leaving no trace, participation, and immediacy – the dogmas that ritual underwrites – as a condition of incorporation (http://www.regionals.burningman.com/networkprinciples.html). The Burning Man Network is likely to produce memetic duplication and factional fission, with the faithful replicating the ethos. The disaffected, already a presence at the annual burn, (in the form of such groups as the Pirates of the Gonorrhean – again, Disney being the ineluctable nexus of subversive semiosis – who perpetuate politico-aesthetic vandalism at the central shrine, posting, for instance, stickers that proclaim "Free the Man"), who feel the event has grown too "large," too "organized," or too "touristy" will form less impious splinter groups charged with rekindling the "authentic" "original" flame.

COMEDY OF THE COMMONS

While a theory of comedy has been usefully applied to the understanding of advertising (Stern, 1995), much more of consumer behavior falls under its purview. In his magisterial survey of the genre, Segal (2001) dissects the dynamics of comedy in a way that illuminates the goings on in Black Rock City. Beginning with etymology, he traces the essence of *komos* to a cluster of meanings centering around a "wild, wine-soaked, no-holds barred revel" or, more preciously, a "revel without a cause," that typically occurred at night. He links *komos* to the dreamworks and the carnivalesque, and judges it to be a superego solvent; it is a state of mind, not merely a performance (2001, pp. 4, 7). He mines such spurious relatives as *kome*, to make a suggestive bridge to the roisterers banned from the ancient city, who pursued their revels in the country, which provided them greater freedom (2001, p. 3). Most helpfully, he detects an "erotic sense of letting go" to underlie the root, and pronounces the essence of *komos* to be its very "irresistibility" (2001, pp. 2, 7). He speculates that the common Indo–European root of words such as *komos* and *kome* connotes communal activity, a sense of "home" as a focus of the "community spirit" (2001, p. 8). Thus, the Black Rock benediction, "Welcome Home," proves an especially apt incantation for the liminoid license to ensue. It is the "happy end" that is the "essential joy" of comedy (2001, p. 10).

Segal proclaims the primal appeal of comedy to be the "unconscious desire to break society's rules" (2001, p. 8), to indulge fantasy in the flesh, to experience a mental orgy. He locates the genre's origin in a "mimetic, cosmogonic ceremony" offering spectators and participants a "fresh, new beginning" (2001, p. 150). This ritual is a stimulative re-enactment of the birth of the world from Chaos and Eros, originally involving orgiastic sex but gradually institutionalized in the form of a festive gamos, or wedding; comic transvestism, involving loss of social and sexual identity, abetted this ritual (2001, pp. 14–16). The genre evolved from the "phallic procession" that celebrated the "metasexual embodiment" of continuity and fertility. Even the licentious verbal abuse encouraged in such ritual produces "invigoration by invective" (2001, p. 21). Each of these elements – world renunciation and world renewing, orgiastic sex and weddings, the fungibility of social and gender status, the fescinine humor of the sacred clowns, and the constant interplay between fantasy and embodiment – is celebrated at Burning Man.

One critic's dismissal of the "Disneyfication" of religion is another's postmodern vindication of the efficacy of syncretism in preserving the relevance of "essential truths" (Eade, 2000, p. xxiii). Indeed, the subversive co-optation or reappropriation of Disneyfication – the contratheming and rememing of Holt's (2002) vampiric capitalism – is part of the culture jamming agenda of such revitalization movements as the Burning Man Project. Think of it as a "Take Back the Night" operation waged on a cultural scale. The sacred center resides in the movement to the limits of the need for intermediaries (Eade & Sallnow, 2000, p. 7), whether from clergy or clerisy, in a way that renders everyman (and woman) his (and her) own (sacred) clown. The coordinates of the center can be described as person, place, and text (Eade & Sallnow, 2000, p. 9), that is burners, installation (mega or micro), and performance (in cyberspace or IRL).

In his chronology, Beckett's *Waiting for Godot* marks the death of comedy for Segal, and Kubrick's *Dr. Strangelove* witnesses its transmogrification, as nuclear annihilation becomes the subject for laughter (2001, pp. 450, 454). This recalls Benjamin's (1968) quip about people being able to experience their own destruction as aesthetic pleasure of the first order. The Burning Man festival suggests that comedy may be revived and rehabilitated toward its original end. In an era when the power of ritual is co-opted and appropriated by the commercial, where the liminoid is siphoned away to become the liminate (Sherry, 2004) as corporate spectacle provides more individuals with their principal source of transcendence, and as art struggles to touch the masses, the promise of revitalization held out by countercultural activists is tantalizingly cogent. Festivals that are able to harness the comedy of the commons, uniting individuals in a lived experience of community devoted to the revisioning of the social order, may be able to restore that primal license that may rehumanize the "world."

NOMADIC ESSENCE OF THE BURN

While the surface structure of Burning Man is well described by a theory of comedy, its deep structure requires a more comprehensive interpretation of the type supported by Berman's (2000a) culturally grounded, panoramic, and provocative theory of nomadic spirituality. At the cost of doing great violence to his eloquent argument, Berman's insights can be reduced to set of observations. In evolutionary perspective, the sedentism giving rise to agricultural civilization, and the corresponding alienation of humans from the natural environment, led to the development of three different types of consciousness to deal with the rift. "Paradox," the nomadic mode of consciousness, is a diffuse or peripheral awareness, an "animal alertness" absent a "quest for meaning" that accepts the world as it is. The sacred and the secular are coterminous. The "sacred authority complex" (SAC), the mode of consciousness of sedentism, projects sacrality out of the world (upward to the gods), tapping spirituality through "ascent" or "oceanic" experience via trance ecstasy, and creates a "psychological cocoon" that assure humans that reality is of a very particular fabric. Finally, "dullardism," the mode of consciousness of industrial society, while maintaining trace activity of ecstatic practice (among the heretical marginal fringe), encourages humans to go unconscious by adopting drugs, television, sport, organized religion, and other compulsive behaviors (consumption being an obvious candidate), and to believe that the sacred lies elsewhere (Berman, 2000a, pp. 3–6). This is the diminished perceptual capacity people have sacrificed to other mental capabilities (Lévi-Strauss, 1979). We imagine Burning Man to represent a flight from dullardism, through a re-engagement with SAC, to a reconnection with paradoxical consciousness. While paradox may be a burner ideal intermittently or cumulatively achieved, it is at the heart of the burn(s).

Imagine the sacred, or, more specifically, the pilgrimage, as the site of a religious "void," an "arena" for complementary or competing interpretations of spirituality where meaning is contested earnestly or playfully (Eade, 2000, p. xiii), and the wisdom of preserving the polysemy of the Man is confirmed. This theater of contending discourses (Eade & Sallnow, 2000, p. 5) comprises both the event and the moment. The "rituals without dogma" positioning (Kozinets, 2002) is disingenuous to the extent that it masks the Burning Man ideology (or dogma): radical self-expression in the service of temporary community, to the purpose of self-transformation, in the absence of marketplace behavior, in the hope of cultural (r)evolution. There can be no ritual without some mythic charter. That ideology, phrased most succinctly as a series of Thou Shalt Nots – no spectating, no vending, no trace – enfranchises innovation. Minimalist prohibition invites a thousand snowflakes to melt.

As pilgrims desert the structural realm of dullardism for the antistructural realms of SAC and paradox, in keeping with Turner's (1974) formulation of the liminoid, they become existential nomads as well, eager to assimilate radically new ideas and experiences. Principally familiar with the fixed perceptions of "certainty" created by sedentism, their journey predisposes them to experiment with the ecstatic modes of SAC that industrial society has suppressed, and to seek the experience of transcendence. Nomadism encourages paradoxical perception, a consciousness that is simultaneously focused and unfocused, such that an intensely personal unique moment feels as if it is also profoundly universally shared in connection with others. This is the experience of immanence produced by nomadism, the sense that movement across landscapes renders religious ritual "superfluous"

(Berman, 2000a, pp. 6, 16, 166). The communitas of the festival, conditioned by the sojourn in the desert and catalyzed by the burn(s), is the immanence the pilgrims feel.

If movement is the "physiological substrate" of paradox, and if movement encourages the grasp of life without mythic or ritual filters (Berman, 2000a, p. 81), then the "rituals without dogma" ideology of the festival (Kozinets, 2002) can be understood as a kind of withering away of the SAC, and the techniques of the ascent experience a collective transitional object, all in the service of recovering, eventually, paradoxical consciousness. If spectacular unmediated aesthetic experience is the manifest impulse to the pilgrimage, the latent satisfactions of the soul at Black Rock City appear to reside in the recovery of sacred/secular unity, and the realization that the "aliveness of the world is all that needs to be worshipped" (Berman, 2000a, p. 188). To the extent that the burner regards the festival not as a "mental theme park," but as a rejection of the "suffocating ideological certainty" and emotionally crippling consequences of sedentism (Berman, 2000a, pp. 151, 157), even temporarily, the desert may afford him the most congenial staging ground for the experience of immanence.

Contemporary nomadism may represent the return of the repressed, the recovery of our mobile genetic heritage, and the recognition that a need for unpredictability and surprise supercedes our need for certainty. It marks as well the recovery of spiritual intelligence (Berman, 2000a, pp. 16, 157, 181, 188; Sherry, 1990). The definition of nomadism offered by Deleuze and Guattari (1987), the "attempt to reterritorialize on deterritorialization," is an accurate description of Black Rock City. To the extent that nomads are able to preserve their experience of paradox upon their return to industrial society, and nurture it until their return migration (or until the organizers acquire enough private land to institutionalize the festival permanently, which will prompt ever more interesting evolution), their pilgrimage promises to remake the world over yet again. In their flight from the dominant tradition, through the countertraditions of primacy of spirit or process and primacy of matter as the vehicle of spirit, burners use art in the service of transcendence. By the end of the week, or by the end of years of weeks, lived somatically in the immediate presence of fellows in a natural environment that demands constant contemplation, burners achieve a mundane apotheosis in a third countertradition, finding truth will emerge only when it is not pursued (Berman, 2000a, pp. 208–209).

Insofar as the postmodern pilgrimage may be construed as a journey of the "suffering soul" rather than the traditional "suffering body" (Eade, 2000, p. xvii), the technological and luxurious ingenuity of the nomads' desert structures, and the sophistication of the cyber-oases they habitually traverse in the off season, seem all the more poignant. While it can be an enormously expensive undertaking to flee to the Black Rock Desert, the event is more than simply an opportunity for elite consumers to use their money to achieve the illusion that money is unnecessary or incidental to life. Money is used pragmatically, as a means to an end. In some fundamental sense, it takes money to un-make money. If the potlatch is to be efficacious, the sacrifice should be considerable. Having money to burn is essential.

Intensive secular commerce frequently attends the sacred commerce of pilgrimage (Eade & Sallnow, 2000, p. 25). Merchant's Row is a common fixture of Neopagan gatherings (Pike, 2001a, p. 75), and vendors are present in such other utopian convocations as the mountain man rendezvous (Belk & Costa, 1998). Indeed, the stalls have traditionally proven felicitous points of entry for ethnographers. Secular commerce (with those few noted exceptions) is banned by fiat from Black Rock City, the little we detected driven underground, and often decried and reported to the Rangers, by affronted observers. Impersonal modes of exchange may be anathema to the world-building agenda of emergent spiritual movements, whereas gift giving appears to abet it.

Recent work in consumer research supports Berman's belief (2000a, p. 18) that contemporary culture is bound for the next incarnation of SAC, and a large uptick in the transcendent outlook. The corporate appropriation of the liminoid and its transmutation to the liminate (Sherry, 2004), encouraging individuals to construe themselves primarily as consumers and to seek transcendence in goods and services is a hallmark of the postmodern era. Like Berman, we believe that paradox should remain a gadfly, not become a tyrannous paradigm itself, to remind people of the abounding alternatives of being. He notes that "oddball spiritual nomads keep rediscovering paradoxical heritage on a mental level" (Berman, 2000a, p. 12). The pilgrims of Black Rock City have converted this mindscape to landscape once again. They have created a postmodern hybrid of the potlatch and the cargo cult. By amassing goods in the wilderness, and by destroying or redistributing them, the pilgrims coax the gods back into lived experience.

In the course of writing our accounts of the festival, the years have witnessed the phenomenal box office profitability of two films of unlikely popular appeal. One (*The Passion of the Christ*) celebrated deicide, the other (*Fahrenheit 9/11*) the conflict between contemporary crusaders and jihadis. This hyperpoliticization of the spiritual has stirred considerable cultural commentary, even though it has been sparked by that quintessential genre of spectacle, the cinema. Concurrently, the Temple (the Temple of the Stars) has evolved to a mega structure covering a quarter-mile surface of the playa. Such synchronicity conspires to remind critics that the spectacular exists in a relation of complementarity to the sacred, and contrariety to the profane (Sherry, 2004), and that our culture can travel from pathos to bathos in less than 60 seconds. We hope our exploration of nomadic spirituality keeps the flame that is the polylogue of utopian discourse in consumer research turned all the way up.

REFERENCES

Belk, R. (2004). Possessions, self, and the sacred. In: A. Griffin & C. Otnes (Eds), *The sixteenth Paul D. Converse symposium*. Chicago: American Marketing Association.

Belk, R., & Costa, J. (1998). The mountain man myth: A contemporary consumer fantasy. *Journal of Consumer Research*, *25*(3), 218–240.

Belk, R., Wallendorf, M., & Sherry, J. F., Jr. (1989). The sacred and profane in consumer behavior: Theory on the Odyssey. *Journal of Consumer Research*, *16*(1), 1–38.

Benjamin, W. (1968). *Illuminations*. New York: Schocken.

Berman, M. (2000a). *Wandering god: A study in nomadic spirituality*. Albany, New York: SUNY Press.

Berman, M. (2000b). *The twilight of American culture*. New York: Norton.

Bey, H. (1994). *Immediatism*. Edinburgh, Scotland: AK Press.

Brill, L., & Bee, L. (2003). The art of burning man. *Leonardo*, *36*(5), 339–370.

Brown, S. (2001). *Marketing: The ratio revolution*. Thousand Oaks, CA: Sage.

Brown, S., Kozinets, R., & Sherry, J. F., Jr. (2003). Teaching old brands new tricks: Retro branding and the revival of brand meaning. *Journal of Marketing*, *67*(3), 19–33.

Chatwin, B. (1987). *The sunglasses*. New York: Penguin.

Coleman, S., & Eade, J. (2004). Introduction: Reframing pilgrimage. In: S. Coleman & J. Eade (Eds), *Reframing pilgrimage: Cultures in motion* (pp. 1–25). New York: Routledge.

Csordas, T. J. (1997). *The sacred self: A cultural phenomenology of charismatic healing*. Berkeley and Los Angeles: University of California Press.

Davis, E. (1998). *Techgnosis: Myth, magic and mysticism in the age of information*. New York: Random House.

Deleuze, G., & Guattari, F. (1987). *A thousand plateaus: Capitalism and schizophrenia*. Minneapolis: University of Minnesota Press.

Doherty, B. (2004). *This is burning man*. New York: Little, Brown and Co.

Dubisch, J. (2004). Heartland of America: Memory, motion and the reconstruction of history on a motorcycle pilgrimage. In: S. Coleman & J. Eade (Eds), *Renaming pilgrimage: Cultures in motion* (pp. 109–132). New York: Routledge.

Eade, J. (2000). Introduction to the Illinois paperback. In: J. Eade & M. Sallnow (Eds), *Contesting the sacred: The anthropology of Christian pilgrimage* (pp. iv–xxx). Urbana, IL: University of Illinois Press.

Eade, J., & Sallnow, M. (2000). Introduction. In: J. Eade & M. Sallnow (Eds), *Contesting the sacred: The anthropology of Christian pilgrimage* (pp. 1–29). Urbana, IL: University of Illinois Press.

Eliade, M. (1954). *The myth of the eternal return*. Princeton, NJ: Princeton University Press.

Fernandez, J. (1982). *Bwiti: An ethnography of the religious imagination in Africa*. Princeton, NJ: Princeton University Press.

Gilmore, L., & van Proyen, M. (Eds) (2005). *AfterBurn: Reflections on burning man*. Albuquerque, NM: University of New Mexico Press.

Graebner, D. (2004). *Fragments of an anarchist anthropology*. Chicago: Prickly Paradigm Press.

Hanegraaff, W. (1998). *New age religion and western culture: Esotericism in the mirror of secular thought*. Albany, New York: SUNY Press.

Harvey, L. (2004). Cover Letter. Retrieved from http://www.regionals.burningman.com/network_coverletters.html

Holt, D. (2002). Why do brands cause trouble? A dialectical theory of consumer culture and branding. *Journal of Consumer Research*, *29*(1), 70–90.

Hyde, L. (1998). *Trickster makes the world*. New York: Farrar, Straus and Giroux.

James, W. (1982). *The varieties of religious experience: A study in human nature*. New York: Penguin.

Kohut, H. (2000). *The analysis of the self*. Guilford, CT: International Universities Press.

Kozinets, R. V. (2002). Can consumers escape the market? Emancipatory illuminations from burning man. *Journal of Consumer Research*, *28*(1), 67–88.

Kozinets, R. V. (2003). The moment of infinite fire. In: S. Brown & J. F. Sherry Jr. (Eds), *Time, space and the market: Retroscapes rising* (pp. 199–216). NY: M. E. Sharpe.

Kozinets, R. V., & Sherry, J. F., Jr. (2003). Dancing on common ground: Exploring the sacred at burning man. In: G. St. John (Ed.), *Rave and religion* (pp. 287–303). New York: Routledge.

Kozinets, R. V., & Sherry, J. F., Jr. (2005). Welcome to the black rock café. In: L. Gilmore & M. van Proyen (Eds), *AfterBurn: Reflections on burning man*. Albuquerque, NM: University of New Mexico Press.

Kreuter, H. (2002). *Drama in the desert*. San Francisco: Raised Barn Press.

Lévi-Strauss, C. (1979). *Myth and meaning: Cracking the code of culture*. New York: Schocken Books.

Naipaul, V. S. (1990). *India: A million mutinies now*. New York: William Heinemann.

Pike, S. (2001a). Desert goddess and apocalyptic art: Making sacred space at the burning man festival. In: E. Mazur & K. McCarthy (Eds), *God in the details: American religion in popular culture* (pp. 155–176). New York: Routledge.

Pike, S. (2001b). *Earthly bodies, magical selves: Contemporary pagans and the search for community*. Berkeley, CA: University of California Press.

Pike, S. (2004). *New age and neopagan religions in America*. New York: Columbia University Press.

Pinchbeck, D. (2002). *Breaking open the head: A psychedelic journey into the heart of contemporary shamanism*. New York: Broadway Books.

Pinchbeck, D. (2003). Heat of the moment: The art and culture of burning man. *Art Forum 42*(November), 174–179.

Roof, W. (1999). *Spiritual marketplace: Baby boomers and the remaking of American religion*. Princeton, NJ: Princeton University Press.

Schramm, K. (2004). Coming home to the motherland. In: S. Coleman & J. Eade (Eds), *Reframing pilgrimage: Cultures in motion* (pp. 133–149). New York: Routledge.

Segal, E. (2001). *The death of comedy*. Cambridge, MA: Harvard University Press.

Sherry, J. F., Jr. (1990). A sociocultural analysis of a midwestern American flea market. *Journal of Consumer Research*, *17*(l), 13–30.

Sherry, J. F., Jr. (2003). Bespectacled and bespoken: The view from Throne Zone and five o'clock and head. In: S. Brown & J. F. Sherry Jr. (Eds), *Time, space and the market: Retroscapes rising* (pp. 19–34). New York: M. E. Sharpe.

Sherry, J. F., Jr. (2004). We might never be post-sacred: A tribute to Russell Belk on the occasion of his acceptance of the converse award. In: A. Griffen & C. Otnes (Eds), *The sixteenth Paul D. Converse symposium*. Chicago: American Marketing Association.

Sherry, J. F., Jr., & Kozinets, R. V. (2003). Sacred iconography in secular space: Altars, alters and alterity at the burning man project. In: C. Otnes & T. Lowrey (Eds), *Contemporary consumption rituals: A research anthropology* (pp. 291–311). NJ: Lawrence Erlbaum.

Stern, B. (1995). Consumer myths: Frye's taxonomy and the structural analysis of consumption text. *Journal of Consumer Research*, *22*(2), 165–185.

Taylor, C. (2001). *Varieties of religion today*. Cambridge, MA: Harvard University Press.

Traub, B., Plunkett, J., Brown, S., & Wieners, B. (Eds) (1997). *Burning man*. San Francisco: Hardwired.

Turner, V. (1974). *Dramas, fields and metaphors*. Ithaca: Cornell University Press.

Turner, V., & Turner, E. (1978). *Image and pilgrimage in Christian culture*. New York: Columbia University Press.

Urry, J. (2002). *The tourist gaze*. Thousand Oaks, CA: Sage.

Wallis, R. (2003). *Shamans/neoshamans: Ecstasy, alternative archaeologies and contemporary pagans*. New York: Routledge.

York, M. (1995). *The emerging network*. Lanham, MD: Rauman and Littlefield.

GLOBALITY

CONSUMING THE DEAD: WAITING FOR BLESSINGS IN A JAVANESE CEMETERY

Kevin Browne

Blessing (*Pangestu*)

Every night for three months
she has come to this
  old cemetery
seeking healing for her lungs

from the spirit
of a revered leader
dead now for
four hundred years.

She rolls out her mat,
talks with other
blessing-seekers,
eats and sleeps.

Consumer Culture Theory
Research in Consumer Behavior, Volume 11, 151–163

ISSN: 0885-2111/doi:10.1016/S0885-2111(06)11007-8

Thursday nights are most
  propitious, she says.
Undeterred by apparent lack of
results, she will return.

The point is
  to be here,
just in case
the blessing comes.

I wrote this poem after participating in a Thursday night vigil at the gravesite of Senopati, the founder of the old Central Javanese kingdom of Mataram, near the present-day city of Yogyakarta, Indonesia. The dozens of supplicants who came to this cemetery on this night were asking blessings from the spirit of Senopati, who died in 1601. They sought a range of favors, including the healing of illness, family harmony, job promotions, and favorable grades for their children. This kind of event is repeated every Thursday night, and to a lesser extent other nights, at this and many other gravesites of famous Javanese persons throughout the island. These sites are included among the many *keramat*, or sacred places, that include certain springs, trees, and other loci of power in the Javanese socio-spiritual landscape. I visited several cemeteries, including the royal tombs of Sultan Agung (the grandson of Senopati) and others, at Imogiri, south of Yogyakarta. I use this phenomenon of gravesite vigils as a springboard for a discussion of alternative ways of sensing and being in the world, of the interanimating power of people and place, and for how these concepts extend Consumer Culture Theory in useful directions.

When I first visited the cemetery in which Senopati is buried, an ancient monumentalized topography of mausoleums amidst the white-walled homes of Kota Gede on the southern fringe of Yogyakarta, I was tempted to agree with Pemberton's (1994) conclusion that these gravesite visits across Java represent a reproduction of state power, a conditioned social quiescence. Even after 10 months of fieldwork at the time, a decade or so after Pemberton's, it was seductive to conclude, as Pemberton did, that "nothing" was happening. Pemberton saw a pervasive sense of static, un-becomingness in these vigil rituals. He argued that blessing-seekers, recognizing that general and ambiguous requests are more likely than highly specific ones to be considered successful, are reduced to asking for generic blessings. Pemberton states that the only requirement for these blessing-seekers is to stay awake during the vigil, in order to be conscious if and when the blessing is dispensed. They enact, in effect, a "landscape of waiting" (Pemberton, 1994, p. 288).

Conducting research during the heart of Suharto's authoritarian New Order rule in Indonesia (1967–1998), Pemberton argued that these visits ultimately served the regime's paramount goals of social control. "Traditional Javanese culture" had become a "metaspook," Pemberton claims, displacing issues of class and power. In this view the grave visits, and the blessing seeking in general, reinforce an idealized hierarchical system, a fetishized attempt to recover the idea of "Java."

Awaiting uncertain blessings among everyday Javanese seeking financial and other favors can give the impression of the kind of lack of climax, of social quiescence, that fulfilled extant political goals. I think that Pemberton's analysis, however, misses a crucial point. There is little sense of agency or the power of place in his post-structural exegesis. In my view these events generate a poetics of place, one that speaks to local concerns with continuity with the past, with health and wealth, and one that extends laterally to connect with regional and global discourses of identity and healing. My concern is with how this consumption of the famous and semi-famous dead reflects a contested socio-moral Javanese landscape infused with longing, sociality, and practices of power. Gravesite vigils enact this engagement among everyday concerns with health, desires for financial advancement, and family harmony with the metonym of "traditional Javanese culture." I offer this alternative to Pemberton's analysis, that the emplacement of persons at these cemetery events generates a poetics of diverse meanings (Basso, 1996) that destabilizes official rhetoric, providing a countermeasure to the reproduction of hierarchy.

DEATH, POWER AND IDENTITY

Writing of Asante death rituals, Bonsu and Belk (2003) argue that contrary to prevailing theory, identity (re)construction projects do not necessarily end at death. They argue that conspicuous consumption at Asante funerals provide a means for the active renegotiation of identity for both the bereaved and the deceased, offering a continuity of relationship.

For the Javanese, where those – such as Senopati – have often been dead for centuries, the blessing vigils go even further in extending identity construction projects. Through these rituals of consuming the power of the dead, ties are extended laterally into broad social identity projects as Javanese, and in time to a diverse range of unrelated and powerful ancestors.

To understand the context of these vigils, we must apprehend that there is a different conception and practices of power at play here. Anderson (1972) writes that in Java power is viewed as concrete and exists independent of possible users. It is also seen as homogenous, with the amount of power in the universe remaining constant. As a result, power can be concentrated in individuals and places, and exists without inherent moral implications. Moreover, the overt pursuit of wealth often meets with social disapproval and reduces one's status. The belief is that money itself should not be the object of pursuit, but that wealth frequently flows to the holder of power.

This conception of power infuses Javanese practices of politics, healing, and everyday life. Many healers I interviewed also used methods based on the idea that power is concentrated and can be detected and dispensed through vibrational energy. And there is a strong belief shared by many people that a loss of energy leads to various illnesses.

The idea that power is finite, is accumulated through the success of an individual, and does not automatically disperse after death, can explain why people might sit and wait for some of this power to be released. It also explains why the blessing energy is assumed to have a limited radius, and so proximity to the place of burial is critical. In the case of Senopati, his legitimation myth and source of power derives from his legendary sexual tryst with Ratu Kidul, the spirit queen of the southern ocean, and his subsequent political success in establishing a dynasty. The power and protection Senopati obtained from this liaison is a founding myth of "traditional" Javanist culture, and was usefully deployed by both the Javanese aristocracy over several centuries, as well as by the New Order regime, both of which benefited greatly by the codification of a hierarchical social system.

Ratu Kidul is a powerful spirit in Java. Stories about her abound throughout the southern coastal regions of the island. Many of these stories deal with people who have reportedly been possessed by her, a condition characterized by confusion, lethargy, and other symptoms similar to some forms of mental illness. Many people I talked with said they knew someone who had been possessed. People seeking spiritual power often meditate on the southern beach in order to gain strength. And Ratu Kidul is propitiated at various times, including, as I witnessed, on the eve of Ramadan. The belief that Senopati embodied the strength and protection of Ratu Kidul necessarily means he concentrated significant power.

Gravesite vigils today, however, are often more about practical concerns such as health and economic advancement than about any idealized seeking of traditional Javanese notions of spiritual power. The social context informing these requests includes a pervasive discourse on the increase in stress in contemporary Indonesian life. This stress is evident in the pressures of family life and changing economic expectations, generational friction, and new media influences challenging social values. This apparent commodification of blessing requests, however, is more reflective of a complex and contested social distress than a complete embracing of capitalist consumption.

The blessing vigils also highlight the social fault lines between the growing presence of modernist Islam in Java, which subscribes to a Quranic interpretation of socio-moral life, and a more indigenous Javanese version of Islam, which embraces a more mystical orientation. It is this latter Javanist worldview which accounts for the belief in the power of the dead to confer blessings on the living. Among my modernist Muslim friends, such beliefs were strictly prohibited.

These practices, then, far from exemplifying a "waiting culture" (Urry, 1995, p. 23), articulate within a global circulation of modernist and postmodern discourses on morality, consumption and desire. During my research these influences included such articulations as the selling of jinn (helpful Islamic spirits) to aid in becoming wealthy, the wide circulation of global psychological concepts of individualism and desires through various media, and global flows of medical and healing discourses. The famous dead in Java have become a repository for the projection of desires for financial gain and personal healing, as well as a social construction of the contemporary contestation for Javanese social and moral values.

EMPLACEMENT

By emplacement I refer to the idea that place, embodying the infusion of agency and culture, is generative of force and meaning. Casey (1996) argues that place is more like an event in its dynamic and uncertain qualities. Place, as a generative event, evokes Soja's (1989) argument that landscapes are socially produced and infused with longing and desire.

This sensual, textured quality of place works against a strict post-structural analysis, in which social landscapes are primarily about relationships of power (Foucault, 1986). While quiet vigils at mausoleums seem to serve the state's insatiable appetite for monumentalism and control, places also engage an everyday resistance through consumption practices. A key concept of this practice is interanimation (Basso, 1996), in which a sense of place reciprocally imbues human participants and landscape features with cultural meanings. This conflation of person with geographic space generates a field of meaning and possibility (Merleau-Ponty, 1962). Thus while consumption of the dead at Javanese cemeteries on one level implicitly binds the supplicant to ideas of traditional Javanese culture, it also provides openings for alternative and disruptive practices. It is this interanimation that provides the generative backdrop for the kind of uncertainty, the sense that something (as opposed to nothing) can happen.

This sensing of place also extends laterally. The practice of blessing seeking occurs within regional and national contexts and conflicts, as well as the global circulation of economic, psychological, and spiritual discourses. The vigils express the contradictions of place in Central Java. As the seat of putative "traditional Javanese culture," the region also swirls with the national discourse on development, with myriad political conflicts, with religio-cultural flows from Malaysia, Saudi Arabia, Egypt, and elsewhere, and with the desires of capitalist consumption and "making it." Tsing (2005) refers to the interconnectedness of these types of intersecting, discordant processes as "friction." Waiting at the gravesite of a dynastic founder, dead for four hundred years, to see if one has the proper luck or timing to receive help with family discord, for example, is necessarily linked to these intersecting flows; fundamentally, it reflects the gathering powers of place (Casey, 1996).

SENSING THE WORLD

I have been speaking here about a way of perceiving (and a way of consuming) that interanimates person and place. Stoller (1989) urges ethnographers to open their senses to how others perceive the world. The Songhay of Niger, whom Stoller studies, for example, orient themselves significantly through taste, sound, and smell in addition to sight. Stoller describes spaces and encounters as textured, a dimension that traditional consumer research often neglects.

The Javanese describe their way of perceiving the world as *rasa*. While we lack a sufficient gloss of rasa in English, it generally refers to a way of sensing the world that includes taste, sight, voice, meaning, desire, mystery, and a kind of inner experience of events. Stange (1984) says that rasa, in addition to having a physical aspect, includes a spiritual, mystical knowing that is integral to Javanese sensibility. One of my consultants, Pak Delik, a respected healer and teacher, described rasa like this:

K: Can you explain the importance of rasa in knowing the world?

D: Rasa is about life in the world, it is felt individually. For me, if my rasa is only good, then I don't ever feel troubled. I can eat anything and I like it, I don't have to say 'don't use eggs, don't use fish', whatever there is we eat. But if I want things that aren't possible, in my rasa emerges the beginning of sickness. Now mostly this is called stress.

For Pak Delik rasa is a perceptual orientation connected to the inner essence of things. The rasa of a situation is based both upon the outer form as well as the inner feeling of the texture of events. This felt sense is often the basis for how the Javanese subjectively interpret a situation. As Pak Delik suggests, many Javanese seek to cultivate an inner sense of calm, a harmonious rasa. At the gravesite vigils, what Pemberton interpreted as social quiescence and "nothing" happening, can also be seen as the enactment of a pervasive Javanese sense of engagement with the world, a quiet rasa of perception.

BLESSING VIGILS

I first went to the gravesite of Senopati on a Monday morning. There were only a few caretakers and self-appointed guides lingering around. Unlike the tomb of Sultan Agung at Imogiri, which is a popular site for Javanese pilgrims as well as tourists and is well maintained and attended by Javanese caretakers, the cemetery of Senopati does not appear to have been significantly "upgraded," as Pemberton phrases it.

Looking at the guest book on display near the entrance, the most common reason given for making the visit is "*ziarah*" (devotional visit). This idealized response reflects intense social pressure toward lofty aspirations, and there is little contradiction felt among most supplicants by combining *ziarah* with asking for real world help. The rasa of the experience for me, during that day with almost no one there, is one of quiet respect, endurance, and longevity.

I returned soon after on a Thursday night around 7 pm. The Muslim holy day (Friday) actually begins on Thursday night in Indonesia, and so this is the most popular time to make the gravesite visit. Over the next several hours many people came and went. Many were older people with various health problems, others were middle-aged people asking for promotions, to resolve family problems, or for their children's success. A number of younger people, some in leather jackets, also showed up. Like at the tomb of Sultan Agung in Imogiri, there was an opportunity to make offerings and prayers. According to one of my consultants, Pak M., who is a healer in the city, it is the attitude of the supplicant that matters most:

PM: They (such as Sultan Agung and Senopati) have a power that carries down to the present day, and people can request blessings…

Q: Is there a certain way someone has to request these blessings?

PM: Only from God. The prayer is up to the person.

Q: Is there a special requirement such as a prayer or offering flowers?

PM: Generally most people there bring flowers.

Several people told me they came every night. The encounter that inspired my opening poem occurred that night as well. The woman, in her 50s, whom I will call Bu Tutik, described her situation like this:

K: How often do you come here?

T: I've been coming every night for three months.

K: Why do you come?

T: For my lungs. They are sick and I come hoping they will be healed.

K: Do you think it has helped?

T: Not yet. But I like to come. My husband has died. During the day I work at the *pasar* (market) in Yogya. At night I come here and ask for help and sleep. I think one day it will work. I plan to keep coming here until they are healed.

Another man, a civil servant whom I'll call Pak Susilo, described the reason for his visit like this:

S: I come often on Thursday nights. I stay only about two hours because I have to work the next day. Otherwise I would be too tired to work.

K: What kind of blessings have you asked for?

S: The first one I asked for was general well-being (*keslametan*).

K: Do you think that request has been granted?

S: Yes, that is pretty good. After that I asked for harmony in the home, especially getting support from my wife.

K: How about that one?

S: (chuckles) Not yet. And the third one was for help in paying for my children's schooling. (chuckles again). That one too, not yet.

We can see in these two excerpts the everyday concerns with health, family harmony, and economic success, articulating within a larger narrative of endurance, continuity and identity construction.

By 9 pm there were perhaps 35 people sitting in small groups and talking quietly. I sat with a small group telling stories and laughing at jokes. Many people brought food to share. Despite the compelling concerns that provoke these visits, the urgency was not overt, but was overlaid with congenial sociality. The rasa quality I had of this night was one of humility and anticipation, a waiting for an ineffable grace, not knowing if and when it will come, nor what it would feel like if it did. There is also a quality of vulnerability to these vigils, of longing and need. It is a mistake to infer from periods of silence and waiting that nothing is happening. Silence is an integral part of many Javanese performance traditions, and is a key element in the development of a harmonious rasa. As de Certeau (1984, p. 106) asserts, there are many "rich silences and wordless stories." The gathering qualities of these blessing events unfold the cultural meanings of places, of their production of Javanese identity.

I decided to get the perspective of another respected practitioner of Javanese healing toward this phenomenon. I discussed the vigils with Romo S., a recognized expert on Javanese culture. Romo confirmed that these *keramat* are indeed places of power, but the approach most people take to obtain blessings is fruitless. The basic mistake is that people just go and wait, not knowing when to be there. According to Romo, each *keramat* has a specific day and time when the blessing is available. For Senopati this is Jumat Pon, a particular Friday (Jumat) in the 35 day Javanese calendar, which combines the typical seven-day week with a five-day market week. Jumat Pon corresponds to the day of Senopati's death, and 9 pm is the time of his death. Being there at other days and times, says Romo, is a waste of time and effort.

Romo says that the blessing comes in the form of electrical energy. At the specific time, some of this electrical energy of the deceased person is discharged and can be absorbed into the body of the living person. The window then closes again until the next time.

POETICS OF PLACE IN JAVA

On much further reflection, I think Romo's dismissal of the blessing seeking at times other than the specific time of death as a waste misses the most important point. He, of course, was merely responding to my question, which reflected my limited understanding of the power of place. He responded to my question literally, whereas I should have been asking metaphorically. It is only much later I saw that it is the emplacement that occurs during these visits that generates meaning, rather than whether there is any verifiable blessing obtained.

Wagner (1991, p. 44) describes poetics as the process by which "cultural forms turn into meaning." As I reflect on my encounters with these people and place, where supposedly nothing happens, I sense the longing, the suffering of ill health, the desire to "make it", or to obtain an otherwise impossible education for one's child. Far from "nothing" happening, I would describe it as a passionate process. These vigils reflect the struggle of the self and community in everyday life. de Certeau (1984, p. 105), described these spatial practices as a "poetic geography," in which the indeterminancy of acts and movements give meaning. Poetics, Brady (1991) claims, is engaging with the process of becoming, in "contact with the spontaneous present." As Tsing (2005, p. 28) puts it, poetics and sensory absorption can sweep away the "common sense" of despair. This poetics of desire, though necessarily rife with slippages and uncertainties, resists encapsulation by totalizing discourses such as tradition and control, as it also resists reduction to a nostalgic fetishization of lost glory or of economic gain.

This poetic context is informed by a tradition of poetic prophecy in Java. The most famous of these poems, the Kalatidha, is a lament about the loss of 19th century court privilege and prophesized a coming age of madness (*jaman edan*). Its author, the court poet Ronggawarsito, wrote reflexively, with an understanding of how words can influence the future (Florida, 1995). This prophetic writing, though little read by average citizens, nevertheless animates Javanese cultural knowledge, the self-conscious awareness of the power of words in the world.

I often saw the metaphor of *jaman edan* being invoked by contemporary commentators to reference the social changes unfolding in the country, in particular the perception of hedonistic consumption and abandonment of traditional morals. Javanese engagement with the jaman edan metaphor, however, and with the dead at *keramat* sites, reflects a much greater degree of indeterminancy than these cautionary laments would suggest. Among the Javanese who gather in such places for blessing-seeking events, many are aware, through their emplacement, that participation, like reading, can move simultaneously both forward and backward in time. This is not the kind of collapsing of space and time that results in fragmented and disillusioned selves, but is more a means of generating meaning and possibility. It suggests a fluidity of boundaries and the interanimation of place and person. As Casey (1996, p. 35) puts it, there is always an "insinuation of wild Being" into the body in place; and the results are sometimes unpredictable.

CONTRIBUTIONS TO CONSUMER CULTURE THEORY

I want to conclude by examining how these practices of consuming the dead in Java might extend Consumer Culture Theory in some useful directions.

Holt (1995), for example, has proposed a typology grid of consumer behavior that includes four categories – consuming as experience, consuming as integration, consuming as classification, and consuming as play. Consuming as experience, as Holt explains it, refers to the subjective and emotional reactions to objects of consumption. I cite this particular contribution as a springboard to ask some questions: What do we mean by experience, or by "emotional reactions?" How do we comprehend how others orient themselves to the world? How do they apprehend and engage with it and each other? And how does place interanimate with persons to generate unique and salient meanings?

Holt developed his typology based on watching numerous American baseball games. He sought an etic understanding in order to generate a cognitive classification schema. Any typology is necessarily reliant on the analytic language that informs it; in other words it contains embedded assumptions about experience and is limited by the linguistic and psychological worldview of the culture. Typologies are not well suited to capturing the rich, messy, and contested practices of everyday life. We cannot assume that such a typology would hold merit in a different cultural context, either within or outside the U.S. I suggest that adopting an emic approach opens greater possibilities of understanding consumption experiences and insight into the emotional and social experiences that generate meanings in everyday life.

The Javanese construction of experience (e.g., Browne, 1999, 2001), for instance, is much different from the one which might inform such a grid. Fernandez (1986) argues that experience consists of words and images (and I would add other senses and textures) and rituals are based on mixed, sometimes discordant metaphors, what he calls the play of tropes. Javanese blessing vigils enact their own play of tropes. The Javanese way of perceiving the world, for example, suggests we need a broader contextualization of sense in consumer research. Similarly, a different conception of power and its transmission may challenge researchers who work among diverse consumers in the U.S. and internationally to rethink their assumptions about how consumers relate to material culture. Javanese practices of emplacement also challenge the modernist (both in the sense of a particular Indonesian modernist movement, as well as a western assumptive category) conception of space and time. If events can generate meaning both forward and backward in time, both inward toward secret desires and outward toward public hierarchies, the horizons of consumer theory may be dimensionally extended.

Ortner (1991, p. 5) has argued that contemporary consumer culture has resulted in a widespread fragmentation of selves and disruption of narrativity. As Strauss (1997) has demonstrated, however, narratives are more often partly integrated than wholly fragmented. And it is emotionally salient experiences that mediate between the self and social discourses, allowing for the preservation and articulation of partly integrated self-narratives. Within the play of tropes that animate the person–place blessing vigils, there are emotionally salient experiences, such as hope, desire, and belonging, that allow participants to construct partly integrated narratives that join with others in the multi-vocal Javanese identity landscape. Rather than Pemberton's empty holding tank for state power, these participants actively engage a way of sensing the world (rasa) and making meaning. As de Certeau (1984, p. 108) puts it, "there is no place not haunted by many different spirits hidden there in silence, spirits one can invoke or not."

Emplacement, whether in a Javanese cemetery, an English "Irish" pub, or a shopping mall, works to fashion selves, whether in a moment of urgency (Wikan, 1995), such as illness, or through play or aesthetic pursuit. As Casey (1996, p. 17) puts it, we are "always already in place." Consumer Culture Theory can delve deeper into these worlds of emplacement through embracing a poetics stance. If we are moved to do so, how do we as researchers engage a poetics, or even receive inspiration from the wisdom of places (Basso, 1996)? Sherry and Schouten (2002) have argued that poetry, as a method of consumer research, helps to generate intersubjectivity in the writing process. To this I would add that poetics in consumer research offers an empathic immediacy of experience, an opportunity to reciprocate the vulnerability we ask of others, and a way of knowing that may be more like the way that many consumers actually generate meaning in their lives.

ACKNOWLEDGMENTS

The author wishes to thank the Indonesian Institute of Sciences (LIPI) for granting permission for this research, and the Center for Southeast Asian Studies at the University of Wisconsin-Madison for providing partial funding.

REFERENCES

Anderson, B. (1972). The idea of power in Javanese culture. In: C. Holt (Ed.), *Culture and politics in Indonesia*. Ithaca. NY: Cornell University Press.

Basso, K. H. (1996). Wisdom sits in places: Notes on a Western Apache landscape. In: S. Feld & K. H. Basso (Eds), *Senses of place* (pp. 53–90). Santa Fe, NM: SAR Press.

Bonsu, S. K., & Belk, R. W. (2003). Do not go cheaply into that good night: Death ritual consumption in Asante Ghana. *Journal of Consumer Research*, *30*(June), 41–55.

Brady, I. (1991). Harmony and argument: Bringing forth the artful science. In: I. Brady (Ed.), *Anthropological poetics*. Savage, MD: Rowman and Littlefield.
Browne, K. O. (1999). *Landscapes of desire and violence: Storied selves and mental affliction in Central Java, Indonesia*. Unpublished dissertation. University of Wisconsin, Madison, WI 53706.
Browne, K. O. (2001). (Ng)amuk revisited: Emotional expression and mental illness in Central Java, Indonesia. *Transcultural Psychiatry*, *38*(2), 147–165.
Casey, E. S. (1996). How to get from space to place in a fairly short stretch of time. In: S. Feld & K. H. Basso (Eds), *Senses of place* (pp. 13–52). Santa Fe, NM: SAR Press.
de Certeau, M. (1984). *The practice of everyday life*. Berkeley: University of California Press.
Fernandez, J. W. (1986). The Argument of images and the experience of returning to the whole. In: V. W. Turner & E. M. Bruner (Eds), *The anthropology of experience* (pp. 159–187). Urbana: University of Illinois Press.
Florida, N. K. (1995). *Writing the past, inscribing the future: History as prophecy in colonial Java*. Durham: Duke University Press.
Foucault, M. (1986). Of other spaces. *Diacritics*, *16*(1), 22–27.
Holt, D. (1995). How consumers consume: A typology of consumption practices. *Journal of Consumer Research*, *22*, 1–16.
Merleau-Ponty, M. (1962). *The phenomenology of perception*. New York: Humanities Press.
Ortner, S. (1991), *Narrativity in history, culture, and lives*. University of Michigan CRSO Working Paper, 457. Ann Arbor, MI.
Pemberton, J. (1994). *On the subject of "Java"*. Ithaca: Cornell University Press.
Sherry, J. F., & Schouten, J. W. (2002). A role for poetry in consumer research. *Journal of Consumer Research*, *29*, 218–234.
Soja, E. W. (1989). *Postmodern geographies*. London: Verso.
Stange, P. (1984). The logic of Rasa in Java. *Indonesia*, *38*, 113–134.
Stoller, P. (1989). *The taste of ethnographic things: The senses in anthropology*. Philadelphia: University of Pennsylvania Press.
Strauss, C. (1997). Partly fragmented, partly integrated: An anthropological examination of 'postmodern fragmented subjects'. *Cultural Anthropology*, *12*(3), 362–404.
Tsing, A. L. (2005). *Friction: An ethnography of global connection*. Princeton: Princeton University Press.
Urry, J. (1995). *Consuming places*. London: Routledge.
Wagner, R. (1991). Poetics and the recentering of anthropology. In: I. Brady (Ed.), *Anthropological poetics*. Savage, MD: Rowman and Littlefield.
Wikan, U. (1995). The self in a world of urgency and necessity. *Ethos*, *23*(5), 259–285.

A HEAVY BURDEN OF IDENTITY: INDIA, FOOD, GLOBALIZATION, AND WOMEN

Jenny Mish

ABSTRACT

India's dynamic turn toward globalization brings new eating practices driven by desires for status and convenience. Traditional expectations of women as keepers of domestic culture persist as fears of a possible loss of Indianness are projected onto women. In the reflexive identity processes of urban middle-class Hindu women, new normative beauty ideals are often impossible to attain, resulting in Western-style food-related health problems. Awareness of these risks may be deflected by matrimonial, body image, and time pressures, as depicted in a preliminary model of food globalization and women's identities.

INTRODUCTION

I will always remember my first forays into the seething aromatic bazaars of old Delhi, in search of food. It was 1981, and I a stubborn 20-year old American girl. At first I ate boiled eggs and raw cucumbers. Later, I found a few Raj-style restaurants with scrupulous waiters, and I eventually became

Consumer Culture Theory
Research in Consumer Behavior, Volume 11, 165–186

ISSN: 0885-2111/doi:10.1016/S0885-2111(06)11008-X

comfortable at the semipublic eating houses, shunned by the higher castes, where itinerant male workers nourished themselves. They would suck air deeply through their mouths to soothe the fiery burn, staring at my blond hair and pale skin. After awhile, I enjoyed scooping soupy lentils into my mouth with a deft stroke of my right thumb. But the gaze continued to haunt me.

Twenty years later, I returned to a different Delhi, where I was offered a McDonald's Maharaja Burger, wrapped, on a plate, in a home. My host eagerly explained that he was unfamiliar with such foods, but he wanted me to feel comfortable, did I like it? It tasted like cardboard, but I thanked him.

Between these visits, televisions appeared everywhere. Eating utensils had become the norm. A whole array of commercial eating options had arisen. I was still treated with deference by male servants, but their attitudes were more often jaded. Perhaps most strikingly, the gaze had shifted – I went from exotic beauty to just another blond.

My experiences in India raised important questions. Among them I chose two for investigation. First, how is the globalization of food affecting Indian culture? Then more specifically, how does it affect the lives and identities of Indian women?

Chapter Overview

This chapter is laid out in six sections, beginning with (1) a brief look at some of the large-scale changes occurring in Indian consumption and media, followed by a description of the urban Hindu middle class, the population of interest for this study. The next section (2) sketches some of the changes in food culture inside and outside the home, especially in response to an accelerating pace of life and increasing status needs.

Next, (3) an introduction to Indian women's changing identities provides the specific context for a secondary-source print media study focused on the effects of food culture changes on women's identities. The method used for this study is introduced, followed by (4) results in three sections, gender relations, beauty and body image, and health issues. Finally, (5) a preliminary model of food globalization and women's identities is presented, with proposed questions for further research. The chapter ends with (6) a brief conclusion.

Consumption, Global Brands, and Media

The total number of brands advertised in India rose from 14,800 in 2000 to 75,900 in 2005 (Cooksey, 2005). Western-style retail malls are springing up, though street markets and small shops remain the dominant retail forms. In general, Indian consumers are value-conscious, often choosing low-priced equivalent products after sampling more than three times as many brands as U.S. shoppers. Status is strongly and increasingly associated with consumption in both urban and rural India, where 70% of the population resides. Yet even in the Communist state of Kerala, most people find nothing inherently problematic in consumption (Osella & Osella, 1999).

Prior to the arrival of television in towns and villages across India in the past 15–20 years, scholars had concluded that media had little influence on social change in India (Johnson, 2001). This was in spite of an enormous film industry and abundant print media. Now, televisions are perceived as a necessity throughout the country and the deprived minority form what Kirk Johnson calls an "information underclass" (2001).

Non-Hindus are rarely depicted in advertising, which remains heavily slanted toward middle-class Hindu audiences (Cayla & Peñaloza, 2005; Mazzarella, 2003; Rajagopal, 1998). This reflects the immaturity of the Indian ad industry as well as the general cultural dominance of Hindus, who comprise 80% of the population. Even so, Indian TV advertising is rapidly changing as the indigenous industry acquires sophistication. For example, children are increasingly targeted, and food is the most common product category advertised. In 1992, an estimated 35% of all Indian TV ads intended children as their audience (Supraja, 2004), a percentage which is certain to have grown in the intervening years. "Parents use TV as an electronic babysitter and bribe them using TV toys or chips seen in ads to get children to behave, eat, or cooperate" (Supraja, 2004, n.p.).

The Urban Hindu Middle Class

Although a quarter of India's 1.1 billion people currently live on less than $1 per day, each year 1% climb out of poverty. If this continues, the middle class, currently estimated at 300 million (Ganapati, 2004), will be 50% of the population by 2025 (Das, 2004). Between 2004 and 2009, household consumption is expected to double to $500 billion (DSP Merrill Lynch in Ganapati, 2004).

The burgeoning of the middle class has arisen from increased access to education and the development of small enterprises among the lower and middle castes, creating what is called "the new rich" (Lakha, 1999). Caste discrimination is illegal and the rhetoric of caste prejudice has hushed, yet caste divisions continue to limit access to resources, similar to the role of race in the West. It is somewhat less true for lower castes that education is a "ticket out of poverty" (Das, 2004, n.p.). Nonetheless, there is indeed "a new social contract whereby talent, hard work, and managerial skill have replaced inherited wealth" (n.p.) as the means by which Indians have attained higher class status.

The urban Hindu middle-class is among the most rapidly changing segments of Indian society, and the most influential vis-à-vis consumption (Lakha, 1999; Venkatesh, 1994). Middle-class urban Hindus play a mediating role between the forces of globalization and other segments of society. For example, in rural India, status is increasingly associated with middle-class norms portrayed on television (Lakha, 1999; Osella & Osella, 1999).

Much of this influential segment cannot be clearly distinguished from its members who travel or work abroad, pollinating culinary innovation. Economic reforms of the 1980s included incentives for "nonresident Indians" to invest capital at home (Breckenridge, 1995), helping to maintain close ties, and with them cross-fertilization. "Generally diasporic Indians in affluent countries are regarded as a reference point by many middle-class people throughout India" (Lakha, 1999, p. 257).

This chapter focuses on urban middle-class Hindus in India and also includes data from members of this group in the U.S. diaspora. Although there is a degree of homogeneity within this group, it must be noted that it contains a great deal of variation, especially by age, region, and social, religious, and political views. These variations merit research beyond the scope of this chapter.

CHANGING FOOD PRACTICES INSIDE AND OUTSIDE THE HOME

Upwardly mobile salaried professionals live within tight schedules and are concerned with positioning themselves conspicuously on the social ladder. Career opportunities often require geographic mobility, altering family structures, and increasing consumption. As one female engineer said, "I don't have my in-laws staying with me. So I feel free to spend when I want, on what I want" (Ganapati, 2004, n.p.). Along with identity changes, which will be discussed below, trends in Indian food culture, both inside and outside the home, are moving in two general directions: toward convenience and status.

Home Cooking

Traditional Indian cooking is well loved and far from endangered, except in the sense that it is increasingly modified "to suit life in the fast lane" (Karen Anand in Bhumika, 2004, n.p.):

> People don't have time any more for slow cooking. We have to simplify our ingredients and change methods of cooking to suit our lifestyle … I think a number of women don't like to cook, which is fair enough. They are forced into the role of cooking because they have to. More and more women are working so there's very little time to cook (n.p.).

New culinary options include Western and Indian snacks and packaged foods, such as MTR's ready-to-eat masala dosa (Riti, 2003). Food blenders, spice grinders, microwave ovens, stoves, and refrigerators are making their way into more and more kitchens.

The refrigerator is a particularly popular addition (Venkatesh, 1994). However, it is largely a status symbol, typically used to cool just a few items (Kemper, 2001). This is due to traditional views emphasizing freshness and purity, a practical approach to food safety in a hot climate, along with heavy spicing. However, the practice of saving leftover food is on the rise and it appears that its widespread acceptance is inevitable. A telling story was written by an Indian woman who was raised in the U.S. and who married a man from India:

> Like any newly married Indian girl, I would get the ubiquitous question from elders in the family. 'What did you cook today?' This was a difficult question to answer, because although I enjoyed cooking, I of course didn't- and still don't- cook everyday. Okay, I've said it. My dirty little secret is out. YES WE EAT LEFTOVERS! AND SOMETIMES, THEY'RE NOT INDIAN! Of course such an idea seemed positively blasphemous to many Indian elders. In the beginning, I was naïve, and I'd take the question at face value, and answer honestly. I still remember the look on my husband's aunt's face when I told her we reheated some pizza from the night before. I might as well have told her I'd served my husband a plate of rubber for dinner. After that, I began noticing more home-cooked Indian meals in Tupperware containers coming our way (Iyengar, 2005, n.p.).

Many authors indicated that leftovers are increasingly accepted, and some cookbooks give tips for using them (Appadurai, 1988). A proliferation of new cookbooks began appearing in the 1970s, often emphasizing that they are "designed to resolve shortages of time and money" (p. 8). The middle-class housewives for whom these books are intended are frequently expected to perform culinary feats in the kitchen. These are women "whose husbands feel the pressure to entertain colleagues and contacts at home" with modern trends (p. 8). At the same time, they are expected to satisfy extended family members who have attachments to regional and other specialized culinary traditions:

> Many middle-class housewives are thus on a perpetual seesaw that alternates between the honing of indigenous culinary skills and the exploration of new culinary regions. It is the tacit function of the new cookbooks to make this process seem a pleasant adventure rather than a tiring grind (p. 8).

In the interests of that pleasant adventure, these cookbooks are filled with enticingly perfect images of delicious food, what Coward (1984, in Lupton, 1996, p. 24) refers to as "food pornography." Appadurai identifies the "*seductiveness of variety* as an important part of the ideological appeal of the new cookbooks, [which] masks the pressures of social mobility, conspicuous consumption, and budgetary stress" (emphasis his, 1988, p. 10). This effort is largely self-directed, as the authors are members of their audience, documenting the oral exchange of recipes across regions and social groups.

Restaurants and Fast Food

This exploration of the culinary Other extends beyond the home to other social settings involving food. Modern middle-class wedding parties have begun to feature a trendy array of international cuisine (Joshi, 2005). In the bigger cities, sushi and tempura are now easily found, as well as pizza parlors and hamburger shops, and a well-established tradition of Chinese eateries. Upscale restaurants may feature celebrities, or have unique décor, such as a backwoods replica of rustic India (Conlon, 1995).

Restaurants in India serve all classes in the sense that they treat everyone to new notions of cuisine and social status. Review columns have proliferated, and this voyeurism helps to create hyper-awareness of status:

> The appeal is not only to our tastebuds, but to our need to differentiate ourselves as culinary adventurers with a highly developed ability to discern style in food and to engage in the luxurious, finer things of life … Dining out is thus an important practice of the self … particularly among the most economically privileged groups [where it] becomes a public demonstration of an individual's possession of both economic and cultural capital, phrased as their sense of taste (Lupton, 1996, p. 98).

For a society fervently engaged in aspirations of upward mobility, the discrimination of status cues must be a refined art.

In addition to meeting growing status demands, restaurant dining has been "encouraged by gradual changes in the timing of meals" (Conlon, 1995, p. 97). The "restructuring of office hours and the physical expansion of Bombay city reduced the possibility that most clerical workers could consume all meals at home" (p. 97). A uniquely Indian service developed in response to this need. About 200,000 office workers in Mumbai (formerly called Bombay) receive home-cooked midday meals delivered daily by 5,000 "dabbawallas" via an elaborate network of street exchanges.

In addition, footpath food vendors represent an indigenous Indian fast food tradition. These tiny businesses offer quick and easy meals and snacks for almost nothing by Western standards. In contrast, a meal at McDonald's or a similar import shop costs as much as a meal at a fine restaurant. Nonetheless, "[Western] fast food is distinctively 'trendy' and 'fashionable' in India" (Narayan, 1995, n.p.), where such shops are frequented by upper class families and youth who can afford to flaunt their sophistication in this way.

Vegetarianism and Caste Prescriptions

Outside the home, and especially in diaspora, vegetarianism is increasingly difficult to maintain (Bhatt, 2002; Sperling, 1999). Most Hindus now eat at least some meat. As of 1998, only 20% of the Indian population was vegetarian (Hinduism Today, 1998). Even so, vegetarianism remains an important dimension of Hindu identity, and less meat is eaten per capita in India than in almost any other country. Thus the meaning of vegetarianism is changing. For some, it is directly tied to religious beliefs, and for others it is seen as a health issue, or a non-religious moral question. One might expect those retaining the practice to be religious Hindus from higher castes. Indeed, a Hindu spiritual leader told a father whose children were allowed to eat meat that "[their] mother was not a mata, a good mother, but a kumata, a mother who promoted evilness" (Hinduism Today, 2004, n.p.).

Unlike vegetarianism, which is approaching personal preference status, caste restrictions on food preparation have become a collectively shunned symbol of archaic bad manners. Those retaining caste rules are portrayed as extremists. One author complained in dismay about a litany of immoral acts in society, including "dowry, lynching women as witches, marrying daughters to dogs, hiring sorcerers' service to tackle malaria, and refusal to eat food cooked by Muslims and lower caste Hindus" (Statesman-India, 2005, n.p.). Even an article interviewing 18 of Hinduism's "top spiritual leaders" found agreement that casteism is no longer a proper Hindu practice. "Today when we travel, do we ask the caste of who is sitting with us? When we have food in the hotel, do we ask them the caste of the cook who has made the food?" (Hinduism Today, 2004, n.p.)

Thus, in many ways the food lives of the Indian middle class are becoming more Westernized. Still, Indian consumers tend to adopt new practices selectively, "without using Western yardsticks of what is acceptable and not" (Venkatesh, 1994, p. 324). This selectivity can be seen in the persistent prevalence of traditional Indian dishes, in the blending or creolization of Indian and other cuisines, and in the selective adaptation of traditional practices such as vegetarianism, caste restrictions, and aversion to leftovers. However, as detailed below, in the case of Western notions of beauty and health, two intertwining normative messages espoused by commercial Western-influenced media, Western yardsticks appear to be difficult to for Indian women to reject.

IDENTITIES IN FLUX

The rapid changes in Indian food culture inside and outside the home reflect a corresponding dynamism in sense of self among middle-class urban Hindus. On the one hand, "contemporary Indian middle-class identity ... is largely constructed through lifestyle practices and media representations centred on the consumption of expensive global commodities" (Lakha, 1999, p. 265). On the other hand, many Indians are concerned about assimilation and a possible loss of Indianness:

> The clash between traditionalism and modernism, or the blending of the two, is a perennial theme ... Among many middle-class Indians this ontological tension exists regardless of age or gender, signifying the fear of a possible loss of cultural identity in moving away from their imagined notions of Indianness. (Venkatesh, 1994, p. 328).

For women, food is at the heart of this identity clash. As an Indian woman in the U.S. wrote, "Every weekend you call home and the first question you end up answering invariably is what you ate and what you cooked that day" (Joshi, 2004). In Hindu scripture, the rules about women and food actually confound the two. "The texts make so many overlapping connections between wives, food, sex (fertility), and hospitality that their implications are difficult to summarize" (Herman, 2000, n.p.). This confounding of food and the feminine is an aspect of the confounding of food with all things spiritual. "For Hindus, food and religious devotion are intricately entwined" (Melwani, 2005, n.p.).

Building on these religious mores, Hindu nationalists, in power from 1998 to 2004, responded to the threat of modernity with a two-part strategy of embracing foreignness in the world outside the home, while attempting to bolster traditionalism in the domestic realm. Partha Chatterjee called this "a new patriarchy" (Chatterjee, 1989, p. 244), distinguished from the prior form by explicitly allowing certain adaptations of dress, food, manners, and education, while insisting that women maintain the home as "the principal site for expressing the spiritual quality of the national culture" (p. 243).

Layered upon this pressure to maintain Indianness and Hinduness with food-based domestic identities, Indian women simultaneously face an onslaught of new normative messages about femininity in the form of Western ideals of beauty, body image, and health. They also face dynamic changes in employment, travel, parenting, entertainment, and extended family relationships. Thus, women's roles and identities are extremely turbulent in India. They are changing so quickly that the views and modes of behavior in establishing identity vary markedly across five-year age cohorts of Indian women (Venkatesh, 1994).

Theoretical Orientation and Research Question

In the context of a post-traditional order, the process of self exploration is described by Anthony Giddens (1991) as a reflexive project of self, a project in which "self and body become the sites of a variety of new lifestyle options" (p. 100). Giddens specifically names the body and its regimes, including presumably everything to do with food, as an essential location of reflexive identity development. Informed by Giddens' theory of the modernizing self, the goal of this research is to understand how middle-class urban Hindu women's identities are changing as a result of food globalization, and what role(s) these changing identities might play in food globalization.

Method

I conducted a written media study, initially reviewing 1,047 articles published between January 1, 1996 and November 30, 2005. These articles were culled from online databases in three phases. The first phase used as keywords *food, cuisine, cooking* AND *identity* or *women*. The second phase sought both additional data related to women's roles and clarification of the

Hindu nationalist discourse regarding women's roles. Keywords used were *women, role, relationships, BJP, Hindutva* AND *identity* or *food*. The final phase sought to fill gaps and investigate disconfirmations, using as keywords *vegetarian, caste, leftovers, health, beauty* AND *identity* or *food*.

The reviewed articles appeared in nine newspapers and magazines, Hinduism Today, India Abroad, India Currents, Indian Express, India Today, Little India, News India Times, The Statesman (India), and Times of India. Five of these sources are published in India, and four in the U.S. Particular attention was given to the balance of data published in India and in the U.S. Through the remainder of this chapter, India may be assumed to be the context unless otherwise indicated. Reliance on secondary data, much of which is published in the U.S., is considered a significant limitation of the study.

Of the total, many articles provided recipes, restaurant reviews, or were otherwise not relevant to the research question. Every relevant article was selected for detailed analysis and coding, for a total of 102 coded articles. The majority of these (87) were published between 2001 and 2005, however in 15 cases, articles published between 1996 and 2000 were used due to inadequate results in the more recent period (six of these relate to vegetarianism, and seven address gender and Hindu nationalism).

Analysis was done iteratively and concurrently with data gathering, using the method of constant comparison. Articles and sections of articles were ultimately coded into 11 categories (beauty, body, caste, diaspora, fusion, health, Hindutva, leftovers, servants, vegetarianism, and women's roles). Data were compared across categories, across time periods, and across successive phases of data gathering. Data from the articles in the written media study were also compared with the sources used in the literature review and with personal observations during June–August of 1981 and January–March of 2001. Disconfirming evidence was investigated, and in several cases this led to additional data gathering. Findings thus emerged from the data.

FOOD GLOBALIZATION AND WOMEN'S IDENTITIES

Gender Relations

The written media study revealed that the official Hindu nationalist discourse is no longer explicitly patriarchal. In 2001, the central leadership of the Hindu nationalist party (the BJP) announced a change to a policy of "gender sensitivity" (Statesman-India, 2001), apparently reversing what Chatterjee called the "nationalist resolution of the women's question" (Chatterjee, 1989).

Although this attempt was ultimately abandoned, the underlying archetypal reasoning persists, and the confounding continues, at least to some degree. Many women feel pressure, if not internally then from family members, to uphold ideals of domestic purity. "For a woman, religion is not just something linked to a god but a cultural practice that she is supposed to preserve" (Lakshmi, 2005, n.p.).

Two important aspects of this underlying pressure should be highlighted. First, Indian men have projected their fears about modernity onto Indian women, at least to some extent. "To handle the threats to their own Indianness, nationalist men insisted that women remain at home cooking, doing puja (religious observances), and maintaining family ties" (Derné, 2002). This implies a projection of at least a portion of the process of reflexive identity development, and with it a rejection of personal responsibility.

Second, it is clear that women are not the only ones defining their own identities. For example, 69% of Hindu women say they need permission from fathers, husbands, or sons to seek employment (Hasan, 2002a), and only 18% report participation in the workforce (Hasan, 2002b). Among middle-class urban Hindus, rising employment among women is widely seen as an indication of increasing autonomy, dignity, and modernization. Yet contradictory if not impossible expectations on the home front are often implicit. One author explained the pivotal role of food in this predicament:

> We have broken the shackles of the kitchen but food still binds us ... We know how little time a career-driven girl has to learn the art of simmering and sizzling. Yet, prospective desi husbands (anywhere in the world) feel free to quiz her on culinary intelligence (Joshi, 2004, n.p.).

The matchmaking game is perhaps the most entrenched arena in which Indian men both define Indian women's identities and project identity conflicts. Indian women seem to be paradoxically expected or allowed to live increasingly modern lives while simultaneously preserving domestic traditions. Most matrimonial ads explicitly request or require specific domestic skills and it is quite common to see ads like this one, in which the writer is apparently unaware of the contradictions in his request:

> My partner should be young, cute, dashing, smart, fair, intelligent in studies, understanding nature, should understand the feelings of her partner and go according tto [sic] him, respect my parents and obey their words, should be good cook i.e. she should cook

> delicious foods because I am very much found [sic] of eating good and tasty foods. she [sic] attend funtions [sic] like marriages, parties and also she should attend the funtions [sic]. she [sic] should be expert in cooking like north indian [sic] foods, south indian [sic] foods, chinese [sic] foods, italian [sic] foods, desserts, ice cream etc. She [sic] can wear jeans (rarely) sari and salwarsuits (she can wear them daily). She can be of any caste, any religion, can talk any language, she can be from any country. Hobbies can be anything, she is free to lead her own life in her own style. Should be in a good position and lead my life in high society (http://www.matrimonialbank.com/cgi-bin/search.cgi, July 26, 2006).

Several media study articles detailed cooking tests for prospective wives. In one, a conservative family tested their daughter's culinary skills because they did not want her to pursue an education, in spite of an exceptional scholarship. "The ability to produce a decent meal is part of that skill set which would assure the family she would never be hungry and miserable in an alien land" (Venkatraman, 2003).

For women in India, divorce and remaining unmarried are not real options. Even in the Indian–American community, divorced women are outcasts (Mankekar, 2005). One divorcée wrote, "Whenever I went back to India, I was shunned by my relatives … [who] prevented me from entering their kitchens and polluting the Gods" (Sarvate, 1999, n.p.).

Several articles discussed the "outsourcing" of spouses. In these cases, Indian men who were raised or schooled abroad seek wives raised in India, presumably for their traditional domestic skills. One article emphasized the poor social skills of such husbands and the sometimes severe abuse received by such wives (Melwani, 2005). In these cases, relationship and gender role expectations are often based on romanticized notions rather than accurate information. One outsourced wife described her expectations when coming to the U.S.:

> I thought I was guaranteed a life without any of the hardships wives in India encounter, such as living with in-laws and constantly tending to house chores … I thought I wouldn't need to lift a finger because I had heard of automatic appliances to cook food and clean dishes … The reality of America was something I was perplexed by – and to a certain extent, I still am (Shah, 1996, n.p.).

Thus, the written media study revealed abundant evidence that Indian women's food-related identities are negotiated *with* the men in their lives, and *by* them to some degree. The evidence additionally suggests the importance of family members as negotiators of women's identities. It is clear that in-laws, especially mothers-in-law, exert significant influence in the food lives and identities of Indian women, particularly in more traditional families. This is consistent with Caplan's (1997) reminder that identity is not purely individual, but is socially constructed, as symbolized by the commensality of food.

This issue raises questions about the imposition of an individualistic notion of identity in a more collectivist cultural context. The collectivist context might, for example, prioritize group-level commitment issues above individual compatibility issues in matchmaking. The data for this study failed to provide sufficient information to analyze this dimension. Instead, the acknowledged emphasis here is on the emergence of stronger individual identities as a response to the globalization of food practices.

Beauty and Body Image

Unsurprisingly, the print media study produced abundant data about new norms for beauty and body image for middle-class urban Hindu women. Overall, representations of women have been shifting "to an increasing emphasis on glamour, sexuality, and appearance" (Munshi, 2001). As in the West, the beauty and body image prescriptions descending upon Indian women set unrealistic if not impossible standards. "In this, India has fast caught up with the West. Today, the muscled, taut body has become something of a cultural icon" (Munshi, 2001, p. 86). The rise of weight control and dieting schemes attests to the adoption of this emphasis in India (Lal, 2005).

Between 1994 and 2000, India produced six Miss Worlds or Miss Universes. In a formula, "worked to the pinnacle of perfection," prospective contestants undergo an exhausting program of undernourishment and exercise (Runkle, 2004, n.p.). "How did these women attain crowns in a country and culture known for its voluptuous, dark eyed, petite, dark skinned beautiful women?" asked one author (Gawle, 2002, n.p.). The traditional Indian beauty ideal presumed a well-fed figure with rounded curves (McGivering, 2003). "Well-fed bodies were more testimony to the fact that the person came from a well-to-do family and ate well" (Munshi, 2001).

These new standards of beauty have serious consequences in the mating game. Once again, the male gaze is never far removed, framing a shared arena of agency and responsibility:

> You can thumb through any number of matrimonial ads in Indian publications, and discover that every Indian man is looking for a 'fair and slim girl' … Are Indian women to be chided for adopting Western notions of beauty, or are Indian men responsible for promoting them? (Sarvate, 2001, n.p.).

In *Food, the Body and the Self*, Deborah Lupton describes the Western emphasis upon appearance as a source of both pride and anxiety. Bodies become "potent physical symbols of the extent to which their 'owners' possess self-control" (1996, p. 16). The need to see ones' self as possessing self-control may be an essential but elusive aspect of a modern individualistic identity for Indian women. Sociologists McIntosh and Zey (1998) argue that although women are the responsible gatekeepers for food in the home (cross-culturally), men control the enactment of that responsibility for food, making an important distinction between responsibility and control. In this context, dysfunctional eating must also be seen as an expression of self-control. "Anorexics and bulimarexics are particularly notable for their overcompliance … Food becomes one sure way they can exert control in the world" (Counihan, 1998, p. 152).

As if to illustrate this, an Indian–American woman writes about the day she decided to start dressing like the other moms at her daughter's school, and goes shopping for new clothes:

> I finally break down and decide to join the ranks of the beautiful people. Beautiful, that is, compared to me … Did I mention that the private-school moms are Atkins-skinny too? … Have they ever heard of idlis or vadas, or banana bread? They must spend their lives on the elliptical trainer, I decide, and head for the bakery, where I order hot chocolate with a double whipped cream. About halfway through, the sugar hits me hard, and I begin to think that the mom-crew isn't so bad after all. After all, they're looking after their health. I guess I should do the same, but right now, I really need an apricot Danish (Pappu, 2004, n.p.).

This narrative makes light of troubling inner conflicts about appearance, health, and identity, conflicts that are expected to resonate among readers. It highlights how these conflicts become confounded with food choices and personal volition. It also reveals the way in which food-related health issues become subsumed by appearance-related aspects of the reflexive identity development process. In order for a process to be reflexive, there must be a degree of self-awareness. When it comes to food-related health issues, this needed awareness may be lacking.

Health Issues

Susie Orbach (1988) and others have pointed out that social pressures to limit food intake in order to conform to norms of feminine body size lead to pathological relationships with food. This emphasis lures women away from other more socially agentic desires they might have. "Because the outward appearance of the body is understood as demonstrating the inner worthiness and personality of its owner, there is a high degree of preoccupation with bodily presentation and management" (Lupton, 1996, p. 137).

In India, the result is a new array of Western-style diseases and social ills, including heart disease, obesity, anorexia, and psychiatric depression (Devgan, 2003; McGivering, 2003; Suchitra, 2002). One doctor explained that, "more and more urban women are leading … 'pressure cooker' lifestyles. They eat wrong (more junk food and frequent meal skipping), don't exercise, sleep less and are constantly worrying about work or tasks they have to finish" (Devgan, 2003, n.p.). The pressure on girls and women to miraculously navigate these impossible expectations is immense:

> Girls at the beginning of their adolescence manifest five times more anxiety than boys … Internet and TV expose the younger generation to a Western, liberal and explosive lifestyle in a society that refuses to shift from orthodox family values. This situation puts a lot of adolescent girls in a state of flux that normally leads to depression (Bhattacharjee, 2003, n.p.).

Dietary factors are clearly critical contributors to these health problems. Ingredients have become less nutritious and higher in calories and salt. In addition, "there has been a change in meal timings … a lopsided load on the digestive tract towards the night" (Akthar, 2005, n.p.). One article complained that "the demand for newer and newer taste sensations to feed a public that hankers for what some writers refer to as 'gastro porn' has led to Indian food being regarded as the 'S & M' of the culinary experience" (Doctor, 2000, n.p.). Exercise, or the lack of it, is another key contributing factor. "Who in our culture goes for exercise?" one author asked rhetorically, and then answered, "Nobody!" (Melwani, 2004, n.p.).

Clearly, many of these health concerns affect both genders. For example, Indians of both genders are at high risk for diabetes, comprising 20% of the world diabetic population, or 33 million people (Akthar, 2005, n.p.). Indian–American men are four times more prone to coronary heart disease than White American men (n.p.). One out of every eight Indian–American women gets breast cancer, the highest ratio in the world (n.p.). On balance, however, Indian women carry a greater burden of responsibility than their male counterparts in attempting to live healthy food lives. This is due both to the role of food in the economic structure of gender relations and to unrealistic internalized and externally imposed ideals of beauty and health.

DISCUSSION AND PRELIMINARY MODEL

These mixed messages and contradictory expectations facing Indian women as they navigate potential identities related to food are exemplified by Jassi.

the star of an Indian TV serial with soaring ratings, who is "well on her way to becoming an icon for Indian womanhood" (Statesman-India, 2004, n.p.). Hardly a realistic role model, Jassi takes a job as a secretary, and within a year she is the CEO of the company:

> Jassi is … the overworked, perpetually burdened 'working woman' with infinitely elastic duties … [She] has her own identity and principles … she is a rational being, not confined to the four walls of the home … [She is] free of household duties because her mother and grandmother are homebodies … Her grandmother lightly tells Purab – the perfect eligible future bridegroom – 'She will learn to cook eventually' (n.p.).

Even CEO Jassi is haunted by the inevitable need for culinary expertise in order to secure a mate. Her postponement of this issue is not portrayed as a source of tension or conflict, but as an adaptive, modern, trendy approach to life. Her appearance somehow appears patently normal, even as it conforms to the new ideals:

> In a way, Jassi is portrayed as a foil to the modern Westernized woman … [who] has a painted face and wears revealing clothes … Her ugly duckling role has worked like magic, reassuring hundreds of ordinary-looking girls about their self-worth. Yet … Jassi is far from 'ugly'. She is slim, tall and fair with a flawless skin and perfect features. The thick spectacles, …braces, … and shapeless salwar kameezes are but an elaborate disguise (Statesman-India, 2004).

Thus Jassi somehow achieves the impossible balance between modern and traditional notions of beauty, independence, time use, and feminine ideals. However, she only attains traditional feminine ideals by postponing marriage. She will eventually learn how to cook, and then she will marry. This is debt financing of one's identity: she is borrowing against future traditional identity payments in order to live more modern today. Meanwhile, a fashion house has a Jassi collection available across India.

Jassi's ease in achieving these impossibilities belittles the actual lives of non-fictionalized Indian women. One divorced woman in California was shunned by the Indian–American community for being divorced, until she proved herself as a successful realtor who put her son and daughter through good universities. Only then was she respected and embraced as a member of the community (Mankekar, 2005). A real life Jassi might have high blood pressure, be obese, or be dependent on anti-depressants. She might live with a violent spouse; an article in *The Hindu* advising women on avoiding domestic violence implicated widely accepted gender roles without providing a practical strategy for addressing them (Bhattacharjee, 2003).

The experiences of Western women facing similar conditions may have helpful lessons to offer. Anthropologist Carole Counihan analyzed five books addressing food-related women's health issues in late 20th century North America. These five authors "concur that the problematical relationship between women and food is invariably linked to women's difficulty being women" (1998, p. 145). These five books all propose the same solution: "developing a strong, positive sense of female identity. It involves teaching women to make their personal problems part of a broader social analysis" (p. 157).

Preliminary Model

Fig. 1 offers a preliminary model of the relationship between women's identities and five overlapping influences: matrimonial pressures, body image pressures, time pressures, the effects of high-fat, low-nutrition foods, and resulting negative health impacts, both physical and psychological. Although I developed this model specifically for the context of middle-class urban Hindu women's lives in India, it may be applicable in other contexts as well.

This preliminary model begins to recognize the factors involved in making even small and apparently insignificant food consumption decisions. Every Indian woman makes dozens of such decisions every day. As seen in the passage above by the mom who decides she needs an apricot Danish, each of these factors is likely to be present to some degree in many daily decisions. A given woman may or may not be aware of the presence or influence of each

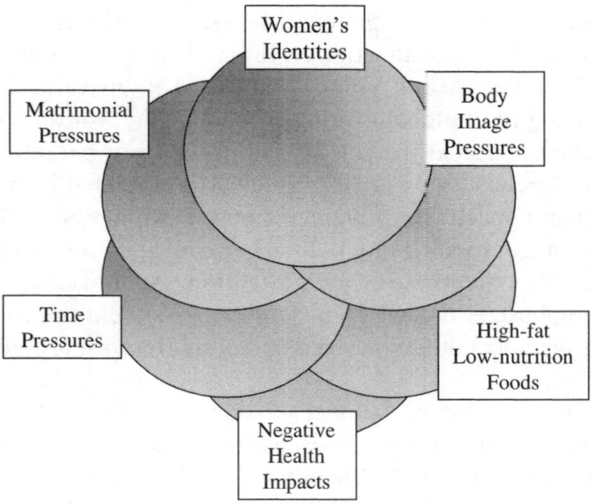

Fig. 1. Food Globalization and Women's Identities Preliminary Model.

of these factors, even though they may actually be quite salient. Food behaviors are used by Western women to suppress awareness of gender-related pressures and unresolved identity conflicts:

> If they feel angry about job discrimination or their husbands' failure to help around the house, they may react by turning their anger against themselves: eating eating eating, or starving starving starving. The food fixation blots out other battles. Many women, in fact, put off living fully until after they have resolved their struggle with food (Counihan, 1998, p. 152).

Thus, each of these factors can be viewed in isolation, but they are more likely to be experienced as intertwining influences of varying salience or awareness in any given situation. The model attempts to avoid the assumption of fragmented rather than unified notions of self in relation to food behaviors (Lupton, 1996), leaving both possibilities open. It would seem likely that a greater awareness of these factors and their cultural embeddedness would lead to a more unified sense of self. Along with a broader social analysis, this might achieve the strong, positive sense of female identity proposed by Counihan's five authors.

Questions for Further Research

The key question for further research raised by this study is whether middle-class urban Hindu women both construct and accept imposed constructions of modern female identity, which deflect social awareness from the negative health impacts of food globalization in India. This question has important implications for public health policy, and may be applicable to privileged women embracing food globalization throughout the world.

This study has neglected the role and importance of parenting, age, and generational differences in women's changing food-related identities. There is also a divergent spectrum of women's experience across the various regions of India, and across varying political, social, and religious views. Each of these dimensions deserves research attention. As previously mentioned, this chapter emphasizes the emergence of women's identities as individuals rather than as members of families and communities; this, too, bears further investigation.

One surprising omission in the data for this study is the silence about the transition from domestic servants in Indian households to none in diasporic households. Although it is briefly mentioned by a few authors, only one article dealt with this topic. It was written by an Indian–American woman who was raised in the U.S. and who then moved to India. She described the challenges of supervising servants and her process of adjustment in the kitchen (Chachra, 2005). It seems inevitable that the loss of domestic help would dramatically influence the food lives of Indian women moving to the U.S., and that this influence would be felt in food-based interactions. Perhaps this silence is associated with a generalized shame about the caste relations of the past, now seen as backward. Further research on this topic may be valuable.

CONCLUSION

Food and food preparation play a pivotal role in India's dynamic turn toward globalization, one which places women at the fulcrum of a whirlwind of change. This central position implies tremendous stress, as women grapple with irreconcilable contradictory expectations. Compared to other deeply-held traditions, such as vegetarianism and caste relations, traditional expectations of women as keepers of the culture persist doggedly, exactly because of their location at the center of the whirlwind, in the kitchen.

Although women's roles are the fulcrum of this debate, it also involves men and their views of women, their identities, and their fears about modernity. The terms of the debate revolve around women's appearance and culinary skills, not around men's sense of self. Women's relationships with food are not simply their own business, but instead belong to their husbands and in-laws. Indeed they belong to the entire society, which relies upon them for stability in a torrent of upheaval.

Thus urban middle-class Hindu women are in a process of reflexive identity development in which individualistic, personal choices and those representing collective traditions and family cannot be easily reconciled. This process is intimately involved with food, and with new normative ideals of health and beauty, ideals that are in most cases impossible to achieve. The resulting health risks will be borne not only by individual women, but also by the society as a whole.

ACKNOWLEDGMENTS

The author would like to thank Russell Belk, Melea Press, Rebecca Gill, Debra Scammon, Shalini Bahl, Kristy Bartley, Cornelia Otnes, Mohammadali Zolfagharian, and the participants of the first Consumer Culture Theory Conference for their comments and suggestions. Any mistakes are the sole responsibility of the author.

REFERENCES

Appadurai, A. (1988). How to make a national cuisine: Cookbooks in contemporary India. *Comparative Studies in Society and History*, *30*(January), 3–24.

Akthar, S. (2005). Eat your way to good health. *India Abroad*, *35*(April 15), M3 Retrieved from ProQuest database December 10, 2005.

Bhatt, S. (2002). Then they leave home. *India Abroad*, *32*(September 27), M5 Retrieved from ProQuest database November 23, 2005.

Bhattacharjee, S. (2003). Why women are depression-prone. *The Hindu*, October 2. Retrieved November 26, 2005, from www.thehindu.com/thehindu/mp/2003/02/10/stories/2003021001200100.htm

Bhumika, K. (2004). Grab an old world bite. *The Hindu*, August 30. Retrieved October 16, 2005, from www.thehindu.com/thehindu/mp/2004/08/30/stories/2004083002790400.htm

Breckenridge, C. A. (1995). *Consuming modernity: Public culture in a South Asian World*. Minneapolis: University of Minnesota Press.

Caplan, P. (1997). Approaches to the study of food, health, and identity. In: P. Caplan (Ed.), *Food, health and identity* (pp. 1–31). London: Routledge.

Cayla, J., & Peñaloza, L. (2005). Domesticating the Indian imagination. Paper presented at the Association for Consumer Research North American Conference, San Antonio, TX.

Chachra, K. (2005). Can you imagine vacuuming? *India Abroad*, *25*(March 25), M12 Retrieved from ProQuest database December 10, 2005.

Chatterjee, P. (1989). The nationalist resolution of the women's question. In: K. Sangari & S. Vaid (Eds), *Recasting women: Essays in Indian colonial history* (pp. 233–253). New Brunswick, NJ: Rutgers University Press.

Conlon, F. F. (1995). Dining out in Bombay. In: C. A. Breckenridge (Ed.), *Consuming modernity: Public culture in a South Asian World* (pp. 90–127). Minneapolis: University of Minnesota Press.

Cooksey, E. (2005). India: The potential from increased consumer choice. *Brand Strategy*, May, (192), 44–45.

Counihan, C. M. (1998). What does it mean to be fat, thin, and female in the United States: A review essay. In: C. M. Counihan & S. L. Kaplan (Eds), *Food and gender: Identity and power* (pp. 145–162). Harwood Academic: Amsterdam, The Netherlands.

Das, G. (2004). The respect they deserve. *Time Asia*, *164*(23). http://www.time.com/time/asia/covers/501041206/two_indias_vpt_das.html, accessed on Dec. 27, 2006.

Derné, S. (2002). Globalization and the reconstitution of local gender arrangements. *Men and Masculinities*, *5*(October), 144–164.

Devgan, K. (2003). Troubled hearts. Women's Feature Service, New Delhi, April 28. Retrieved from ProQuest database October 14, 2005

Doctor, G. (2000). Celebrating food: Let's do an Indian. *The Hindu Folio*, April 30. Retrieved November 26, 2005, from www.hinduonnet.com/folio/fo0004/00040060.htm

Ganapati, P. (2004). Indians shop till they drop. *India Abroad*, *34*(February 27), A28 Retrieved from ProQuest database October 14, 2005.

Gawle, R. (2002). Mirror, mirror on the wall: The Indian obsession with Western beauty standards just isn't fair. *India Abroad*, *32*(January 11), M7 Retrieved from ProQuest database December 10, 2005.

Giddens, A. (1991). *Modernity and self-identity: Self and society in the late modern age*. Stanford, CA: Stanford University Press.

Hasan, Z. (2002a). Analysis: Choice, little freedom. *The Indian Express,* Dec. 20. Retrieved November 23, 2005, from www.indianexpress.com/full_story.php?content_id = 15079

Hasan, Z. (2002b). Analysis: Women interrupted. *The Indian Express,* Dec. 19. Retrieved November 23, 2005, from www.indianexpress.com/full_story.php?content_id = 15024

Herman, P. K. (2000). Sita in the kitchen. *Manushi, 120*(September–October). Retrieved October 14, 2005, from www.indiatogether.org/manushi/issue120/sita.htm

Hinduism Today. (1998). Biggest-ever survey of India. *8*(May 31). Retrieved from ProQuest database December 10, 2005.

Hinduism Today. (2004). Dharma discussions. 28(March 31). Retrieved from ProQuest database December 10, 2005.

Iyengar, A. (2005). Fun fusion. *India Abroad, 35*(July 22), M10 Retrieved from ProQuest database December 10, 2005.

Johnson, K. (2001). Media and social change: The modernizing influences of television in rural India. *Media, Culture and Society, 23*(2), 147–169.

Joshi, M. (2004). Desi voices: Hot rotis off the tava. *India Currents, 18*(August), 25 Retrieved from ProQuest database December 10, 2005.

Joshi, M. (2005). What's on the menu? *India Abroad: Wedding Special, 35*(April 15), S6 Retrieved from ProQuest database October 14, 2005.

Kemper, S. (2001). *Buying and Believing.* Chicago: University of Chicago Press.

Lakha, S. (1999). The state, globalization, and Indian middle-class identity. In: M. Pinches (Ed.), *Culture and privilege in capitalist Asia* (pp. 251–274). London: Routledge.

Lakshmi, C. S. (2005). Different registers: Women and religion in a secular society. *The Hindu,* July 8. Retrieved November 26, 2005, from www.thehindu.com/thehindu/lr/2005/08/07/stories/2005080700180400.htm

Lal, N. (2005). India: Veggie blues. *Women's Feature Service*, New Delhi, June 27. Retrieved from ProQuest database October 14, 2005

Lupton, D. (1996). *Food, the body and the self.* London: Sage.

Mankekar, P. (2005). India shopping: Indian grocery stores and transnational configurations of belonging. In: J. L. Watson & M. L. Caldwell (Eds), *The cultural politics of food and eating: A reader* (pp. 197–214). Malden, MA: Blackwell.

Mazzarella, W. (2003). *Shoveling smoke: Advertising and globalization in contemporary India* Durham, NC: Duke University Press.

McGivering, J. (2003). Anorexia takes hold in India. *BBC News*, June 17. Retrieved October 14, 2005, from http://news.bbc.co.uk/go/pr/fr/-/2/hi/south_asia/2978216.stm

McIntosh, Wm. A., & Zey, M. (1998). Women as gatekeepers. In: C. M. Counihan & S. L. Kaplan (Eds), *Food and gender: Identity and power* (pp. 125–144). Amsterdam, The Netherlands: Harwood Academic.

Melwani, L. (2004). What a stretch. *Little India*, January. Retrieved November 22, 2005, from www.littleindia.com/january2004/WhatAStretch.htm

Melwani, L. (2005). Dishonor and abandon: Marry an NRI at your own peril. *Little India,* February. Retrieved November 22, 2005, from www.littleindia.com/february2005/DishonorAbandon.htm

Munshi, S. (2001). Marvellous me: The beauty industry and the construction of the 'Modern' Indian woman. In: S. Munshi (Ed.), *Images of the 'Modern Woman' in Asia: Global media, local meanings* (pp. 78–93). Surrey, UK: Curzon Press.

Narayan, U. (1995). Eating cultures: Incorporation, identity, and Indian food. *Social Identities, 1*(1), 63–87.

Orbach, S. (1988). *Fat is a feminist issue*. London: Arrow Books.
Osella, F., & Osella, C. (1999). From transience to immanence: Consumption, life-cycle and social mobility in Kerala, South India. *Modern Asian Studies*, *33*(October), 989–1020.
Pappu, N. (2004). Reflections of an Indian-American mom. *News India-Times*, *35*(November 26), 28 Retrieved from ProQuest database December 10, 2005.
Rajagopal, A. (1998). Advertising, politics and the sentimental education of the Indian consumer. *Visual Anthropology Review*, *14*(Fall-Winter), 14–31.
Riti, M. D. (2003). MTR seeks to go mainstream with ready-to-eat curries. *India Abroad*, *33*(May 9), B4 Retrieved from ProQuest database October 14, 2005.
Runkle, S. (2004). Manufacturing beauties. *Manushi, 143*(September). Retrieved October 14, 2005, from www.indiatogether.org/manushi/issue143/beauties.htm
Sarvate, S. (1999). The ugly face of patriarchy: How I became a victim of domestic violence. *India Currents*, *13*(July 31), 64 Retrieved from ProQuest database November 26, 2005.
Sarvate, S. (2001). The last word: Indian chic is causing angst. *India Currents*, *15*(June 30), 72 Retrieved from ProQuest database December 10, 2005.
Shah, B. (1996). Indian American dreams: Lost and found. *Little India*, *6*(September 30), 28 Retrieved from ProQuest database November 26, 2005.
Sperling, V. (1999). Food: Friend or foe? Hinduism Today, April 30, 41 Retrieved from ProQuest database December 10, 2005.
Statesman-India. (2001). BJP to be gender-sensitive from the grassroots. March 10. Retrieved from LexisNexis Academic database November 26, 2005.
Statesman-India. (2004). A mixed message. October 5. Retrieved from LexisNexis Academic database November 26, 2005.
Statesman-India. (2005). Secular claims. January 21. Retrieved from LexisNexis Academic database December 10, 2005.
Suchitra, M. (2002). In the grip of depression. *Manushi,* December. Retrieved October 14, 2005, from www.indiatogether.org/women/health/ker_depn.htm
Supraja, C. (2004). India: 'Buy-Buy' kids. *Women's Feature Service,* New Delhi, Aug 9. Retrieved from ProQuest database October 14, 2005.
Venkatesh, A. (1994). India's changing consumer economy: A cultural perspective. In: C. T. Allen & D. R. John (Eds), *Advances in Consumer Research* (Vol. 21, pp. 323–328). Provo, UT: Association for Consumer Research.
Venkatraman, V. (2003). A literary feast: Understanding the culture that made the cuisine possible. *India Currents*, *17*(July), 44 Retrieved from ProQuest database November 26, 2005.

CONSUMPTION AND CLASS DURING AND AFTER STATE SOCIALISM

Katherine Sredl

Consumer culture in Croatia presents a challenge to some of the received notions about consumption and class during and after state socialism in Eastern Europe. Class and consumer culture during state socialism might seem to contradict notions of socialist equality and communist shortages; their appearance in Eastern Europe after 1989 could be easily assigned to westernization. Even so, after World War II, the party created a large, urban middle class and provided a high level of consumption to signal a new era of equality and comfort. The political dynamics of transformation mostly abolished this structure, bringing heightened awareness to consumption as a sign of political and social place in the new order, as ethnographic research conducted in Zagreb in 2002–2003 suggests. Thus, consumer culture during transformation is rooted in prior social tensions and the political upheavals of transformation.

Consumer culture in Croatia presents a challenge to some of the incumbent notions of consumption and class during state socialism and marketization in Eastern Europe. Class and consumer culture during state socialism might seem to contradict notions of socialist equality and communist shortages; their appearance in Eastern Europe after 1989 could be

Consumer Culture Theory
Research in Consumer Behavior, Volume 11, 187–205

ISSN: 0885-2111/doi:10.1016/S0885-2111(06)11009-1

easily assigned to westernization. Even so, after World War II, the state created a large, urban middle class, outfitted with modern, urban housing as a way of manifesting the promised era of social equality. They also endorsed the small nomenclature and its higher standard of living as an example of the benefits of working for the state. The dynamics shifted in the 1970s as youth sought self-expression outside the conformity of the socialist middle class, but such criticism did not distract from general norms of middle class, socialist equality (Ramet, 1984/1992).

The state supported this structure financially through balancing its Cold War geo-political position between NATO and the Warsaw Pact. Yugoslavia was outside the Warsaw Pact, received aid from the US, and traded with other state socialist countries as well as Germany and neighboring Italy. Citizens could work and travel abroad and bring home goods. Marketing theory was taught at the Economics Faculty in Zagreb starting in 1970 and practiced in promotions agencies starting after World War II (Pecotich, Renko, & Shultz, 1994). Thus, participation in consumer culture, both global and local, was not new after state socialism. The political dynamics of transformation mostly abolished the class structure, bringing heightened awareness to consumption as a sign of place in the new state, as ethnographic research conducted in Zagreb in 2002–2003 suggests.

In spite of these locally grounded, historical, norms of consumption and class in Eastern Europe, as well as the dynamics of the transformation, the consumer behavior literature on the region tends to interpret consumer culture as the movement "from socialism to capitalism" (Coulter, Price, & Feick, 2003, p. 151). When contemporary consumer behaviors in Eastern Europe resemble those in the US, they are quickly labeled as the "westernization" or "glocalization" of local consumer behavior (Ger & Belk, 1996). This rests on assumptions about the transformation that are, for the most part, not explored with local informants. Although richly contextualized research is consistently demanded of consumer culture theory scholars working on consumer behavior in the US (for example Crockett & Wallendorf, 2004), studies of consumers in Eastern Europe seem to be exempt from the same standard.

This article asks how the social processes of privatization in Croatia have influenced class and consumption in Croatia. As much as contemporary cultural forms and social stratification might, at first glance, look like homogenization or hybridization of consumer culture and market structures in Croatia, consumption and class have specifically local meanings with roots in the dynamics of consumption in the socialist era.

LITERATURE REVIEW OF TRANSFORMATIONS

As Comaroff and Comaroff argue, in their discussion of the intersection of ethnographical research and historical perspectives, social change is a dynamic process in which existing social and political tensions, local and global, are played out, with an uncertain outcome. Change is often about how competing groups come to power (Comaroff & Comaroff, 1992). Consumer researchers have already applied this perspective on class, consumption, and change in places as widespread as Niger and the US, but not to Eastern Europe.

Changes in markets in these two cases heralded changes in existing social class structures and norms of consumption. Arnould describes how marketization in Niger among the Hausa from the 1920s to the 1940s altered class dynamics so that status and wealth became less related to networks of personal relationships and more to market access (Arnould, 1989). This shift also explains relaxation of laws about who would wear which clothes – looking smart could no longer be just for the old elites as a new social group could afford this standard, if not better. Scott examines the growth of the textile industry in the US in the 1840s and the social role of the immigrant Irish women who worked in the factories. These women earned money dressed fashionably. Many married men who were members of the elites, thus challenging the dominance of wealthy New England Puritan women over social class structures and norms of dress (Scott, 2005). The expansion of the textile mills brought with it a new means of entry into the class that makes the rules – through money and fashion. In both cases, changes in the local market structure – the peanut market or the textile mill – did not bring class and consumption, but brought changes to its dynamic. Extending these perspectives to Croatia, this research looks at how privatization brought changes to local class relationships in ways that influence socio-cultural beliefs about consumption.

Although class is generally understood in the literature as dynamic, consumer research in Eastern Europe tends to view it as static (Holt, 1998). Interpretive consumer research seems to approach social stratification in Eastern Europe in a binary of party members/everyone else or urban/rural. These binaries tend to focus on how the state maintained power through defining who was in or out of its favor, or how it maintained its ideology of equality (Belk & Ger, 1994). It overlooks the ways that people gave meanings to subjective positions of class through consumption. There is little interrogation of class, like the pre-war bourgeoisie culture or domestic production of agriculture that has been a continued influence before and after state socialism. It also tends to overlook the urban professional class that emerged in the early 1970s and its influence on class dynamics (Reid & Crowley, 2000; Drazin, 2002; Švab, 2002). Thus, class dynamics are an important but as yet overlooked influence understanding consumers in transformation in Eastern Europe. A specific area of inquiry of this article is how local social dynamics frame socio-cultural beliefs about consumption during transformation.

Consumer artifacts of state socialism, for example urban housing, have been described in the consumer behavior literature as if they were necessarily products of a broken system, "apartment blocs built to house workers looked old before their time as poor quality paint faded" (Belk & Ger, 1994, p. 127). The focus is on how the state structured conditions of consumption rather than how consumers made sense of it. Shortages tend to be the focus in interpretations of consumption during state socialism, "Shopping became a matter of connections, hours in lines, and constant vigilance to find goods that might unexpectedly turn up in stores and markets" (Ger, Belk, & Lascu, 1993, pp. 102–103). Few researchers investigate consumer practices of forging connections, time management, of maintaining some of the customs of pre-war bourgeoisie culture, and even small scale farming – the consumer behaviors of state socialism – and how they might also be a part of socio-cultural beliefs about consumption (Ditchev, 2004).

Consumer research tends to focus on class differences as examples of the ideological contradiction or inefficiency of state socialism, "Cars and televisions available to the nomenclatura, but even factory directors had to wait months or years to get theirs" (Belk & Ger, 1994, p. 127). This article, however, interprets status differences in consumption not as a by-product of the problems of communist ideology or state socialist central planning, but as a taken for granted part of the system in which people lived (Reid & Crowley, 2000).

Thus, what providing guests in your home with green toilet paper from Austria meant during state socialism tells something of what consumer culture was like. It was stratified and display was important. Meanings resonated with pre-war and contemporary notions of culture and class (Drakulić, 1992). There was also a specific value judgment about how people consumed in the context of state socialist consumer culture. Consumption during state socialism was not strictly a by-product of broken economic structure. It was part of socio-cultural beliefs about consumption, within a historical and political moment. The interpretive consumer research approach to transformation consumers – the focus on linear change and the arrival of Western goods as discussed in this section – has left unasked many theoretical questions that are at the center of interpretive consumer research.

RESEARCH METHODS

Research took place through observation of and participation in consumption in multiple sites throughout Zagreb and by composing field notes – observations, thick descriptions, emerging analysis, and reflections – and visual ethnography, during the summers of 2000–2001 and from June 2002 to August 2003. I sought triangulation across sources in Balkan history and sociology scholarship, both cross-cultural and inter-cultural works, and Croatian literature and art. Participation in consumption rituals included co-shopping for women's and men's clothing and shoes, women's cosmetics, in elegant city center stores as well as flea markets at the edge of town, at new malls in the new suburbs, as well the second economy. Analysis and interpretation of data developed as informants repeated themes and stories, especially of surprise and frustration with transformation, across interviews. Emergent design, purposive sampling, depth interviews, and focus groups explored and tested analysis. Member checks brought to light insights from observations and directed the research to important new areas of exploration (Lincoln & Guba 1985; McCracken, 1988; Belk, Wallendorf, & Sherry, 1989).

Depth interviews and focus groups with consumers centered on the socialist and postsocialist consumption experience, consumption aspirations, political influences, the new social structure and social values, and ethnicity. I accessed consumers from different ethnic groups and regions of Croatia. I believe that my access to informants and their stories was greatly enhanced as I told them about my background – my parents are from Croatia. Interviews were conducted in Croatian (I speak Croatian) and English, tape-recorded, and transcribed. A total of 52 informants participated. I accessed them through the snowball method, starting with my network of friends, relatives, and colleagues at the University of Zagreb, Dept. of Marketing. Some interviews were conducted at the home of the informant or the interviewer, some in the work place of the informant, and some in cafes. The duration of each interview was between one and two hours, and I interviewed many informants more than once.

CONSUMPTION IN CROATIA

Most interpretive consumer researcher acknowledges that not only market structures but also socio-cultural beliefs influence consumption (Arnould & Thompson, 2005). At the center of consumer culture in Croatia, therefore, we would expect to find socio-cultural beliefs about consumption. Most consumers would use these norms as a heuristic of how to consume. They might understand consumption as a way to construct a self through the brands they choose (Belk, 1988). These heuristics may form a theory for interpreting consumer behaviors, for example how subjective class positions might influence consumption (Holt, 1998). Even so, the interpretive consumer research on this region tends to focus on structural change (Ger & Belk, 1996; Coulter, Price, & Feick, 2002). There is little interrogation of the complexities the social processes of consumption past or present, or interpretation from a grounded understanding of that world. This section explores how the social and political relationships of state socialism were articulated through consumption, and with what consequences for post-socialist consumer culture. To begin with, this section outlines how consumer culture developed in Yugoslavia.

Consumer culture in Croatia was an essential part of its political, social, and economic system of social equality (Švab, 2002, p. 67). Consumer culture developed in Yugoslavia much earlier than in other socialist states. This was partly due to the unique political situation of Yugoslavia. Josip Broz Tito, President of Yugoslavia, officially parted ways with Stalin in 1948, and by 1950 moved to an independent line from Moscow in its interpretation of Marxism, international politics, and economic organization (Allcock, 2000). Yugoslavia remained outside the Warsaw Pact and started the Non-Aligned Movement in 1955. It maintained trade within the block, but Yugoslavia also entered into trade agreements with Italy and Germany in 1954. The state issued passports and allowed citizens to hold foreign currency, which allowed consumers to work and shop abroad (Szerbhorvath, 2002). The state condoned less formal trade relations. Satellite television exposed consumers to German and Italian broadcasts. Švarceri, or black market traders, sold foreign goods in the local informal exchange networks (Švab, 2002). Border crossing provided high quality imported equipment and consumer goods.

Loans and imported goods also allowed the party to direct production investment from consumer goods to armaments, making Yugoslavia one of the most armed countries in Europe in the Cold War (Lampe, 2000). Although the state did produce some goods, especially agricultural products, domestically, the party justified its investment in armaments and its foreign trade within the rhetoric of the Cold War. It needed armaments to defend its form of national socialism against the threat of takeover by other powers, specifically the Soviet Union, especially after its invasion of neighboring Hungary in 1958 (Lampe, 2000). Open borders facilitated the development of tourism, especially on Croatia's Adriatic Coast, with the influx of foreign tourists and currency, specifically German marks (Rusinow, 1978). Participation in global networks of trade was, therefore, part of the everyday experience of consumption in Yugoslavia as well as part of Yugoslav official ideology and political practice. As an informant in her mid-forties recalled,

> There were some brands that were produced by Croats under the license of their original owners [during state socialism] but some of the brands that were not present on the market were present because they were bought in Austria or in Italy then, and imported by the consumers themselves, so of course the brand concept was known to Croats long before it really opened in 1990 when we actually started our transitioning to capitalism from a different way of working through the socialistic system, so basically there is a general acceptance and knowledge of the of the system of communication.

The Yugoslav government, like many others state socialist governments, promoted a specific consumer ethic. The state publicized its scientifically developed recommendations of consumption per person, usually related to industrial goods and services such as electricity or "basic needs" such as meat, that inevitably were met yearly. Through the rhetoric of quantity and science surrounding consumption, the state sought to demonstrate the historical progress of state socialism over the pre-socialist, peasant lives of most people in Yugoslavia, the high standard of living of socialist workers and the morality of the paternalistic state that provided equally for basic needs (Kligman, 1998). Consumption was a social process in which the ideology articulated by the state met with subjective experiences of class in Croatia to create consumer culture during state socialism. Yugoslav consumer culture was about the morality of material and social equality and socialist progress.

Consumer culture in Eastern Europe during state socialism was also organized to facilitate the involvement of consumers in the production and allocation process (Verdery, 1996). This was most pronounced in Yugoslavia. The participation of self-managing enterprises in the economy was a way to include consumers in decision making. Worker's self management in 1950 was an effort to decentralize economic organization into units of decision making, including management of profits and wages, at the enterprise level rather than through the federal bureaucracy. Yugoslav promotions agencies, for example Oglasni Zavod Hrvatske (OZEHA) (Advertising Bureau of Croatia), started in the 1950s as state organs for promoting official ideology, and by the 1970s were creating national campaigns for global and local clients like Pepsi, American Express, and Podravka (Pecotich et al., 1994). Central planning included less formal mechanisms of decision making as well. For example, the party tended to tacitly condone the unofficial economy, for example firm directors traded state resources privately. Thus, participating in the second economy was less about resistance and more about how people used social capital to consume.

At the same time, Yugoslav consumer culture, even with its focus on progress and equality, had some resonance with the pre-war, bourgeoisie culture, especially when it came to questions of style and self-presentation in public. A woman, a pensioner, who had been a pharmaceuticals professional remembered, "It was the custom, that everyone, maybe they didn't have [money] to buy whatever [things], but to dress, to dress very nicely and fashionably. I could find nice fabrics from Italy and dressmaker would sew a dress from a picture I would bring her from a fashion magazine. Zagreb was very fashionable … during second war and after the war, when socialism came this was little bit vanished, but very soon, maybe 10 years later, again it started in Zagreb."

CLASS IN CROATIA

One of the main criticisms in Croatia by scholars and politicians of Yugoslav economic and political arrangement was usually the centralized control by the League of Communists of Yugoslavia over the Republic's political and economic institutions (Ramet, 1984/1992). This referred to the ways that party power structures were embedded in social and political dynamics. For example, all members of worker's self management decision making units, all directors of banks and managers of foreign investment funds, were party members, and almost all party members participated in economic decision making (Rusinow, 1978). The men at the top of the Party – it was usually men – who made decisions in the Central Committee were peasants who fought for Josip Broz Tito's partizan resistance movement in World War II in the remote hills of southeastern Yugoslavia, especially Montenegro, Bosnia, and mountain regions of Serbia. Tito brought them into leadership positions in the party as a reward for their sacrifices during the war. This group formed the new social elites of Yugoslavia, the red bourgeoisie. Thus, the ruling elite had a specific ethnic and cultural interpretation, not only in Zagreb, but also in the other cities in the north of Yugoslavia: Belgrade and Ljubljana (Lampe, 2000).

The structure of class and political power had a specific influence on consumer culture. An informant described markers of social class during state socialism as, "how easy can you get a job, a better job, if you have connections … the place where you live, the car you're driving, education."

Connections to the elites determined who would get top jobs and apartments. In the immediate post-war period, the elites organized University admission by a student's political orientation or regional origins so that the children of the former bourgeoisie were denied admittance. The party attempted to secure its future political legitimacy by creating a newly educated class that would be friendly to the system and to reverse the pre-war class structure (Lampe, 2000). The party, therefore, organized class as red bourgeoisie and middle class. Within the middle class, it favored workers over the ex-bourgeoisie.

By the 1950s, the party had brought tens of thousands of migrants from rural regions to the cities of Yugoslavia (Ramet, 1984/1992). As one informant put it, "Zagreb was cosmopolitan, continental before the War. After World War II, people from the forest [northeast region of Croatia] came here, and after the last war, people from stones [Hercegovina, southeast] came" (Marko, bank executive, Zagreb, age 65). The party created a new aesthetic for the middle class. For example, the state advocated through popular magazines like *Globus* a sense of aesthetic style, especially for women's dress, that was appropriate for specific rituals and times of day, like afternoon coffee. It supported differentiations in social and political power by suggesting how a woman prominent in the party or a working woman might dress for theater or meeting a friend at home. It blended socialist concepts of modesty and utility with Western trends to demonstrate communism's membership in the pantheon of historical progress (Bartlett, 2004). The consumption ethic approved of fashion within the constructs of socialist good taste.

To ease political and class tensions that came with socialist industrialization and urbanization starting in the late 1940s, for example between the pre-war urban middle class, and the newly urbanized, the party in Yugoslavia and other countries sought to create a specific aesthetic, ritual, luxury, and technology of consumption. One of the first signs of the new classes and consumption culture were state-provided apartments for the newly urbanized villagers (Buchli, 1999). The state promised living quarters to all workers as a way to legitimate its ideology of equality. The state-provided apartments were also a way to promote modern aesthetics and urban styles of living as a break from the agrarian and bourgeoisie past. Creating Yugoslav domesticity allowed the party to establish its ideology within timeless notions of domesticity and fashion. Still, housing was often in short supply and of limited comfort, and party leaders lived in the best apartments in the best locations. Even so, state socialism created a sense of entitlement to equality in living standards.

These homes and clothes were designed by people unfamiliar with urban life, making do in the rush to create a middle class. Aesthetics tended to be a shoddy duplication of pre-war local fashions or styles reported from Paris. Many consumers in Zagreb who had lived there before the war understood housing quality or availability not as a problem of central planning but as an outcome of the lack of cultural know-how of the red bourgeoisie (Bartlett, 2004). However, they also understood the Yugoslav system's political and economic success through consumption experiences they considered "European" or "Western" like use of charge cards, owning cars, and vacation homes, as well as modern domestic goods. Alongside the home and dress, signs of the material progress of communism, equal access to housing and an absence of poverty signified the officially acclaimed moral superiority of state socialism over capitalism. The state promoted middle class consumption just as high as the west, but without the problems of poverty and homelessness as in the capitalist west (Ditchev, 2004; Verdery, 1996).

Decorating the home was a way to show pre-war class and regional origins – city or peasant family – by the books in the shelves, the types of decorations on the walls, or even the cleanliness of the apartment (Drazin, 2002). In the mid-1960s through the late 1970s, after the post-war rebuilding, yet before the recessions of the late 1980s, consumers had it all: state-provided housing, hi-fis from Austria, and clothes from Italy, all guaranteed by the state. An informant described that her husband, because he worked for a state company involved in international trade, traveled to West Germany frequently and brought home the best German appliances that she still uses.

Consumption was a competitive display of middle class status, especially in Yugoslavia, with its access to goods in Italy and Austria (Švab, 2002). Participation in second economy trade networks required a woman to demonstrate she had goods (coffee, cloth, lipstick) or services (i.e., hair-styling, a husband who repaired cars) to trade (Berdahl, 1999). It was also a way to show knowledge of fashion and elegance, of what was good, and when and how to consume it, a knowledge the party lacked. As an informant, a woman manager aged 45 looked back on it, "if you were going to visit someone [at home] and bring them some liquor, you know you brought Chivas Regal, that was considered top style." In Croatia, a Western standard of living was a sign not only that people "beat the system" and its scarcity, but also that local culture was surviving the state's notions of culture, and that they lived in a more Western country than their neighbors to the east (Drakulić, 1992).

Status was not so much about comparison to the elites, but to other people in the middle class. If the party leaders had more, that was fine.

Those who were most dedicated to achieving Marxist goals – the red bourgeoisie and the newly urbanized party officials – received goods equal to their efforts. They had the best apartments, cars, and other luxuries like colored toilet paper (Drakulić, 1992). Because everyone else was theoretically equal, standing out as unequal, as having less, drew suspicion. This drove a specific sort of status competition: if your neighbor had it, you had to have it, too, just to prove you were as good as anyone else (Ivan, MBA student, early 30s, Zagreb). Thus, there was a sense of acquisitiveness and status, funded on specific networks of credit, to project not an image of upward mobility, but an image of membership in a mass middle class (Pecotich et al., 1994).

The young urban professionals who emerged in the affluent early 1970s were a new strata within the middle class. They re-introduced bourgeoisie individualist style to local consumption practices and challenged what it meant to be middle class: not just modern and affluent, but also an individual. They wanted to show, especially through wearing Italian fashion, "that they were different, that they had different needs than you know vast majority, so this need for difference just forced them to save money and to go to Trieste or to Graz and buy something else" (Zagreb woman, 40, marketing director). Goods were a sign of individuality and access in a system in which social equality was the ideal (Švab, 2002). This search for something else had a political dimension in that it sought liberalization of the system, and an aesthetic dimension in stylistic forms of expression, yet it was not a criticism of state socialist ideals of equality.

Within the official rhetoric of class and consumption in Yugoslavia and its participation in global trade, consumption had less to do with shortages or subversion and more to do with identity and status. Consumption as display of membership in a class – the red bourgeoisie (communist elite), the middle class, youth culture, and the working class – was embedded in everyday life. It was not isolated to the elites or to political resistance or subversion by the rest. Its meanings were hidden and collective, related to historical nuances of differences as well as party rhetoric of equality and progress.

The system allowed very little social mobility, except for those who participated in party leadership, or state companies. The most obvious class differences would have been between the communist elite and the rest, but perhaps the most nuanced differences were within this large group. These differences were communicated through consumption oriented to private and public spheres – the home and education or on clothes or cars. Differences in the public sphere referred to an awareness of Western fashion and in the private sphere more towards Western ways of living. Consumption was a way to show individuality within a larger social group. (Bartlett, 2004; Švab, 2002).

Official consumption rhetoric and class stratification was set against a backdrop of urbanization and political change that brought pronounced cultural differences together in Zagreb. Consumption during state socialism was about how demographic shifts of urbanization and political changes of power influenced subjective positions of class. Thus, consumption after state socialism has much less to do with influx of forms and ideologies of Western advertising and consumer culture like brands and class as Croat consumer were participating in global consumer culture throughout state socialism and lived with local class dynamics that influenced consumption. Similar dynamics of class would continue to influence consumption after state socialism.

The next section examines how subjective positions of class and socio-cultural beliefs about consumption influence interpretations of the social processes of privatization. It also explores how marketization – the transfer of much of the socialist state's structuring of the market and consumption through ideologies and practices like equal rights to housing – has influenced interpretations of consumption of goods for public and private display. One of the most striking similarities between socialism and postsocialism in Croatia has been the rule of politically connected elites from rural areas. Often, some of these elites are former communists who have become nationalist capitalists. One of the most important differences between state socialism and postsocialism is the role of the state and its class ideology in organizing consumer culture.

PRIVATIZATION IN CROATIA

One of the main issues of marketization in Croatia was not the introduction of Western advertising and brands. As this article has discussed, Croatia was integrated into the global consumer economy during state socialism, and developed a specific consumer culture and aesthetic. Thus, unlike prior research, the focus of privatization in this article is not the influx of advertising and brands. The focus of understanding privatization asking how, as this informant phrased living with the socialist market situation people are adjusting from "working through the socialistic system" to working through the market system. This raises new questions about how the system has changed and how it influences consumer behaviors.

Yugoslavia, like most countries in Eastern Europe, was already in a recession by the late 1980s. The end of Yugoslavia and the Soviet Union meant the end of established trade relations across Eastern Europe. In Croatia, the war caused serious damage to infrastructure and trade. Tourism, the most profitable economic sector in Croatia, had been in decline in the late 1980s. The war more or less brought travel to Croatia to a halt. War damaged existing infrastructure and the expense of war eliminated the possibility of updating the transportation infrastructure, on which not only tourism but also market distribution relies (Pecotich et al., 1994). Critics in Croatia have pointed out that regardless of the economic problems of independence and war the way privatization was carried out exacerbated the economic problems of the transformation era (Glavaš, 1994).

Many Croats expected market liberalization to facilitate economic growth. However, the ways that it was carried out have still not harnessed that expectation. After independence, migrants from Hercegovina, a region that covers the southeastern border of Croatia and Bosnia that was part of the Republic of Bosnia–Hercegovina during the Yugoslav era, moved to Zagreb, consolidated political power within the Hrvatska Demokratska Zajednica (HDZ) (Croatian Democratic Union), the majority party, and privatized state assets. Privatization was organized to consolidate Croatia's economic assets and natural resources within the control of 200 Croat families, many of whom were from Hercegovina or had party connections (Glavaš, 1994). Asserting national control of resources rather than marketization was a reaction against party control of the economy during state socialism. It happened in other countries as well, but the case of Croatia has been criticized as the least transparent (Verdery, 1996). Informants generally saw privatization similarly to this woman, a media professional in her early 30s: "The war and that period when the, uh, HDZ was in the government and all of privatization, and all that happened with it was horrible."

Privatization in its first phase was an unregulated consolidation of power among a new group of elites. Political connections, especially within people from a rural region, continued to determine social class. The economic problems and the cultural clash that came with privatization and independence were a problem for many Zagreb natives. Many middle class, urban Croats anticipated postsocialism would be a combination of socialist and pre-war norms of consumption, like the emphasis on the home and a "Western" aesthetic, within a market economy. As the prior section described, privatization fell short of many people's expectations for restructuring the economy. Jagoda, an informant in Zagreb, a professional woman in her late 30s, summed up the reaction of many people in Zagreb to the new structures of class and patterns of consumption, "Young girls driving BMW at the University, things like that, that's usually the mafia – the ones responsible for the pillage of Croatia." This resonated with an experience I had. In the second floor bathroom of the Philosophy Faculty of Zagreb University, I read graffiti written in English on the wall of the women's stall, "Hercegovci Go Home." The next section discusses further how privatization re-organized the context of consumption.

The process of privatization ended the state structure and ideology of morality and consumer entitlement. Consumers no longer progress as they did through the state socialist system: education, employment, and housing. The pressures of privatization could be felt in the new education requirements for the job market, for example requiring a University degree, the new uncertainty of the job market, and the new expenses of housing. These pressures of privatization pushed many consumers into poverty, especially those who had been in the working class during state socialism. Many people who had been in the professional middle class – who could capitalize on their connections, education, or homes-managed to maintain or enhance their positions, but still regret the loss of the socialist middle class. A retired professional woman remembered: "We have, now [society] is very layered. Always before there was very, before in the time of socialism, we had a middle class, very big and powerful enough. But these poor people, there weren't many, and now we have very many poor people, the middle class we practically don't have, and we have again one small group of people who are very rich, but that [former] layering has left very suddenly and now after this most recent war."

Subjective positions of class during state socialism have been an important influence on how consumers experience postsocialist transformations. The processes of marketization have influenced the meanings of social capital in Croatia (Bourdieu, 1984). Their positions of maintaining the status quo in Zagreb are challenged by the new structuring of class and consumption. The next section discusses how the new organizations of class have influenced socio-cultural beliefs about consuming for display in public and private spaces.

Many informants ask how the new elite can afford consumption for both the public and private spheres. An informant, a woman in her early 30s, a professional, summed it up, "people from that part of Croatia and Bosnia, they do not invest in some real values like homes, having friends, et cetera, they just want to show how well they've done and how much money they have, but it's totally wrong logic, I don't know, I will never understand it, but whatever." This describes the shifting class relationships in the context of socio-cultural beliefs about consumption. Public display causes many to wonder how others can afford to maintain a home as well – how well they can adhere to "normal" beliefs about consumption. Those who have the social capital to know the "right" way to consume in Zagreb are in conflict with those who have the political and economic capital to assert new definitions of what is "correct."

Most consumers feel the pressures of the privatization of housing, as they now have to buy an apartment in Zagreb. This translates into public display, according to informants, as many people would lie about where they lived and say they lived somewhere better. Because home phone numbers indicate the neighborhood in which one lives, for example 46 is for the exclusive center of town, while 35 is for the less affluent eastern suburbs, giving an acquaintance a mobile number only is a good alibi. For locals, telling someone you are "from Zagreb" has a specific meaning, implying that you are not a newcomer, you are an established person. These are also the people who commented that they missed the old practice of inviting people into your home. Thus, there is a tension between new and old socio-cultural beliefs of consumption and between old and new structures of consumer culture. Just as the new elite has mastered generating envy through their consumption of goods to display in the public sphere, especially of cars, the old middle class is trying to translate its consumption in the private realm into public display.

Consumption during postsocialist transformations is about how social relationships are contested through consumption. For the prior middle class, public display of cultural know-how, of envy provocation, and individualism expressed through consuming for the home or public display continues. Many Zagreb locals, both working class and middle class, see the new elite as a challenge to their norms of consumption from state socialism and their expectations of consumption after marketization. The elites have established their position as consumers of luxury.

The remaining middle class argues for its position as the carriers of morals of social equality bourgeoisie consumption aesthetics. Consumption is also about how the structural changes of privatization – the influx of people from Hercegovina and the consolidation of economic capital among this group – challenge socio-cultural beliefs about consumption and morals about spending. The new economic capital of membership in the political and economic elite challenges the social capital of state socialist, urban middle class consumer culture know-how. Consumers are not responding to the arrival of Western advertising and goods, but to new norms of spending and consumption brought by the cultural, political, and economic dislocations of the privatization and democratization process in Croatia.

DISCUSSION

Most of the consumer behavior research in Eastern Europe tends to overlook how social class relationships frame consumption patterns in transformation. Still, class is acknowledged as a central framework for consumer practices (Holt, 1998). Moreover, Arnould and Scott, in examining market transformations, point to the ways that social class dynamics are part of the ways the consumers contest socio-cultural beliefs about consumption – who can consume what and how (Arnould, 1989; Scott, 2005). This research takes such views of class and transformation and applies them to Eastern Europe. It does so by looking at the transformation as the uncertain outcome of the changing dynamics of consumption patterns, social relationships, and market structures of state socialism. Thus, research in Croatia followed the lead of prior work on class. Rather than following the lines of questioning that have previously been asked in Eastern Europe, it follows the lead of prior historical work on marketization outside of Eastern Europe.

During state socialism, consumer culture was a way to demonstrate Marxist progress and the moral superiority of state socialism through entitlement to a high standard of living for the proletariat. Class differences were only a manifestation of this notion of progress: most people were equal, while those who were most devoted to Marxism were so rewarded. Consumption was a way to show the political power of Yugoslavia as a state that managed to be independent, yet maintain ties to both Soviet and market economies. Consumer culture during state socialism was about how consumers expressed their subjective class positions, responded to envy and expressed notions of cultural know-how of the west. Consumption for the domestic sphere fit in with notions of socialist domesticity, but also with prewar cultural understandings of consuming for the home as appropriate. Socialist consumption ideology, for example providing housing, sought to fit in with local norms of consumption and socio-cultural beliefs about consumption.

Structural and cultural changes of postsocialism have challenged these norms about consumption, especially as they relate to the domestic sphere. New patterns of consuming for the public display of the private space are likely to emerge from the transformation. In the context of transformation, it would allow the continued articulation of cultural values about the home and socio-cultural beliefs about the domestic space as a sphere of investment within the context of class tensions. Postsocialist consumer culture is less about adjusting to westernization or global consumer culture. It is more about adjusting the spheres in which competitive consumption is played out. This takes place as privatization and democratization alters the structures of consumer culture. It introduces new structures of power to define consumption norms, in this case the new elites, who are kept on the outside, but work from the center of power. Middle class consumers make sense of these changes through their historical experiences, expectations of the future, and socio-cultural beliefs about consumption.

Other postsocialist countries in the region experienced similar structures of consumption during state socialism, like the morality and entitlement of equality. Within the socialist middle class in East Germany, showing western brands was a way of communicating subjective positions of social and economic capital – for example, access to these goods through relatives in western Germany (Berdahl, 1999). Processes of transformation in other countries, for example Bulgaria, have not brought the expected outcomes. Many consumers in Eastern Europe are similarly negotiating marketization with many of the same skills they used as consumers in their everyday experiences of state socialism (Creed, 1998). Even though this article provides some pointed questions to understanding postsocialist consumption – looking at its roots in the consumer culture of state socialism and pre-war culture, looking for continuity with the past, exploring local social class relationships, taking apart the processes of marketization – this research has a broader implication for consumer behavior scholarship.

This research looked for the roots of contemporary consumption practices and market structures in Eastern Europe in everyday experiences of consumption during state socialism, socio-cultural beliefs about consumption, and state policy and rhetoric of consumption. Moving beyond Cold War constructs of planned and market opened a window on what is happening from the point of view of locals and their notions of class and socio-cultural beliefs about consumption. Thus, the roots of postsocialist consumer behavior lie in state socialist consumer culture. Marketization is not a natural outgrowth of this system or a sign of the failure of planned economies and their replacement by a better system. Its future success or failure is not a reflection of the totalizing and empty or liberating nature of market globalization. As the dashed hopes of many consumers describe, marketization has been mostly a national process of addressing local social, cultural, and political relationships of state socialism. It was the structures and processes of state socialist consumer culture that laid the groundwork for consumer culture after state socialism. Thus, consumer behavior in the region is much more the debris of state socialism than a forecast of the future.

ACKNOWLEDGMENT

Research for this article was supported in part by a grant from the International Research & Exchanges Board (IREX) with funds provided by the National Endowment for the Humanities, the United States Department of State, which administers the Title VIII Program, and the IREX Scholar Support Fund. None of these organizations is responsible for the views expressed.

REFERENCES

Allcock, J. (2000). *Explaining Yugoslavia.* New York: Columbia University Press.

Arnould, E. (1989). Toward a broadened theory of preference formation and the diffusion of innovations: Cases from Zinder Province, Niger Republic. *Journal of Consumer Research, 16*(September), 239–267.

Arnould, E., & Thompson, C. (2005). Consumer culture theory: Twenty years of research. *Journal of Consumer Research, 31*(March), 868–882.

Bartlett, D. (2004). Let them wear beige: The petit-bourgeois world of official socialist dress. *Fashion Theory, 8*(2), 127–164.

Belk, R. (1988). Possessions and the extended self. *Journal of Consumer Research, 15* (September), 139–168.

Belk, R., & Ger, G. (1994). Problems of marketization in Romania and Turkey: Consumption in marketizing economies. In: C. J. Shultz II, R. Belk & G. Ger (Eds), *Research in consumer behavior* (Vol. 7, pp. 123–155). Greenwich, CT: JAI Press.

Belk, R. W., Wallendorf, M., & Sherry, J. F., Jr. (1989). The sacred and the profane in consumer behavior: Theodicy on the odyssey. *Journal of Consumer Research, 16*(June), 1–38.

Berdahl, D. (1999). *Where the world ended: Re-unification and identity in the German borderland.* Berkeley: University of California Press.

Bourdieu, P. (1984). *Distinction: A social critique of the judgment of taste.* In: R. Nice (Trans.). Cambridge: Harvard University Press.

Buchli, V. (1999). *An archaeology of socialism.* Berg: Oxford and New York.

Comaroff, J., & Comaroff, J. (1992). *Ethnography and the historical imagination.* Oxford: Westview Press.

Coulter, R. A., Price, L. L., & Feick, L. (2003). Rethinking the origins of involvement and brand commitment: insights from postsocialist Central Europe. *Journal of Consumer Research, 30*(September), 151–169.

Coulter, R. A., Price, L. L., & Feick, L. F. (2002). Changing faces: Cosmetics opinion leadership among women in the new Hungary. *European Journal of Marketing, 36*(11/12), 1287–1308.

Creed, G. W. (1998). *Domesticating revolution: From socialist reform to ambivalent transition in a Bulgarian village.* University Park, Pennsylvania: The Pennsylvania State University Press.

Crockett, D., & Wallendorf, M. (2004). The role of normative political ideology in consumer behavior. *Journal of Consumer Research, 31*(December), 511–528.

Ditchev, I. (2004). The forge of consumers. An essay on communist desire. In: B. Groys (Ed.), *The post-communist condition*. Karlsruhe: ZKM.

Drakulić, S. (1992). *How we survived communism and even laughed*. New York: Harper-Perennial.

Drazin, A. (2002). Chasing moths: Cleanliness, intimacy, and progress in Romania. In: R. Manel & C. Humphrey (Eds), *Markets and moralities: Ethnographies of postsocialism*. Oxford: Berg.

Ger, G., & Belk, R. W. (1996). I'd like to buy the world a coke: Consumptionscapes of the "Less affluent world". *Journal of Consumer Policy*, *19*, 271–304.

Ger, G., Belk, R. W., & Lascu, D. (1993). The development of consumer desire in marketizing and developing economies: The cases of Romania and Turkey. In: L. McAlister & M. Rothschild (Eds), *Advances in consumer research* (Vol. 20, pp. 103–107). Provo, UT: Association for Consumer Research.

Glavaš, D. (1994). The roots of Croatian extremism. *Mediterranean Quarterly*, *5*(Spring (2)), 37–50.

Holt, D. B. (1998). Does cultural capital structure American consumption? *Journal of Consumer Research*, *25*(June), 1–25.

Kligman, G. (1998). *The politics of duplicity: Controlling reproduction in Ceausescu's Romania*. Berkeley: University of California Press.

Lampe, J. R. (2000). *Yugoslavia as history: Twice there was a country*. Cambridge: Cambridge University Press.

Lincoln, Y. S., & Guba, E. G. (1985). *Naturalistic inquiry*. Beverly Hills, CA: Sage.

McCracken, G. (1988). *The long interview*. Newbury Park, CA: Sage Publications.

Pecotich, A., Renko, N., & Shultz, C. J. (1994). Yugoslav disintegration, war, and consumption in Croatia. *Research in Consumer Behavior*, *7*, 1–27.

Ramet, S. P. (1984/1992). *Nationalism and federalism in Yugoslavia, 1962–1991* (2nd ed.). Bloomington and Indianapolis: Indiana University Press.

Reid, S. E., & Crowley, D. (Eds) (2000). *Style and socialism: Modernity and material culture in post-war eastern Europe*. Oxford, UK: Berg.

Rusinow, D. I. (1978). *The Yugoslav experiment 1948–1974*. Berkeley, CA: University of California Press.

Scott, L. M. (2005). *Fresh lipstick: redressing feminism and fashion*. New York: Palgrave Macmillan.

Švab, A. (2002). Consuming western image of well-being – Shopping tourism in socialist Slovenia. *Cultural Studies*, *16*(1), 63–97.

Szerbhorvath, G. (2002). Suffering and legitimacy. *Cultural Studies*, *1*(16), 127–144.

Verdery, K. (1996). *What was socialism and what comes next?* Princeton, NJ: Princeton University Press.

IDENTITY

HAPPINESS, CONSUMPTION, AND BEING

Carolyn Costley, Lorraine Friend, Emily Meese, Carl Ebbers and Li-Jen Wang

This chapter presents a photo-essay of happiness. Participants provided photographs of what happiness means to them. Through phenomenological interviews and thematic analyses of both the photos and the interviews, we saw two major themes: personal relationships and nature. Close relationships and nature both contributed to the women's sense of being themselves and made them happy. Consumption played an instrumental role. The women did not consume to be happy, but consumption was part of their relationships with others. Consumption also manifest as detrimental to happiness in their perceptions of its damage to nature. Thus, consumption can contribute favorably to happiness, but consumers need to know more about its unhappy consequences.

HAPPINESS IN A CONSUMER CULTURE

Does having things make people happy; does buying, consuming, or giving bring happiness? In an increasingly materialistic era, it seems that people might believe so. Despite our consumption culture, research tells us that the desire for material possessions relates more to unhappiness than to happiness (Belk, 1985; Burroughs & Rindfleisch, 2002; Csikszentmihalyi, 2000;

Consumer Culture Theory
Research in Consumer Behavior, Volume 11, 209–240

ISSN: 0885-2111/doi:10.1016/S0885-2111(06)11010-8

La Barbera & Gürhan, 1997; Mick, 1996; Richins, 1987; Sirgy et al., 1998). Economists find that subjective well-being increases, then levels off as national levels of discretionary income increase (Csikszentmihalyi, 1999; Diener, 2000; Meyers, 2000). Furthermore, many economists cite correspondence between happiness and relative income (Blanchflower & Oswald, 2004; Solnick & Hemenway, 1998; Stutzer, 2003) to explain the stagnation of average happiness despite rises in national incomes. Increasing one person's income relative to others decreases the others' happiness so that pursuing money to achieve happiness becomes a zero-sum affair; average national happiness does not change (Lee, 2006).

Although materialism – as the pursuit of more material things – may not enhance average happiness, few studies have tried to understand how consumption may contribute to happiness at an individual level. People do report engaging in consumption activities to achieve happiness. They go clubbing, go out for entertainment, shop, go to movies, drink alcohol, and take illegal drugs specifically to increase their happiness (Tkach & Lyubomirsky, 2006). The dynamics of consuming and happiness are likely to be complex. Having a fun day out shopping with friends, finding pleasure in giving gifts, and stressing over a maxed out credit card are likely to affect individual subjective well-being (e.g., happiness) in different and complex ways. We wondered whether there could be some affirmative links between consumption activities – rather than the quantity of goods or money acquired – and individual happiness.

Our work explores the dynamics of consumption and happiness from the perspectives of individuals. We studied what people say makes them happy to find out what role consumption might play in their subjective well-being. Scholars commonly use "happiness" and "subjective well-being" synonymously. Happiness is an experience of positive affect and life satisfaction – good feelings that one wants to maintain (Layard, 2005). We asked people to tell us about what they think makes them happy. We did not ask about consumption, but we searched their photos and interviews for evidence of consumption in their happiness. This is part of our effort to answer the call to do relevant research on big picture questions about consumption in people's lives.

METHOD

This research consisted of auto-photography and phenomenological interviews. It combined Ziller's (1990) and Heisley and Levy's (1991) uses of photography as a data collection medium. Descriptions are deepened and stories embellished when participants take pictures of a phenomenon

(Ziller, 1990) and researchers use photos to elicit information in interviews (Heisley & Levy, 1991). Photographs can express the artistic, emotional, and or experiential aspects of a phenomenon (Harper, 2000) and humanize the participants (Belk, 1998) in ways that words alone cannot. Moreover, this collaborative process allows participants to help interpret and represent the phenomenon (Belk, 1998) as well as improves the interview's flow and depth (Heisley & Levy, 1991).

Over two weeks, 10 participants snapped or collected photographs representing "what makes you happy or unhappy in your life?" We set no limits on the number of photographs, allowing participants to bring as many as seemed right for them. We interviewed each participant about her photos in relation to the happiness theme. We first asked them to "tell us about" each picture (Thompson, Locander, & Pollio, 1989; van Manen, 1997) and then compose a note or caption that best described the photo (Goldberg, 1985) in terms of happiness. This allowed the participants to guide the interview and interpretations we drew from the photos.

We sought volunteers with interests in photography through photography clubs and the local community, university, and polytechnic courses. Ultimately, 10 women between the ages of 20 and 30 participated. Homogeneity of gender and age alleviated problems with anticipated gender and age differences and was intended to ease the possible stress of discussing this personal topic with the 20-something woman interviewer. In this chapter, we report analyses based on data from four women.

THE PARTICIPANTS

The four women ranged in age from 20 to 25. Three were visiting New Zealand from other countries. Two of them were studying at the university. Just one of the four was employed full time. They all expressed interests in photography and willingness to talk about what makes them happy.

"Sally" is 21 years old and from Germany. She is well traveled and had been studying in New Zealand for about four months. Sally is passionate about nature. She hates to see animals and nature adversely affected by humans. Although she does not like crowds of people – over population, as she put it – she likes to feel connected with people and she likes to feel that people understand her. Sally was our most prolific photographer. She brought 50 photos to the interview, some of which came from her collection of photos she had taken during her travels and some taken specifically for this project.

"Di" is 20 years old and from China. She came to live and study in New Zealand – planning to stay 3–4 years, but had been in the country only two months so far. She notes that everything is new and different compared to China. Bearing witness to that, her 12 photos contained themes of adjusting to life in New Zealand.

"Kay" is 25 years old, originally from New Zealand, and works full time in a customer service and administration role. She feels she is in a settled stage of life and is looking to buy her own home soon. She enjoys nature and spending time with friends and family. Kay took 25 photos. Her happiness themes revolved around solving problems and her unhappiness themes around inabilities to see solutions.

"Hannah" is 23 years old, originally from Australia, and has a degree in psychology. She describes herself as keen on self-expression and creativity. She lived and worked in Sydney for several years and is now living with family in New Zealand, having come for some time out. She is searching for meaning in her life and her 38 photos reflect this. Through her photos, she conveyed that lack of meaning and feeling empty makes her unhappy and finding meaning makes her happy. Feeling connected with the world around her makes her happy; feeling isolated makes her unhappy.

After the interviews and transcriptions, three researchers analyzed the photos and stories for common themes and evidence of consumption associated with being happy or unhappy. The following photo-essay illustrates what we found. Hear the participants' words as they talk about their photos.

HAPPINESS IN THE WOMEN'S PHOTOS

Two main themes emerged from the women's photos and discussions. They spoke of their happiness in relation to personal relationships and nature. We have organized their photographs and their words into these two themes.

Relationships

For these young women, happiness comes from close connections with family, friends, and boyfriends. These connections are deeper than day-to-day acquaintances. They involve deep bonds where they understand, support, and care for each other. They share their feelings, and thoughts, and they experience good, fun, and peaceful times together. They play, relax, and enjoy each other. Comfort in these relationships allows them to be free to be themselves. At the same time, they rely on these relationships to give them senses of self and being in the world because of connections to family, friends, and social communities. They feel unhappy when they become disconnected or isolated from their close friends and family.

Photo 1 represents Hannah's feelings of happiness in having a close relationship. She explains:

> It's funny, actually. Even though I'm taking the photo, it's almost as if she is just looking at me. I really like her expression. We are very close. We have an understanding and have the same type of ideas – like we want to go traveling and do all this stuff .... (Hannah)

Similarly, Di brought a picture of one of her close friends from China to show her happiness in having this relationship (Photo 2). Her comments also show the emotional elements in happiness. She notes,

> This young woman is one of my best friends. We always chatted and laughed a lot when together. ... I miss her. The picture reminds me of those memories with her. It cheers me up. (Di)

Like Hannah and Di, Sally also expresses the importance of having friends to be happy in life (Photo 3).

> This reminds me of my trip [to the Coromandel] and the importance friends actually have on me. … because when I came … to New Zealand, I didn't know anybody … so I really had to make friends. And, I got to know people who kind of understand me … and … could support me here. Yeah, that's what it's actually all about … to meet people everywhere around the world … [and to] have international friends. (Sally)

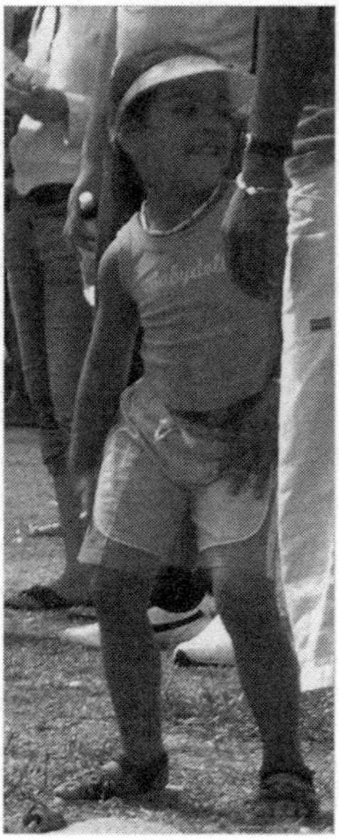

As Sally continues about friends, she delivers insights into the connections between intimate relationships, freedom of being, and individual happiness (Photo 4).

> [It's important to have friends where I can] just let myself go, and be myself basically – like this kid dancing. Because, I think you play different roles in society, and you are never completely yourself, except around those special people, like family and maybe two or three friends. And, that's what I really appreciate and what I'm missing in New Zealand because I don't have those people here. I realize how important it actually is that you have people that know you ... that can actually see when I'm feeling bad, and ask some questions and show their concern. (Sally)

Hannah depicts themes of both relationships and nature when she says that this picture (Photo 5) represents:

> very simply, that going for a walk with the family is satisfying. ... This is actually my sister and she is holding her baby ... and the others are my nieces. We are actually just going for a walk, being in the nature .... It's quite fun having kids in nature. ... Being around them and getting to know them .... Yeah, just the interaction. They make me happy. (Hannah)

All four of these young women took pictures that represented how being lonely and isolated from close friends and family made them feel unhappy. Hannah specifically painted a copy of the famous painting "The Scream" and then photographed it out of focus to illustrate her feelings of unhappiness (Photo 6). She explained:

> This is actually negative, an unhappy photo. It really means something to me. It describes a lot of mood and emotion – like depression and anxiety. It's the feeling of being alienated from what is going on ... the stress of being cut off ... [being disconnected], and not getting anywhere. You [don't or] can't communicate. It's all too much and you can't cope with that feeling – the anxiety. (Hannah)

Like Hannah, Sally experiences how being disconnected – when she chooses not to be on her own – feels lonely and isolating, making her feel unhappy (Photo 7).

> I went on a class trip and all my friends were drinking all day. I really felt lonely, because like all my friends were drunk and I couldn't really talk to them properly. (Sally)

Sally contrasted the unhappy feelings of loneliness in a group with good feelings associated with choosing to be alone in nature.

But, I really like being by myself, especially in nature. … If you are free to choose, and for instance, decide to watch the sea for a couple of hours, I really love that. (Sally)

Nature

Nature featured as a main theme of happiness for all these young women. The women in this study seemed to find freedom in the natural environment, which allowed them to balance the restrictions and stresses of relationships. Nature grounds them. It gives them a sense of space and freedom for being and becoming in the world. See Photo 8.

I really love the sea … probably because … if you look at the horizon … it's so far away. You don't see anything. [There's] … this small movement. But apart from that, nothing. It's just freedom. It just represents … I don't know … how big the world actually is … You can't see the end … You can dream … [about] what's on the other side …. It gives so much space for your thoughts … Yeah.

And, it's the sound of the sea … It calms me down. You know, the sun, the sea, the birds, the fresh air, and like the silence … just the whole environment actually makes me happy and relaxed. I forget all my problems – well not all my problems, just all my thoughts. It just cleans up everything … And I have energy to proceed. I really love it. (Sally)

The spiritual and natural aspects of being in the environment make Kay happy (Photo 9).

> [After arriving at this cabin late Friday night], we got up in the morning and looked outside. I saw this rainbow and this really fantastic place .... You can see in the background, there are these really, I would say, quite spiritual hills. They've got [native] vegetation all over them. And, because it's so near the mountains – Tongariro National Park – the air is really crisp. It's really refreshing air .... And of course, being the middle of winter, it was really pleasant .... There was snow just a few kilometers south .... It was very quiet. ... It was just a really great way of getting up. And the rainbow just kind of topped it off. I thought, "Wow, this is a really cool place. This is really cool." (Kay)

After talking about nature in many of her photos, Sally summarized with this one (Photo 10).

> [This] ... was just a point ... where we sat down and just enjoyed the view. It is the kind of nature I really appreciate ... the hills, the grass ... the small river, and the sea.... (Sally)

Hannah took Photo 11 in the Chinese Scholars' garden at Hamilton Gardens, the public garden in Hamilton, New Zealand. Her explanation of this photo resonates with themes of balance. She speaks of inner balance derived from nature as well as happiness experienced when human impositions complement nature and confirm balance. About this photo, she said:

> This is very peaceful ... the symmetry, the reflection in the water .... This is the most important thing [being represented here]. It's not just the peacefulness; it's the beauty of it. It complements nature; it adds to it. I like the idea of man-made things complementing nature, rather than disregarding nature.
>
> And it's ... about appreciating another culture and their way of life – the ideas about living in harmony and being in peace. I found this part of the garden felt like that. When I look at this picture, it makes me feel at peace. (Hannah)

Di, who came to New Zealand from China, seemed to associate nature with happiness partly because nature is precious and rare in her home country (Photo 12).

> I love the color, the blue color; I love New Zealand's blue skies and clouds. ... The environment can easily delight me, because I never see this clean environment in China – never. (Di)

CONSUMPTION IN THE WOMEN'S PHOTOS

The women and their photos did not express consumption as central to what makes them happy, but consumption materialized in two secondary roles, which we refer to as destruction and maintenance. Consumption creates conditions that disrupt and destroy nature and thus, make these women unhappy. They observed that, globally, mass consumption damages nature and they said this makes them personally unhappy. We labeled this a secondary role, even though they connected it directly with their personal unhappiness, because they primarily spoke of anonymous others' consumption, not of their own. From their photos and discussion, we also learned that consumption is part of these women's relationship maintenance activities – part of their relationships with others, which make them happy.

Consumption, Destruction, and Unhappiness

Consumption first appears in the women's expressions of distress at mass consumption's destructive consequences to nature. They spoke of how consumption adversely affects nature, particularly in developed countries, and they expressed unhappiness. They connected unhappy feelings and unhappy thoughts with unsightly evidence of consumption. Sally brought this photograph of a car import site viewed from a plane over Auckland, New Zealand (Photo 13).

> I was just shocked to see this. Because for me a car is really representing the destroying, the destruction of nature. [It is] the way people are using cars and exploit the technology without thinking about nature and the consequences. (Sally)

Sally provided the unhappy image in Photo 14 from her collection of travel photos.

> In big cities [in Europe] the traffic is crazy … it's dirty air. You can smell it, and feel it as well. I haven't smelled it in New Zealand yet – not even in Auckland. [And] it's so noisy. I find it disgusting. I hate big cities. (Sally)

Although it is not their own consumption per se that makes them unhappy, but irresponsible consumption by masses of anonymous others, they admitted their membership in the mass. They expressed some guilt at driving their cars, for instance, but often not enough to change their behaviors.

> I've got a car. I'm part of humans. I'm not saying that I'm not like that. I'm just saying the mass is what makes me unhappy. I can't change; I need my car. … I'm taking part in destroying nature. I'm pretty depressed – well more frustrated – that I'm actually part of this whole thing. (Sally)

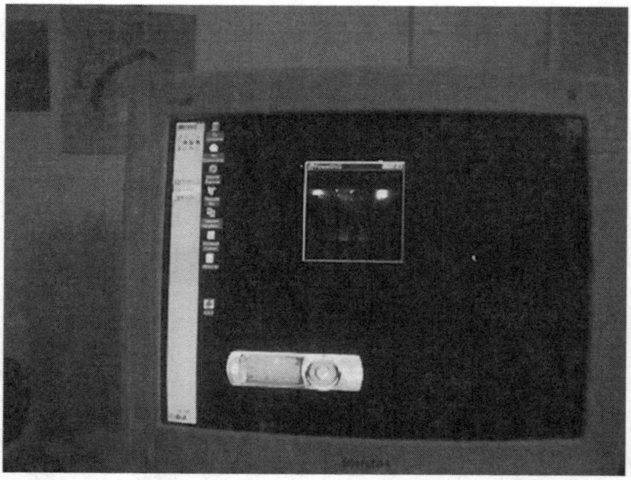

Kay tries to avoid damaging the environment (Photo 15).

> One of the major reasons why I don't update my computer is the environment. I just hate the fact that when you upgrade a computer, you've got all these components that people aren't going to want anymore. This is one of the major issues with society today that technology is improving so fast that you can't keep on top of it; And, who is going to use the old stuff? What happens to the old stuff? … [It] must be almost impossible to pull all the components apart so you can actually reuse those resources and it must be so expensive. Someone's got to come up with a solution to that. (Kay)

Sally brought Photo 16 to show consumption's impact on the environment.

> This has been there for years. There's no color on it anymore and there's a lot of moss on it. ... It's just crazy. This expresses the whole thing – the negative impact of mass consumption on society. The contamination, the destruction, the loss of color, being squashed, and covering over of the problem. (Sally)

Hannah attributed negative consequences to the instant gratification that comes from mass consumption (Photo 17).

> With the supermarket, there is just this ultra-convenience life-style: open seven days, 24 hours, and often a crowded environment. You can just buy anything anytime and people get frustrated when they have to wait. Your ego just wants the entire world, rather than putting yourself in perspective. We believe we are entitled to things now. And, these are the things ... that don't really buy happiness, but instant gratification. They are not really a good investment. (Hannah)

Consumption, Maintenance, and Happiness

Consumption emerged as part of relationships with others. These women did not directly speak about consumption making them happy. However, their photos and talk about their relationships incorporated consumption activities in relationship activities. It appears that consuming together – especially food – maintains personal connectedness. Photo 18 and the corresponding interview discussion illustrate how consumption is part of relationships, but not necessarily the most important part of Sally's experience.

This photo symbolizes how I like sitting in cafés with friends and just drinking coffee and eating the chocolate that comes along with it. … [Is it a brand?] Yeah, it is, but I don't know which one it is. My roommate gave that cup of coffee to me. It was pretty expensive … He is one of those people who just enjoys consuming good coffee and stuff. But I don't know what it was. He prepared it at home. But, it looks nice. It looks like it's from a café. That is why I took the picture. (Sally)

Di talked about how she shops, cooks, and eats with her Chinese friends in New Zealand to connect with both friends and culture. She illustrated this with Photo 19.

> When I came here [to New Zealand], I have a single room. I found that too lonely. Sometimes, just nobody call me, no one ask me to go out, and I got bored. My Chinese friends were very friendly and asked me out. We cook a lot … because we miss our Chinese food. We just tell our favorite foods … [and then] go to different supermarkets to pick up the … most cheap things. It takes a long time to cook. But the process is fun. We just make jokes and laugh. I didn't find cooking so fun when I was in China. Here I find it very fun. (Di)

Relatively few photos connected material goods with happiness and those that did also connected them with interpersonal relationships. For Sally, possessions show a connection between friends (Photo 20).

> This picture is symbolizing friends or friendship. These are the same people, actually [from the shadow picture (Photo 3)]. We just at that moment … realized we were all wearing the same shoes basically – the same style (laughing). It shows this connectivity among us. (Sally)

Only one woman, Kay, expressed happiness in certain specific purchases and possessions – a new handbag, a new duvet, and a favorite scarf. Even for Kay, it is not the possessions alone that bring happiness. She linked her happiness in having these things with the conversations they provoke with others. See her pink purse in Photo 21.

> I'm just really happy with … this purse. I thought it was so cute. I never have really been a pink person until recently, so I was quite proud of the fact that it was pink. And, it makes life easier. I have less clutter in my life now. It's about half the size of the one I used to have. And, just the fact that it was so affordable. Like … you just wouldn't expect bags to be as cheap as it was. It's kind of a conversational starter. They're like, "Oh, where did you get that from?" (Kay)

Di expresses a similar yet somewhat weaker consumption theme when she talks about her pleasure in the act of going shopping – both on her own and with friends. Like Kay, she likes to receive compliments on what she buys. See Photo 22.

> Well, I love shopping. I just love shopping. I like looking around the place … I spend lots of money shopping. That's not good. … I sometimes feel guilty (laughing). But I still enjoy browsing these things, especially clothes – on my own [and] with friends sometimes. It's more fun to shop with another friend because you can talk, "Oh, it's cute! I like that." Yeah, when I *buy* clothes, that makes me happy; that [is] another type of happiness. When somebody told me the top I wear today is pretty, I will be happy. (Di)

In addition to bonding with others during shopping or conversing about possessions, these women experience happiness in gifts, given and received. Giving and receiving gifts allows these women to create, manage, and sustain their relationships. Sally indicates that it is not the giving that is important to her happiness but the evidence of a close bond represented in the giver's choice of gift. The floral bouquet in Photo 23 shows

> this connection between us … our good relationship. I just think that flowers can mean and express so much. Maybe it's a female thing, I don't know. Just the colors, like it's nature, just beautiful and it's a nice gesture. [They were sent for no particular reason, just] to show that I mean a lot to him. And these are my [favorite]; I just love these flowers the most. And the color, like purple and yellow are just complementary colors. And I like most complementary colors. And, yeah, that's probably because that person really knows me. He just knows the flowers I really love. It showed me that this person really stands behind me. I always get [and give] small presents during the year. … It's not like I get [or give] huge presents. … [It is just showing] this connection between us. (Sally)

Although gift giving is an important way to manage relationships, Kay corroborates Sally's message that it is more than the gift itself that is important. The processes of deciding on, shopping, and giving the gift are also important in their experiences of happiness. Kay tells a story about Photo 24.

> This is my friend and the tiger I gave to him as a present [for upgrading my computer] … He gave me all the parts for free. And you know, he spent quite a number of hours setting it all up … so I thought I should get him a gift. No one had ever given him soft toys before. They saw him as being too tough. So I thought, "Well, that's going to be perfect …" Anyways, I went shopping in my lunch break and found this cute tiger, like the size of a newborn baby – quite a huggable size … fluffy ears and stuff. He received it in the mail at his work. And he sent me a text message when he got it …. I can just imagine him smiling away when he was texting me. … Then he sent me this pxt [Photo 24]. It was this photo introducing Charlie the tiger! Just the look on his face is absolute classic. … I was just smiling away thinking that's awesome. I have this thing that I really wanna give people gifts that they're gonna care about. (Kay)

Of Sally's 50 pictures, consuming was the main reason for taking only a few. In Photo 25, she linked her experiences of enjoying the concert atmosphere and the music to having fun. Although she was with others at the event, consuming this experience had more to do with inner freedom – like these women found in nature – than with relationships with the others present.

> It was just an amazing atmosphere in there …. It was a German singer – quite popular …. It's a huge stadium, like the biggest in Germany and it was completely sold [out] ….

He's sold so many CD's .... His songs ... are pretty thoughtful and he is singing about family and those kinds of things. And, I don't know it's just happiness as well. In a different way, because it's not nature at all .... But, it's just a different way to get rid of reality for a couple of hours .... It's not escape, because it's not like I've got so many problems that I really have to escape or anything. It's more ... I don't know, experiencing something different for a couple of hours .... It was the atmosphere. Like, so many people are happy that they are just enjoying their time. [You went with your parents and your boyfriend?] Yeah, although I didn't really have a lot to do with them .... We were actually more focused on the concert .... It was not like a social thing, it was more just everybody was just enjoying the time. (Sally)

Sally makes a point about money in general, which corresponds remarkably well with the literature on income and happiness. She brought Photo 26 and explained how a certain lifestyle can make you happy or unhappy.

Being upper middle class, I think that's really good. It can really make you happy. ... You need a certain amount of money to make you happy. For instance, that's why I had the chance to come to New Zealand, and can afford my car. I think in Germany you need a certain standard to be happy, to have convenience, and to actually function in society without bothering or being worried about lacking in money. But, I think as soon as you're upper class, I don't think it makes you really happy. (Sally)

Di also talked about lifestyle and social norms and extended Sally's broad points. Di talks about how she sees New Zealanders being happy compared to the Chinese because, "they have obtained 'American dream'." See Photo 27.

> New Zealanders just don't worry about pressure; they have cars, big houses, and cats. But in China, life is more complicated and pressured. We have tied relationships with people; we have peer pressure [to achieve]. We have to care too much, too much, about how other people treat us. But here, I'm free. (Di)

After talking about nature in relation to Photo 28, Hannah summarized her big picture on happiness.

> You can get lost in the aspects of contemporary culture and it's so nice to look at nature; it's so superior, you know. I feel sad when I watch people who are caught up in [the consumption] world. … They are being lied to about what makes them happy; … lies that if you look a certain way, it will make you happy. I just think it is important that people should be more critical of that sort of thing. (Hannah)

DISCUSSION

Happiness Themes

Relationships and nature emerged as the main two themes in happiness. By taking photographs, discussing, and labeling their photos, the women in this study helped identify these themes. They came from four different countries and shared common experiences of happiness in personal relationships and in nature. They did not experience happiness in just any relationship, but in close ones, which encompassed mutual understanding, caring, and support. In this kind of relationship, they found freedom to be themselves. This closely matches the happiness literature, which reports that happiness depends primarily on the quality of relationships (Kahneman, Krueger, Schkade, Schwarz, & Stone, 2004; Layard, 2005). However, while the happiness literature speaks of ones relational situation (married, divorced, etc.) our data speak of relational experiences and processes. These women described their happiness in being with their family and friends, not merely the fact that they have family and friends.

Relationships can be constraining and stressful (Lane, 2000; Schwartz, 2004; Suh & Oishi, 2002) and these women seemed to turn to nature for balance; in nature, they refresh their freedom to be themselves and be happy. They spoke about feeling calm, peaceful, clean, and refreshed in nature. It sounded almost meditative and seemed to describe the absence of stress as an experience of happiness. This is consistent with the common definition of happiness as including absence of negative emotional experience (Suh & Oishi, 2002). This sort of happiness illustrates contentment, which is just as happy but less aroused than joyful feelings of happiness (Layard, 2005).

The women also experience frustration and unhappiness at environmental destruction, which disrupts the balancing effect of nature in their lives. Frustration, anxiety, and loss of connection in this spoiled space contaminate and threaten their identities (Goffman, 1971). The idea of dirt, smell, noise, and congestion of the city pollutes their personal space and being. Hectic lifestyles, excessive choice (Schwartz, 2004), and clutter of the marketplace (Strasser, 1999) have ruined the environment and their ways of being. Their message suggests that caring for nature may be relevant to everyone's long-term well-being.

> The *traffic is crazy* … it's *dirty* air. You can *smell* it, and *feel* it as well. I haven't smelled it in New Zealand yet – not even in Auckland. [And] it's so *noisy*." … "[O]pen seven days, 24 h, and often a *crowded* environment. You can just *buy anything anytime* and people get *frustrated* when they have to wait." … "This is one of the *major issues with society today that technology is improving so fast that you can't keep on top of it*; And, who is going to use the old stuff? *What happens to the old stuff?*" … "This has been there for years. There's *no color* on it anymore and there's a *lot of moss* on it. … It's just crazy. This *expresses the whole thing* – the *negative impact* of mass consumption on society. The *contamination*, the *destruction*, the *loss of color, being squashed, and covering over* of the problem.

Despite the fact that relationships between environmental changes, climate, and happiness are beginning to emerge in the happiness literature (Rehdanz & Maddison, 2003), the New Zealand context may be partly accountable for the nature theme. We consider the possibility that in this place of natural beauty and outdoor activities, nature is how these women expressed freedom. In discussing their photos, they tell us about their senses of peace and personal freedom that they experienced in nature. The literature reports that peace and freedom link to happiness (Layard, 2005). However, the literature refers to governments that allow personal freedoms and are not at war while our women speak of a more personal individual freedom. Their experiences of happiness suggest that freedom to be who they are rather than construct special identities makes them happy.

Freedom of being (one's innate identity) may be a more important source of happiness than research has yet revealed. These women find this freedom in nature where there is little clutter of things, fewer expectations, and requirements. Di, from China, may be creating a metaphor for the freedom she feels in being away from the pressures of China's collectivist society (Suh & Oishi, 2002). Sally also found this sort of freedom in her concert experience as she became absorbed in the music and the atmosphere (and forgot about her identity requirements). Their happiness in close relationships – the leading source of happiness – seemed to come partly from the support to be themselves that they felt in these close (as opposed to casual) relationships.

The dynamics of freedom and happiness are likely to be complex. Suh and Oishi (2002) note that a sense of personal freedom may be more important to ones happiness than close relationships with others are. At the same time, others argue that desire for individual freedom is what has disconnected people from relationships, caused materialistic behavior, and reduced happiness (O'Shaughnessy & O'Shaughnessy, 2002; Putnam, 2000). Our data single out freedom related to identity, which includes human relationships, from the value for unrestrained freedom for individualistic endeavors, which separates people. The relation between freedom and happiness clearly needs further exploration.

The Dynamics of Consumption and Happiness

Consumption played an instrumental role, rather than a terminal role, in happiness for the women in this study. We sought evidence of consumption in their representations and experiences of happiness. They rarely mentioned consumption per se. They did not talk about happy meanings, value, status, pride, or achievement experienced in material possessions. No one mentioned brands. There were few social comparisons, which would indicate that happiness derived from having relatively more than other people have (Blanchflower & Oswald, 2004; Lee, 2006; Stutzer, 2003) was not central for them. Naturally, they may have omitted these sources of happiness if they perceived them to be socially unfavorable representations of themselves (Mick, 1996). If that is the case, then we underestimate the role of consumption in their happiness. On the other hand, perhaps they recognize that putting material things as end goals for happiness does not work or at least does not last (Csikszentmihalyi, 2000; Lee, 2006).

These women did not consume to be happy, but they consumed to facilitate and maintain relationships, which made them happy. Consumption was part of their relationships with others – eating together, giving and receiving gifts, shopping and complimenting purchases. They used it as a tool and a context for managing relationships. Furthermore, they passionately declared that consumption – excessive mass consumption – destroys nature and that makes them unhappy. This has implications for sustainability initiatives and for educating consumers about the harmful effects of consumerism on things that make them happy (Abela, 2006; Csikszentmihalyi, 2000).

In addition, these women did not mention looks, beauty, or body image. This is an interesting omission because of society's current and increasing focus on the body and its perfection (Askegaard, Gertsen, & Langer, 2002). We have created a standard of femininity that is impossible to attain and that has led to women feeling insecure and unhappy with themselves and consumption practices to measure up. It is common for women to believe that loosing weight, toning their bodies, or altering their appearance through cosmetics, fashion, or cosmetic surgery will make them happy. Society equates thinness, a tone body, and beauty to happiness (Jeffreys, 2005; Wolf, 1991).

The literature has noted some interesting developments in contemporary consumer societies, which relate to happiness and which raise questions. First, a consumer culture reduces the time that people spend with people (O'Shaughnessy & O'Shaughnessy, 2002; Putnam, 1995, 2000). Because of the documented importance of relationships to happiness, this trend is detrimental to well-being. Second, people can relate to brands in ways similar to human relationships (Fournier, 1998). Because society has become less intimate, are people turning to brands for connection? They could possibly turn to brands as substitutes for human relationships. Alternatively, people could turn to brands as a way to (re)connect with people – to signal to others that they are part of their group – and develop relationships with people (Scott & Johnson, 2005). What is it about these people that lead them to turn to brands or consumption for relational happiness? What is happiness like for these people? We need to study the dynamics between brand relationships, people relationships, and happiness.

Happiness scholars call for more research on antecedents and consequences of happiness as well as mediators and moderators. In particular, they note that individual traits affect what people do to pursue happiness, which of course affects their happiness (Diener, Suh, Lucas, & Smith, 1999). We note that emotional intelligence is an individual trait that would seem to matter to both materialism and happiness and that no one has investigated in this context. People who are able to manage their emotions (i.e., people high in emotional intelligence) may be able to connect with people and build intimate relationships better than people whose emotional intelligence is lower (Goleman, 1995). They may be less materialistic, too. Moreover, we could expect them to be happier than other people are. Because both materialism and emotional intelligence correlate with subjective well-being and relationships, it is unclear what drives what. The dynamics between emotional intelligence, materialism, and happiness is worthy of exploration.

Conclusions and Contribution

All in all, we learned that consumption plays a supporting role in happiness. Thus, we add to the debate about whether or not consumption has any positive role in creating or sustaining happiness. Our study indicates that relationship-enhancing activities include consumption. Consuming with friends is a happy event. These women used consumption activities to maintain relationships and derive happiness from their close relationships. From this, we conclude that not all consumption is "dark side" behavior when it comes to happiness and therefore not all marketing is bad.

We also learned that nature contributes to happiness – at least for these women in this place. Csikszentmihalyi (2000) says that people are happy when "doing," but not when "having." We suggest that there is a happiness ceiling in "doing." Over-doing impedes happiness and produces a need for retreat. In this era in which so much seems to be happening and there are so many choices, these women find relief, refreshment, and balance in nature. The peace and freedom they feel in nature seem to balance the stresses in the rest of their lives and nourish their identities and their happiness. Not only do they feel happy when they experience the natural world, but the idea of contaminating it makes them unhappy. In particular, damage that they attribute to excessive mass consumption makes them unhappy. This suggests important avenues for the consumer education that Abela (2006) suggested to curb materialistic consumption. We should consider ways to make people aware of what makes them happy and link that to ways to preserve or enhance the environment and social relationships.

REFERENCES

Abela, A. V. (2006). Marketing and consumerism: A response to O'Shaughnessy and O'Shaughnessy. *European Journal of Marketing*, *40*(1/2), 5–16.

Askegaard, S., Gertsen, M. C., & Langer, R. (2002). The body consumed: Reflexivity and cosmetic surgery. *Psychology & Marketing*, *19*(October), 793–812.

Belk, R. W. (1985). Materialism: Trait aspects of living in the material world. *Journal of Consumer Research*, *12*(December), 265–280.

Belk, R. W. (1998). Multimedia approaches to qualitative data and representations. In: B. B. Stern (Ed.), *Representing consumers: Voices, views and visions* (pp. 308–338). London: Routledge.

Blanchflower, D. G., & Oswald, A. J. (2004). Well-being over time in Britain and the U.S.A. *Journal of Public Economics*, *88*(July), 1359–1386.

Burroughs, J. E., & Rindfleisch, A. (2002). Materialism and well-being: A conflicting values perspective. *Journal of Consumer Research*, *29*(December), 348–370.

Csikszentmihalyi, M. (1999). If we are so rich, why aren't we happy? *American Psychologist*, *54*(October), 821–827.

Csikszentmihalyi, M. (2000). The costs and benefits of consuming. *Journal of Consumer Research*, *27*(September), 267–272.

Diener, E. (2000). Subjective well-being: The science of happiness and a proposal for a national index. *American Psychologist*, *55*(January), 34–43.

Diener, E., Suh, E. M., Lucas, R. E., & Smith, H. L. (1999). Subjective well-being: Three decades of progress. *Psychological Bulletin*, *125*(January), 276–302.

Fournier, S. (1998). Consumers and their brands: Developing relationship theory in consumer research. *Journal of Consumer Research*, *24*(March), 343–373.

Goffman, E. (1971). *Relations in public*. New York: Basic Books.

Goldberg, J. (1985). *Rich and poor*. New York: Random House.

Goleman, D. (1995). *Emotional intelligence: Why it can matter more than IQ*. London: Bloomsbury.

Harper, D. (2000). Reimagining visual methods: Galileo to *Neuromancer*. In: N. K. Denzin & Y. S. Lincoln (Eds), *Handbook of qualitative research* (2nd ed., pp. 717–732). London: Sage.

Heisley, D. D., & Levy, S. J. (1991). Autodriving: A photoelicitation technique. *Journal of Consumer Research*, *18*(December), 257–272.

Jeffreys, S. (2005). *Beauty and misogyny*. London: Routledge.

Kahneman, D., Krueger, A. B., Schkade, D. A., Schwarz, N., & Stone, A. A. (2004). A survey method for characterizing daily life experience: The day reconstruction method. *Science*, *306*(December, 3), 1776–1780.

La Barbera, P. A., & Gürhan, Z. (1997). The role of materialism, religiosity, and demographics in subjective well-being. *Psychology & Marketing*, *14*(January), 71–97.

Lane, R. (2000). *The loss of happiness in market democracies*. New Haven, CT: Yale University Press.

Layard, R. (2005). *Happiness*. London: Penguin Books.

Lee, D. R. (2006). Who says money cannot buy happiness? *The Independent Review*, *10*(Winter), 385–400.

Meyers, D. (2000). The funds, friends, and faith of happy people. *American Psychologist*, *55*(January), 56–67.

Mick, D. G. (1996). Are studies of dark side variables confounded by socially desirable responding? The case of materialism. *Journal of Consumer Research*, *23*(September), 106–119.

O'Shaughnessy, J., & O'Shaughnessy, N. J. (2002). Marketing, the consumer society and hedonism. *European Journal of Marketing*, *36*(5/6), 524–547.

Putnam, R. D. (1995). Bowling alone: America's declining social capital. *Journal of Democracy*, *6*(January), 65–78.

Putnam, R. D. (2000). *Bowling alone: The collapse and revival of American community*. London: Simon & Schuster.

Rehdanz, K., & Maddison, D. (2003). Climate and happiness. Working paper FNU-20, Centre for Marine and Climate Research, Hamburg, Germany.

Richins, M. L. (1987). Media, materialism and human happiness. In: M. Wallendorf & P. Anderson (Eds), *Advances in Consumer Research* (Vol. 14, pp. 352–356). Provo, UT: Association for Consumer Research.

Schwartz, B. (2004). *The paradox of choice: Why more is less*. New York: HarperCollins.

Scott, J. K., & Johnson, T. G. (2005). Bowling alone, but online together: Social capital in e-communities. *Community Development: Journal of the Community Development Society*, *36*(1), 9–27.

Sirgy, M. J., Lee, D.-J., Kosenko, R., Meadow, H. L., Rhatz, D., Cicic, M., Xi Jin, G., Yarsuvat, D., Blenkhorn, D. L., & Wright, N. (1998). Does television viewership play a role in the perception of quality of life? *Journal of Advertising*, *27*(Spring), 125–143.

Solnick, S. J., & Hemenway, D. (1998). Is more always better? A survey on positional concerns. *Journal of Economic Behavior and Organization*, *37*(November), 373–383.

Strasser, S. (1999). *Waste and want: A social history of trash*. New York: Henry Holt.

Stutzer, A. (2003). The role of income aspirations in individual happiness. *Journal of Economic Behavior and Organization*, *54*(May), 89–109.

Suh, E. M., & Oishi, S. (2002). Subjective well-being across cultures. In: W. J. Lonner, D. L. Dinnel, S. A. Hayes & D. N. Sattler (Eds), *Online Readings in Psychology and Culture*, Unit 7, Bellingham, WA: Center for Cross-Cultural Research, Western Washington University. Retrieved from http://www.wwu.edu/~culture

Thompson, C. J., Locander, W. B., & Pollio, H. R. (1989). Putting consumer experience back into consumer research: The philosophy and method of existential-phenomenology. *Journal of Consumer Research*, *16*(September), 133–146.

Tkach, C., & Lyubomirsky, S. (2006). How do people pursue happiness?: Relating personality, happiness-increasing strategies, and well-being. *Journal of Happiness Studies*, *7*(June), 183–225.

van Manen, M. (1997). *Researching lived experience*. London, Canada: The Althouse Press.

Wolf, N. (1991). *The beauty myth: How images of beauty are used against women*. London: Vintage.

Ziller, R. C. (1990). *Photographing the self*. Newbury Park, CA: Sage.

SUDDENLY MELUNGEON! RECONSTRUCTING CONSUMER IDENTITY ACROSS THE COLOR LINE

Elizabeth C. Hirschman and Donald Panther-Yates

ABSTRACT

The Melungeons, a person-of-color ethnic group dwelling in southern Appalachia, have recently discovered their multi-racial, non-Christian ancestry. We describe the process of ethnogenesis via consumption undertaken by Melungeons to connect their identities to this newfound ancestry. We also examine the social evolution of the Melungeon ethnic label to become a valued personal possession and the public identification of certain physical features as markers of Melungeon ethnicity. It is proposed that these may serve as exemplars for consumer behaviors among other mestizo ethnic groups.

One day she came, quite by accident, across an old, iron key. It was a curious object; she was not sure if it belonged to her or not. What lock could it fit into? She carried it into her parents' bedroom to a closet rarely opened. Within the closet were all the trappings of the family's life – piles of furniture, rugs, black & white and color television sets, the swing set and sandbox in the backyard, the summer trips to Florida, Merry the dog, all

Consumer Culture Theory
Research in Consumer Behavior, Volume 11, 241–259

ISSN: 0885-2111/doi:10.1016/S0885-2111(06)11011-X

the clothes bought at JC Penney, the Ford and Chevrolet sedans, the girl scout uniforms with their merit badge sashes, the Christmas trees, Easter eggs, summer camp in North Carolina, the father's trout fishing gear, the mother's bridge table; they were all there.

Did she really want to unpack all that material, to disrupt it, so tightly crammed and wedged into the past? She slowly began pulling it out piece by piece. It was laborious to do by herself; no one else was around to help. Several times she sat down on a dislodged armchair to rest and think. Maybe she should just stop, put it all back in place. It was a stupid effort; her parent's bedroom was now littered with the stuff pulled from the closet, everything was in disarray and for what?

Her parents sat like mannequins on the living room couch; next to them were her grandparents and brother; they were silent, still, muted. She observed them for a while and then returned to the bedroom closet. She worked systematically now, obsessively; gathering up the smaller items in her arms and tossing them out, pulling and tugging the larger ones – the aluminum boat from which she and her brother had fished for blue gills, the old blue bicycle, the tennis and swimming lessons, the pony rides, the Thanksgiving dinners with all their kin.

Finally, the closet was cleared to the back. A small wooden door with a lock was now visible in the dim light. She knew now that the mysterious key would fit into it. She was scared. Behind her lay the chaotic piles of the family's life, dragged loose and littering the room. In front stood the small wooden door. She fit the key into the lock and turned it. The little door squeaked open as she pushed it.

On the other side was an extraordinary scene. There was a golden afternoon sun and a light breeze blowing toward her face. In front of her were lush green meadows, soft hills and a quaint village filled with men, women, and children dressed in long, loose clothing; they were dark skinned – a sort of medium brown – with dark hair that hung past the women's shoulders. They talked in languages she could not understand: Hebrew and Portuguese and Arabic and Spanish. Their faces looked friendly, but she was invisible to them. The foods they were eating were unknown to her – the roasted meats and vegetables smelled of spices and leeks, all cooking in black iron pots. Surrounding the village were beautiful vineyards full of grape arbors; the village houses were of cream-colored stucco; there were horses and burros and cattle and chickens. To the left of the village was a steep, forested hillside. A family lived there in a bark-covered lodge – a father and mother and their two black haired children; they were dressed in deerskin pants and cloaks, embroidered with geometric patterned shell beads. They seemed happy and content. These were her ancestors. Why had she never been told?

INTRODUCTION

The Melungeons are a people-of-color ethnic group dwelling in the south-central Appalachian Mountains (Ball, 1992; Bible, 1975; Burnett, 1889; Kennedy, 1994/1997). Their heaviest concentration lies in the rural, mountainous intersection of eastern Tennessee, western North Carolina, eastern Kentucky, western Virginia, and southern West Virginia. Other Melungeon communities are found in southern Ohio (the Mt. Carmel Indians), central Tennessee near Chattanooga (Graysville Melungeons), and Sand Mountain, Alabama (Kessler & Ball, 2001). Estimates of the size of the Melungeon population range from 50,000 to 250,000+ (Kennedy, 1997). The importance of the Melungeons to consumer behavior theory is their origin as a people and "rediscovery" both by themselves and by social scientists in the 1970s, 1980s, and 1990s.

Most recently, researchers (Hirschman, 2003, 2005; Kennedy, 1997) have argued that the Melungeons descend from early Spanish settlers who arrived in North America from 1492 onward. Most were likely Sephardic Jews and Muslim Moors who had superficially converted to Christianity in order to escape the Spanish Inquisition and then made their way to the New World as colonists (and away from possible religious persecution in Europe). The presence of Sephardic and Moorish surnames among the Melungeons such as Chavis, Blackamoor, Driggers (Rodrigues), Looney (Luna), Perry (Perrira), Rivas/Reeves, Lopes, and Steel (Castille) lends support to this argument. Once in the mountains, these Spanish colonists would have intermarried with the resident Indian population, forming a bi-cultural/bi-racial community.

ETHNOGENESIS AND CONSUMER RESEARCH

Inquiries into ethnicity have a lengthy history in consumer research. Beginning with early attempts to describe racially-defined market segments (Bauer & Cunningham, 1970), investigations became increasingly sophisticated, addressing issues such as consumer acculturation (Penaloza, 1989, 1994) and post-assimilationist strategies (Askegaard, Arnould, & Kjeldgaard, 2005). Ethnic identities enmeshed within this research tradition have included African–American (Oswald, 1999), Hispanics (Deshpande, Hoyer, & Donthu, 1986), Indo–Pakistanis (Mehta & Belk, 1991) and Inuit (Askegaard et al., 2005).

In contrast to these studies, we use a theoretical stance that seems better suited to the Melungeons – ethnogenesis. Hill (1996, p. 1) describes ethnogenesis as "the historical emergence of a people who define themselves in relation to a socio-cultural ... heritage" and further notes that "ethnogenesis can also serve as an analytical tool for developing critical historical approaches to culture as an ongoing process of conflict and struggle over a people's existence ... within ... a general history of domination." Most commonly, the term ethnogenesis and its evolving theoretical framework have been used to ground research on the responses of indigenous and African-originating persons to the European colonization of the New World (see e.g., Albers, 1996; Hickerson, 1996). Since the Melungeon people are situated within exactly this historical and cultural nexus, the framework is highly appropriate for them.

PURPOSES

The purposes of the present inquiry are threefold: first, we examine within an ethnogenic framework how persons of Melungeon ancestry are reconstructing their identity through purposeful changes in consumer behavior. We explore, for example, how foodways, medical practices, and musical styles have been used to redefine these individuals' sense of self and community, resulting in an emergent ethnic culture of consumption.

Second, our inquiry explores the social and personal struggles within the Melungeon community over the past five years resulting from access to newly available DNA data, genealogical records, and historical writings. This knowledge is being used to construct ethnic boundaries regarding who and what is a Melungeon.

Third, the idea of ethnicity as a possession is carried more deeply into a consideration of physical traits becoming publicly recognized markers of ethnic membership. We develop a discussion of the ethnicized body as an heirloom possession and specific physical markers as valued attributes (Curasi, Price, & Arnould, 2004).

METHOD

We two authors are of Melungeon descent, something we became aware of around six years ago. Prior to that, we had identified ourselves ethnically as a WASP and an American Indian, respectively. Since learning of this ancestry, we have attended seven Melungeon Gatherings during the summers of 2000–2006 both as observers and participants. Additionally, extensive personal correspondence via e-mail, telephone, face-to-face conversations, and written mail/fax has been carried on between the two authors and several key members of the Melungeon community. In constructing the present interpretation, we combined insights gained from direct discussions with informants, Melungeon e-bulletin board postings, Melungeon Gathering presentations by diverse speakers and extensive readings in Appalachian regional history.

CONSUMPTION ETHNOGENESIS: LEARNING TO CONSUME LIKE A MELUNGEON

In our view, the originally-formed Melungeon community (1540–1890) constituted an emergent ethnic community; one which combined aspects of Sephardic Jewish, Muslim Moorish, and Indigenous culture (see Hirschman, 2005). Supporting this classification is the fact that among the Melungeon communities in Appalachia there were shared conventions of worship (Old Primitive Baptist), funerary procedures, foodways (e.g., "tomato" and "chocolate" gravy) and child-rearing patterns that set them apart from both white and indigenous settlements in the area (Bible, 1975; Ball, 1969; Kennedy, 1997).

This original community was largely destroyed during the late 1800s to early 1900s as a result of racist activities which occurred at the local, state, and federal levels. The present Melungeon community, in our view, is in the early stages of ethnogenesis – it is attempting to learn what it means to be a Melungeon. As we shall show, learning to consume like a Melungeon is a key ingredient in the ethnogenic process.

Early in the Melungeon Movement (1995–2000) efforts were made to extend consumption boundaries to the products and practices of those groups from which particular Melungeons believed themselves to be descended (see also Kennedy, 1997). At gatherings and on the Melungeon web-boards commonly discussed topics included specific foodstuffs, musical styles, herbal remedies deemed to be of Melungeon origin. As Melungeon ethnogenesis evolved from 2000 to the present, attention increasingly has turned to melding these newly-adopted ethnic folkways with the traditions of southern Appalachian regional culture with which most Melungeons grew up. Occasionally, pre-existing Appalachian practices have been imbued with new meanings, as they became recognized as links to a previously invisible Melungeon ancestral past. For example, the recollection that one's grandparents strictly avoided pork had not been previously recognized as indicating potential Jewish or Muslim ethnicity.

Herbal Remedies

In several instances herbal remedies present in Appalachian culture for many generations have been retraced to Melungeon and American Indian roots. Because both of these ancestries were deemed a negative status within the southeastern U.S. until recently, the use of herbal medicines prior to

Melungeon ethnogenesis usually was not attributed to one's own ancestors, but rather said to be the province of a specific "herb doctor" or "herb healer" unrelated to oneself. Postings from the Melungeons @ Topic-A (MTA) community bulletin board describe some of these remedies which now are publicly being claimed as part of the poster's Melungeon ancestral history:

> My great aunt got so aggravated when we couldn't get her any more Swamp Root and Black Root. My father-in-law used slippery elm, yellow root, burdock root, calmus, and others. Catnip tea has a calming effect on the stomach ... You can tie a piece of potato on a wart for a day or two and it will go away ..., or [you can] go to one of our people here in the hills and they will rub it and it will go away. My wife can attest to that from experience. My wife's elderly cousin once kissed our newborn infant, so that she would not have thrush mouth. (March 16, 2003, MTA)

> I know grandpa grew herbs and used a cut stick just a little longer than my son was to cure him of asthma, and it worked ... He could dowse for water, but his brother, Richmond Brewer, could not only dowse for it, but tell you how deep to dig. And of course, we had our 'dreams' and 'feelings' that came true. I still have them. It was never called magic in our family, but a gift from God to be used for good. If you used it for evil, it was dangerous. Grandma could take a needle, put it on a string, and it would go in a circle if you were having a girl and back and forth if you were having a boy ... She was always right. Didn't have ultra-sound back then, but didn't need it. (January 28, 2004, MTA)

> My father taught me some about Cherokee medicine ... We'd spend time looking for herbs in the woods together. Some of the herbal stuff he taught me has been tremendously useful in my life, and he taught me some of the Native spirituality he learned growing up ... My friends when I was young were weirded out by some of the foods we ate, like pokeweed Jellico, roasted cat tails (young cattail plants can be cooked like corn on the cob, the roots can be made into a starchy flour), and venison jerky ... "My father was a Spencer who lived in North Carolina around the Grassy Creek area ... He had ruddy skin, black hair and ice blue eyes ... Had very Indian-looking features." (April 27, 2003, MTA)

The attribution in the quote directly above to "Cherokee medicine" is what Albers (1996) would term an "umbilical link" to one of the Melungeons' founding ethnicities. Because the Cherokee, by default, became the dominant indigenous nation in the area inhabited by Melungeons, those Melungeons who believe they have Native ancestors often label them as "Cherokee." In actuality, by the 1700s the Cherokee were a collection of several surviving Native peoples; likely their folkways and genetics reflected a diversity gained from both Indigenous and European inputs.

The current willingness to not only publicly announce these practices, but to attest to their efficacy speaks to a newfound confidence in the wisdom of one's forebears. On a different level, it gives voice to an anger and resentment toward the larger culture outside Appalachia, whose dominance and repressive ways led to ethnic abandonment or concealment over the past two to three generations. On yet an additional level, the reclamation of such practices signifies a bond across all those indigenous peoples made to feel less worthy, less desirable, and less culturally "evolved" than the colonizing populations who engulfed them (Bell, 2005).

Cooking & Foodways

Several Melungeons have now discovered that they have Sephardic Jewish and Moorish Muslim ancestry, as well as American Indian. There have been discussions on e-boards and at Melungeon Gatherings of how Appalachian foodways may relate to Judaic kashrut and Islamic halal practices. One tradition frequently described is the draining of blood from chickens during the slaughtering process.[1] The posting below was titled "Doesn't everybody hang their chickens on the clothesline?"

> I think this is pretty universal [among Melungeons]. It's the most effective way to drain meat. My dad raised hens down over the river bank for their eggs ... When a hen stopped laying, she went in the pot and daddy would kill her out in the back yard. First, he 'wrung' her neck to kill her quickly, and then he hung her by her feet on the clothesline. He pulled the hen's head back and with a very sharp knife, he cut her head off ... By hanging the hen, the meat is not bruised, it is cleaner, and all the blood was spilt from the chicken's body. This part may be a Jewish custom by the way ... The hen was removed from the line and dipped in boiling water, [so] her feathers were easily plucked ... Then the hen was dipped in boiling water again and held over an open flame to remove any pinfeathers. I know that Grandma Mary ... would soak chicken in saltwater to "purify" it before frying: I do this still ... Grandma Mary was a faith healer and "fasted" on occasion ... I remember my mom checking out the matzoh in the grocery store when I was a kid and telling me about fasting. (January 17, 2004, MTA)

Others recalled special rituals used to purify cooking utensils:

> ... all pans were washed in boiling water before the first use, as well as any dishes and all cast iron pans/skillets [which] were coated with oil and then put in the oven for several hours to 'cure'. (September 28, 2002, MTA)

> Another custom from my dad's family was that when it was a woman's time of the month, she shouldn't cook – that the food wouldn't taste right. (September 29, 2002, MTA)

> I've been waiting for one of y'all to mention hummus. It's my favorite ... My daughter loves Mediterranean food. She is pretty good at cooking it, and I always have it when I go to her house. By the way, people who meet her often think she is Jewish or Arabic. She does look like it, and so much like my mother's family from Floyd County,

> Kentucky. Almost black hair, olive skin, and brown eyes with green highlights. She never sunburns, and I don't either! (July 10, 2003, MTA)

Sephardic and Muslim ties were also explored via recipes linked to specific holidays, which some Melungeons are now beginning to celebrate. For example, one Melungeon website presented a lengthy set of recipes appropriate for Purim, along with a discussion of the history of Sephardim in Persia, Morocco, Egypt, and other Middle Eastern countries (MTA, February 12, 2003). As with the allusions to Cherokee practices discussed earlier, these would represent what Albers (1996) terms the "umbilical" connection to founding ethnicities. This strategy rests on the assumption that one can learn to be Melungeon by consuming in ethnically appropriate ways; indeed, as one reviewer pointed out, Barth (1969) pioneered the identification of consumption behaviors as an ethnic boundary marker.

Musical Traditions

Melungeons also have attempted to retrospectively trace the traditional Appalachian musical forms they grew up with to their newly discovered ethnic antecedents. The quote below concerns the dulcimer, an instrument indigenous to Appalachia.

> I have a hammer dulcimer at home … I fell in love with the hammer dulcimer a few years back, thanks to the late Rich Mullins. I have heard the hammer dulcimer used in some of the newer TV commercials. My husband Dan tells me the hammer dulcimer is also a Jewish instrument, and around our house a lot of Jewish and Klezmer music is [now] being played – quite a change from being raised up in a country/bluegrass/folk music background. (August 4, 2004, MTA)

Other Melungeons, who additionally have Roma/Gypsy heritage, claim to discern retrospective ethnic connections to traditional Appalachian musical forms, as well:

> Musically speaking certainly there is a connection of the people of Roma and the stylings of the mountain music which evolved into bluegrass music. If you go to my ethnomusical site and click on the link for a sample of a Turkish man playing a Roma song, you can hear something very familiar. (May 9, 2003, MTA)

MELUNGEON ETHNICITY AS STATUS POSSESSION: FROM PARIAH TO PRIZE

In this section we explore Melungeon ethnicity as a social label that has been transformed over the past decade from a stigmatic identity, one that was hidden, denied and (if possible) discarded, to a prized personal possession, one that is displayed publicly with pride. We believe the lessons learned from the Melungeon experience are ones that are transferable to other multi-ethnic and multicultural ethnogenesis contexts and which expand the theoretical comprehension of consumers' possessions to include one's physical embodiment and social persona (Daniel, 1992; Thompson & Hirschman, 1995).

With increasing societal acceptance and, upon occasion, celebration of multicultural/multi-racial ancestry, the Melungeon Movement has flourished during the past decade. Indeed, Melungeon ethnicity has become a prized asset to such an extent that there are now social, political, and personal conflicts within the community over who has the right to claim this ethnic label. The core of the conflict lies in the geographic areas and ancestral lineages deemed to constitute "true," "pure," or "authentic" Melungeon-ness.

Because several early magazine and newspaper articles (e.g., Dromgoole, 1890, 1891a, 1891b) specified the Newman's Ridge/Vardy area of Hancock County, Tennessee as a geographic area in which Melungeons lived, some of the present day residents in this area began claiming that only they are genuine Melungeons. As will be illustrated in texts below, these advocates viewed Melungeon ethnicity as restricted to only three or four ancestral lines and additionally proposed that one must live on Newman's Ridge currently to be considered a Melungeon – this became labeled the "Ridge-only" criterion. Not having ancestry from one of the proposed founding lines or having ancestors who had migrated away from the Newman's Ridge/Vardy community rendered one non-Melungeon.

Because Melungeon ethnicity was now valuable, those persons who viewed themselves as Melungeons, but did not meet the "Ridge-only" geographic/ancestral criteria, responded with counter arguments supporting their claims to the ethnic label. For example, Curtis Christie, a Melungeon not from Newman's Ridge, wrote to the Melungeon-List (Mel-L) at Rootsweb:

> No one person: not a Ridge-only and not the [list] moderator should be allowed to (1) [let] the M-List to be used as someone's-or some clique's-little hobby horse with which to trample on the rights of others, or (2) to allow some philosophy to use it as a kind of power base from which to attempt a hostile takeover of Melungeon-ness, or (3) to unsub people as a way of proving who's in charge ...(March 27, 2004)

Rick Stewart, a Melungeon and Cherokee descendant living in West Virginia, and also not from Newman's Ridge, responded to this posting by stating:

> Curtis, this was a very interesting post ... Of the leaders in this Melungeon research, I trust only Nancy [Sparks Morrison], you, and Brent [Kennedy] and y'all's opinions.

> From what I recall of the last definition, West Virginia and most of VA and NC were excluded from the term Melungeon … I have a fair amount of ancestry from Scott Co., VA, but have no desire to connect with the "Ridgers." "[My ancestors] cleared out of Scott Co. for WVA and KY anyway with their dark complexions in the early 1800's …" (Rick Stewart, Mel-L, March 27, 2004)

Tim Hashaw, an African American and Melungeon descendant now living in Texas, voiced a similar response:

> Curtis, we have lost numerous West Virginians, Virginians, eastern Kentuckians and others from Melungeon research [due] to the vagueness of the term Melungeon and the downright dismissal of our being Melungeons by the Ridge Onlys and others. These people could have contributed much to this research and are now gone due to bigotry … (Mel-L, 2003)

The exchange below between Melungeon researcher Brent Kennedy and Jack Goins, a Newman's Ridge "born and bred" Melungeon, illustrates well the internecine bickering over the now-prized possession of Melungeonness.[2]

> Brent Kennedy to Jack Goins (Mel-L, 2003): Jack, you seem here, as opposed to your book (Goins, 2003), to be defining the Melungeons as a very few families from which only you and a few others are descended. This is extraordinarily restrictive and, in my strong opinion, extraordinarily incorrect (and, again, in direct conflict with what you have written in your book). And, importantly, quite a few historians would vehemently disagree with this rather limited approach.
>
> JG: I believe everyone should have the right to self-identification, but what comes with this right is the obligation to show proof of that identification, this is where family history and genealogy can be used to locate your possible Melungeon ancestors.
>
> BK: I agree to some degree, but you can't selectively toss out evidence that runs counter to your agenda. The URL links above provide a wealth of documentation, pre-Brent Kennedy, to confirm this point …
>
> JG: … I have forefathers who are named by historians, one by Walter Plecker in 1924, as Melungeons. They suffered the discrimination that came with this label, so I have an obligation and the determination to seek the truth …
>
> BK: Walter Plecker was not a historian. He was a racist [Virginia] state registrar intent on driving all people of color out of the accepted social structure. The fact that you call this man a "historian" is troubling. Regarding family involvement, I also have an emotional stake here. My Mullinses, among others, are documented Virginia Melungeons with East Tennessee roots. My Bollings came from Hancock County and helped start the Melungeons on High Knob/Stone Mountain. A lot of my family are also on Plecker's lists … But, most importantly, I have no problem in remembering and honoring all my ancestors, regardless of where they migrated and settled. Newman's Ridge, or High Knob, or Stone Mountain, or Coeburn Mountain are all wonderful places, but pride in family shouldn't begin and end on these mountaintops.

At this point the Melungeon-List moderator, Dennis Maggard, stepped in to comment:

> One can always define the word Melungeon to mean only the residents of one particular ridge – this is a common propaganda technique known as "victory by definition" – but in so doing you have defined Melungeons to be a very small and relatively uninteresting group, except to itself and its family historians ... It is the larger, broader group from which the residents of this one ridge sprang and to which they are related which is of real interest and of real significance in the history of colonial Virginia ... and southern Appalachia. In my opinion this broader group has just as much claim to the name Melungeon as the residents of one ridge who just happened to be the first Melungeons identified as such to the outside world. It's not about living on one ridge or another; it's about a group of interrelated families sharing a common socio-economic status and common hardships, because of their common mixed race ancestry. (Mel-L, 2003)

Because few present day Melungeons experience racial or ethnic discrimination and are not generally classified as minority group members qualified for special consideration under Federal and State affirmative action policies, the struggle over the label Melungeon represents one's right to claim this title as a personal possession, in and of itself. This position stands in contrast to the internecine struggles within American Indian communities where being designated Cherokee or Lumbee or Lakota does imply access to valuable economic resources. Further, because even "Ridge-only" Melungeons are rarely able to assert their Melungeon ethnicity in everyday life by displaying, say, their genealogies or other social "proofs" of their ethnic status, other physically visible personal markers have come into play as evidence of Melungeon identity. These are discussed in the next section.

"WRITTEN ON THE FLESH": ASCRIBED STATUS AND THE PHYSIOLOGY OF ETHNICITY

Perhaps one of the most theoretically intriguing aspects of Melungeon ethnogenesis is that the majority of present day group members have "passed" for "white" over the course of their lives. It is only during the past decade that most have discovered that they are carrying Iberian, Semitic, American Indian, Roma, and sub-Saharan African ancestry and had grandparents, great grandparents, or more distant ancestors who were publicly viewed as non-white and classified as Free Persons of Color (FPC) or Mulatto.

While some contemporary Melungeons are quite light complexioned, even having blonde or red hair and fair skin, the majority are darker, with what is commonly described as "olive" or "copper" toned skin, brunette or black hair, and dark brown eyes. Ironically, despite having Mediterranean or Middle Eastern physiognomies, many Melungeons grew up confident of their ostensibly Northern or Western European ancestry. This self-deception often originated with parents or grandparents who told the individual that s/he was Scotch–Irish, English, French, and/or German. If challenged by the skeptical child that s/he seemed to be darker than most Scottish or German persons, the parent/grandparent might reply that this was due to some Black Dutch or Black Irish ancestry.

As Melungeon ethnogenesis progressed, more distinctive physical markers than dark coloring were sought to determine if one had Melungeon ancestry. For example, Hispanics and bi-racial persons (mulattos) were already "known" entities. How could Melungeons be differentiated from other dark colored persons? Were there physical characteristics other than coloring which set them apart?

The answer was "yes." Beginning in 1994, a set of physical characteristics began to be circulated both within and outside the Melungeon community, which was deemed indicative of Melungeon ancestry. These included (1) a cranial ridge or protuberance at the rear of the skull attributed to Anatolian and/or American Indian ancestry, (2) sinodonty ("shovel teeth"), a non-European tooth form found in East Asians, Inuit, and American Indians, (3) polydactilism (most commonly in the form of six digits on hands and/or feet), (4) Thallasemia, a genetically transmitted anemic condition most common in persons of Mediterranean, African, and East Asian descent, (5) Familial Mediterranean Fever (FMF), a genetically-restricted disease found among North African Jews, Armenians, Kurds, Turks, and Arabs, and (6) palatal and mandibular mouth tori; these are bony growths in the roof of the mouth found among the Inuit, American Indians, and East Asians (palatal) and along the lower jaw among sub-Saharan Africans (mandibular), (see Melungeon Health Education and Support Network, www.Melungeonhealth.org).

Because these features came to be identified as Melungeon ethnic signifiers, they soon acquired the status of sought after personal attributes. Possessing at least one or more, and preferably all, of these physical markers served to signal one's authenticity as a Melungeon. Absence of the markers on one's physical being cast doubt on one's Melungeon ethnicity. These features expanded into a wider set, as additional markers were reported and linked to the specific ethnicities which fed into the Melungeon community. A September 26, 2002 post to MTA states,

> I am a great believer in the efficacy of accepted anthropological traits. I have the mandibular tori of African-Americans. I have a textbook-perfect set of shovel teeth, proven to be connected to Native American ancestry. And although the following traits are more suggestive than "provable," I have olive skin, high cheekbones, crooked fingers ...

> The Indian and Black came from somewhere! Just haven't found where (April 30, 2004, MTA).

> I have the teeth, the mandibular tori-bilateral, the Asian cranial bump, and I understand my (maternal) mtDNA will come back as Haplotype U ... It was supposed to be NA (Native American) ... Well, I guess not, even though [my grandmother] sure looked it and it was stated in her family papers. I have her portrait: 4 feet tall, black hair, black eyes, olive complexion, no lips, round face, "hook" nose, Asian eyes. I look forward to a detailed explanation of the U haplotype. (September 30, 2002, MTA)

The reference to DNA haplotypes in the latter posting leads us to a second significant – and very recent – set of Melungeon markers. In 1998, the first public commercial DNA testing service was launched (www.OxfordAncestors.com), and was shortly followed by several others. These services offered consumers – for the first time in history – the opportunity to privately order DNA testing of bodily tissues in order to link oneself to specific geographic areas and ethnic groups. For Melungeons, this seemed like a godsend: finally, a scientific method to prove one's Melungeon ethnicity.

Earlier DNA studies using medical blood samples collected from 177 Appalachian Melungeons found that their closest matches to present world populations were in Libya, the Canary Islands, Malta, Veneto and Trentino (Italy), Cyprus, and Galicia (Spain)[3] (Guthrie, 1990). Yet specific Melungeons still did not know who, exactly, their ancestors were among these several possibilities. The availability of inexpensive ($99 y-chromosome, $149 mtDNA; $175 autosomal) personalized DNA tests permitted individual Melungeons to send in samples and find out "who am I" genetically. Persons receiving back results that were consistent with Iberian, Semitic, Turkish, American Indian, and so forth, ancestry now had tangible evidence that they "were" Melungeon. Kennedy, the early Melungeon researcher, was one of the first to send in his DNA sample and receive his genetic vindication.

> My mitochondrial DNA, which I inherited from my mother, matches the Siddis of India. The dark-skinned Siddis likely originated from what today is Ethiopia, Eritrea, or Somalia – sub-Saharan, east Africa. They were transported to India in a variety of ways, most not so pleasant, and formed a major component of what became known as the Untouchable Caste. Their lives – and the life of my ancestral Mother – must have been horribly difficult. But she survived long enough to have at least one daughter and that daughter did likewise. And generation after generation this original ... girl's DNA was passed along until, in 1950, it came to me ... (September 2002, MTA)

One Melungeon list administrator stated:

> Given the scientific validity of the DNA study, ... its results are not a matter of opinion, but of fact. That is the beauty of science. And one of the beauties of DNA analysis is that

> it can shed the light of scientific fact on questions long fraught with opinions and conjectures. Dennis Maggard (Mel-L, 2002)

The use of DNA testing by Melungeons to determine their ethnic ancestry has a troubling side for the social sciences. Over the past 30 years, several of the social sciences, most notably anthropology, have adopted the position that "race" and "colored" are solely socially constructed phenomenon, having no basis in biology (Stojanowski, 2005). Ironically, this position grew out of a moral commitment intended to protect persons of racial minority status, whose classification as "colored" was used to oppress and segregate them.

Yet, here are the Melungeons who, contradictorally, are seeking DNA testing in order to confirm their colored status by validating their ancestry in various ethnic/racial minorities, e.g., sub-Saharan African, Native American, Gypsy, Spanish. Although this paper is not the appropriate forum to address these issues in depth, it is the authors' position that DNA testing voluntarily undertaken by consumers to gain knowledge of their ancestral identity is a positive phenomenon, because it provides access to personally significant information unavailable through other means.

Thus, the Melungeon experience opens a potentially very significant new avenue for the study of ethnogenesis and consumption. By problematizing both body features and genetic endowments, it brings to the foreground aspects of ethnicity that previously had been backgrounded in recent anthropology and consumer research. With some notable exceptions (e.g., Stojanowski, 2005), the physical features of an ethnic group have not been attended to in either literature. Often it is simply "taken for granted" that group membership is readily apparent through visible, but unspoken, cues. By delineating a community-circulated set of physical traits, the Melungeons have de-naturalized their own bodies and identified specific "pieces" as having ethnic meaning. Because these ethnic features are passed forward to future generations through genetic-linkage, they can be viewed as a type of bequest or heirloom (Curasi et al., 2004). Notably, Melungeons now report inspecting infants and children for these physical features, and express satisfaction if they have been "carried forward."

Dennis Maggard's statements above regarding DNA testing and the perceived validity of science in determining ethnicity also points to another novel aspect of Melungeon ethnogenesis. Very probably, the Melungeons are the first ethnic group to avail themselves of commercial DNA testing to determine community origins and, ultimately, individual membership. The community's hybrid racial ancestry and purposely obfuscated genealogical records made the acquisition of personal ethnic knowledge difficult, if not impossible, using traditional genealogical and census techniques. DNA testing seems to have helped many answer the "who am I?" question, at least in a partial sense. We believe that the Melungeon experience is likely to be a forerunner to the widespread use of DNA testing to determine ethnic membership.

DISCUSSION

First we will consider what the process of learning to consume like a Melungeon might teach us about the role of consumption in constructing ethnic identity. Second, we suggest that the journey of Melungeon ethnicity from racial epithet to hidden identity to valued personal possession should stimulate a reconsideration of the ontological, social, and personal nature of ethnicity in consumer research. Finally the Melungeon experience suggests additionally that we should not just problematize the physical characteristics of the human body (e.g., Thompson & Hirschman, 1995), but rather re-cast them as personal possessions capable of signaling ethnic status and community membership.

Can Consumption Create Ethnicity?

One of the primary arguments advanced in the present study is that individuals and groups can use their behavior as consumers to construct an ethnic identity. This proposition reverses the causality usually observed and assumed between ethnicity and consumption, i.e., that a person's ethnicity will direct his/her consumption preferences, practices, and behaviors. In virtually all consumer research on ethnicity, as well as the sociological and anthropological literatures, ethnicity is seen as preceding consumption. Even in studies of national culture and subcultures, the pre-existence of one's membership is taken as the starting point for inquiry, with the attitudes and behaviors observed then being attributed to one's cultural membership.

Conversely, the Melungeon experience is more akin to the process of assimilation experienced by persons coming to a new country. Like recent immigrants, they have arrived in a novel land and must choose how to make sense of it. Sampling the food, the music, and observing the folkways are among the most common means of "opting in" to a new culture (e.g., Penaloza, 1994).

The Melungeon experience, however, is not fully consistent with an assimilationist model. Rather than being strangers in a strange land who must choose either to cluster together into a community and retain (and perhaps even celebrate) their strangeness, the Melungeons are strangers in their own land. They have been given sudden knowledge that estranges them from their own identity.

Significantly, one of the central ways in which these people chose to be reborn as Melungeons was through consumption. Recipes and herbal remedies are shared at the annual gatherings and over the Internet, providing a material basis for community. Photograph albums, candlesticks, pieces of apparel, and jewelry are brought to meetings and displayed, helping to create a communal set of images and artifacts. Ethnogenesis is shown to be both a forward and backward looking process, assisted in both directions by consumption choices.

Race and Religion

The persons composing the Melungeon community are by and large regular people. Their understandings of race, religion, and genetics are probably similar to those shared by most Americans. In this view, race (e.g., black, white, Indian, Asian) and religion (e.g., Christian (Protestant), Jewish, Muslim, Hindu, Buddhist) are conceived as fundamental qualities that are a permanent feature of the individual, in much the same way that one's hair, fingerprints, or voice are. The sense that emerges from Melungeon discussions of race is that it is not an optional feature; rather race is a key, fundamental aspect of one's identity and existence. Further, Melungeons' multi-racial ancestry means to them that they belong to each of the races that has contributed to their existence. They share an ancestral affinity; they are kin.

This is one of the reasons why it was (and is) so important to many Melungoens to "have their DNA tested" to see who they are related to; to learn what they are "made up of." This is essentialism at its most basic, grounded level; but it seems for these people a genuine expression of self.

Akin to this is the view of religion as expressed by Melungeons at their gatherings and in the website postings we have quoted. Contra social science norms, religion within the Melungeon ethnogenesis experience often is something that is deemed to be hereditable from ancestors; it is "in the blood," at least in an emotional sense.

This leads us to the third theoretical contribution of the present study. Although other consumer research inquiries have addressed the problematization of the body's physical features (e.g., Thompson & Hirschman, 1995; Schouten, 1991), these were situated within the context of comparing the body to a cultural or gender-based normative standard.

If the Melungeon embracing of coloredness is generalizable to other people-of-color groups, then we may witness a movement away from white cultural standards of appearance in apparel, hair style, facial features (e.g., reduced cosmetic procedures or plastic surgeries to lighten skin, widen eyes, alter noses), food preferences, and the like, among adult Americans, as opposed to the mimicry of cultures-of-color by American white youth as a form of resistance and rebellion. Ultimately, "whiteness" may become viewed simply as European ethnicity, rather than as a standard to be emulated.

Melungeon ethnogenesis has also directed our attention to the ways – and depths – to which the body may become a contested site of ethnic identity. On the body's surface, this group has problematized features such as eyelid shape (positively valuing epicanthic folds). However, perhaps more theoretically profound than these surface markers are Melungeons' recent efforts at delving into their genetic structures in the hopes of identifying – at the molecular level – definitive proof of personal identity. What are we to make of this? Surely it is as dramatic a departure from consumer research's focus upon the Goffmanesque self-costuming of apparel, automobiles, leisure activities, socio-economic status, and other external forms of cultural capital as one could imagine. The notion that consumer identity may arise, in some cases, from physical sources within the individual, as much as from material entities external to the self is, in our estimation, as fundamental a challenge as consumer research has yet encountered.

NOTES

1. Remarkably, Melungeons seem to have also attempted to "kosher" or "halal" slaughtered hogs, by first draining all blood from the carcass, then soaking it in water and finally rubbing it with salt. Because feral and domestic hogs were a primary protein source in pre-colonial and colonial times, they were often incorporated into the diets of even crypto-Jewish and crypto-Muslim settlers.
2. Ironically, Walter Plecker was one of the architects of Virginia's Racial Integrity Law in 1924, the very law that was used to disenfranchise Melungeons. Here Melungeon Jack Goins cites Plecker as proof of Goin's Melungeon ethnicity.
3. All these areas are known to have populations of Spanish Jews and Muslims who fled the Inquisition from 1500 to 1600; further, in and of themselves, Guthrie's findings were remarkable, considering the donors were all Appalachian and not expected to match, say, Libyans.

REFERENCES

Albers, P. C. (1996). Changing patterns of ethnicity in the Northeastern Plains, 1780–1870. In: J. D. Hill (Ed.), *History, power and identity* (pp. 90–118). Iowa City: Iowa University Press.

Askegaard, S., Arnould, E. J., & Kjelgaard, D. (2005). Post assimilationist ethnic consumer research: Qualificans and extensions. *Journal of Consumer Research*, *32*(June), 160–174.

Ball, B. S. (1969 revised 1992). *Melungeons: Their origin and kin*. Johnson City, Tennessee: Overmountain Press.

Barth, F. (1969). *Ethnic groups and boundaries: The social organization of cultural differences*. Boston: Little, Brown.

Bauer, R., & Cunningham, S. (1970). The negro market. *Journal of Advertising Research*, *10*(2), 1–13.

Bell, A. (2005). White ethnogenesis and gradual capitalism: Perspectives from colonial archaeological sites in the Chesapeake. *American Anthropologist*, *107*(3), 446–460.

Bible, J. P. (1975). *Melungeons yesterday and today*. Rogersville, Tennessee: East Tennessee Printing Company.

Burnett, S. (1889). Note on the Melungeons. *American Anthropologist*, *1*(October), 347.

Curasi, C. F., Price, L. L., & Arnould, E. J. (2004). How individuals' cherished possessions become families' inalienable wealth. *Journal of Consumer Research*, *31*(December), 609–622.

Daniel, G. R. (1992). Passers and pluralists: Subverting the racial divide. In: M. Root (Ed.), *Racially mixed people in America*. Newbury Park, California: Sage Publications.

Deshpande, R., Hoyer, W., & Donthu, N. (1986). The intensity of ethnic affiliation: A study of the sociology of Hispanic consumption. *Journal of Consumer Research*, *13*, 214–220.

Dromgoole, W. A. (1890). Land of the Malungeons. *Nashville Sunday American*, August 31, 10.

Dromgoole, W. A. (1891a). The Malungeons. *The Arena*, *3*(March), 470–479.

Dromgoole, W. A. (1891b). The Malungeon tree and its four branches. *The Arena*, *3*(June), 745–751.

Goins, J. H. (2003). *Melungeons and other pioneer families*. Rogersville, Tennessee.

Guthrie, J. L. (1990). Melungeons: Comparison of gene frequency distributions to those of worldwide populations. *Tennessee Anthropologist*, *XV*(1) Spring.

Hickerson, N. P. (1996). Ethnogenesis in the South Plains. In: J. D. Hill (Ed.), *History, power and identity* (pp. 70–89). Iowa City: Iowa University Press.

Hill, J. D. (Ed.) (1996). *History, power and identity: Ethnogenesis in the Americas, 1492–1992*. Iowa City: University of Iowa Press.

Hirschman, E. C. (2003). Consumer behavior among the melungeons; reconstructing a lost heritage. *Advances in Consumer Research*, *30*, 161.

Hirschman, E. C. (2005). *Melungeons: The last lost tribe in America*. Macon, GA: Mercer University Press.

Kennedy, N. B., with Kennedy, R. V. (1994, revised 1997). The Melungeons: The resurrection of a proud people; An untold story of ethnic cleansing in America, Mercer University Press, Macon, Georgia.

Kessler, J. S., & Ball, D. B. (2001). *North from the mountains: A folk history of the Carmel Melungeon Settlement*. Highland County, Ohio, & Macon, Georgia: Mercer University Press.

Mehta, R., & Belk, R. W. (1991). Artifacts, identity, and transition: Favorite possessions of Indians and Indian immigrants to the United States. *Journal of Consumer Research*, *17*(March), 398–411.

Oswald, L. R. (1999). Culture swapping: Consumption and the ethnogenesis of middle-class Haitian immigrants. *Journal of Consumer Research*, *21*(June), 32–54.

Penaloza, L. (1989). Immigrant consumer acculturation. *Advances in Consumer Research*, *16*, 110–118.

Penaloza, L. (1994). Atravesando Fronteras/border crossings: A critical ethnographic exploration of the consumer acculturation of mexican immigrants. *Journal of Consumer Research*, *21*(June), 32–44.

Schouten, J. W. (1991). Selves in transition: Symbolic consumption in personal rits of passage and identity reconstruction. *Journal of Consumer Research*, *17*(March), 412–425.

Stojanowski, C. M. (2005). The bioarchaeology of identity in Spanish colonial Florida: Social and evolutionary transformation before, during and after demographic collapse. *American Anthropologist*, *107*(3), 417–431.

Thompson, C. J., & Hirschman, E. C. (1995). Understanding the socialized body. *Journal of Consumer Research*, *22*(September), 139–153.

REAPING IDENTITY MEANINGS FROM AN AGRARIAN PAST: SOUTHERN HARVESTERS OF COMMERCIALLY CULTIVATED REGIONAL HERITAGE

Kelly Tian and Craig Thompson

ABSTRACT

Extending knowledge of the cultural shaping and variegating of white identity that occurs through the commercial diffusion of identity myths, we examine the reception of Southern identity myths promoted in the oppositional narratives of New South commercial media. We characterize oppositional narratives as texts which operate by eliciting an interpretive reading that devalues rather than supports the surface narrative, and explain the duplicitous text as one intended to seduce a dominant power, while empowering and bolstering identity of a marginalized group. After elaborating how oppositional discourse can serve to reinforce the identity frame constructed by regional media producers, we report on a study examining how urban and rural Southerners read and respond to this discourse. Our findings highlight mediators in the relationship between individuals' oppositional readings and their alignment of identity in a manner responsive to it.

Consumer Culture Theory
Research in Consumer Behavior, Volume 11, 261–295

ISSN: 0885-2111/doi:10.1016/S0885-2111(06)11012-1

> The stratification of power and privilege within whiteness hinges upon rural versus urban identity and the relative degrees of education versus "backwardness;" these labels all work to animate these key contours of difference within whiteness. – Hartigan (2003, p. 96).

Scholars of American history share a clear consensus that the socio-political legacy of the Civil War, and most particularly the cultural rifts exacerbated and solidified during the era of Congressional Reconstruction (circa 1867–1877), have exerted a profound influence on American society (Blight, 2001; Foner, 1988). Although the historical and mythic underpinnings of contemporary consumer culture have garnered considerable theoretical interest in recent years (see Arnould & Thompson, 2005 for a review), the nexus of regional identifications, romantic venerations, social stigmas, and, most controversially, the racial significations encoded in Southern consumption symbols, lifestyle idealizations, and archetypical characters have, much like the proverbial elephant in the room, been conspicuously ignored.

In a closely related theoretical vein, the role that commercial representations play in creating feelings of collective identification among white Americans has been largely overlooked by consumer researchers, with the notable exception of Peñaloza (2001), who discusses how Western Stock Shows glorify the cultural role of white settlers in their promotional staging of the American West. This disciplinary oversight exemplifies a broader tendency in the social sciences to treat whiteness as a natural condition, in need of no further explanation, rather than as a socially constructed category exhibiting shifting symbolic boundaries, differing gradations of membership, and internal diversity that engenders ideological instability and transformative conflicts (Perry, 2001; Roediger, 1999). Consumer researchers have analyzed identity myths in the context of gender (Holt & Thompson, 2004; Thompson, 1996), (non-white) ethnicity (Crockett & Wallendorf, 2004; Mehta & Belk, 1991; Peñaloza, 1994), and most prominently, consumer-centric identifications, such as being a biker (Schouten & McAlexander, 1995) or a trekkie (Kozinets, 2001), but they have given scant attention to the white identity myths which are conveyed through consumer culture.

In this paper, we propose that an historically informed analysis of the commercial diffusion (and reception) of Southern identity myths can provide important insights into the cultural shaping and variegating of white identity, which occurs in relation to rural versus urban designations. With the post-Civil War Reconstruction era, white Americans of the urban north were held to be different to an inferior class of white Americans residing in the more rural, agrarian south (Menken, 1920). This regional ordering of white race status continued in the New South manufacturing economy, fueled by the moral approbations leveled against the South and Southerners as a result of segregationist policies and practices. Of particular import were the nationally televised 1950s and 1960s Civil Rights struggles, which propelled the media creation and dissemination of two iconic Southern characters, the hillbilly and the redneck. While differentiated in their propensity toward violence (the hillbilly being less volatile and more affable), both caricaturized Southerners as backward, uneducated, and bound to a rural landscape (Doane & Bonilla-Silva, 2003; Graham, 2001), and serve as the present-day repositories for the Celtic myth, by which Southerners were once held to be descendants from an inferior bloodline (McWhiney, 1989). Through this multiplicity of representations, the South has been positioned as the symbolic cultural "other" of the rest of the nation (Graham, 2001). Notwithstanding the present-day far-reaching audiences who identify with redneck culture through the humor of comedians like Jeff Foxworthy, the lyrics of country music singers such as Gretchen Wilson, and the popularity of redneck sports like NASCAR, these still hold currency as markers of Southern culture and the South's inhabitants (see Cobb, 2005).

In a related investigation we have highlighted how commercial producers, who profit from cosmopolitan portrayals of the South seek to cultivate Southern identity as a source of valued distinctiveness (Thompson & Tian, 2006). Cultivate, here doubles in meaning referring to both the tilling and overturning of the historical terrain to give rise to ground deemed fertile for sowing a regional identity, as well as, advancing an educated, mannered regional identity. In particular, commercial producers that trade on an upscale, materially affluent yet distinctive image of South attempt to create what Chambers (1991) calls "room for maneuver" within the dominant structure imposed by national media portrayals of the region in the figures of rural rednecks and hillbillies. They enact practices of discursive resistance, which rather than being revolutionary, are instead complicitous, and make use of dominant national discourse to provide a position from which they may defend, and to a degree liberate, middle-upper class white Southerners from oppressive images.

While these self-positioned commercial redeemers of Southern culture experience the power of national structures of dominance as inescapable and limiting, these powers are also enabling: "Historically situated in spite of themselves, they speak of the presence and obsessive power of a social context that they conjure up by their very attempts to deny it, by their refusal to acknowledge it" (Chambers, 1993, p. 13). In the overarching narrative message of a highly materially affluent yet distinctive South, these texts pose a contradiction, read in recognition of material affluence as the effect of modernism. To be highly modern is to disappear into what is commonplace or normal, and to be distinctive from modern is to be marginal (Hartigan, 2003; Shields, 1991). Such a contradiction is a device used by producers to invite readers' interpretation of the text, as an activity essential to rendering their texts as "oppositional discourse" (cf. Chambers, 1993). As conceptualized by Chambers (1991, 1993), oppositional discourse is a text written in such a way that it encourages readers to contest and devalue the surface narrative, as explicitly told or written. Such texts are produced by embedding cultural codes within the narrative which are discernable to members of a marginalized group and which subtly mark the discourse as possessing ambiguity, contradictions, and ironies; the combinatory effect of which produces an interpreted narrative that is in opposition to the explicitly written narrative.

Extending our initial examination that focuses on the myth-endowed oppositional narratives constructed by producers of Southern lifestyle media (see Thompson & Tian, 2006), here we look to white upper/middle-class Southern residents as the intended readers of such texts and seek to understand what identity meanings and benefits they harvest from commercial cultivations of regional heritage. Our research questions and method are designed to delve broadly into white Southerners' oppositional readings of commercial texts that promote an upscale, materially affluent yet distinctive South, rather than an in-the-moment reading of a specific commercial text (cf. Mick & Buhl, 1992).[1]

THE IDENTITY FRAME OF THE SOUTH'S OPPOSITIONAL DISCOURSE

The South's Oppositional Discourse

The texts of New South media that promote a materially upscale yet distinctive South, such as offered by *Southern Living* magazine (Logue & McCalla, 2000; McPherson, 2003), operate through the practice of "oppositional discourse," characterized by a duplicitous text (Chambers, 1991). The text is duplicitous in the sense that it renders a double reading: one of the text as narrated to a narratee; and the other, as an interpretation of the text, prompted by a sense of irony, that leads to a reading between the lines of a different message (Chambers, 1991, 1993). Oppositional discourse is also duplicitous in the sense of being deceptive; that is, the message of the surface reading is a cover or disguise for the text's covert, oppositional message (Chambers, 1991, 1993).

The split narrative performance of these New South media producers emerges from playing to different audiences (cf. Chambers, 1991). As we elaborate in our prior work (Thompson & Tian, 2006), the overarching quest of these media producers' oppositional discourse is to solve an immediate problem: maintaining their media positioning of the South as a distinctive cultural region, which is increasingly challenged with the effects of modernization and globalization. There are also broader ramifications. As modernization/globalization forces visibly efface much distinctiveness from the landscape (Reed, 2003), the regional media industry plays a critical role in protecting the South's economic base that thrives on a tourism industry which stages a romanticized image of the South's culture (see also McPherson, 2003). Beyond targeting the South's urban and rural populations, the discourse of these producers is also intended for an audience outside the region, in particular national advertisers, business investors, and national and international tourists (e.g., Logue & McCalla, 2000; McPherson, 2003).

As Chambers (1984) reminds us, the same story can afford different meanings and moral implications depending on the situation in which it is told. Adapting one of his examples, consider a "redneck" joke told by Southerners among themselves, by Northerners among themselves, by a Northerner to a Southerner, and by a Southerner to a Northerner. In each instance, the story is determined less by the content and more by "the point of its being told, that is, the relationships mediated by the act of narration" (p. 3). The point of regional media producers telling the story of an upscale, affluent yet distinctive South is different for their different audiences. Yet for both audiences, the story possesses the power to change human situations, producing reversals of situations or offering reinforcement of values or beliefs which may prompt action (Chambers, 1984). A split performance of the text – that is, one that exhibits duplicity in presenting a narrated text, the more surface reading of which is countered by the interpretative reading – provides two paths of seduction, such that oppositional discourse may seduce the powerful while empowering the excluded or marginal (Chambers, 1991).

Consider the surface narrative of Southern lifestyle media texts that promote a materially affluent yet distinctive New South. The surface narrative respects the dominant power of modernism, asserting its values in a quest for national advertising dollars. On terms of exchange set by this power, regional media producers seduce national advertisers by promising a region that is economically affluent, able to afford national luxury brands. Yet their survival is conditioned upon positing a South of nuanced tastes, whose population does not subscribe to national lifestyle publications (see Logue & McCalla, 2000). In our earlier analysis, we highlight that select commercial producers of Southern lifestyle magazines assert regional distinctiveness by disseminating traces of the region's historical myths, particularly Old South/ Lost Cause myths tied to a "moonlight and magnolias" romantic imagining of the agrarian region, reviving and reconstructing these to suit contemporary contexts (Thompson & Tian, 2006). As noted by Cash (1941, p. xlix), "What the Old South of the legend in its classical form was like is more or less familiar to everyone."

> It was a sort of stage piece out of the eighteenth century, wherein gesturing gentlemen move soft-spokenly against a background of rose gardens and dueling grounds, through always gallant deeds, and lovely ladies, in farthingales, never for a moment lost that exquisite remoteness ...Its social pattern was manorial, its civilization that of the Cavalier, its ruling class coextensive with the planter group ... They dwelt in large and stately mansions, preferably white with columns and Grecian entablature. Their estates were feudal baronies, their slaves quite too numerous ever to be counted, and their social life a thing of Old World splendor and delicacy...a world singularly polished and mellow and poised...

In their reconstructions, cultural producers, in an act akin to winnowing chaff from grain, cast off historical representations which precipitated the region's stigmatization and oppression nationally, particularly those associated with race and class inequities instantiated by cultural practices associated with its agrarian past. They neatly glean from the romanticized antebellum period, its aristocratic images of a gracious lifestyle of home entertaining carried out in interiors of lavishly textiled and nature-adorned homes, which in appropriating the agrarian landscape (and the historical fruits of its terrain, primarily cotton) offer a one-with-nature imagery that contests modernization, despite exhibiting all its material benefits. These traces of an agrarian antebellum heritage are covert in regional oppositional discourse, facilitated by a media cover story, in which these are material markers of an affluent population thriving in a New South economy, and possessing a particular, regionally nuanced taste. This is the surface narrative intended for the national business community and those residing outside the region. In this regard, New South oppositional narratives follow early or traditional oppositional narratives identified by Chambers (1991), in that the surface narrative addresses the dominant power.

For the audience of readers residing in the region, however, the recognition of this historical trace introduces the element of irony. Irony emerges in representations of a cosmopolitan New South that claims cultural capital in a modern/global economy through the material symbols of its agrarian Old South heritage (cf. Holt, 1998). Such an interpretation would negate the cover story of a New South that asserts its modernization and progressive affluence through upscale if peculiar tastes, because the material markers of distinctiveness are recognizably from the pre-modernization period. As the media-conjured historical moment is the antebellum South prior to Civil War defeat, it is one when being distinctive did not imply being marginal. The Old South, rather than supplanted by a modern cosmopolitan New South, has in the more ironic reading remained permanently elusive, and within the pages of such regional discourse, "The Old South rises again." For media producers, cultivating such an oppositional reading among targeted regional residents offers an historical basis for authenticating the various cultural practices for enacting a Southern identity that they promote.

Readers may also discern irony in other themes of these texts. For instance, these texts heavily tout the region's upscale cultural amenities, often as "well kept secrets," to a regional readership able to see and experience these. The contradiction in the text of advertising "secrets" which, residents can see, pulls for its regional audience to read between the lines to recognize oppositional intent – that of contesting nationally disseminated Celtic myths of the South iconized through cinematic depictions of poor backward, rural rednecks, and hillbillies. Although the assertion of regional status, in general, implies there is a power that oppresses it (cf. Chambers, 1991). There is, however, no direct or explicit confrontation with these stigmatizing national representations; rather, they are left latent, unspoken.[2] The value to media producers of this oppositional reading among targeted regional residents is that it may create a sense of solidarity through a shared tribal stigma (Goffman, 1963), which creates a defensive, reactionary desire to enact a Southern identity, through means prescribed in their media offerings.

The Identity Frame of the Discourse

The "room for maneuver" constructed with oppositional narrative, or counter discourse, thus is a space which may, beyond producers' immediate quest for economic survival, also shape people's mentalities, inclusive of ideas, values, attitudes, and feelings, as the manifestations of desires which may propel them to altered behavior (Chambers, 1991). Producers of Southern lifestyle media, through various discursive practices attempt to shape the desire for "other," that is, for a southern identity, shared with a collective of Southerners, and rendered identifiable through participation in a set of prescribed consumption practices (Thompson & Tian, 2006). Stated differently, in the creation of the oppositional narrative, the commercial producer creates a frame for identity (cf. Goffman, 1974; e.g., Martin, 2002).

While Cash (1941, p. 3), held long ago that "Nobody of any considerable information ... any longer believes in the legend of the Old South," we have found that regional commercial producers of oppositional texts, nonetheless, cultivate this heritage as the basis for white Southern identity (Thompson & Tian, 2006).

The regional oppositional discourse we have described presupposes a readership that will read the discursive text as an oppositional narrative; that is, a readership able to read between the lines to discern in the subtlety of the discourse's subtexts, the traces of the Old South/Lost Cause myth that underpins the privileged regional representations, and/or to recognize the implicit stigmatizing national myths that the discourse counters.

> For it is the ongoing *readability* of texts (and works of art), their ability to transcend the context of their production, that enables them to make all the necessary concessions and compromises with the prevailing power of the moment – ...so that their oppositional readability can become available ... to a readership that is the true object of their "address." [address in the French language holding the additional meaning of adroitness]... that is *other than it seems*; and it is adroitness in the management of address that defines the oppositional text... (Chambers, 1991, p. 2)

An oppositional narrative, to be so, then requires that readers – usually the marginalized or oppressed, "condemned to silence" in their exclusion from the media – critically interpret these dominant texts in ways that call forth the oppositional elements embedded in the narrative (Chambers, 1991, pp. 3–4). This reading produces the oppositionality; if targeted readers do not perceive irony but instead read only the surface text, then the discourse is not oppositional. Chambers' works highlight how the duplicitous role of oppositional discourse facilitates the seduction of members of the dominant culture (via the surface narrative), while seducing readers from the marginalized culture with collective identity meanings (via the interpretive reading of the narrative). Following Chambers' (1991, 1993) conceptualization of this form of discourse, other works have suggested that commercially produced oppositional discourse can assist their target audience of marginalized individuals in self understanding and sense making of lived experiences (Martin, 2002; Snow, Rochford, Worden, & Benford, 1986).

Individuals' reading and responding to opposition in narratives may also be situationally mediated (Chambers, 1991). One such mediator in our context of the South's oppositional texts would seem to be Southern readers' sense of "home" within the Southern region, which is characterized by both large urban metropolitan cities and the small towns, many of which exist on their periphery. Although national media representations of the South, as well as nationally disseminated tourist texts published by Southern media producers, often portray the South as the North's oppositional agrarian and rural other (Graham, 2001; McPherson, 2003), places within the region are further marked, ranked, and characterized in polar terms of urban and rural, city and country, modern and not modern, inflected as either backward or quaint. This type of place-based status ordering has been noted by sociologist Rob Shields (1991, p. 3).

> Marginal places, those towns and regions which have been 'left behind' in the modern race for progress, evoke both nostalgia and fascination. Their marginal status may come from out-of-the-way geographic locations…being the Other pole to a great cultural center. In all cases the type of geographic marginality … is a mark of being a social periphery. That is, the marginal places that are of interest are not necessarily on geographical peripheries, but, first and foremost, they have been placed on the periphery of cultural systems of space in which places are ranked relative to each other. They all carry the image, and stigma of their marginality which become indistinguishable from any basic empirical identity they might once have had. From this *primary* ranking of cultural status they may also end up being classified in what geographers have mapped as systems of 'centres and peripheries.'

Our research questions follow this line of inquiry into the ways, which oppositional narratives operate through these contested mythic constructions of place and with them racialized consumer identifications. As a precondition to reading regional oppositional discourse, do white Southerners read national media representations of the Southern region and its inhabitants as stigmatizing and oppressive? That is, are they sensitive to the Celtic myth, and thus able to read between the lines of what is left latent by media producers in proffering a materially affluent yet distinctive South? Preconditioning to the Old South/Lost Cause myths which are carried forward in regional media representations, would also seem to advantage readers' oppositional readings, enabling them to follow the often implicit text intended to conjure this local heritage as a means of rendering promoted lifestyle choices as regionally distinctive. Are imaginings of the antebellum South and the event of the Civil War salient aspects of cultural heritage to present day white Southerners? How do individuals, Southerners, respond to regional oppositional discourse? In what ways do individuals align their identity with the identity frame created by regional oppositional discourse?

METHOD

Informants and observations were drawn from two culturally interconnected Southern locals – one a large urban center and the other a small town on its periphery. The two locals differ further in their geographical proximity to and economic dependence on agricultural farming and in the ways they are positioned in national discourses of the Civil War and the Civil Rights struggles. The larger of the two, Birmingham, Alabama is home to over a million inhabitants. Noted for its production of cast iron pipe and mineral based industries which dominated until the 1960s (Morris, 1994), Birmingham's economy today is further comprised of service industries, banking and finance, and health related technological research. Its economy is not dependent on agricultural production, and indeed from its very post Civil War founding in 1871 and subsequent growth, it was upheld as an icon of the emerging New South. In contradiction to at least the social equality meanings of the New South, the city was a focal site of racial violence and Civil Rights protests during the 1960s, with many of these images nationally televised.

Our second site is 45 miles outside of Birmingham, in a town we disguise here under the name of "Springville." A small town of a little over 5,000 residents, the town emerged to offer services to the local farming community, which it continues to serve. While many of its population can trace their ancestry to a frontier predating the Civil War, the landscape bears no traces of the antebellum period as might be seen in other Southern towns whose histories traverse this period (e.g., Natchez, Mississippi; Natchitoches, Louisiana; or Clemson, South Carolina). Nonetheless, like many small towns throughout the southeastern region, it has begun to market its quaint culture (Cobb, 2005), drawing largely from the population of Birmingham residents who seek out its quiet main street and its natural surroundings, into which they are drawn by the town's covered bridges, as well as, the local art festivals held on the riverbanks beneath them. The seemingly fresh from the field produce of its farmers' market is also a draw.

As a result of its proximity to Birmingham, Springville's cultural identity has since the beginning of the last century, been defined largely in opposition to it. Birmingham is the modern "other" of a different way of life to that of Springville. The population of Springville is interchanged with that of Birmingham, as some Springville residents have sought employment in the Birmingham job market, while some Birmingham workers have sought escape in Springville's small town life. Readers of commercially produced oppositional discourse of the region are drawn from both rural and urban populations (e.g., Logue & McCalla, 2000), while representations of the South in this discourse often use rural scenes as backdrops to the affluent lifestyles more characteristic of urban markets (Thompson & Tian, 2006).

In representing the informants of this presentation, we dispense with the traditional use of "consumer" designations, consistent with Firat's (2006) recognition of the conceptual contradictions this terminology engenders in the face of the post modern experience in which boundaries between consumption and production have become blurred or porous.[3] This criticism is particularly relevant in this context. To the extent that regional culture is produced in everyday life and the occupations that sustain it (e.g., the production of food, clothing, housing, education, and entertainment), all individuals participate in the production of their local culture. Further, to varying degrees, all carry consumption activities into the realm of work (cf. Tian & Belk, 2005). Our 12 informants are upper- and middle-class white Southerners of the babyboom generation, who as a group differ in occupations, age, interests, and travel experiences. All but one were born and reared in the South, with more than half possessing college degrees. Six are residents of Springville, and six dwell in Birmingham.

Interviews resulted from approaching individuals during extended stays. These ranged from half an hour to several hours and followed a general guideline. Discussions were initiated with questions to learn about informants' personal history, inclusive of experiences traveling outside the region, and their personal values and consumption experiences. Subsequently, questions were asked to elicit their views of the distinguishing aspects of life in the Deep South, inclusive of regional cultural values and consumption practices. Additional questioning obtained their impressions of cultural changes that had occurred in the South during their life. These areas of inquiry often prompted informants to spontaneously share their views of how the South is depicted in regional and the national media and popular culture. Regional commercial texts that we report on here are those that informants chose to feature in their discussions of the South's culture and their personal life histories. Thus, our findings reference commercial cultivations of the region via lifestyle media publications, televised series, popular films, and tourist promotions, the oppositional texts of which we were able to identify and which have, although through different emphases, been noted in prior research or acknowledged in corporate biographies (e.g., respectively, *Southern Living*, *Designing Women*, *Steel Magnolias*, and riverboat casino promotions and tours; Logue & McCalla, 2000; McPherson, 2003; Roberts, 1996). Hereafter, we refer to these in aggregate as regional oppositional discourse.

Our analysis features four cases followed by an integrative analysis. The selected cases are purposively highlighted to elaborate the mediating role of rural/urban sense of home or identity, and its accompanying cultural heritage, in individuals' readings of and responsiveness to regional oppositional discourse.

PROCESSES OF HARVESTING COMMERCIALLY CULTIVATED HERITAGE

Individual Cases

Doreen, a Lifetime Rural Resident

Doreen is the third generation owner of a county paper operated out of an office extension of her home in the small town of Springville. While she has traveled outside the region for vacation, for all but a few years in another Southern state, she has resided in or on the outskirts of Springville. She considers it and the surrounding county "home." In speaking of national media's portrayal of the region, she appears sensitive to the Southern region as "other" in a national discourse that biases presentations to maintain this "otherness" (see 1.1 in appendix). Notably she does so without explicit mention of "rednecks" or "hillbillies," terms completely absent from her interview vocabulary. While she sees the more desirable aspects of the South as deserving of more media attention, she makes clear in her argument that she is not challenging the credibility of national media reports. As a result of her editorial experiences tied to reporting on the politics and economic challenges of the region, she recognizes that culture, as enacted through lifestyle practices, is influenced by economic resources, such that the poor and affluent experience a different sense of Southern culture. In her words, "there is no single Southern culture" (see 1.2 in appendix).

Doreen does, however, find common ground across poor and affluent Southerners, locating this in a culturally inherited "tenacious attitude" stemming from the Civil War (see 1.3 in appendix). Reference to the Civil War emerges spontaneously in her discussion of the South's nonunion labor, which she considers a present-day cultural effect of this heritage. She shares, a story passed on through oral history of her Civil War ancestors who fought for the Union rather than the Confederacy, adding to this "they're [mountain people] a tough rugged people, they're survivors. You let the economy crash, you let everything we depend on come tumbling down and they'll survive."

The genealogy she offers, linking herself and Springville back to Union rather than Confederate soldiers of the Civil War, seems a useful perceptual lens for reading, and granting authority to those media publications that separate a gracious Old South lifestyle from its production via the institution of slavery (McPherson, 2003).

> *Southern Living* is our Bible, I don't know if you're heard of it. It's the Bible. We just call it that, we don't want to throw it away. We hold on to them for fear there's something in there we didn't catch. As the South becomes more affluent, we see it in our construction,

we see it in our larger gracious houses, we see it the increasingly gracious and even excessive entertaining. I think it's still in us. We hunger for it. Those maybe who never knew it want it, those of us who experienced it hunger for it. [By that you're talking about?] Graciousness, the big porches. The porches they're building now are too small, if you're going to have a porch it's gotta be a veranda. But, there's still a hunger for it.

Apparent in her reading of the magazine, is its ability to conjure a lost past of gracious living tied to veranda-skirted homes in which affluent Southerners entertain. Contrasting her ancestral claim as a descendant of rugged mountain people, in other stories that Doreen tells from her personal history, she counts herself among those who knew a more gracious affluent Southern life and now "hunger" for this as a lost heritage.

I do want to tell you two stories when I think about the South that I love. I was reared by two truly Southern ladies. Of course, mother is, but these were older. We lived in a modest house, and when you're in town you'll see Ace Hardware, and her home is a brown brick with a beautiful veranda going around the side. I spent my summers there. Her daughter had gone off to college so I had the run of the house. Gracious, so gracious. But she was a character, just like what you see in southern novels. She introduced me to alcohol when we were just 12. She had made these crème de mint. She had decided it was time to introduce us to alcohol. Always there with food. Getting to have dinner, that would be lunch, in those dining rooms just transported you to another world. Atmosphere, the food, the setting, it's just, among my finest memories ... Florence was a fabulous story teller.

...I truly do not believe the woman was afraid of the devil himself... [The film Steel Magnolia] It's very much on target. You have this gracious façade and you have all this strength down under. Southern women are very strong women. And I think that became wired in with the Civil War. I was interviewed by public radio after 9–11. They were wanting a take on how a small town, a small county reacted. I told them that our people would be ready to lock and load, that we often forget that we have had war in this country. We forget that-that our people had known war on their, in their home. And that becomes a part of you whether you realize that or not. The subconscious of the brain absorbs so much and so much is passed on...

And we're fighters. I find that fascinating. And southerners make up such a high percentage of the military. Our men are fighters, they're gun people. There are fewer places to hunt, so they play more golf but it's still there. They still line up at the Walmart at Christmas to give guns to the boys at Christmas, which I always think is so weird to give a kid a gun at Christmas. But it's still the big thing, you've got to start this boy out with his first gun...

Church is still very much a social, it's where you go to meet friends. We don't have a lot of entertainment. We're a dry county. You can't buy alcoholic beverages here, except now you can at the clubs. We have two golf clubs, and we managed to get legislation through last year, it just tickled the stew out of me, so now you can go to the club, and I can have my gin and tonic. I feel like I've just died and gone to heaven.

Although Doreen lays claim to a more gracious Southern past through episodic experiences rather than an affluent family background, she bolsters her membership with claims to having attained a level education higher than most in the Springville community. In conjuring life memories of a gracious *Gone With the Wind* – inspired affluent Southern culture, *Southern Living* becomes, like the Bible, the timeless guide to Southern culture. Following its regional representations (Cobb, 2005; Logue & McCalla, 2000; Roberts, 1996), hunting falls to golf as the competitive masculine sport, while Church gives over its congregation to the country club, with its members able to toast a return to gracious life. Doreen, throughout, places this upscale gracious life not in opposition to aspects of culture, such as hunting, often associated with national Celtic stereotypes of the rural poor, but rather as the natural evolution of these cultural practices. The town's Civil War heritage likewise becomes the foundational base of a media-shaped "steel magnolia" ideology of southern womanhood, in which inner strength is masked in highly feminized "ladies," though no such explicit linkages are made in the film of this title (see McPherson, 2003).

Doreen's ability to privilege a *Southern Living* inspired landscape as "authentic" despite the patchwork rural–modern and poor–affluent terrain of present-day Springville, is achieved by a selective imagining of the effects of modernization. Doreen easily traces her heritage backward to the Civil War devastation and then forward to the modernization of the rural agrarian community. In this narrative recounting, the practice of hunting, for example, evolves in the modern/global world into playing golf, and driving out to the Country Club is cast idyllically in a way that glosses over the presence of Wal-Mart super stores and strip mall centers that line the way. In reckoning with the reality that golf clubs have not entirely supplanted firearms as recreational possessions, Doreen links the latter to a present day nationalism asserted through military participation. The genealogical threads of cultural evolution she selects, are however ones well informed, and thus seemingly more authentic to her, as a result of her gleaning these from historical texts. Early in the interview, she offers that to truly understand the culture, we should read Cash's (1941) *Mind of the South*, and Flynt's (2004) most recent chronicle of Alabama history, which she claims are the two most credible references on the subject.

Through this discourse, Doreen is revealed as conscious of reading the opposition in commercial Southern culture texts, such as *Southern Living* magazine and the film *Steel Magnolias*, that promote an affluent but distinct South. Her oppositional reading derives from general knowledge of national media stereotypes (see 1.1 in appendix), and a sensitivity to this given the rural place of her upbringing and her lived experience of the everyday interactions between the affluent and poor in her small town (see 1.2 in appendix). Despite her acknowledgement that "there is no single Southern culture," she grants authority to regional media producers, like *Southern Living*, in representing an affluent culture as authentic Southern culture. As she sums up, "This is the southern culture we all like to think about."

Doreen's elective affinity (e.g., Holt, 1998) for this ideological framing of Southern identity and culture is mediated by several factors. A combination of oral history and readings of historical texts enable her to trace to the antebellum period the prescribed cultural practices and lifestyles of media promoting an upscale South. She recognizes the Old South/Lost Cause myths that are implicit in these media representations. Further, she is able to align her lived experiences with the frame, which gives weight to its authenticity. This alignment is facilitated by her adoption of the vocabulary and material markers for Southern identity and culture offered in regional oppositional discourse which privileges Southern vernacular (e.g., Logue & McCalla, 2000; cf. Martin, 2002).

Specifically, the personal narrative that she reconstructs from the past becomes aligned through references to "Southern ladies" whose "gracious" entertaining, transports guests to another world, providing her "finest" memory. Her office interior to some extent mirrors her narrative and representations of Southern lifestyle in regional oppositional discourse. The large open office opposes a modern aesthetic, and instead features low lamp-lit lighting and arrangements of fresh flowers on the desks that align the walls, leaving the center available for the large traditional dining table, on which is offered a cornucopia of fruit. Prints of the county's surrounding natural landscape are arranged throughout, and in places positioned next to decorative plates, some revealed to be family heirlooms. Ongoing identity alignment during the interview also seemed evident. In keeping with her interpretation of *Steel Magnolias* as women imbued with inner strength inherited as descendants from Civil War survivors, she subtly aligns her identity, revealing her advanced stage of cancer only near the end of the lengthy interview. Doreen also views as authentically Southern those cities, such as Savannah and Sea Island, that offer "a smell, a taste, a feel" of Southern culture (see 1.4 in appendix), eliding the tourism-motivated commercial production of these (Brundage, 2005). Preconditioned by her self categorization as affluent/educated and different from Springville's rural poor ("the Bubba" she claims she has "grown to appreciate"), she is seduced by the narrative of regional media producers whose oppositional discourse contests national stereotypes which cast all white Southerners in terms of its rural poor. Instead, she embraces the identity frame for being Southern offered by these oppositional discourses.

Danny, a Vacillating Rural–Urban–Rural Resident

Danny, who grew up in Springville, is in his mid 40s and is a married father of two boys. He moved to Birmingham to attend college, after which he was employed in the business field by a large Birmingham-based corporation for 14 years. He and his family relocated their place of residence to Springville eight years ago while Danny continued to commute to Birmingham, until last year, when he opened a postal service franchise with a storefront along Springville's Main Street. In elaborating his relocation of residence, Danny highlights the draw of the natural environment, slower pace of life, and the more intimate community relations, contrasting this with the stress he experienced in his former Birmingham job. He highlights these same rural features, in speaking about the broader culture of the South.

> I love it here. It's a rural area. Just decided this is a slower pace of life and I enjoy it, I enjoy the people more…I bought some land. [in talking about valued aspects of culture] First of all I love the geography. I think it's a beautiful state. We have beaches, we have flat woodlands, we have swamps, we have mountains, we have fast moving rivers, slow lakes, we have a lot of wildlife, we have a diverse population different people different backgrounds and that blend creates ah, I think makes a very interesting group of people.

Finding enjoyment in the diversity of the South, Danny finds that national media's portrayal of the South's race problems are "blown out of proportion." Like Doreen, Danny seems largely oblivious to commonplace media portrayals of "rednecks" and "hillbillies." Rather, he focuses on the representation of race relations that portray the South as a segregated region, dominated by racist social attitudes. Danny routinely points to signs of cultural diversity as a rebuke to these media images (see 1.5 in appendix). To bolster his view that the South enjoys a much higher degree of racial harmony than recognized by the national media, he returns to the past, discussing first the diversity of Alabama's pioneer period in terms of its Caucasian and Native American populations, followed by the disclosure that one of his ancestors was Native American, a respected community member and Civil War General.

Danny too takes pride in the extensive knowledge of Southern history he has consciously cultivated (1.6, 1.7).

> I majored in history. I've always had a fondness for history, especially Southern and American History. And that goes back to my childhood here and hearing stories about my forefathers and actually having some artifacts from when my family migrated here during the early 1800's… most of my family were poor farmers. Most of them came

> from South Carolina, most came from Georgia, some came from Tennessee. My mother's side, we know that some of our forefathers actually participated in the War of 1812, they participated in the Creek and Indian War, and that's how they became fascinated with Alabama. They came down here and fought in the war, and then went and got their families and settled down here before Alabama was a state... We had family names in a Bible, and I actually did some research.

While Danny reports that he is most fascinated with the pioneer history which precedes the Civil War, he nonetheless demonstrates extensive knowledge of his Civil War ancestors. He tells an extended narrative of a large family of brothers, divided in their decision to participate in the War, one hiding out, one fighting and dying at Gettysburg, and the remaining brothers also dying in battle. His story weaves oral history, passed down from his grandmother, together with additional information he uncovered in his attempts to verify the facts and contexts of the story. His story is detailed with names, dates, and battle sites. He highlights a number of inherited keepsakes, which he uses to authenticate his story: a letter from one of the brothers discussing the politics of the Civil War; a button and a coin from the pockets of the brother who fought and died at Gettysburg; and $100 Confederate bill, sent by the Confederate government to the mother following his death. Throughout, he expresses an identity-affirming confidence in this oral history because he was able to verify much of his grandmother's tale with historical records (see 1.7 in appendix).

> What is unique about this, you hear all these stories about the South and the Civil War, my family was just regular farmers, not slave holders. And actually two of my great great grandfathers hid out during the Civil War to avoid going in the army. And one of these was the brother of the six or seven brothers who were in the War. The ones that hid out. That was passed on through oral history. But you don't hear about, everyone just wasn't gung-ho about the war.

In these ancestral reflections, Danny's claim to the lineage of the rural poor of Springville takes a central narrative role. The research-reinforced oral history in which he is invested is the place from which he contests popular, affluent representations of Southern culture as is present in regional oppositional discourse.

> My wife's a big *Gone With the Wind* fan, and I've always told her that I want to rewrite it cause I, there were a few people who lived that type of lifestyle, but in college we learned that one third of one percent of the white population in the South lived like the people in *Gone with the Wind* did. That was a minority. If you think about it, it makes sense, everybody is not rich. So, I would like to, I've always teased her about rewriting *Gone with the Wind* and showing your average farmer, toiling, sweating in the fields, and the children out there working with him and living in a log cabin. ... being a lady you don't necessarily have to be wealthy, to be a lady or a gentleman. It doesn't matter. But I think

a lot of people think of having money and arrogance to be a southern lady or gentleman and that's not always the case.

As a college educated, business owner, Danny's socio-economic standing is quite comparable to that of Doreen. However, his possession of this richly articulated oral history leads him to identify differently with the regionally dominant portrayal of Southern culture's affluent white citizenry. He does not grant these oppositional discourses authority. Danny's assertion of a Southern heritage of "toiling, sweating in the field" adjoining a log cabin do not reflect the alignments with Southern oppositional discourse invoked by Doreen in her vocabulary of gracious leisurely living from expansive verandas. Rather, he challenges the meaning of cultural terms such as Southern lady or Southern gentlemen as being inherently linked to class standing.

Furthermore, his postal franchise exhibits a very symbolic contestation. While one side contains the greeting cards, stationary, and mailing supplies that might be found in any such service place in the country, the front entrance features home-made and home-canned preserves and sauces, and the left side hosts an elaborate wall display of Mayberry branded t-shirts, hats, and handbags (in reference to the fictional town made iconic by the widely popular *Andy Griffith Show*). The line extends into Mayberry recipe books in the display case, arranged such that Aunt Bee's image flanks on both sides a chess set, the opposing pieces of which are cast as Confederate and Union Civil War soldiers (see Figs. 1 and 2). The latter arrangement is emblematic of Danny's discourse concerning his poor farmer ancestors who

Fig. 1. Civil War Chess Set Displayed for Sale in Danny's Postal Service Franchise.

Fig. 2. Mayberry Branded Merchandise Sold in Danny's Postal Service Franchise.

were pawns of the slave holding planter class. Notably, there are no other symbols of the Confederacy, save this one, focally displayed, which in presenting both parties invokes Civil War heritage in a way that buffers against "redneck" labeling, a buffering enhanced by the guarding and disarming presence of the feminized, always well-meaning Aunt Bee. Mediated by his oral history, Danny embraces what he deems as the heritage of rural folk – a slow pace of life where people enjoy nature and know their community members well enough to light heartedly poke fun at them.

> Well, I like Andy Griffith myself, and I thought, that's something that you don't see everyday and I think a lot of people still keep up and watch Andy Griffith and Mayberry. It's just something unique that you don't see in a lot of places…[it's the] Humor. I think a lot of times people take life too serious and that show kind of, you know a lot of people you can relate with a lot of characters in that show, I think it helps you enjoy life more. …I think most southerners don't mind poking fun at themselves if its done in a certain way, not a disrespectful way.

Lorna, a Vacillating Urban–Rural Resident

Lorna, a small business owner in her mid 40s, grew up in Birmingham where she resided until three years ago. In the reverse pattern of Danny's move, Lorna maintained a Birmingham residence and commuted to her office in Springville for more than a decade before finally relocating there. She acknowledges that despite the stress and inconvenience of the long drive, her long-sustained reluctance to relocate reflected her desire to avoid being identified with a rural, small town. Her move was finally prompted to accommodate the wishes of her school-age child, who attended a Springville school, and wanted to be near friends. Unlike Doreen and Danny, Lorna's comments on national media portrayals are explicit in referencing depictions of "rednecks" (see 1.8 in appendix). She interprets the "redneck" icon, not as a symbolic character, but rather as a legitimate social category that designates the South's rural poor who live in trailers and in her narrative, they assume the role of the marginalized "other" who stand in invidious comparison to more affluent Birmingham residents.

Also in contrast to Doreen and Danny, in speaking about the South's culture, Lorna makes few references to either family heritage or Civil War history, and makes no claims to having read historical texts. The only reference to the Civil War occurs in her attempt to clarify the meaning of "redneck." Beyond linking the redneck to a rural place, she asserts that such a label applies to someone who passionately holds to an idea irrespective of how it impacts other people, and uses as illustration, the practice of holding to the Confederate flag as a symbol of the South. In her ambivalence toward history, Lorna expresses the present, forward looking perspective of modernism, the foundational ideology which inspired the South's bulldozer revolution and the urban development projects that dramatically transformed Birmingham (Morris, 1994).

As an urban born and reared Southern middle/upper-class business owner, and daughter of a middle/upper-class business owner, Lorna is easily able to align her identity with the oppositional discourse of regional commercial productions of culture that emphasizes an aristocratic vision of Southernness and which traces back to antebellum plantation economy. For Lorna, being Southern means acquiring and exhibiting class-based manners:

> I think a southern lady is someone, and I know this is going to sound real old school, but its someone who likes having the door opened for her, like having the man take care of the things that you generally think men take care of, the cars and the yard, that likes dressing up to go out, that's what I think… I think what you see in movies, yeah that's your typical southernness about it, they [Southern women] want to be treated like a lady, they want their doors opened, seats pulled out at restaurants. It's manners. I'm teaching my son that… Now that's southern that's not "redneck."

However, as a function of her work, Lorna routinely interacts with rural residents, both affluent and poor. Through these encounters, her sense of Southern graciousness has been altered. In her reformulated view, dressing down (as opposed to "up") is the gracious way to maintain social harmony and interactional southern comfort, as the distinctive mantras of Southern culture and she decouples these regional traits from any necessary connection to class status (see 1.9 in appendix). Her reconstructed meaning of Southern grace is one drawn from the lived experience of navigating and floating between interactions with the poor and affluent that characterizes much of Southern culture, particularly rural areas in which farmers reside in close proximity to those seeking escape from the urban environment. However such interactions are absent from regional oppositional discourse, which asserts a more homogeneously affluent South (e.g., Thompson & Tian, 2006).

Betty, a Lifelong Urban Resident

Betty, a married empty nester over the age of 60, has resided in Birmingham her entire life. Betty's parents ran a service-oriented "mom and pop" business that provided for Betty's middle-class upbringing. Although she never attended college, Betty claims this was her choice and not one of limited financial means. While Betty has been firmly situated within the middle-upper class for several decades, her early married life cast her as wife of a working class spouse who without a college education matriculated to the middle/upper-class upon entering a marketing profession. Corresponding with her husband's rise in income, Betty gave up her early clerical job to become a full time homemaker, and after rearing her children, began her present career as an interior design consultant. Betty and her husband were among the upwardly mobile Southerners of the babyboom generation, outside the circle of old money Birmingham elites, yet able to enjoy some of the same types of cultural amenities.

Like Lorna, Betty's reports of national media portrayals of the South are explicit in their references to hillbillies and rednecks (see 1.10 in appendix). Having traveled more outside the region than Lorna, she is sensitive to how these representations have influenced negative impressions among individuals living in other regions (see 1.10 in appendix). Betty's travels have not, however, provided much exposure to the South's rural poor. Betty reports that both her parents, and grandparents were Birmingham residents, and that only her grandparents had spent their youth in rural farming communities. Betty has few significant remembrances of rural life, with the exception of a few childhood memories of accompanying her grandparents' return on special occasions like Church Homecomings. Having less exposure to the rural South, Betty is less cognizant of the reality of the rural poor than Lorna. Challenging the authenticity of national media representations, she remarks of the poor, rural interviewees chosen by media agents in national news stories: "You just wonder how long they have to look to find these people."

Also, like Lorna she makes no references to Civil War history, either in discussing her personal heritage or broader cultural heritage. Even while her reflections on unfair media portrayals mention the recurrent replays of the

Civil Rights struggles of the 1960s, she does not link these events to the plantation past and its precipitation of the Civil War. In reflecting upon portrayals of the South which she deems to be positive, such as the film *Steel Magnolias*, she does not link representations to the Civil War as does Doreen, but rather comments on the beautiful home that served as the stage for much of the filming. Likewise in her discussion of Southern homes and the characteristics that she views render them distinct from homes in other regions of the country, Betty notes the greater use of textiles, particularly window draperies. However, she links this to neither the antebellum plantation past and the cotton crops which supplied Southern textile mills, nor to the media-constructed interiors, in films such as *Gone with the Wind* (a film Betty claims not to have seen), or televised series such as *Designing Women* that feature this interior design element (see McPherson, 2003).

> Oh yeah, the South is big on that [window draperies]. That's southern… what it does it warms the house. A house with window treatments is always a cozier, it gives it a better feeling than one that is stark and bare… Southern homes usually are much warmer to people [relative to Western and Northeastern homes] because of the things people have accumulated. We're not a throwaway part of the country. We accumulate and many times it's things that have been handed down through the family, antiques or special glass ware. Southern homes are just full of those kinds of things. You very seldom see a home that's ultra contemporary. That just doesn't fit the southern lifestyle. If you see a home like that most likely it's someone who has moved here from the North.

For Betty, the defining cultural traits of Southern lifestyles have not been lost to the antebellum past (and awaiting revival), but rather they have emerged in conjunction with the modern New South, and the achievement and material aspirations that it fueled. Betty's perception has been framed by her historical reliance upon regional lifestyle media and their stylized representations of legitimate Southern domestic taste.

> It [*Southern Living* magazine] is the be all and end all of interior design, cooking, and gardening. It's a comprehensive magazine that covers anything that a southern man or woman would want to find out. [Do you know, did your mom have them?] No, I don't know, it probably was, but she didn't have it. I started collecting them when my sister-in-law's sister worked for *Southern Living*, …So that's what I got for Christmas every year for years and years and years was the *Southern Living* subscription plus their cookbook. At the end of every year they take all the recipes that have been in all the magazines for the year and they put them in a hardback cookbook and you can buy that.

Betty's narrative, however, does express a sense of loss over some of the lifestyle changes that she sees as accompanying the economic modernization, such as reduced leisure time and compromised enjoyment of the natural environment. For example, she traces leisure time from her childhood, when she attended day-long picnics on the banks of rivers where she swam, to her parenthood when, because the rivers and springs had become polluted with modernization, she carried her children to a country club swimming pool. Observing from the point of view of a grandparent, she believes the success-oriented, individualistic extracurricular activities of children (e.g., team sports, individualistic sports like skateboarding, music, etc.) make it difficult for large families to unite in the leisure activities offered by country clubs.

Similarly, in discussing the preparation of traditional Southern foods, Betty suggests that the South's culinary traditions have been debased by the time-pressed quest for convenience. She recalls the coconut cakes her grandmother sold at Christmas when she was a child, noting that while the desert had survived as a traditional Christmas sweet, it is no longer a double-layer cake made from fresh grated coconut, but a single-layered Pyrex "sheet" desert topped with canned coconut (see 1.11 in appendix). Likewise the ambrosia of the past is now mimicked with canned fruit cocktail with a few diced pecans and apples tossed in. She traces this debasement further, from the *Southern Living* inspired recipes that hastened the cooking process with nationally branded food preparations to the convenience of franchised restaurants (see 1.12 in appendix).

While Betty, like Doreen, traces the evolution of Southern culture noting its transformation, her rendering highlights that ostentatious facades of affluence now stand at odds with hallowed Southern traditions of neighborliness and gracious home entertaining:

> Very few homes are designed with a front porch because people don't sit out any more. We're so spoiled with air conditioning, we ride with it in the car with it on to wherever we go, we work in it all day. People don't use them anymore. That's why you don't see them on houses. TV and air conditioning ruined the front porch... I think people in neighborhoods don't know each other anymore because people don't sit outside. Most people don't even do their own yard work anymore. So there's none of that contact. And most neighborhoods, new neighborhoods, your generation, they both work so they're gone all day, so there's no contact there ... How well off people are, is more an image than a reality. The people that you think are very very well off sometimes are just ah, I think a lot of times, the people, addresses, the type houses they build, it's all about the image, of people perceiving them well off and having everything. In most cases that's not the truth. There are people spending up every dime they have trying to look good. In the South, the home tends to be the ah, I don't even know the word for it but the "I have arrived" sort of thing." People build homes that they can't afford and you go inside and they have absolutely nothing in them. You'll drive up to a home and you'll think "this is going to be a really good job." And you go in there and the furnishings are so, they're just nothing, and old. And it's because they've bought the address or the size house that makes them, that gives everybody the idea that they are doing well. [What about entertaining?] I don't think they do like they used to.

For Betty, these symbols of marketplace legitimization represent concessions to modernism that have compromised some essential features of Southern culture. Lost are community front-porch gatherings for entertainment during which guests may be offered relatively unique if time intensive cuisine as a result of honoring family recipes. Like Doreen, Betty's reading reflects her culturally situated understanding of the differences between what is represented and what is lived and observed in daily life. By contrast to Doreen who takes this discrepancy as being emblematic of a lost heritage, Betty sees the deleterious social influences exerted by progressive modernism, its material rewards, and the resulting invidious comparisons which prompt present-day Southerners to live beyond their means. Homes have become status symbols rather than places to constitute community and friendship. Betty describes these grandiose McMansions as "empty" and as where people "don't entertain anymore, like they used to." Betty's reading brings to the surface the irony of Southern homes, as depicted in *Southern Living* magazine among others, requiring a two-income household, leaving little time or money for home entertaining in lavish interiors and contradicting the slow-pace of life often noted as distinguishing qualities of Southern culture.

While Betty grants authority to regional oppositional discourse in dictating taste and representing Southern in terms of the taste of the more affluent classes, and while much of Betty's domestic displays are aligned with this cosmopolitan discourse of the New South, she nonetheless does not see this as traditional Southern culture. Rather, this is a particular class-centered New South taste for which the material markers have escalated over the course of her life (cf. Schor, 1998), with the result that the quest for their conspicuous display now competes with Southern traditions that are focused around home production of food and community interactions.

Integrative Analysis

Preconditioning to Oppositional Reading as a Function of Rural/Urban Identity

While all of our Southern informants spontaneously presented national media portrayals of the region as disparaging, the manner in which they articulated this perception differed according to their self-ascribed identity as rural versus urban. Doreen and Danny, who considered Springville their home and place of heritage, use general expressions which are noticeably absent of specific references to portrayals of hillbillies and rednecks. This narrative elision was manifested among all those we interviewed who accepted a rural identity, with the exception of one resident who grew up on the west coast. In contrast, our two informants with stronger identifications to the metropolitan South, Lorna and Betty, spontaneously invoke these terms in their narratives about the national media's unfair portrayals of the region. In their respective narratives, rednecks and hillbillies are understood as the stigmatized rural "other," which national media seek out, for the purpose of affirming national stereotypes of the southern region. Similar meanings of rednecks and hillbillies were conveyed by our other metropolitan informants. The finding is something akin to the socialization noted by Hartigan (2003, p. 97) whereby "…white, middle-class liberals learn very young not to use epithets with racial connotations while they receive different messages from their parents concerning labels for poor whites."

Recognition of the implicit Old South/Lost Cause myths in regional oppositional discourse also varied across those expressing rural versus urban identifications. Doreen and Danny were well versed in Civil War history and were able to trace their personal genealogy to Civil War ancestors. Augmenting the oral history from this period which they were able to recount, they had extensively read socio-cultural historical texts that articulated both the causes and cultural effects of the Civil War. By contrast, neither Lorna nor Betty knew their Civil War ancestors, had ever traced their genealogy or read much of the South's history from this period or others. Their ambivalence toward regional and local history is consistent with the positioning of Birmingham, as a forward looking New South (Morris, 1994), as well as, is explicable in terms of distancing identity from the backwards and backward-looking traits attached to Southern rednecks and hillbillies (see Graham, 2001). This pattern held in the broader set of interviews. Whereas all of the Springville born informants recited Civil War history, both personal and cultural, only one of those who identified with Birmingham did so, his readings and research prompted by finding a family Bible with names from that period.

Mode of Oppositional Reading as a Function of Rural/Urban Identity

Informants possessing rural versus urban identity attend to different information in regional oppositional discourse reflecting two different modes of reading opposition in narrative. The two types have been recognized by Chambers (1991, p. 45) as stylistic modes in producing oppositional narratives; that is, in writing them. The first is a surface narrative that overtly acknowledges a dominant power wherein can be read a covert opposition to it. The second offers an overtly oppositional writing wherein is the covert acknowledgement of dominant power. Chambers labels the latter a "melancholic appeal," reflecting that the oppositional writing is non-autonomous because it is necessarily produced by the other (p. 45). Irony, in this mode is not eclipsed but its functioning is transformed. Rather than negating an address to power, this irony functions as mode of appropriation. Its address to power is used less as a disguise and more as a hook, to seduce the readerly interpretation, turning the discourse of power to the purposes of oppositional seduction. Chambers (1991) positions these as temporally ordered, characteristic of ancien régime and nouveau régime oppositional writing, respectively.

We suggest here, however, that in *reading* opposition, either mode may be invoked from the same text as a function of the readers' selective attention to the explicitly written narrative and preconditioning to historical meanings in the text. As we have presented, both selective attention and historical preconditioning in our context are linked to place-based identities as rural or urban. Further, individuals, as a function of their selective attention to the surface narrative and their historical preconditioning, may engage a mode of oppositional reading unattended to and unintended by the media producer. We illustrate with our two cases that represent the strongest opposing identities as rural and urban – Doreen and Betty.

Doreen, possessing a rural identity, rural residence, and few lived experiences outside of this place, reads regional oppositional discourse with sensitivities toward the representations of modernism in the narrative text. Springville's relative lack of modernization is the basis on which her rural identity and rural place of residence have been labeled marginal, both nationally, and locally stemming from Springville's proximity to the more metropolitan Birmingham. Thus, she selectively attends to information about the South's modernization and its accompanying affluence depicted in regional discourse such as *Southern Living* Magazine. Stated in Chambers' (1991) terms, she reads celebrations of modernism as the explicit or surface narrative. The explicitly written, if selectively extracted message is, "The South, like the nation, is now modern." (This is the surface message addressed to the dominant power, the representatives of which are national advertisers and business investors). Yet, Doreen reads beneath these opulent representations to discern references to the Old South/Lost Cause myth (as a covert oppositional message). This interpretive reading is aided by her knowledge of Southern history, which she leverages to explain the disparities between media portrayed images of the South and those of her surrounding landscape as reflections of a lost heritage.

Betty, possessing a metropolitan identity and having traveled in all other regions of the nation, in contrast to Doreen, reads the same discourse of

Southern Living magazine, yet selectively attends to what is both distinctive and positive about the South. In Chambers' (1991) terms, Betty reads the text as being explicit or overt in its oppositional message – the South is a desirable exotic other of the rest of the nation. Southernness is the basis on which her identity and place of residence have been labeled marginal through national media's homogeneous depiction of the South and Southerners in terms of the rural poor. Given this, a positively depicted upscale South resonates with Betty who is sensitive to the national media's disparaging portrayals of the region. Selectively echoing the themes of the magazine's surface narrative, Betty reiterates belief in a Southern distinctiveness that is natural and ever present, with nuances passed on by "mamma" rather than the antebellum past (cf. Thompson & Tian, 2006).

Apparent in Betty's discourse, however, is her reading of a "melancholic appeal" in the regional oppositional discourse. Beneath the claims of a distinct yet materially upscale South, Betty reads the discourse as covertly containing in vestigial narrative form, the acknowledgement of a regional culture succumbing to the material allure of modernization, at the cost of practices which she deems authenticates and distinguishes the South. In her interpretive reading, the upscale facade of the South, iconized in the grand Southern home, has been acquired through the forces of modernization, but at the expense of hollowing out its inner traditions. In Chambers' (1991) terms, Betty is "hooked" by the modern themes (the text she subordinates in her selective attention and the one addressed to the national advertising community) to look beneath the transparent narrative of an "upscale yet distinctive South" (in Betty's case, the surface narrative) to arrive at a more complex oppositional reading. Her more complex reading is preconditioned by her extensive exposure to the homes, home interiors, and working home owners she has encountered in the course of her daily work experiences, though also by her lived-experience of the cultural transformations of the region.

This oppositional reading is one that media producers of texts such as *Southern Living* would neither intend nor deem desirable. Indeed, *Southern Living's* producers have remained persistent over the course of nearly half a century in eliding that the forces of modernization challenge the South's distinctiveness (see Logue & McCalla, 2000). We have in an earlier study, however, recognized that producers of regional culture have emerged in the new millennium who, perhaps intuitively, recognize Southerners' readings of a "melancholic appeal" in regional discourse, and have incorporated this predilection into the overt oppositional narrative (see Thompson & Tian, 2006). That is, they create a written text that explicitly contests modernism but goes beyond *Southern Living's* discourse by explicitly incorporating a call for readers to return to home production (e.g., home-cooking and craft production) and home entertaining.

Responsiveness to Oppositional Reading

Responsiveness to regional oppositional discourse occurred in two directions – aligning identity with the identity frame provided by regional oppositional discourse and aligning identity with a counter frame to that of the dominant regional oppositional discourse. Insights into the processes underlying the alignment of identity with or counter to the frame provided by regional oppositional discourse are offered by comparison of the cases of Doreen and Danny. While their depth historical grounding enable them both to read opposition in regional discourse and its traces of the Old South/Lost Cause Myth, they respond differently to it. Doreen embraces it as authentic, whereas Danny rejects its authenticity, with the difference seeming to lie in their self-categorizations as descendants of the South's rural affluent or of the South's rural poor.

Doreen, who first claims descent from "mountain people," uses episodic lived experience and education to re-imagine herself as a descendant of the South's rural affluent, given to leisurely wiling away hours on verandas, while sipping cocktails and telling stories. Her mythic reconstruction of identity makes ready use of Southern vernacular, cultural terms, and meanings that correspond with those appearing in regional oppositional discourse. Danny's personal narrative aligns with regional oppositional discourse only in the sense of desiring ties to the land. His place-based identity is situated lower in a tiered hierarchy of white status, marginalized in relation to the urban North, and still further marginalized in relation to the elitist, metropolitan South. Danny's response is counter to this dual experience of "symbolic violence" (Bourdieu, 1990) by identifying with a reconstructed and civilized transformation of the hillbilly icon, reflected in both his small town Mayberry displays, and his choice to represent Civil War heritage in a chess set, that imbues dignity and virtue to this white heritage.

Life experiences tied to contrasting rural–metropolitan life experiences also are revealed as mediating individuals' alignment of identity with the frame offered by regional oppositional discourse. These differing culture experiences are linked to contesting and reconstructing the historical cultural terms of Southern identity as expressed in oppositional discourse. Danny and Lorna, whose work/home experiences led them to travel between the cultures of rural Springville and urban Birmingham, challenged the class-based meanings of cultural terms appearing in regional oppositional discourse. In particular, they sought to remove the material expressions of affluence from meanings of Southern grace, Southern lady, and Southern gentleman. Doreen and Betty as life residents of their respective rural/urban places did not engage in this reconstruction. For Danny, who embraces his poor rural heritage, the reconstruction of key cultural terms facilitates his identity project of rebuking the (dominant) regional oppositional narrative; in contrast, Lorna's reconstructions facilitate a more interactional coding of class that is, nonetheless consistent the upscale Southern culture promoted in regional oppositional discourse.

CONCLUSION

Our findings suggest that regional oppositional discourse creates a space for a Southern identity that is deemed positive by some middle-class Southern residents who seek escape or to distance themselves from national media portrayals of Southerners as rural poor rednecks and hillbillies (cf. Hartigan, 2003). Our findings contribute to understanding of the role of commercial producers in the construction of white identity (e.g., Holt & Thompson, 2004; Peñaloza, 2001), by highlighting their role in creating room for maneuver (Chambers, 1991) that is outside the regional and rural/urban stratification of whiteness represented in national discourse.

We have undertaken an examination of how regional oppositional discourse, produced commercially, is read by its intended audience. Our analysis reveals that such texts are read as oppositional, and further that interpretations are nonetheless nuanced, reflecting different levels of preconditioning by cultural memory, eliciting different modes of reading opposition in narrative, and prompting different responses to the identity frame created by this text. Further, we highlight both general and context specific mediators of the relationship between individuals' oppositional readings and their alignment of identity in a manner responsive to it.

While such oppositional texts have rarely been the focus of commercial discourse analysis or readings of commercial texts within consumer research, various other disciplines have examined how such texts address women oppressed by masculine norms (Sellnow, 1999), and non-white races oppressed by white race's dominance (Aboriginals, Chambers, 1991; African Americans, Walters, 1999). Further, beyond texts we identify here and in our prior work as oppositional discourse (i.e., lifestyle magazines, television series, popular culture films; see also Thompson & Tian, 2006), other works have recognized that such discourse may take the form of recorded music (e.g., Mary Chapin Carpenter's "He Thinks He'll Keep Her;" Sellnow, 1999), as well as, the promotional materials of consumer organizations that draw membership from individuals with a stigmatized status (e.g., Overeaters Anonymous; Martin, 2002). By offering insights into how oppositional discourse is read by its intended audience, we hope to stimulate further research of commercial texts that target different marginalized identities.

NOTES

1. Our focus on a broader oppositional discourse that is dispersed through a variety of commercial texts follows the illustration of Chambers (1993) whose work recognizes that a thematically related body of works situated historically in the same moment and similarly in relation to a dominant power, exhibit the same modus operandi of opposition, though there are nuanced differences in execution across these texts.

2. Oppositional discourse relies on readers' cultural memory to activate its oppositional narrative through reading between the lines to recognize messages of resistance to or oppression by a dominant power. This discourse may be usefully contrasted with texts, which overtly represent their opposition to domination, and use the juxtaposition of explicit symbols of liberation/oppression to convey this. An example is the brand NuSouth, with its logo of the rebel flag re-colored in black and green, the colors of African liberation. The branded clothing merchandise is further promoted under the brand driver: "For the sons and daughters of former slaves, for the sons and daughters of former slave owners" (see McPherson, 2003, p. 37). As Chambers (1991) notes, overt representations are more likely when the dominant institution does not possess legitimacy in the eyes of the marginalized or weaker party. That is, the dominant institution represents a "force" to be confronted and overcome, rather than a "power," deemed legitimate and from which the marginalized seek only escape from its negative effects.

3. The informants we report on here are independent of the editors-in-chief of regional lifestyle media whose discourse we have previously analyzed (Thompson & Tian, 2006). The latter, in acting strictly as agents of their respective media corporations, spoke solely on topics related to business visions, strategic perspectives, and disclosed few if any aspects of their personal history.

REFERENCES

Arnould, E. J., & Thompson, C. J. (2005). Consumer culture theory (CCT): Twenty years of research. *Journal of Consumer Research*, *31*(March), 868–882.

Blight, D. W. (2001). *Race and reunion: The Civil War in American memory*. Cambridge, MA: Belknap Press.

Bourdieu, P. (1990). *The logic of practice*. Cambridge, UK: Polity Press.

Brundage, W. F. (2005). *The southern past: A clash of race and memory*. Cambridge, MA: Harvard University Press.

Cash, W. J. (1941). *Mind of the South*. New York: Knopf.

Chambers, R. (1984). *Story and situation: Narrative seduction and the power of fiction*. Minneapolis, MN: University of Minnesota Press.

Chambers, R. (1991). *Room for maneuver: Reading oppositional narrative*. Chicago, IL: University of Chicago Press.

Chambers, R. (1993). *The writing of melancholy: Modes of opposition in early French modernism* (M. S. Trouille, Trans.). Chicago, IL: University of Chicago Press.

Cobb, J. C. (2005). Beyond the "Y'all Wall": The American South goes global. In: J. C. Cobb & W. Stueck (Eds), *Globalization and the American South* (pp. 1–18). Athens, GA: University of Georgia Press.

Crockett, D. X., & Wallendorf, M. (2004). The role of normative political ideology in consumer behavior. *Journal of Consumer Research*, *31*(December), 511–528.

Doane, A. W., & Bonilla-Silva, E. (Eds) (2003). *White out: The continuing significance of racism*. New York: Routledge.

Firat, F. A. (2006). *Consumption culture theory: What it is and what it should not be(come)!* Presentation at the Consumer Culture Theory Conference, Southbend, IN: University of Notre Dame.

Flynt, W. (2004). *Alabama in the twentieth century*. Tuscaloosa, AL: University of Alabama Press.

Foner, E. (1988). *Reconstruction: America's unfinished revolution, 1863–1877*. New York: HarperCollins.

Goffman, E. (1963). *Stigma: Notes on the management of spoiled identity*. Englewood Cliffs, NJ: Prentice Hall.

Goffman, E. (1974). *Frame analysis*. Garden City, NY: Anchor.

Graham, A. (2001). *Framing the South: Hollywood, television, and race during the Civil Rights Struggle*. Baltimore, MD: John Hopkins University Press.

Hartigan, J., Jr. (2003). Who are these white people?: "Rednecks," "Hillbillies," and "White Trash" as marked racial subjects. In: A. W. Doane & E. Bonilla-Silva (Eds), *White out: The continuing significance of racism* (pp. 95–112). New York: Routledge.

Holt, D. (1998). Does cultural capital structure American consumption? *Journal of Consumer Research*, *25*(June), 1–25.

Holt, D., & Thompson, C. J. (2004). Man-of-action heroes: The pursuit of heroic masculinity in everyday consumption. *Journal of Consumer Research*, *31*(September), 425–449.

Kozinets, R. V. (2001). Utopian enterprise: Articulating the meaning of Star Trek's culture of consumption. *Journal of Consumer Research*, *28*(June), 67–89.

Logue, J., & McCalla, G. (2000). *Life at Southern Living: A sort of memoir*. Baton Rouge, LA: Louisiana State University Press.

Martin, D. D. (2002). From appearance tales to oppression tales: Frame alignment and organizational identity. *Journal of Consumer Ethnography*, *31*(April), 158–206.

McPherson, T. (2003). *Reconstructing Dixie: Race, gender and nostalgia in the imagined south*. Durham, NC: Duke University Press.

McWhiney, G. (1989). *Cracker culture: Celtic ways in the Old South*. Tuscaloosa, AL: University of Alabama Press.

Mehta, R., & Belk, R. W. (1991). Artifacts, identity, and transition: Favorite possessions of Indians and Indian immigrants to the United States. *Journal of Consumer Research*, *17*(March), 398–411.

Menken, H. L. (1920). The Sahara of the Bozart. *Prejudices: Second Series.* New York, NY: Alfred A. Knopf.

Mick, D. G., & Buhl, C. (1992). A meaning-based model of advertising experiences. *Journal of Consumer Research, 19*(December), 317–338.

Morris, P. (1994). The Birmingham industrial heritage district. *Alabama Heritage, 33*(Summer), 44–46.

Peñaloza, L. (1994). Atravesando fronteras/border crossings: A critical ethnographic study of the consumer acculturation of Mexican immigrants. *Journal of Consumer Research, 21*(June), 32–53.

Peñaloza, L. (2001). Consuming the American West: Animating cultural meaning at a stock show and rodeo. *Journal of Consumer Research, 28*(December), 369–398.

Perry, P. (2001). White means never having to say you're ethnic. *Journal of Contemporary Ethnography, 30*(February), 56–91.

Reed, J. S. (2003). *Minding the south.* Columbia, MO: University of Missouri Press.

Roberts, D. (1996). Living southern in *Southern Living.* In: R. H. King & H. Taylor (Eds), *Dixie debates: Perspectives on southern cultures* (pp. 85–98). UK: Pluto Press.

Roediger, D. R. (1999). *The wages of whiteness: Race and the making of the American working class.* London: Verso.

Schor, J. B. (1998). *The overspent American: Upscaling, downshifting, and the new consumer.* New York: Basic Books.

Schouten, J., & McAlexander, J. H. (1995). Subcultures of consumption: An ethnography of the new bikers. *Journal of Consumer Research, 22*(June), 43–61.

Sellnow, D. D. (1999). Music as persuasion: Refuting hegemonic masculinity in "He Thinks He'll Keep Her". *Women's Studies in Communication, 22*(Spring), 66–84.

Shields, R. (1991). *Places on the margin: Alternative geographies of modernity.* New York: Routledge.

Snow, D. A., Rochford, E. B., Jr., Worden, S. K., & Benford, R. D. (1986). Frame alignment processes, micromobilization, and movement participation. *American Sociological Review, 51*, 464–481.

Thompson, C. J. (1996). Caring consumers: Gendered consumption meanings and the juggling lifestyle. *Journal of Consumer Research, 22*(March), 388–407.

Thompson, C., & Tian, K. (2006). *Reconstructing the south: How commercial myths compete for identity value through the ideological shaping of popular memories and countermemories.* Unpublished working paper.

Tian, K., & Belk, R. (2005). Extended self and possessions in the workplace. *Journal of Consumer Research, 32*(September), 297–310.

Walters, K. (1999). He can read my writing but he sho' can't read my mind: Zora Neale Hurston's revenge in Mules and Men. *Journal of American Folklore, 112*, 343–371.

APPENDIX

Doreen Lifetime Springville resident	Danny Vacillating rural-urban–rural resident	Lorna Vacillating urban–rural resident	Betty Lifetime Birmingham resident
(1.1) I think [the South is depicted] very unfairly. They tend to focus on the sensational. The things that make us look bad, I mean they're accurate. But there's so much more here that deserves attention, but I think we're all used to it. (1.2) When I think about Southern culture, there is no single Southern culture. The lifestyle of the poor and the lifestyle of the well to do like in any culture is so very different, that it would depend on what part of the culture you are talking about.	(1.5) There's a lot of truth [national media portrayals of the South], but a lot is blown out of proportion. That's just my perspective. I know a lot of people, if Alabama was such a negative place that looked down on different races if they were other than Caucasian, then why are there so many different races. (1.6) I think the early years of Alabama, it was a pioneer world and people were just worried about surviving. And then once they started establishing Alabama as a cultivated society and started establishing towns, then you had the Civil War which disrupted everyone's family and home. So I think people were	(1.8) I think most people perceive most people in Alabama as "rednecks" living in manufactured homes. I mean wouldn't you think? If there's ever a bad weather event that's who they go out to interview. There could be homes over in Mountain Brook demolished, but yet the people they choose to put on TV are those that are less fortunate, and maybe aren't quite as well educated, so their speech is though, you know. (1.9) All of them [clients] address me as Miss [maiden name] or Miss	(1.10) And she [an air flight passenger] asked me where I was I was from. And I said "Birmingham." And she said "Oh, the South." She said "Is the South really c-o-u-n-t-r-y (draws it out)?" And I could tell by the way she wrinkled up her nose she meant hillbilly country, I knew that's what she meant. And I said no it's not, we get a bum rap a lot in the South.... It's not how the media portrays us when they interview people after tornadoes. (1.11) Just like fresh coconut cake. My

APPENDIX (*Continued*)

Doreen Lifetime Springville resident	Danny Vacillating rural-urban–rural resident	Lorna Vacillating urban–rural resident	Betty Lifetime Birmingham resident
(1.3) We're ones that refuse to be unionized. I think that's more of this independent attitude that's still very prevalent in the South. We're a stubborn people, had to have been to have survived the Civil War, the devastation, the poverty, to overcome what had to be overcome. The whole culture was decimated and then had to be rebuilt. So you've got a very stubborn people and that's good and that's bad… We're tenacious, but we're reluctant to change… "My father was mountain people, so I have some of that in me.	more worried about surviving than keeping up with a lot of their history. Now we do have some history…. (1.7) …And through oral history passed down by my grand mother and she was a very very intelligent person, she had heard that he was shot while getting water, it was very hot in Pennsylvania at this time. And she said he was killed early, early in the morning, right before daybreak getting water. And I went and pulled the military records some, I did some research and actually saw that he did get killed by a gunshot wound, that was in the military records. And I went and did the history on the regiment, and that battle at Culps Hill took place was actually an early morning, night battle that ended the next	[married name] even now [after 20 years]…I don't sit there and think, he makes a lot of money, he's a CEO of a big company in Birmingham, I need to change my presentation of myself to him in relation to someone who is a laborer or something like that, or a farmer. It's just natural… You don't want to be way up here and [also] you don't want them to perceive you to be not as competent as you should be as their representative. It's instinctive when someone walks into the office, I react to them however they're coming	Dad's mom made them and sold them her whole life. I mean people clamored for those things. They were the from scratch cake with the real grated coconut, I mean the whole nine yards. And I still make those but only at Christmas. But you don't find those any more. When you buy them from some one who says [they're homemade] they're the frozen coconut out of the freezer at the store and they've bought the can of coconut milk and poured over it to make it look like it's the real thing. It's usually a yellow or white cake mix that they're done

(1.4) In Mobile, you'll find a sense of southern culture. That part of the world still has a smell, a taste, and a feel… I think the Carolinas, the Sea Island, that part of the world, Savannah, I think you would find more of a sense of the Southern culture that we all like to think about.	morning. So what she had passed along was historically [accurate]… I doubt she did the research. It was just passed along."	across to me. That's grace… you do not overdress your clientele. And I do think that's a grace thing, because you don't want to put them ill at ease. I know I have a lot of customers that if I wore a suit everyday and high heel shoes and my staff dressed like that, they would feel very uncomfortable coming and sitting down in my office.	out of, far removed from the real thing…. Now they even do it, it's even more convenient to do it in a big sheet pan, like a Pyrex dish, you know, and they just ice the top of it just so they have coconut cake a Christmas. (1.12) Kentucky Fried Chicken, all the grocery stores have great fried chicken, nobody fries chicken in the South anymore. That's something you expect at a picnic or a Sunday dinner is fried chicken and nobody cooks it any more.

MEMBRANE OF THE SELF: MARKETING, BOUNDARIES, AND THE CONSUMER-INCORPORATED SELF

Eugene Halton and Joseph D. Rumbo

CREATING THE CONSUMPTIVE SELF

> Advertising treats all products with the reverence and the seriousness due to sacraments.
>
> Thomas Merton

Much has been written about the various strategies that marketers use to target variously situated consumers in contemporary society. The more sophisticated of these strategies rest upon the notion that each consumer, as a *self*, represents a site of contestation over the very definition of his/her selfhood. Whereas the marketers' objective is to create selling messages designed to colonize each and every self in accordance with the desires of their corporate clients, such messages may be at odds with the development of a healthy, uncorporatized self.

Marketers use widely varied demographic and psychographic (lifestyle) techniques to group consumers into narrowly defined and purportedly unique market segments. Celebrants of advertising and consumer culture tend to argue that the sphere of consumption offers consumers untold liberating possibilities for constructing identities and projecting unique, highly

Consumer Culture Theory
Research in Consumer Behavior, Volume 11, 297–318

ISSN: 0885-2111/doi:10.1016/S0885-2111(06)11024-8

personalized images of self (Firat & Venkatesh, 1995). We contend that all of these purportedly unique constructions of selfhood are nothing more than permutations of what we call the *consumer-incorporated self*, a self compromised by marketing ideology and brand affiliations in which consumption practices displace self-autonomy.

Unsurprisingly, the myriad strategies that marketers have developed for reaching different consumers typically derive from the predominant model of the self found in college-level textbooks on marketing management. Across the pages of these touchstones of marketing wisdom unfolds the template for the *consumer-incorporated self*, an idealized model of self that renders the consumer in largely behaviorist and cognitivist terms, subject to manipulation. Sprinkling marketing theory with influences culled from motivational psychology and neoclassical economics, this dehumanizing notion of self reduces the consumer to a combination of rational calculator *and* passive recipient of marketer manipulation.

One widely influential book that has impacted the thinking of countless college business majors and practicing marketing professionals is Philip Kotler's (2003) popular college text *Marketing Management*.[1] An examination of this text is presented in this inquiry to serve as a cultural indicator of the marketer's conception of self. Kotler succinctly describes this conception in a section entitled "personality and self-concept:"

> Each person has personality characteristics that influence his or her buying behavior. By personality, we mean a set of distinguishing human psychological traits that lead to relatively consistent and enduring *responses* to environmental *stimuli* ... Personality can be a useful variable in analyzing consumer brand choices. The idea is that *brands also have personalities*, and that consumers are likely to choose brands whose personalities match their own. We define brand personality as the specific mix of human traits that may be attributed to a particular brand. (p. 193, emphasis added)

In the highly segmented world of narrowly defined "clusters" of consumers, marketers try to develop brand personalities that "will attract consumers with the same self-concept" (p. 195).

For Kotler (2003), "the marketer's task is to understand what happens in the *buyer's consciousness* between the arrival of outside stimuli and the purchase decisions" (p. 183, emphasis added). Yet the marketer is only concerned with understanding the consumer's consciousness insofar as it informs his/her "buying behavior," which is "influenced by cultural, social, personal, and psychological factors" (p. 183). Consequently, differences in the consumer's most individuated and innately felt attributes, such as attitudes, beliefs, and opinions, are measured as a function of certain personal/psychological and social/cultural variables. Clearly, such a model of self has profound implications for how marketers target consumers with their selling messages, and we will turn to Kotler's text in more detail later to explore the implications of this *consumer-incorporated self*. But first, let us outline the theoretical background for this inquiry and introduce some key terms.

THE MEMBRANE, THE STIMULUS-RESPONSE SELF, AND SELF-ORIGINATED EXPERIENCE

We argue that advertising operates from a model of a "stimulus-response self" for whom material acts of consumption bring rewards of symbolized social relations incarnated in commodities. Successful advertising involves an ideal of a consumer-incorporated self, responsive to marketing stimuli. But to achieve this, advertising, and marketing more broadly, must first breach what we will term the *membrane of the self*, that boundary organ of communication through which the self (1) qualitatively attunes itself to its environment; (2) selectively attends to and filters out various aspects of its environment; and (3) enacts its purposes in transaction with its environment. We will describe how corporate marketing culture attempts to colonize and replace the self with its consumptive model, and how the membrane of the self can help to resist these incursions.

On the corporate side, the explicit function of advertising is to make a profit for the advertiser by developing effective mixes of promotional campaigns for its clients. It can be argued that the implicit function of advertising, however, is to envelop consumers in a matrix of selling messages designed to provide them with low-grade, adrenylated "experience" in micro-melodramas whose form depicts one's pre-consumption self as inadequate and one's post-consumption self as invulnerable. Both depictions are dehumanizing: the former reduces the self to an addictive-like impulsivity requiring consumption for closure; the latter reduces the self to the commodity sign, to an omnipotent amalgamation of materialized corporate logos.

As the amount of selling messages that the average consumer "experiences" has increased dramatically over the past two decades, the struggle to breach or disable the membrane of the self and target consumers has intensified. One estimate states that the average consumer was exposed to 3,600 selling messages (TV ads, radio ads, internet banners, logos, product placements, outdoor ads, etc.) per day in 1996, as compared with 1,500 per day in 1984 (Jhally, 1998). Subsequent estimates of the American consumer's average daily regimen of advertising exposure range anywhere from 2,500 selling messages per day to well over 5,000 (Pappas, 2000). Faced with an increasingly fast-paced world in which consumers have less free time and more ads vying for their attention, marketers are relying more on shock value to reach consumers. As a result, the content of ads is secondary to their melodramatic form, and tends toward attention-seeking techniques. When viewed cumulatively, these ads produce conditioned sleepwalkers, seemingly content with the constantly intruding distractions and their soul-numbing message of inadequacy bought out by material nirvana. The mantra-like repetition of omnipresent ads forms a calculus of anxiety and jovial conformity, which are key ingredients of the conditioned stimulus-response self.

As Georg Simmel (1950) pointed out, the increasingly quantitative ordering of life in the modern metropolis involves an intensification of both the rational or "calculating character" of consciousness and also of everyday stimuli pouring in on the self. Hence the metropolitan must create a protective organ of rational indifference in order to be free to pursue his or her interests. An individual must develop what he called the "blasé attitude," a shield of indifference, to avoid over-stimulation: in short, a protective membrane of self, calibrated to urban life.

And in today's televised, wired and wireless world, this metropolitan mindset is no longer bounded by the city, but has become the accepted norm of Megatechnic America. Only worse: the blasé attitude itself has become the focus of marketers, who must find new ways to penetrate its indifference and attract its attention. Within a consumer culture marked by heightened degrees of "advertising clutter," a premium is placed upon a marketer's ability to create stimuli that can even break through the marketer-matrix to produce a consumptive response (see Rumbo, 2002). They must produce a self whose blasé attitude will shield it from its very own deepest needs for *self-originated experience*, while yet open to the seductions of marketing. This means that marketing must produce a controllable *stimulus-response self*, which it will then consume, a consumer-incorporated self.

By *stimulus-response self*, we mean a model of self based on externally stimulated conditioned responses. In the model of the 19th century reflex arc that dominated behaviorist psychology, a stimulus produces a response and that stimulus can be modified in various ways to condition a response. The self, in this outlook, is a conditioned response. By analogy, one can view this self as a dyadic conditioned response to psychological stimuli, to neuro-brain matrices – "wired-in" or not, to socialization, to cultural conventions, etc. But the flip side of the traditional marketing view of the self are the various postmodern views in which the self is simply an arbitrary or conventional social construction, constructed by the conventions of its culture or its contingent activities, both individual and relational. Perhaps we can call this the "post-stimulus-response self." In these views the self is a function of that which determines it, and the possibility of purposive self-determination is generally excluded. Such views typically ignore the human body itself, that extraordinary organic basis of the self and its sign-making abilities, which remains very much present in human communication and culture. The human self involves developmental natural constructions, which yet require social constructions. To be a self is to be a social construction worker, actively engaged in meaning-making.

By *self-originated experience*, we mean that the self, though conditionable and though developed through habits of conduct, involves a spontaneous, sensing reasonableness not reducible to its habits and conditioning, one whose purport is self-determination. This self requires the bodily involvement in the moment and the availability of feelings, needs, desires, and goals to make sense of that moment. It requires the awareness needed to continue to be itself in the moment, that is, to determine itself in its environment as a socially autonomous being. It is through the capacity for self-originated experience that we find our freedom (see Halton, 2000, 2005).

Consumer culture, in contrast, promises that the self will find freedom in discarding self-originated experience, in becoming a stimulus-response self. As such, it represents the modern myth of the machine, of the idea that machines will progressively bring freedom. Only here the machine is the marketing system-induced stimulus-response self. Entranced by the magical advertised fetishism of commodities, which target our capacity for self-originated experience, our inner wildness, the stimulus-response self is literally the machine-made flesh.

The living self involves a triadic social transaction with its environment, not a dyadic stimulus response. That transaction with the environment is mediated by what we term the "membrane of the self," that boundary organ of communication through which the self (1) qualitatively attunes itself to its environment; (2) selectively attends to and filters out various aspects of its environment; and (3) enacts its purposes in transaction with its environment.[2] Allow us to briefly illustrate each of these functions.

(1) *Qualitative Attunement*: Just how does the self qualitatively attune itself to its environment? Consider the example of an Amazonian Amahuaca man, hunting the tinamou bird. He describes the dangers of using birdcalls to capture the tinamou bird:

> I backed up between the buttresses of a big tree where the ground could be seen for a good distance in front of me, and I started calling the birds to me. You know that it is dangerous to call the tinamou without the protection of a big tree. The jaguar sometimes comes in to answer the call! The tinamou is also his favorite bird. (Abram, 1996, p. 143)

He needed to become the tinamou sound while also not becoming a tinamou sounding prey for the jaguar. This man's attunement was literally the tune, the birdcall, the sign, which related his self to the tinamou. Like an advertiser, he had to create a stimulus whose response would put the bird in his hands. The responding tinamou walking within range of his arrow was the interpretation of his bird-call sign. But the possible responding jaguar stalking him was also a potential interpretation, one requiring him to back up between the buttresses of a tree, creating a literal defensive "membrane," which was also part of his attunement.

In this example we see the significance of empathic intelligence in qualitative attunement to the environment, and how the loss of such an ability could spell the difference between life and death. A "culture of narcissism," as Lasch (1991) has characterized consumer culture, involves precisely the loss of empathic intelligence as an organ of the membrane of self. This mode of the membrane involves qualitative signification, not reducible to conventional signification. Oddly, many qualitative approaches often appeal to cognitivist and post-structuralist theories which cannot account for qualitative signification, including what Charles Peirce termed "iconic signs."

(2) *Selective Attention*: Life would be a booming, buzzing confusion – as William James characterized the newborn's world – if we could not selectively attend to the inpouring information from the environment, including the inner environment of mind. Processing an experience involves more than mechanically recording perceptions like a seismograph, for that is the world of consumption-induced autism. As James (1890) put it:

> But the moment one thinks of the matter, one sees how false a notion of experience that is which would make it tantamount to the mere presence to the senses of an outward order. Millions of items of the outward order are present to my senses which never properly enter into my experience. Why? Because they have no *interest* for me. *My experience is what I agree to attend to*. Only those items which I *notice* shape my mind – without selective interest, experience is an utter chaos. (p. 402)

One can view the Amahuaca man again from the viewpoint of selective attention, and realize that his concentration on tinamous, jaguars, and protective tree shields involves a transaction that filters out information not relevant to this particular hunt. The same man in the same place on another occasion might select a quite different focus of attention. He might be seeing the food plants or medicinal herbs he needs to consume, and so his attention – and attunement – will require a different transaction. In effect, his membrane of self will put him in a different place while he remains in the same physical space. The ability to pay attention is crucial to autonomy, as attention-deficit disorder (ADD) demonstrates.

(3) *Goals of Transactions*: If the self were no more than that which attends "to the mere presence to the senses of an outward order," it would resemble the model of the stimulus-response self we have criticized. But the self is also capable of self-determination, of enacting its purposes in transaction with its environment. We carry purposive habits of conduct into situations, habits that combine cultural values, personal experience and deep-rooted needs, purposive habits to be bodied forth. This third modality of the membrane of the self involves how goals of the self meet a given situation, that is, are realized or revised in a situation, whose larger context is the good life.

Given that we are all immersed in cultural conventions with competing goals, the question is: whose goals are good goals? In the transactional model we are arguing for, those goals which allow self-determination within the context of a good social life provide a basis for an authentic self. Such goals should culminate in a freely acting self, able to be itself with its empathic, spontaneous, and critical intelligence available.

On the other hand, consumer culture offers pseudo-relationships in a pseudo-society of commodities with "brands whose personalities match (the consumers') own," as Kotler (2003) asserts. The stimulus-response model of the self follows utilitarian philosopher Jeremy Bentham's (1948) dictum that "nature has placed mankind under the governance of two sovereign masters, pain and pleasure. It is for them alone to point out what we ought to do, as well as to determine what we shall do." That is, individual sensations determine the goal of life in the stimulus-response model, which does not qualify the sources of sensations and is focused on the consumption moment as goal. In contrast, the chief goal of the free self is something more. It is happiness, as opposed to pleasure, and happiness is basically social, deriving primarily from the way we love our family, friends, and neighbors. Pleasure (or pain) is a dyadic individual response, but happiness is a triadic social relation, inherently relating individual to the social realities of the good life.

And the good life ultimately involves more than a good family life, or neighborhood, or city, or society. It involves a felt-connectedness to the community of life of which we remain a part, on which we depend, and whose filaments reach deeply into the very way our human, primate, mammalian bodies are made. That is, a truly sustainable and interconnected happiness entails relation to and respect for "the others" of the living environment that we are consuming and therefore are responsible to (Shepard,

1996; Halton, 2006). We contend that such a self, intrinsically embedded in social relations, is capable of self-originated experience and real selfhood.

MARKETING MANAGEMENT AND THE CORPORATE MODEL OF SELF

We now turn to a critical analysis of Kotler's (2003) *Marketing Management*[3] that will illustrate how applications of a corporate model of self have informed marketers' strategies. Kotler lucidly outlines this model in a chapter entitled "Analyzing Consumer Markets and Buyer Behavior" (pp. 182–214). Specifically, the "model of buyer behavior" that unfolds in this chapter hinges upon the relationship between *stimuli* (whether from marketing or other sources) and the consumer's *response* (pp. 183–184). Here response refers to the buyer's actual purchases, which are linked to outside stimuli by the two main components of what Kotler calls "the buyer's consciousness:" the consumer's various sociocultural and personal "characteristics," and his/her purchase-driven "decision process."

This is not to suggest that decision processes are consistent across all consumers and all products. Kotler notes that consumer buying behavior varies according to the degree of differentiation among brands in a certain product class *and* the degree of involvement typically required of the consumer for that product (pp. 200–202). Goods that are more expensive, durable, self-expressive, infrequently purchased, and/or whose purchase involves greater risk are more likely to warrant "high involvement" in the buying process, while cheaper and more frequently purchased items tend toward "low involvement" (see Assael, 1987). Buying behaviors are then divided according to whether there are significant differences between brands in a given product class.

Especially for lower involvement items in which there are fewer differences between brands, the composite sketch of the consumer is that of a passive recipient of marketer-controlled stimuli designed to condition her/him to "behave" accordingly through the successive stages of the buying decision process. In order, these stages are "problem recognition," "information search," "evaluation of alternatives," "purchase decision," and lastly "post-purchase behavior" (p. 204).

Marketers specialize in creating specific selling messages whose stimuli are designed to prompt consumers to move forward through the first three of these stages. Although Kotler notes that the recognition of a consumer problem or need "can be triggered by internal or external stimuli" (p. 204), advertising messages that prey upon our inadequacies, anxieties, and/or insecurities have a rich history of "triggering a particular need." As they meticulously craft representations of consumers that portray the self as a deficient social atom to be completed through specific acts of consumption, marketers provide the external impetus for converting shortcomings into problems (e.g., a lack of sexual drive becomes a "dysfunction" to be treated with Viagra), and wants into needs. Consuming to remedy such "problems" and meet such "needs" frequently creates socially legitimized norms. Consequently, goods that were formerly considered luxuries (like cell phones, DVD players, or palm pilots) become "must-have" accessories for today's technologically savvy consumer.

In the succeeding "information search" stage, Kotler allows for the more deliberative components of the "buyer's consciousness." Despite this, he maintains that the marketer's primary task is to develop strategies (stimuli) to impact consumers' purchase decisions (responses). Depending on the amount and types of information sought for a given product, the hypothetical consumer narrows his/her choices from an "awareness set," to a "consideration set," to a "choice set" from which the final purchase decision is made (p. 205). Marketers design selling messages in order to ensure that consumers will: (1) become aware of their product; (2) consider purchasing their product; and (3) prefer their product above other competing alternatives. These messages resemble the three modalities of the membrane of the self; with specific marketing stimuli prompting the consumer to (1) qualitatively attune to a perceived problem in social relations; (2) selectively filter out competing products; and (3) enact the marketer's desired purpose, which is to imprint and habituate the preferred or chosen product as part of the consumer's own values and image of self.

For Kotler, once consumers have narrowed their alternatives to a "choice set," they must evaluate the alternatives within that set by calculating the salience and importance of various product attributes (p. 205). Again, the marketer is there to "assist" the consumer throughout the evaluation process with advertisements that highlight a product's attributes in order to alert the consumer to their benefits (pp. 205–206). For example, a car that features a more powerful engine delivers the benefits of increased acceleration, greater maneuverability through traffic, and the projection of a "sporty" image for the driver. Marketers also influence the evaluation process by developing marketing campaigns designed to inculcate a positive "set of brand beliefs" or "brand image" in the consumer's mind (p. 206). With diminished consumer attention spans and increased competition from competing advertisers, the cultivation of brand images is ultimately cumulative, involving repetitive, long-term exposure to a brand's ads, logos, and other selling messages.

The better the marketing mix that urges consumers through these steps in the decision process, the greater likelihood that more consumers will eventually decide to purchase a given product. Once the consumer passes through the two intervening factors between intent and actual purchase ("attitudes of others" and "unanticipated situational factors") to arrive at a purchase decision, the marketer has met his/her ultimate explicit objective of inducing purchase (p. 207), and the consumer responds by buying say, a Toyota, a Pepsi, some Nikes, or a Big Mac.

REFINING THE MODEL: NEW CORPORATE STRATEGIES FOR COLONIZING THE SELF

Although the relationship between marketing stimuli and consumer response would suggest that the marketer-matrix is a fairly reliable and proven system for inducing consumers to purchase sponsored goods and services, recent changes in society and its intensified marketing communications environment suggest otherwise. A consumer socialization process involving exposure to an ever-increasing gauntlet of selling messages has prompted seasoned and wary consumers to develop a plethora of "ad avoidance" strategies to evade marketer colonization (Speck & Elliott, 1997; Rumbo, 2002). Amidst heightened competition and greater advertising clutter, marketers have had to confront the fact that today's jaded consumer is more likely to circumvent, abandon, and/or avoid each stage of the buyer decision process. Having grown weary from having to manage excess marketing stimuli, such a consumer is markedly more evasive and difficult for marketers to reach.

Marketer strategies have evolved in response to this consumer's more "blasé attitude" toward advertising. Consider the words of Mark Gobé (2001) who appropriates the critical term "branding," transforming it from a negative description of consumers habituated to brand names to a desirable goal of the advertiser:

> Regardless of the medium, from the perspective of Emotional Branding *it is essential to start any advertising endeavor with the acknowledgment that there is a new and savvy and marketing-tefloned consumer out there* who is ready to act as a tough interlocutor. In your face visibility and brand dominance was a very nineties idea, but consumers in the new

> millennium expect more sensitivity and honesty from the brands they like and will appreciate those that will respect their spiritual and physical environment. (p. 222)

Gobé calls this "a new sincerity," but it is just the marketer-matrix's response of increased calculation to the stimulus of blasé-fied consumers. Dullness to "in your face visibility," not awareness of it, was the apparent problem marketers needed to address, even as they disguise it from themselves as "sensitivity and honesty." In our view it was simply the increased complexity of the stimulus-field presented by emergent electronic media and by increased competition between marketers themselves.

Marketers are thus faced with the reality that consumers are more likely to resist their efforts on numerous fronts. Kotler alludes to some of these resistance efforts in his section on "learning," which "involves changes in an individual's behavior arising from experience" (p. 197). According to Kotler, through cumulative experiences of sifting through largely superfluous and unsolicited marketing information, the consumer learns to develop strategies for filtering out unwanted selling messages and, in our estimation, for protecting the self against corporate colonization. For example, consumers have learned to use their remote controls to "zap" particular ads, whether by changing channels, pressing "mute," or, for videotaped programs, hitting the "fast-forward" button. In these and other "ad avoidance" strategies (e.g., throwing away junk mail or deleting internet "pop-up" ads), experience gained by responding to marketing stimuli supplants self-originated experience.

In response to this, marketers have refined their matrix by developing more manipulative and captivating strategies for reaching consumers with their selling messages, such as the use of perceptual cues "that determine when, where, and how a person responds" (p. 197). In turn, these strategies have informed a more nuanced reformulation of the corporate model of self. In responding to the rapidly proliferating stimuli from today's marketing landscape, this model views the self as being marginally engaged in the management of his/her protective membrane.

Kotler's discussion of "perception" (p. 197) further illustrates the obstacles that a cluttered marketing environment poses for marketers trying to reach today's consumer. In it, he identifies three reasons why different people may not come to perceive the same stimulus object consistently: "selective attention," "selective distortion," and "selective retention." The first of these, "selective attention," is comparable to our second modality of the membrane of the self. Echoing James (1890), this principle simply states that each consumer tends to notice certain types of stimuli, such as those that he/she anticipates, or that relate to a consumer's current need. Again, marketers must ensure that the stimuli in their selling messages stand out amidst ad clutter and cut through the blasé attitude of their targeted message recipients, thus giving each ad a greater likelihood of penetrating the membrane's selective filtering process.

Next, Kotler's notion of "selective distortion" refers to "the tendency to twist information into personal meanings and interpret information in a way that will fit our preconceptions" (p. 197). This obviously poses problems for marketers who depend heavily on an undiluted transference of their intended selling message to consumers. Even when a message successfully eludes the membrane of the self, it can still be altered by its recipient. Although Kotler concedes that selective distortion is beyond marketer control (p. 197), many ads convey meanings that are either impossible to misinterpret or intentionally vague, ensuring that most consumers' interpretations neither overshadow nor dilute the ad's central message.

Lastly, Kotler's notion of "selective retention" concedes that a message may be forgotten by the consumer once it is successfully delivered. To alleviate this, marketers frequently rely on "drama and repetition in sending messages to their target markets" (p. 197). Additionally, violence, shocking or odd subject matter, fast-paced imagery, and loud music – which also seek the consumer's "selective attention" – are formulaic elements used increasingly by marketers to raise the likelihood that an ad will make an enduring impression in the minds and bodies of its targeted recipients.

The use of these devices to target the impulsive openings of the self demonstrates how cutting-edge marketing strategies extend beyond rational cognition and stimulus-response manipulation to the realm of affect and emotion. Whether used to trigger positive attitudes toward a particular product or negative reactions toward a competing alternative, these strategies attempt to simulate an affective state or touch an emotional chord. In so doing, they seek out impulsive openings in the habituated consumer-incorporated self. Moreover, the use of more visceral avenues for manipulating the consumer's sense of perception extends to other biosocially rooted aspects of the self, as evidenced by marketers who study the "facial response system" in order to elicit desired bodily sensations (Cacioppo, Losch, Tassinary, & Petty, 1986).

Having thus refined their model of the consumer into a "consumer-incorporated" self, today's marketers systematically navigate the self's psychological and biophysical components as integrated pathways for the delivery of selling messages. Ironically, the many deft constructions of the expanding marketer-matrix ape the real self to produce substitute "gut reactions" for their targeted recipients. As this matrix continues to adapt and "evolve," the dynamic struggle over selfhood between consumers and marketers has intensified. The following section examines "lifestyle marketing" as a contemporary arena in which this struggle is currently being contested.

LIFESTYLE MARKETING: BRANDING THE SELF THROUGH CLUSTERING

To reiterate, the reception of marketing communication is mediated by the membrane of the self, that boundary that lies between the real self and the idealized "consumer-incorporated" self. Everyday attempts to resist corporate colonization dictate that the membrane of the self is an ongoing site of contestation; a site wherein the self's in-tempered psychological and biophysical aspects meet the seductive allure of incorporeal images of self represented in ads and in commodities. For in this space between the real self and consumer-incorporated self lay vigorously and perpetually renegotiated sites of struggle over meaning, and ultimately, over definitions of self.

Consumers struggling to protect the sanctity of their selfhood against the relentless incursions of marketers must nurture this protective membrane, constantly adapting it to remedy perceptual gaps that are exposed by new marketing strategies. Nurturing this membrane requires the advent of filters for weeding out superfluous and unwanted selling messages. These filters constitute the membrane's innermost layer of defense against corporate colonization, a boundary that, much like Kotler's "buyer's consciousness," is situated between marketing (and other external) stimuli and the consumer's purchase decisions (pp. 183–184).

As the corporate players struggle to colonize consumers, marketers are rewarded on the basis of their ability to successfully evade the filtering membrane of the self in order to deliver a selling message to targeted recipients. For a selling message to get through these filters, it must locate *points of entry* at which the ad's depicted lifestyle practices resonate closely with the consumer's innermost desires and consumptive preferences. Having safely passed through the membrane's filters, the good or service that a selling message promotes can be intricately woven into the consumer's lifestyle practices and "identity constructions" and, consequently, into his/her idealized image of self. To the extent that the self's identity is bound up with consumer culture, the membrane itself is compromised, no longer serving the autonomous needs of the self but increasingly attuned to the means of consumption as the basis for experience.

The idea that the membrane of the self contains "points of entry" for corporate selling messages follows from the notion that, as consumers, each of us has certain lifestyle-based preferences that implicate us squarely within the sphere of mass-marketed consumption. Evidencing a twentieth century shift in marketing practices away from the predominance of demographic categories and toward more individuated "taste cultures," locating various points of entry has largely become the purview of "lifestyle marketing" or *psychographics* (Leiss, Kline, & Jhally, 1997). To take the example of the auto, a point of entry emerges (and filters are penetrated) when a marketing message persuades the consumer that a certain brand or class of autos is most congruent with his/her lifestyle and image of self. Accordingly, a yuppie corporate climber prefers BMWs, a teenage girl seeking her first car wants a Geo Prizm, an assimilated rebel from the 1970s covets a new VW beetle, a "soccer mom" housewife desires a minivan, a young musician gravitates toward a cool new Pontiac Vibe, and a rugged outdoorsman just has to have a Ford Expedition sport-utility vehicle (SUV).[4]

Advertising the commodity as though it were made for *your* unique lifestyle, corporate culture further differentiates the "Sloanism," the replication of the American class system through automobiles developed in the 1950s by longtime General Motors CEO Alfred P. Sloan. Paradoxically, while Americans do not like to admit the existence of class, a "unique" lifestyle is a badge of honor and status, even when it is associated with a mass-produced brand of auto. Individuals are expected to own automobiles in America, and every auto is both a statement of self and a vulnerable zone for the membrane of self. The very term "automobile" means self-moving, and the auto is a commodity that too easily lends itself to use as an externally projected image of self. Ironically, the auto informs marketing constructions designed to "move" the consumer to incorporate the automobile as a necessary part of his/her identity and image of self.

Lifestyle marketers mine the latest trends in fashion and culture in order to target different *market clusters*. These clusters are grouped according to psychographic classification systems, including the popular VALS (values and lifestyle systems) typology and the "technographics" framework (see Kotler, p. 194). Reflecting the zeitgeist of contemporary marketing thought, both of these systems view consumer resources as a function of knowledge and income. VALS divides consumers into eight basic categories according to whether one has high or low resources, and whether one is principle-, status-, or action-oriented, while technographics segments technology markets into nine consumer groups on the basis of affluence, optimism versus pessimism, and whether consumers are more career-, family-, or entertainment-oriented (pp. 192–194). A more variegated typology is the PRIZM system, which consists of 62 clusters divided into 15 socioeconomic groupings (Weiss, 2000, pp. 11–13). The increased differentiation in psychographic typologies gives testimony both to the purported fragmentation of consumer society into more particularistic lifestyle-based clusters, and to the abilities of the all-devouring consumption complex to find, target, and assimilate the citizenry to its "consumer-incorporated" model of self.

Exemplifying trends toward the increased individuation of consumers and the personalization of strategies used to reach them, Kotler defines the consumer's lifestyle as "the person's pattern of living in the world as expressed in the person's activities, interests, and opinions" (p. 191). More significantly, Kotler's assertion that "Lifestyle portrays the 'whole person' interacting with his or her environment" (pp. 191–192) assumes that the quantifiable consumer genuinely exhibits the whole person. We contend that this assumption further illustrates the mechanized, dehumanizing pathos of consumer culture.

Once the membrane's filters are eluded and the self has been colonized, the consumer-incorporated self tends to "interact" passively with the *marketing* environment in lieu of cultivating purposeful transactions with *natural* and *social* environments. Having had its filters penetrated, new vulnerabilities in the membrane of the self are exposed. This exposure weakens boundaries between the real self and the consumer-incorporated self to enable a more efficient and thorough colonization.

This corporate model of self seems closer to Gergen's (1991) "saturated self," which is a malleable product of social construction (see Halton, 2004). Lifestyle marketers seize upon the consumer's desire to "construct" multiple, situation-specific subjectivities to locate points of entry for "identity marketing" strategies (Klein, 1999). This pseudo-personalization constitutes nothing less than the "branding" of selfhood, which is a cumulative process of corporate logo indoctrination that begins with the targeting of young children and a socializing process that merges the real biosocial needs of the pre-consumption self with those of the marketer-matrix.

Lifestyle marketers forge this merger by skillfully combining an admixture of scholarly research efforts (ranging from psychology, demography, sociology, and physiology to psychoanalysis, literary criticism, and cultural studies) in order to blur people's perceptual boundaries and obfuscate the social and environmental consequences of consumption culture. As core architects of the marketer-matrix, their relentless onslaught of selling messages animates the lifeless world of corporate goods with a certain spectatorial pseudo-reverence that numbs the self's critical faculties and bodily reactions. The end result is that Megatechnic America produces drone-like consumption-based identities that are at odds with the active citizenry required by a democracy.

However, we hold that the ultimate goal of lifestyle marketers' slickly packaged formulae is to install consumption-based identities that desire pleasure and comfort while eschewing self-originated experience and happiness. Consequently, authentic and purposive experiences are supplanted in favor of the conditioned consumptive experiences of the stimulus-response self. The following transcript of a televised ad for Ford's line of SUVs and an imagined consumer's commentary on it are presented to provide an example of how lifestyle marketers' stimuli seek to condition consumers to cultivate identities through lifestyle-based consumption and, ultimately, to supplant self-originated experience.

FORD'S "NO BOUNDARIES" SUV ADS: TARGETING THE WILD SELF WITHIN

Stimulus

A lush green canopy of trees … a breathtaking view of a green valley set against a snow-capped mountainous backdrop … a rugged middle-aged fisherman baits his hook and casts his line into the water … a wistful mountain crooner wails over slow, mournful guitar chords … as a Ford Expedition SUV appears by the river, the fisherman confides: "To me, this isn't a hobby … or even a sport. It's an obsession. So if I can't get out to this exact spot, at this exact time of year, I may as well be bowling." A Ford Expedition rambles through lush off-road countryside... then the entire line of Ford SUVs darts across the majestic landscape … "Get out there! In Expedition, from your Ford Outfitter – outfitting you with the most far-reaching sport-utilities on earth. Ford Outfitters: no boundaries." Lastly, the fisherman releases a trout into the river.

Response of Armchair Ad Critic: Joe Sixpack's Revelation

Would you get a load of *this* ad? I mean, don't get me wrong, I like nature and all. But what is this ad trying to sell *me*, in the middle of my sports watching weekend? It seems to be the idea that I can easily "get out there" if I would only go and visit my local Ford Outfitter. But I'm a city guy, a burned-out weekend couch potato who is sick and tired of all these ads. And I could care less about this fisherman and his "obsession." Hell, I've got my own obsessions. Fantasy Football. Porn. Beer. Pizza. (Just to name a few.)

But what's up with this guy and his fishing obsession? Why does he need to "get out there" into the wild frontier? Judging by the looks of him, I wonder how this fat old guy even gets out of the house. Boundaries? I've got boundaries for ya, pal. Why don't you put a padlock on your fridge? Or your snack cupboard?

And while I'm on the subject, what is up with this campfire music? It does seem a bit out of place, especially when they show that manly fisherman. Peter, Paul, and Mary meet Grizzly Adams? And finally, am I really supposed to believe this guy just catches fish so that he can release them back into the river? Obviously it doesn't look like he's missed a meal in a long time. Why the sudden change of heart?

That's *it*. This ad is probably about that shit I keep hearing in the news. About SUVs polluting the environment, and how car companies keep on making them and consumers like me keep on buying them, even though tree-hugger groups keep on protesting against them. Maybe Ford thinks that if their ad shows some fisherman putting a fish back into the river, then their customers will think that buying a Ford SUV is good for the environment.

I don't know, but then again I don't really care. After all, there are too many car ads anyway, and many of them are even worse than this one. And this stuff about global warming and spotted owls isn't my problem. I'm just one consumer among billions. I just want them to get back to the playoffs so that I don't have to sit through all these ads. Because in the end, all I need to know is the score of my ballgame, not what Ford SUVs look like. Oh yeah, I forgot, I'm gonna have to tape this game. My wife's at the in-laws this weekend, and I've got to hop in my Jeep and take the kids to their soccer game. Oh well, happy viewing! And if you're shopping for an SUV, happy consuming, and happy polluting too! Gas away, if you can pay for it! Tell the next tree hugger you see out there protesting that Ford sent ya.

(Fade from the Living Room ...)

As our armchair ad critic illustrates, the stylistic elements in this thirty-second network television spot are readily observable: accompanied by campfire-like guitar and emotive tenor vocals, shots of our rogue fishing protagonist are woven into an exhilarating sequence of natural settings. The juxtaposition of the SUV with nature is another common formulaic device found in SUV ads. The main narrative that emerges is that the "far reaching" Ford Expedition makes it possible for the driver to forage deeper into the wilderness. In so doing, this ad symbolically obliterates geographical boundaries separating consumers from nature.

However, what is most illuminating is the extent to which the ad uses the language of necessity to forge a deep connection between the Ford Expedition and the fisherman's self-image, a connection that obliterates the boundaries between his real and consumer-incorporated selves. Spurred by burgeoning SUV sales and the widespread popularity of outdoor leisure pursuits, Ford adopted the moniker "outfitters" to position their line of SUVs as another logical extension to the "outfitting" of recreating consumers. In this ad, the fisherman's "far reaching" SUV constitutes the mechanized conduit to nature that enables him to "get out there" and pursue his recreational drug of choice, fishing. Accordingly, our fisherman readily concedes that, for him, fishing is "an obsession," a lifestyle pursuit upon which his consumption-based identity is predicated. The language of addiction here is more than arbitrary or unmotivated; it evidences a merging of the fisherman's needs to the promotional needs of the advertiser. Having undergone this merger, the fisherman's life would be utterly meaningless without his Ford Expedition and the annual rendezvous with his favorite fishing hole that it makes possible: "So if I can't get out to this exact spot, at this exact time of year, I may as well be *bowling*."

Perhaps no other advertising genre better exemplifies the many intersecting boundary problematics in the struggle for selfhood in consumer culture than ads for big sport-utility vehicles (SUVs). As the autonomous social self struggles to breathe under the weight of the marketer-matrix and its consumptive trappings, nature becomes a nameless, faceless, and voiceless "other" that exists merely to provide humans with entertainment and to fuel the production of consumer goods. As a result, the autonomous self becomes further alienated from its real biosocial sources, even as it is blitzed with ersatz images of them.

CONCLUSION: MARKETING MUZZLES, ADVERTISING LEASHES

Consumer culture's marketer-matrix has colonized American public space to such an extent that it is an invisible opiate: people do not complain that they pay to see a movie, and then are subjected to paid commercials in the movie theater; educators willingly install the means of commercial seduction in schools, as though "free," so that children can be conditioned to McBurgermind in the classroom. People do not see this as the child pornography it is, nor do they see advertising as the soul-sucking it is. Would that Joe Sixpack could respond with the revelation we depicted earlier.

Advertising is the opiate of the people, and corporate arm of a vast megamachine system that would reduce the live self to stimulus-response closure. It is a cultural form of electro-chemical indoctrination, feeding the self with virtual emotions, with effects on the self similar to that of biochemical dependencies (see Halton, 2000). Yet the human self is far more than a servo-mechanism, a meat computer.

How could the dehumanized conception of the self taught to marketers and used in making the advertising propaganda machine be reformed to better accord with democratic values and the relatively autonomous selves democracy requires? In our view they probably cannot be internally reformed. The American marketing machine is a virtual pit-bull, which needs to be muzzled from without. Show it an emotional view of the self, and it targets it for manipulation. Show it human needs for empathy and common decency in social relations, and it makes of them the stuff to sell stuff. Show it the argument for self-originated experience we are making here, and it would simply incorporate the idea in the service of selling an ersatz version of it back to people, further separating them from themselves.

Instead, we need to create *marketing muzzles*, *advertising leashes*, means of protecting citizens from being brain-rinsed (the soft form of brain-washing that is advertising) into becoming consumer-incorporated selves. How to do this? By limiting the infiltration of ads into schools, by reversing the ever-increased amount of time given to television advertising per hour, by creating "advertising-free" environments modeled after "smoke-free" ones, by placing severe constraints on the form and content of children's advertising. In short, by promoting institutional membranes which serve the needs of the autonomous self.

Advertising for children should be treated as a direct assault on the indigenous developmental needs of the growing child. It should be treated as virtual child pornography. The former president of the Kids-R-Us clothing store once famously said, "If you own this child at an early age, you can own this child for years to come. Companies are saying, 'Hey, I want to own the kid younger and younger.'" Such attitudes need to be muzzled by democratic sanctions to protect the sacrosanct developing self. And if it means no financial support for children's television programming, then public promotion of shows should enlarge, or the shows, and the sugarizing and fast food industries which sponsor them, should bow out. Either way means that the citizenry needs to step up to the plate to protect its youth from the culture that would consume them.

A society of "owned" consumers, programmed to consume, is the death of democracy. And it is precisely the society we are in the final stages of perfecting today. The great enemy of America is not the outer terrorist, but the inner automaton, corporately conditioned to respond to commercial stimuli, and to ignore non-commercial basics of everyday life, the arts and crafts of domestic and civic life. It knows how to buy, but has forgotten how to live.

America today is the dream of invulnerability. Americans are scrambling to find the equivalent of "security" through material and technical invulnerability, through the pseudo-choice world of consumption: McMore is McBetter. The problem is that material invulnerability is the equivalent of the zombie, who has defected from living, from being vulnerable to life. The truly invulnerable humans are the living dead, imprisoned within a false consumer-incorporated membrane of self. "To change for the better" demands vulnerability, the capability of being moved, of empathy, of criticism: all capacities of the autonomous self. Democracy demands both awareness and vulnerability, as a life in common. Yet Megatechnic America seems bent on dimming or eradicating both.

Against the great propaganda apparatus that fuels Megatechnic America, matrix-like, with the virtual batteries of consumer-incorporated selves, stands a great potential adversary: the living human body-mind, manifest in the developmental needs and capacities of the autonomous self. That self, when allowed to develop, finds the capacity for empathy in the crucial bonding and separation from the mother between the ages of about one and half and three. It finds bases for emotional sensing, imaginative awareness, self-originated experience, and autonomy when reared in nurturing conditions. Those conditions require a vulnerability to the child's surrounds, one that cannot be allowed to be exploited by marketing socialization. And a truly autonomous adult self is one engaged in, and vulnerable to, its surrounds, to loved ones, to everyday life.

In the great battle for the soul of the self that is the site of consumer culture, the autonomous social self, rooted deeply in our evolutionary past, is virtually an endangered "species," apparently overpowered by "consumer incorporated" and the automatic culture of "invulnerability" it represents. Yet it remains our greatest resource. The autonomous self is one capable of qualitative awareness, of selective attention, of self-determining its goals and of revising them when needed: all aspects of what we have called the membrane of self, through which we mediate our contact with the world without and within. The autonomous self is one capable of consuming, and of taking joy in consuming, without being itself consumed.

NOTES

1. Kotler is a world-renowned marketing authority and professor of International Marketing at Northwestern University's Kellogg School of Management.
2. An earlier variation of this three-fold distinction was developed in Chapter 7 of Csikszentmihalyi and Rochberg-Halton (1981). See Rochberg-Halton (1986) for a discussion of Peirce's three-fold semiotic distinctions.

3. All unnamed page citations and mentions of Kotler in the following sections refer to Kotler (2003).

4. As B. Joseph Pine, a business consultant and author of the forthcoming book, *Authenticity: The New Consumer Sensibility*, earnestly put it in an interview with *The New York Times* concerning vintage brands, "Authenticity is becoming the new buying criterion. If people remember them from their youth, they perceive them as authentic. That's when they formed much of their own self-image. Their identity matches the product's identity" (LaFerla, 2006).

REFERENCES

Abram, D. (1996). *The spell of the sensuous: Perception and language in a more-than-human world*. New York: Vintage Books.

Assael, H. (1987). *Consumer behavior and marketing action*. Boston: Kent Publishing.

Bentham, J. (1948). *The principles of morals and legislation*. New York: Harper and Row.

Cacioppo, J. T. C., Losch, M. E., Tassinary, L. G., & Petty, R. E. (1986). Properties of affect and affect-laden information processing as viewed through the facial response system. In: R. A. Peterson, W. D. Hoyer & W. R. Wilson (Eds), *The role of affect in consumer behavior* (pp. 87–118). Toronto: D.C. Heath.

Csikszentmihalyi, M., & Rochberg-Halton, E. (1981). *The meaning of things: Domestic symbols and the self*. Cambridge: Cambridge University Press.

Firat, F., & Venkatesh, A. (1995). Liberatory postmodernism and the reenchantment of consumption. *Journal of Consumer Research*, *22*(3), 239–267.

Gergen, K. (1991). *The saturated self: Dilemmas of identity in contemporary life*. New York, NY: Basic Books.

Gobé, M. (2001). *Emotional branding: The new paradigm for connecting brands to people*. New York: Allworth Press.

Halton, E. (2000). Brain suck. In: M. Gottdiener (Ed.), *New forms of consumption* (pp. 93–109). New York: Rowman and Littlefield.

Halton, E. (2004). The living gesture and the signifying moment. *Symbolic Interaction*, *27*(1), 89–113.

Halton, E. (2005). Peircean animism and the end of civilization. *Contemporary Pragmatism*, *2*(1), 135–166.

Halton, E. (2006). The cosmic fantasia of life. In: D. K. Scott, S. M. Awbrey & D. Dana (Eds), *Integrative learning and action: A call to wholeness* (pp. 91–114). New York: Peter Lang Publishing.

James, W. (1890). *Principles of psychology* (Vol. 1). New York: W.W. Holt and Co.

Jhally, S. (Ed.) (1998). *Advertising and the end of the world [Film]*. Northhampton, MA: Media Education Foundation.

Klein, N. (1999). *No logo: Taking aim at the brand bullies*. New York, NY: Picador.

Kotler, P. (2003). *Kotler, marketing management* (11th ed.). Englewood Cliffs, NJ: Prentice-Hall.

LaFerla, R. (2006). Hooked on a feeling. *The New York Times*, April 27, G1.

Lasch, C. (1991). *The culture of narcissism: American life in an age of diminishing expectations* (revised edition). New York: W. W. Norton.

Leiss, W., Kline, S., & Jhally, S. (1997). *Social communication in advertising: Persons, products, and images of well-being* (2nd ed.). London, UK: Routledge.

Pappas, C. (2000). Ad nauseam; ad creep: Ads are literally everywhere today, and an increase in venues only promises more for the future. *Advertising Age*, July 10, pp. 16–17.

Rochberg-Halton, E. (1986). *Meaning and modernity*. Chicago: University of Chicago Press.

Rumbo, J. (2002). Consumer resistance in an age of advertising clutter. *Journal of Psychology and Marketing*, *19*(2), 127–148.

Shepard, P. (1996). *The others: How animals made us human*. Washington, DC: Island Press.

Simmel, G. (1950). The metropolis and mental life. In: K. Wolff (Trans.), *The sociology of Georg Simmel* (pp. 47–60). New York, NY: Free Press.

Speck, P. S., & Elliott, M. T. (1997). Predictors of advertising avoidance in print and broadcast media. *Journal of Advertising*, *26*(3), 61–76.

Weiss, M. J. (2000). *The clustered world: How we live, what we buy, and what it all means about who we are*. Boston: Little, Brown, and Co.

ARTISTRY

CULTURE AND CO-CREATION: EXPLORING CONSUMERS' INSPIRATIONS AND ASPIRATIONS FOR WRITING AND POSTING ON-LINE FAN FICTION

Clinton D. Lanier, Jr. and Hope Jensen Schau

ABSTRACT

This paper explores how consumers use the media products of mass culture to co-create the meanings of popular culture. Specifically, we examine both why and how Harry Potter fans utilize the primary texts written by J.K. Rowling to co-create their own fan fiction. Towards this end, we utilize Kenneth Burke's dramatistic method to explore the pattern of literary elements in both the original texts and the fan fiction. We argue that the primary impetus for consumers to engage in the co-creation of these texts is found in their ability to emphasize different ratios of literary elements in order to express their individual and collective desires. Through this process, fans utilize and contribute to the meta-textual meaning surrounding these primary focal texts and propel the original products of mass culture to the cultural texts of popular culture.

Consumer Culture Theory
Research in Consumer Behavior, Volume 11, 321–342

ISSN: 0885-2111/doi:10.1016/S0885-2111(06)11013-3

As we arrive at the movie theater an hour early for the premier of the new Harry Potter movie, I am already struck by how long the line has grown. We all comment on our foresight for having purchased the tickets ahead of time. On our way from the car to the theater, we pass numerous people in robes and hats in a highly excited state. The attendant at the door tears our tickets and we get in line. As we wait in anticipation, the doors of the theater finally open and we all scramble inside. Though not the perfect seats, we settle in and start swapping our favorite Harry Potter stories. The lights finally dim, the main title appears, and everyone begins to cheer.

After the usual introductory scenes, we watch as the students make their way into the Great Hall at Hogwarts. I notice immediately that Professor McGonagall is sitting in the headmaster's chair. That's interesting because Dumbledore doesn't die until book six, and this is the movie for book four. As the students take their seats, Professor McGonagall rises and addresses the students. "The war is going badly. Since Professor Dumbledore's death, things have taken a turn for the worse." Whoa, did she just reference book six? "As you know, the Death Eaters have destroyed most of Hogsmead and have made several attempts to take over Hogwarts." I look around the theater and notice the other stunned faces. McGonagall turns and looks directly at the audience, "That is why I am asking all of you, our most loyal fans, to help us in our battle against the Dark Lord." My jaw drops. Was she just talking to me? As I look around again, I notice that we are no longer in the theater, but are seated in the Great Hall. McGonagall resumes, "We normally don't reveal our world to muggles, but we desperately need your help. Your loyal devotion proves that you can be trusted and granted access to our world."

Just at that moment, the doors to the great hall burst open and Voldemort appears in the entrance. As the professor and the rest of us look around in shock, Voldemort points his wand at Professor McGonagall and shouts, "Avada Kedavra…" (Disclaimer: all characters are the property of J. K. Rowling.)

As many societies have evolved from production-based to consumption-based economies (Baudrillard, 1998; Miller, 1987; Simmel, 1997), there has been a corresponding shift in the idea of value as embedded in a product to value as co-created by both the consumer and the producer (Vargo & Lusch, 2004). This economic transformation has also been accompanied by a cultural transformation in which consumers are not only involved in value creation, but also in meaning creation (Firat & Dholakia, 1998; McCracken, 1988). Consumer culture theory (CCT) research into this cultural transformation is driven by a key question: how do consumers participate in this meaning creation process (Arnould & Thompson, 2005)? We argue that another important question is why do consumers engage in this co-creation process? We acknowledge this "why" question has two distinct parts: (1) what inspires or triggers the process; and (2) what do consumers aspire or hope to achieve through the process? This paper explores the inspiration and aspirations underlying the co-creation process of appropriating and altering media-based products through the writing and posting of online fan fiction (Hellekson & Busse, 2006; Jenkins, 1992). The paper takes a cultural perspective by examining both how and why this co-creation process turns the media-based products of mass culture into the meaningful texts of popular culture.

This paper specifically explores the cultural inspirations and aspirations relating to consumer co-creation of online Harry Potter fan fiction. J. K. Rowling's fictional Harry Potter series has created an extremely fertile universe for consumer engagement (Brown, 2005) and is the context that we have chosen to demonstrate how and why consumers participate in meaning creation through the transformation of texts from mass to popular culture. As represented by the opening vignette, Harry Potter fan fiction are fictional stories written by fans based on some aspect of the Harry Potter universe. Jenkins (1992) calls this source of reference on which fans base their stories the "meta-text" because it includes not just the official information that has been provided or sanctioned by the primary author, but also the unofficial interpretations and speculations of this world that are developed and shared in the fan community. Because these stories are based on elements of both the primary text and consumers' imagination, we consider the writing of fan fiction a co-creative process. In addition, because consumers utilize mass-marketed products to co-create stories that add to the "meta-text" surrounding these products, we also consider the writing of fan fiction a cultural phenomenon in which consumers transform the products of mass culture into the broader meanings of popular culture (Fiske, 1989).

The implicit assumption in this consumer co-creation orientation towards mass and popular culture is the idea that popular culture cannot be unilaterally "produced" (Levine, 1993). Producers manufacture the products of mass culture and consumers transform them into the symbols of popular culture. This paper argues that the source of this transformative process is the co-creation of meaning. This co-creative process is based on the symbolic richness of the product, the inherent limitations of the product to fully expound this richness, and the degree to which the product can be appropriated and reconstructed by the consumer. We argue that although all three contribute to the writing of Harry Potter fan fiction, the key to uncovering the cultural inspirations and aspirations underlying this co-creative process lies in the limitations of the primary text to address all of the issues important to fans.

The primary purpose of the paper is to try to understand both why (i.e., the inspirations/triggers and aspirations/hopes) and how Harry Potter fans use the focal texts written by J. K. Rowling to co-create their own fan fiction, which in turn contributes to the meta-text that propels the original products of mass culture to the cultural texts of popular culture. Towards this end, we employ Burke's (1989) dramatistic method to explore the pattern of literary elements in both the original Harry Potter books and consumer generated fan fiction. We argue that the primary impetus for consumers to engage in the co-creation of these texts is found in their ability to emphasize different ratios of these elements in order to express their individual and collective concerns and desires. In this way, fans take a more active role in the primary text, create meanings that are more relevant, and contribute to the "meta-text" that binds the Harry Potter community together. The result of this process is the creation of the symbolic structures and meanings of a particular form of popular culture.

THEORETICAL ORIENTATION

If we believe that we have moved from a production-centric logic to a consumption-centric logic and that meaning is no longer embedded in a product but assigned to the product (Baudrillard, 1998; Firat & Dholakia, 1998), then we must not only rethink this impact on the broader concept of culture (McCracken, 1988; Miller, 1987), but also on the more specific conceptualizations of mass culture and popular culture. Likewise, we must also reconsider the processes that underlie and connect these concepts. That is, if this new consumer culture is the site in which consumers actively create meaning, develop communities around these meanings, and potentially transmute the dominant ideologies imposed upon them, then we need to understand how culture influences, and is influenced by, these processes.

Conceptualizations of Culture

Williams (1983) suggests that there are three levels of culture. At the macro-level, culture "describes a general process of intellectual, spiritual and aesthetic development;" at the intermediate level, culture "indicates a particular way of life, whether of a people, a period, [or] a group," and at the micro-level, culture "describes the works and practices of intellectual and especially artistic activity" (p. 90). Although the advancement of CCT requires that scholars address all three of these conceptualizations from a broader marketing perspective, this paper focuses on the micro-level of culture represented by the specific products and practices of human activity.

Micro-level culture is often divided into four types – high culture, folk culture, mass culture, and popular culture. Like the broader concept of culture, the definitions of these terms have been hotly debated. The traditional perspective has been to view high and folk culture as authentic forms of culture that originate from an enlightened intellectual or artistic minority and which express deeper meanings and truths (Hoggart, 1957; Leavis, 1930). Mass and popular culture are viewed as inauthentic forms of culture that are fabricated by a few unenlightened producers and which express distilled and predigested meanings (Lowenthal, 1961; Marcuse, 1968). With this shift from the logic of production to the logic of consumption, a new perspective has evolved which now views high and folk culture as exclusive and elitist forms of culture in which meanings become fixed and rarefied (Gans, 1999; Levine, 1990), and mass and popular culture as the site in which the masses, who have been effectively excluded from the realm of high and folk culture, create meaning (Fiske, 1989; McGuigan, 1992).

Although there is a tendency to view mass and popular culture as the same thing, only varying in their degree of collective appeal, some cultural critics view these two manifestations of consumer culture differently. A close examination of consumer culture reveals that there is often a difference between the intended uses of mass-marketed products and the actual uses that consumers make of these commodities (Hall & Whannel, 1964; Hoggart, 1957; Levine, 1993). These critics argue that what distinguishes mass culture from popular culture is both the use and the meaning of a product. Mass culture is characterized by the passive acceptance of both the meaning and the intended use of a product. Popular culture is distinguished by the active appropriation, modification, and elaboration of a product that alters both its meaning and intended use. By parsing the concept of consumer culture, we see that mass culture is fundamentally different from popular culture, and that it is the power of the consumer that transforms mass culture into popular culture.

But as Levine (1993) argues, not all the products of mass culture become popular culture. This is not meant to imply that these products fail; it just means that they are not appropriated and altered by consumers to construct broader meaning structures. Likewise, even if consumers actively engage products, they are still confined to the products provided by the producers of mass culture in their quest to construct meaning (Fiske, 1989). The products of mass culture put broad parameters around what meanings can be realistically associated with the commodity, but they do not necessarily dictate what these meanings will be. In order to understand this aspect of consumer culture, we must also examine the process in which consumers transform the products of mass culture into the culturally shared meaning systems of popular culture and the inspirations and aspirations that underlie this process.

Co-Creation of Meaning

Although there appears to be widespread agreement in the field of marketing that consumers engage in the process of co-creation (Lusch & Vargo, 2006), there appears to be little consensus on what this concept actually means. Consumer co-creation has been used to describe everything from engaging in self-service activities, to navigating firm systems, to participating in a marketing experience (Prahalad, 2004). In order to advance the CCT and to be of value to the field of marketing, we provide a more focused definition of this concept.

The marketing literature often refers to this process of active participation by the consumer as co-production (Bendapudi & Leone, 2003; Song & Adams, 1993). Co-production, or joint production, is usually defined as the process in which producers and consumers work together to jointly design and/or produce a product (Bendapudi & Leone, 2003). This process is similar to that of personalization in which the producer allows the consumer to choose from a set of options and assists the consumer in attaining the product that best fits his/her needs (Surprenant & Solomon, 1987). At best, this process implies a shared meaning structure that enhances the utility and value creation for both producers and consumers (Normann & Ramierez, 1993; Prahalad & Ramaswamy, 2000). At worst, it implies a means by which producers impose their own meanings and processes on consumers in order to reduce costs and increase productivity (Fitzsimmons, 1985; Lovelock & Young, 1979). Research that has attempted to examine why customers participate in the co-production process has focused primarily on the conditions that are necessary for this process to take place, as well as the shared meanings and resources that are needed for it to be effective and efficient (Bateson, 1985; Dabholkar, 1990; Goodwin, 1988).

A review of the co-production literature reveals that although "value" is jointly created by both the producer and consumer, "meanings" are inherently stable and agreed upon by both parties. That is, co-production involves pre-specified options and fixed parameters in which the product can be personalized. Co-production takes place when the consumer and the producer both understand these conditions and work together to satisfy each other's needs. The producer is still in control of the form and meaning of the product, but is now willing to adapt and modify the product and its meaning, within limits, to better satisfy the customer. Unfortunately, this explanation fails to explain why consumers want to alter the form and meaning of a commodity or why these commodities are often taken beyond the uses originally imposed on them by their producers to become the source of the symbolic structures of popular culture and the cohesive glue that binds a particular subculture together.

Although the "co-creation" literature addresses many of the same issues as the "co-production" literature, it seems to suggest more control over the process by the consumer and emphasizes the total experience that results from the process, rather than just the value provided by the good or service (Prahalad & Ramaswamy, 2004). In order to distinguish co-creation from co-production, we argue that whereas co-production is the process in which consumers and producers work together within a prescribed set of options or choices to jointly design or produce a product, co-creation is the process in which consumers take a product that has been produced by others and extend, modify, and/or alter its form, meaning, and/or uses in ways not foreseen or prescribed by its producers. That is, co-creation suggests that consumers have more control over the product than does co-production, in that it allows them to "play" with the product through their imagination and creativity in ways not intended by the producers.

In order to focus on the cultural dimension of the co-creation process, we move away from the strict focus on "value creation," which often implies an economic and utilitarian goal to the process, to the idea of "meaning creation," which suggests the development or restructuring of the underlying symbolic base of a product from which different utilities or value can be achieved. As a result, we conceptualize our approach as the "co-creation of meaning" because it implies the development of new symbolic structures and meanings rather than conformity to existing symbols and meanings. Consumers should no longer be thought of as agents who merely try to maximize the value of commodities within defined limits, but as potentially active participants who engage in the dynamic manipulation of these products to create new ways of thinking (Levine, 1993). As such, we define the co-creation of meaning as the process in which consumers actively appropriate, extend, and/or modify products in ways that differ from the predefined or prescribed form and/or use in order to create new symbolic structures and meanings that have both personal and communal significance.

In order to understand why consumers engage in the co-creation of meaning, we argue that this process is driven by three things: (1) the symbolic richness of the product; (2) the inherent limitations of the product to fully expound this richness; and (3) the degree to which the product can be appropriated and reconstructed by the consumer. The symbolic richness of the product refers to the depth of meaning associated with aspects of the product. For example, Star Wars often refers to worlds, characters, and events that make up the broader context in which the stories unfold. The limitations of the product refers to the fact that a single product can rarely articulate every aspect associated with it. The producer typically emphasizes certain aspects and de-emphasizes others. Even with six movies, George Lucas could only describe and explain a very small portion of this particular universe. The degree to which the product can be appropriated refers to the extent to which the essence of the product allows for assimilation, extension, and alteration. The essence of Star Wars is the story, which allows it to be easily appropriated by fans by means of fan fiction, artwork, and even amateur movies. We argue that although all three contribute to the co-creation process, the key to uncovering the inspirations and aspirations behind this process lies in the limitations of the product to expound the richness and address all of the issues important to fans.

FAN FICTION

Fan fiction are fictional stories written by media fans that are both based on and contribute to the meta-textual elements associated with a focal text (Bacon-Smith, 1992; Jenkins, 1992). The meta-textual elements include the official focal text(s), ancillary material written and/or sanctioned by the original producer(s) of the text, and the unofficial texts and supplemental material created by fans. According to Jenkins (1992, p. 162), "fan writers do not so much reproduce the primary text as they rework and rewrite it, repairing or dismissing unsatisfying aspects, developing interests not sufficiently explored." Writers of fan fiction draw on and add to these meta-textual elements to clarify, alter, and/or extend the focal text(s). With the advent of the Internet, fan fiction websites now give consumers a place to post their stories for free and receive feedback from anyone who has access to a computer. This allows more people to participate in the process and for the various fan communities to extend themselves beyond their traditional boundaries (Hellekson & Busse, 2006).

The context that we have chosen to examine for this paper is online Harry Potter fan fiction. The Harry Potter books[1] by J.K. Rowling have become one of the largest pop-culture phenomena since Star Wars and The Beatles. In fact, it is hard to think of another popular book series that has generated such fervor among such a diverse group of fans. Of the seven books in the series, six have been published so far. These six books have been translated into over 50 different languages, have been published in multiple formats, and have topped the literary charts in many countries (Blake, 2002). The books have been made into four motion pictures, the last of which grossed over 230 million at the box office during its first two weeks. The cultural influence of the books has grown to such a proportion that many of the terms coined by Rowling (e.g., muggle and quidditch) have been added to the Oxford English Dictionary (Brown, 2002).

Although this paper assumes that the reader is familiar with the Harry Potter stories, we provide a short summary of the overall plotline. Harry Potter is a seven book fictional series about an orphaned boy who, after the murder of his parents by the arch-evil wizard Lord Voldemort, is left to live with his abusive aunt and uncle. On Harry's 11th birthday, he learns that he is a wizard and is invited to attend Hogwarts School of Witchcraft and Wizardry by Albus Dumbledore, the headmaster and somewhat enigmatic figure in the wizarding world. During his first year at Hogwarts, Harry becomes best friends with Ronald Weasley and Hermione Granger, and is immediately confronted by his soon to be nemesis, Draco Malfoy. Harry learns that it was Voldemort who murdered his parents, and also that Voldemort had tried to murder him. Through a magical protection given to him by his mother, Harry survived this attempt on his life while Voldemort was almost destroyed. In the process, though, the curse left Harry with a lightening shaped scar on his forehead and a mental connection to the Dark Lord. The series unfolds as Harry learns more about the circumstances surrounding his life, finds himself in various situations in which he is tested, and witnesses Voldemort's return to power. Harry confronts Voldemort and/or his followers in all of the stories, with the last book in the series, though not yet released at this time, bringing this final confrontation to a dramatic conclusion.

The mass-marketed phenomenon of Harry Potter has not been merely passively received by consumers. Many fans have developed reading groups, created Internet tribute sites, produced and traded art (e.g., sketches, watercolors, cartoons), and even filmed amateur videos (Brown, 2005). Another active consumer engagement with the Harry Potter texts is online fan fiction. These are stories that fans create and post to the Internet based on the meta-text of Harry Potter. To date, there are over 250,000 consumer generated Harry Potter fan fiction postings on the Internet. Considering that many of these stories are as long as, or longer, than the original text, fan fiction represents a significant amount of time, commitment, and creativity on the part of Harry Potter fans. Also, this active engagement of the focal text, the extension of its meaning beyond the original work, and the development of an extremely loyal brand community suggests that Harry Potter has been transformed by means of co-creation from a mass-marketed product into a symbolic text of popular culture.

METHODOLOGY

In order to examine both consumers' inspirations and aspirations for writing Harry Potter fan fiction, we utilize Kenneth Burke's dramatistic method (Burke, 1989). The dramatistic method examines how human intentions are manifested through symbolic language. Burke (1989, p. 135) writes, "Dramatism is a method of analysis and a corresponding critique of terminology designed to show that the most direct route to the study of human relations and human motives is via a methodological inquiry into cycles or clusters of terms and their functions." For Burke, humans interpret lived experience through the patterns of symbols that they use. By examining these patterns, we can get a sense of how humans' intentions are directed by, and manifested in, the terms that they use. For this paper, we apply this method in order to discern both how and why consumers utilize the products of mass culture in order to co-create the meanings of popular culture.

Burke (1969) argues that human intentions can be captured in five basic elements of action – act (what was done), scene (where it was done), agent (who did it), agency (how it was done), and purpose (why it was done). Each of these terms is connected in a pentadic framework in which dyadic combinations (or ratios) of terms are emphasized while others are de-emphasized. The five terms form a total of 10 different pentadic ratios – act–scene, act–agent, act–agency, act–purpose, scene–agent, scene–agency, scene–purpose, agent–agency, agent–purpose, and agency–purpose. Burke (1989) refers to these ratios as "principles of determination" because the ratios that are emphasized direct the attention and convey different meanings than the ratios that are de-emphasized. These ratios also constitute the "terministic screens" through which humans filter experience and create meaning, thus constituting the perspective of a particular culture or subculture (Burke, 1966).

When individuals filter experience and creating meaning, the distinctiveness and complexity of the language of the cultural groups to which they belong to cause them to emphasize certain pentadic ratios and de-emphasize others (Burke, 1984). Burke (1966, p. 55) writes, "We discern situational patterns by means of the particular vocabulary of the cultural group into which we are born. Our minds, as linguistic products, are composed of concepts (verbally molded) which select certain relationships as meaningful … though we may privately manipulate this linguistic texture to formulate still other relationships." As a result, any interpretation of experience does not simultaneously emphasize and define all five elements, but rather considers three of the elements through the lens of the other two (Burke, 1969).

This does not deny that all five elements are present in any situation; it just means that in order to make sense of lived experience, certain aspects are interpreted in terms of other aspects. As Burke (1989, p. 115, italics in original) writes, "Even if any given terminology is a *reflection* of reality, by its very nature as a terminology it must be a *selection* of reality; and to this extent it must function also as a *deflection* of reality." As a result, both intention and meaning are influenced by what combinations of terms are emphasized and de-emphasized.

Burke used his dramatistic method primarily to examine the intentions of the producer, and not the consumer, of the text. By analyzing a text, he could discern both the producer's intentions and the meaning of the text. From a marketing perspective, when producers create a product, they understand the product based on a particular pentadic ratio. By examining the product, we should be able to uncover the underlying ratio, as well as the meanings ascribed to the product. In addition, the producer also intends for consumers to interpret the product from this particular ratio of determination. Because the meaning of a product is arbitrary and is ultimately determined by the terministic screen through which the consumer interprets the product (and not by the symbolic terms in which it was created), we argue that consumers can alter the intended meaning of a product by emphasizing a different pentadic ratio by which it is understood. This allows the consumers to reinterpret the intended meaning of a product to better fit their personal and communal understanding and play with different possible meanings. These new meanings may challenge the intended meaning or extend it, but they allow the consumer to dictate the terms of the interaction. By examining how consumers alter the implicit pentadic ratio of a product and use the product as a resource to co-create meaning, we can understand how consumers actively create meaning in a consumer society.

Applying the dramatistic method to fan fiction, we argue that the underlying pentadic ratio of the original stories limits the meaning and application of the focal text for the consumers of these texts. Fans who actively engage the focal text understand these limitations (either explicitly or implicitly) and are inspired to create their own meanings by emphasizing different pentadic ratios in their own stories. By focusing on those ratios that have been de-emphasized by the primary author but are primary to the particular culture/subculture to which the consumers belong, the consumers are able to create new meanings that are relevant both to them personally and to their particular social community. This paper argues that through fan fiction, the focal text becomes the context in which consumers aspire to work out issues that are important to them and to their particular community of fans.

Applying the dramatistic method to fan fiction is thus a two-part process. The first part involves an analysis of the focal text(s) in order to determine the particular pentadic ratio emphasized by the primary author(s). The second part involves an analysis of the fan fiction stories in order to determine the particular pentadic ratio emphasized in these stories. A comparison of the pentadic ratio utilized in both the focal text and the fan fiction allows us to understand the inspirations and the aspirations of the media fans to engage in this co-creation process. We also witness how these fans contribute to the meta-textual meaning surrounding the focal text(s) and, in the process, convert the products of mass culture into the symbols and meanings of popular culture.

CRITICAL DISCOVERIES

Using the two-part process outlined above, this section begins with an analysis of the Harry Potter texts written by J.K. Rowling. Through this analysis, we explain the pentadic ratio emphasized by Rowling in the original book series. In the next part of the section, we explore three different fan fiction stories that were posted to one of the largest fan fiction websites on the Internet (fanfiction.net). We used three criteria to choose the stories: (1) popular (i.e., heavily downloaded and discussed); (2) rich (i.e., fully developed story with multiple chapters); and (3) illustrative (i.e., clearly demonstrate the variance in literary elements). We examine the pentadic ratio in each of these stories, how it is different from the ratio emphasized in the primary focal text, and the intentions behind using this particular ratio.

Harry Potter Texts

In the original Harry Potter texts, the pentadic ratio that is emphasized in the entire series is the agent–act ratio. Each of the books focuses on a year in the life of Harry Potter, the primary agent in the story. The fact that all of the stories have "Harry Potter" in the title is indicative of this focus on the agent. The first book (Rowling, 1997) begins with "The Boy Who Lived" and the reader follows Harry's life for the next seven years. The concept of agent is expanded in the books to include both co-agents and counter-agents (Burke, 1969). In addition to Harry, the stories also focus on and fully develop, among others, the co-agents of Hermione and Ron and the counter-agents of Voldemort and Draco Malfoy. Dumbledore plays a unique role as a separate agent that acts as a mediator between these two groups. The personal properties of all these characters are explored in each of the books and we gain a deeper understanding of each of them as the series unfolds. Although Harry remains the primary agent, this element becomes more complicated as the social network is developed in the stories and becomes integrated into the plotline.

In terms of the act element of the ratio, the plot of each of the books is tied together by the ongoing battle between Harry and Voldemort. The first book begins with the fear that the newly orphaned Harry may be attacked and killed by Voldemort's followers, progresses through a series of encounters between Harry and Voldemort (and/or his accomplices), and currently ends with Dumbledore giving his life to protect Harry from these evil forces. Although the scene of this battle and the agency employed changes in each of the books, this act remains the driving force of the plot line. In fact, in book five, *Harry Potter and the Order of the Phoenix* (*2003*), the act is solidified in the plot through the revelation of a prophecy that states that either Harry or Voldemort is going to die in order for the other to live. The purpose of this battle is de-emphasized in the series in order for it to be slowly revealed through each story. By de-emphasizing the element of purpose, it is used as a literary device to entice the reader to search for clues to unravel this mystery.

Because Rowling focuses primarily on the agent–act ratio in developing the Harry Potter stories, fan fiction writers have nine other combinations that they can chose from to appropriate and rework the primary focal text. In fact, this ratio may be expanded to 18 depending on which of the dyadic elements is dominant in the ratio. Although the fan authors have many different strategies that they can employ to write their stories, it is by changing the pentadic ratio that they truly participate in the stories and move beyond merely conforming to the meaning of the original stories. We next examine how fans utilize this process in three separate fan stories.

Harry Potter Fan Fiction

In *Harry Potter and the Veil of Darkness* (hereafter referred to as HPVD), the fan author (Wiseacre, 2004) inserts himself into the story as a new professor (Max Wiseacre) that has been recruited to teach the students "Creation of Magical Devices." With the professor's help, Harry learns the skills he needs to battle Voldemort once again. The fan author attempts to produce a story that mimics Rowling's style by focusing primarily on the agent pentadic element, hence "Harry Potter" in the title. The difference, though, is that the author is more concerned with how Harry learns to defeat Voldemort (agency) than with the actual battle that takes place (act). As a result, this fan author emphasizes an agent–agency, rather than an agent–act, pentadic ratio in his story. The agent element is dominant in this ratio because the story ultimately is about the fan author and his ability to influence the other elements in the story.

Although the primary agent in HPVD is still Harry, the new important co-agent is the author himself (Max Wiseacre). The author, as the new professor, possesses the necessary skills to help Harry in his battle against Voldemort. In the story, Harry, because of his connection with Voldemort's mind, decides that he needs to learn legilimency (the ability to read minds) in order to interpret the increasingly ominous visions he is having and discover Voldemort's new evil plans. Although Dumbledore is the best legilimens in the wizarding world, we are told that he has too much valuable information in his head for Harry to learn with him. The new professor decides to create a replica of Dumbledore in order for Harry to learn the art of legilimency.

> "Yes, it's pretty amazing, if I do say so myself." Max added as he appraised his work. "Especially when you consider that the whole thing is made out of clay. I started out with a golem spell and evolved it a bit, then added some of the properties of the pensieve. Professor Dumbledore came by to add the necessary mental components. I really should write a book on the technique when I get the chance. Anyways, the Dumbledore Doppelganger here will be leading your lessons. I will supervise just to make sure things go as planned" (Wiseacre, 2004).

Through this and other similar passages, we learn about the new professor's (and perhaps the author's) personal traits and character. We learn about his skills, his views on the battle between the two sides of the wizarding world, and his vital role in the events. Although only a secondary character (or co-agent), the author is able to engage himself more actively in the story by directly helping Harry rather than merely witnessing (or writing about) the events that unfold.

Max not only makes it possible for Harry to learn this new skill of legilimency, but he also protects Harry from Voldemort while he learns this skill. This related aspect of the story allows us to understand how the author employs the element of agency.

> "Using a fake Dumbledore isn't the only security measure we have to take." Max continued. "This may be a bit difficult for you, but since Voldemort still has a connection to your mind I will need to monitor you. This will require me to kind of ... sit in the back of your mind for a short time. Don't worry, I won't have access to any of your thoughts or memories. It's just that it will be much more difficult for the Dark Lord to

> control you if someone else is already in your head. He would still be able to see what you see and send thoughts to you, but I can make sure that he doesn't make you harm yourself or anyone else" (Wiseacre, 2004).

Agency takes on two roles in the story. First, we encounter the agency of Max on Harry. Max makes it possible for Harry to learn legilimency through his skills in the creation of magic devices. Max builds the replica of Dumbledore and protects Harry during his lessons. Second, legilimency becomes the agency by which Harry learns what Voldemort is doing and the means for Harry to prevent Voldemort from carrying out his evil plans. As a result of this dual aspect of agency, the author not only helps Harry, but also battles, though indirectly, with Voldemort. What more could a fan want?

By focusing on the agent–agency pentadic ratio, this fan author is able to contribute to the meta-text surrounding Harry Potter by suggesting ways that fans can take a more active role in the stories. Although Jenkins (1992) reveals that many members in the fan fiction community disdain personalization stories, our broader analysis found that many fan fiction stories reveal some attempt by the fan authors to forge a deeper connection with aspects of the original story. One way to do this is by altering the pentadic ratio to focus on how the act is performed (i.e., agency) and by directly influencing this aspect of the story.

In *Eternal Sunshine of the Scourgified Mind* (hereafter referred to as ESSM), the fan author (Muse, 2005) describes what happens to Harry, Hermione, and Ron after they ultimately defeat Voldemort. The story describes how, in the final battle with Voldemort, all of the main characters have their minds erased and must figure out how to exist with fragmented identities in the non-wizarding world. In writing this story, the fan author emphasizes the agency–scene ratio. Each of the characters has to learn how to act (agency) in a world that is now completely foreign to them (scene). The element of agency is dominant in this ratio because the story ultimately focuses on how the characters cope, with the scene providing the different contexts for the agency to be enacted. Agency also serves as a subtext in the story as the reader slowly learns the full story of how the characters ended up in their current state of affairs.

In the beginning of ESSM, we discover that each of the characters has had their minds erased of everything associated with the wizarding world. Although this crucial bit of information could be interpreted in terms of the element of act, this information basically serves as the context for the story and is provided primarily through the other elements of agency and scene. In Chapter 3 of ESSM, we encounter Harry in a park contemplating his situation.

> He felt his stomach grumble and snapped out of his contemplative state. He didn't know what he was going to do about food, or a place to stay tonight and suddenly panicked about his predicament. He left the park in a hurry. He wasn't exactly sure where he was hurrying to but he liked to feel as if he was doing something rather than waiting for his problems to solve themselves. He was eighteen, he was homeless, he was unemployed, he was broke and he was hungry. He needed to grow up fast (Muse, 2005).

Here we encounter Harry in a scene that is both unfamiliar to the readers of the primary texts and to the character himself. Harry does not know what to do or how to overcome this situation. In the original stories, Harry is constantly trying to figure out how to respond to situations in which he finds himself, and these actions are often driven by Harry's particular talents (agent) and the task (act) that needs to be accomplished. In ESSM, because of his memory loss, Harry is not able to rely on his knowledge (agent), nor does he know what to do (act). Those characteristics that make Harry, as well as Hermione and Ron, so strong and determined in the original stories are stripped from them in this particular fan fiction. Instead, all of them have to learn how to survive without their familiar internal and external supports.

Although Harry still has memories of living with the Dursleys, his uncle tells him that he cannot return home and that he has to make his own way in the world. He ends up taking a job as a pot scrubber and lives in a room at the YMCA. Hermione, who was also left with all of her "muggle" memories intact, is able to find her way home. Because her memories of school have been completely erased, she begins taking courses from a private teacher and volunteers as a phone counselor for a psychiatric hotline. Ron, because he does not have any memories of the non-wizarding world, finds himself seriously injured with slashes across his wrists and at the mercy of strangers. Someone finds him and takes him to a hospital where he has his arms treated.

> Ron had discharged himself from the Royal London hospital and had been wandering aimlessly for a couple of hours now. His wrists were still very sore. He tugged at his sleeve to be sure that the bandages were covered-up. Everybody seemed to see them and immediately know what he had done to himself. He couldn't bare the looks he had been getting from people. He couldn't take one more person asking him why he had done it … He hated this, he hated not having anywhere to be, and he hated not feeling as if he belonged anywhere (Muse, 2005).

Having been given the name of a free psychiatric clinic, Ron decides to check himself into the clinic in order to try to reorient himself with the world and to figure out how to rebuild his life. Interestingly enough, Ron calls the psychiatric hotline and talks to Hermione. Although they do not recognize each other, their common ailments allow them to commiserate with each other and establish a friendship. For all the characters, in the end, it is through their relationships with others and the situations in which they find themselves (scenes) that they learn to adapt and regain control over their lives (agency).

By focusing on the agency–scene pentadic ratio, this fan author is able to contribute to the meta-text surrounding Harry Potter by exploring how the main characters would act in different situations. The primary stories become somewhat predictable because the broader context in which they act is relatively stable. Likewise, the underlying means by which they act (i.e., agency) is established in the stories. Since the reader, presumably, will never have access to this world, fans often want to explore what these characters would do in situations in which fans might find themselves. The agency–scene ratio allows this fan author to explore this aspect of the Harry Potter phenomenon that cannot be addressed in the primary focal texts. Through the fan fiction, the author connects with other fans who are also curious about these issues. The beauty of the online forum is that other fans can provide feedback, comments, and suggestions about these issues and relate them to their personal lives.

Lastly, in *The Pain Within* (hereafter referred to as TPW), the fan author (Wonderr, 2004) changes the perspective of the primary text from the protagonist (Harry Potter) to the antagonist (Draco Malfoy). While maintaining the strategic focus on the agent as in the original stories, the author chooses to explore both the acts that have led to the development of Draco's character and their influence on his current behavior. Throughout the story, the reader is exposed to various events in Draco's life, as well as his thoughts and reactions to these events. Through these devices, the author is able to provide a deeper explanation of why Draco thinks and behaves the way that he does. As a result, the author employs the act–purpose pentadic ratio to develop the story. The act element is dominant in this ratio because the story ultimately focuses on Draco's internal struggle with these forces and its ultimate resolution.

The story begins at the wizard hospital, St. Mungo's, and Draco's birth. His father, Lucius, in an early effort to forge Draco's character, decides to name the child after the Latin word for dragon. In the next episode, Lucius teaches the four-year-old Draco about their master, Lord Voldemort, and their mission as Death Eaters (i.e., followers of Voldemort) to torture and kill muggles and mudbloods (i.e., those born of mixed parents). Lucius beats Draco when he tells his father that he does not want to become a Death Eater. In the third episode, eight-year-old Draco witnesses a fight between Lucius and his wife Narcissa. Narcissa criticizes Lucius for his blind devotion to Voldemort, and Lucius retaliates by viciously abusing his wife.

> The result of Lucius Malfoy's cruel beatings and haughty influence was an arrogant little eleven year old full of pain and fear. Unable to display these emotions, they came off as a nasty attitude full of insults and mockery. Instead of presenting his inner agonies to someone, to anyone, Draco buried them and closed off the world to his emotions. He had stopped crying long ago, finding it was useless along with screaming or yelling because it only subjected him to more abuse. His mother was no longer his source of comfort, for she had to wage her own war, and Draco didn't want to burden her with his own. The pain and fear stayed locked inside, behind walls of mistrust and shame, and under a roof of confusion. Draco was emotionally unreachable, and intended to keep it that way. For the more pain that is let out, the more pain that is brought in (Wonderr, 2004).

Through this and other passages, we get a view into Draco's life that is not provided in the original texts. We are easily led in the focal texts to believe that Draco is simply an evil person who enjoys hurting others. But instead of viewing Draco as inherently malevolence, we get a glimpse at some of the acts that have led to the development of Draco's negative personality.

Interestingly, in the focal texts, the focus is primarily on how Harry's character allows him to perform certain acts. In TPW, it is the acts in Draco's life that impact his character. In a sense, Harry "acts upon" life whereas Draco is "acted upon." From this point of view, the moral universe has clearly been inverted as Harry takes on the symbolic role of the oppressor and Draco the oppressed. Harry has been able to escape the attempt on his life and the abusive environment of the Dursleys relatively unscathed. Love, the magical shield provided by his mother that saved his life, has not only made Harry seemingly invincible, but immune to the effects of the world. Draco, though, has not been so fortunate. He does not have any magical protection from the abusive acts of his past and has internalized his pain and fear. The effect of this process is a young man whose only shield against the world is arrogance and contempt.

In the end, Draco summons up the courage to resist the horrible abuse. Unlike Harry, whose critical actions are always external to him, Draco decides to confront "The Pain Within" and battle not some opposing evil, but the oppressive forces in his life.

> Draco could never, would never, live for himself. He was just a puppet, controlled on tight strings by his father. He would always live in his father's shadow and be forced into things; nothing would ever be his own choice. Like becoming a Death Eater. He glanced down at the black ink of the Dark Mark. He had never wanted that and still didn't want it. Suddenly, the urge to get rid of it overwhelmed him. It repulsed him; he wanted it gone. He crawled through the glass until he found a large, sharp fragment.... Sitting up, he put the edge at the top of the Dark Mark. Slowly, he applied pressure and ran the point along the shape of the skull (Wonderr, 2004).

The author not only describes the actions in Draco's past (act) to explain why Draco behaves the way he does (purpose), but she also uses this explanation to drive Draco's future actions (i.e., defying his father and Voldemort). As a result, the author is able to redefine Draco from being an evil villain to a tragic hero, whose battle is in many ways more dangerous and courageous than Harry Potter's.

By focusing on the act–purpose pentadic ratio, this fan author is able to contribute to the meta-text by exploring the interrelationship between particular acts in Draco's life and the results of these acts. By exploring a character who we think we understand, the fan author forces the reader to reassess this person by filling in those aspects of the pentadic ratio associated with this character that were left out of the original texts. Although it is easy to carve the world up into good and evil, this story reveals that things are often not what they seem and that individuals (i.e., agents) and their social situations are much more complicated than we often assume. The focus on the act–purpose ratio allows the fan author to shift the essence of the story from action-adventure to psychological drama. By shifting the focus from the external struggles of the protagonist to the internal struggles of the antagonist, we get a deeper view into at least one of the characters and the struggles that he must deal with. Based on an analysis of the comments to this story, this is an issue with which many fans personally identify.

CONCLUSION

Although fan fiction writers often profess a fidelity to the focal text on which they base their stories, we show that they are not constrained by the pentadic ratio emphasized by the original author. In fact, we argue that the main impetus for fan fiction authors to write these types of stories is to expand the meaning of the primary text by emphasizing a different pentadic ratio. The focal text becomes merely the cultural resource that these consumers use to co-create meaning. The focal text sets the boundaries of this process, but is unable to control what takes place within these boundaries. Those texts, which provide enough richness and complexity to allow for manipulation of the pentadic ratio and development of multiple meanings are often elevated from their status as mass cultural commodities to popular cultural texts. Although this process ultimately comes to an end, the co-created popular cultural texts often outlive the original production of the mass-marketed commodity.

We highlight three examples of the ways in which the meaning of the original Harry Potter texts have been consumed and co-created by the writers of fan fiction. The original pentadic ratio is changed, either partially or totally, to emphasize certain aspects of the focal text that are meaningful to the fan writer and the subculture of fans that read and critique the stories. Fan fiction stories that significantly alter or extend the meaning of the focal text in ways which are acceptable to the fan community become part of the meta-text that surrounds the focal text. It is the process of creating and updating the meta-textual elements and meanings of a focal text that ultimately transforms the products of mass culture into the symbolic texts of popular culture.

In order to flesh out the heterogeneous nature of consumer culture (Arnould & Thompson, 2005), we have found it beneficial to examine consumer culture through the more focused lenses of mass and popular culture. Moving away from the production-based view of both of these cultures as inauthentic manifestations of higher culture, we argue that they are the primary sites of meaning creation in modern consumer culture. We do not imply that mass culture is bad, but that its meanings are determined in advance of consumption and set certain limits on how the products of mass culture can be assimilated. In many cases and for many consumers, this is unproblematic. For those products that are especially rich in meaning and resonate with consumers, they are often appropriated and altered in ways that extends or changes the original meanings. Through the co-creation process of focusing on the elements of the pentadic ratio that have been de-emphasized in the original text, these market-based products become the cultural resources through which consumers both create and instantiate the meanings of popular culture.

NOTE

1. Rowling (2003), Harry Potter and the Sorcerer's Stone (1997), Harry Potter and the Chamber of Secrets (1998), Harry Potter and the Prisoner of Azkaban (1999), Harry Potter and the Goblet of Fire (2000), Harry Potter and the Order of the Phoenix (2003), and Harry Potter and the Half-Blood Prince (2005), New York, Scholastic Press.

REFERENCES

Arnould, E. J., & Thompson, C. J. (2005). Consumer culture theory (CCT): Twenty years of research. *Journal of Consumer Research*, *31*(March), 868–882.

Bacon-Smith, C. (1992). *Enterprising women*. Philadelphia: University of Pennsylvania Press.
Bateson, J. E. (1985). Self-service consumer: An exploratory study. *Journal of Retailing*, *61*(3), 49–76.
Baudrillard, J. (1998). *The consumer society: Myths and structures* (Chris Turner, Trans.). London: Sage.
Bendapudi, N., & Leone, R. P. (2003). Psychological implications of customer participation in co-production. *Journal of Marketing*, *67*(January), 14–28.
Blake, A. (2002). *The irresistible rise of Harry Potter*. London: Verso.
Brown, S. (2002). Harry Potter and the marketing mystery: A review and critical assessment of the Harry Potter books. *Journal of Marketing*, *66*(Jan), 126–130.
Brown, S. (2005). *Harry Potter's brand magic*. London: Cyan.
Burke, K. (1966). *Language as symbolic action*. Berkeley: University of California Press.
Burke, K. (1969). *A grammar of motives*. Berkeley: University of California Press.
Burke, K. (1984). *Permanence and change: An anatomy of purpose* (3rd ed.). Berkeley: University of California Press.
Burke, K. (1989). Dramatistic analysis. In: J. R. Gusfield (Ed.), *On symbols and society* (pp. 135–176). Chicago: The University of Chicago Press.
Dabholkar, P. (1990). How to improve perceived service quality by improving customer participation. In: B. J. Dunlap (Ed.), *Developments in marketing science* (pp. 483–487). Cullowhee, NC: Academy of Marketing Science.
Firat, A. F., & Dholakia, N. (1998). *Consuming people: From political economy to theaters of consumption*. New York: Routledge.
Fiske, J. (1989). *Understanding popular culture*. Boston: Unwin Hyman.
Fitzsimmons, J. A. (1985). Consumer participation and productivity in service operations. *Interfaces*, *15*(3), 60–67.
Gans, H. J. (1999). *Popular culture and high culture: An analysis and evaluation of taste*. New York: Basic Books.
Goodwin, C. (1988). I can do it myself: Training the service consumer to contribute. *The Journal of Services Marketing*, *2*(4), 71–78.
Hall, S., & Whannel, P. (1964). *The popular arts*. London: Hutchinson.
Hellekson, K., & Busse, K. (Eds) (2006). *Fan fiction and fan communities in the age of the Internet*. Jefferson, NC: McFarland & Company.
Hoggart, R. (1957). *The uses of literacy*. London: Chatto & Windus.
Jenkins, H. (1992). *Textual Poachers: Television fans and participatory culture*. New York: Routledge.
Leavis, F. R. (1930). *Mass civilization and minority culture*. Cambridge: Minority Press.
Levine, L. W. (1990). *Highbrow/lowbrow: The emergence of cultural hierarchy in America*. Boston: Harvard University Press.
Levine, L. W. (1993). *The unpredictable past: Explorations in American cultural history*. New York: Oxford University Press.
Lovelock, C. H., & Young, R. F. (1979). Look to consumers to increase productivity. *Harvard Business Review*, *57*(May-June), 168–178.
Lowenthal, L. (1961). *Literature, popular culture and society*. Palo Alto, CA: Pacific Books.
Lusch, R. F., & Vargo, S. L. (Eds) (2006). *The service-dominant logic of marketing: Dialog, debate, and directions*. New York: M.E. Sharpe.
Marcuse, H. (1968). *One dimensional man*. London: Sphere.
McCracken, G. (1988). *Culture and consumption: New approaches to the symbolism of consumer goods and activities*. Bloomington: Indiana University Press.

McGuigan, J. (1992). *Cultural populism*. New York: Routledge.

Miller, D. (1987). *Material culture and mass consumption*. Oxford: Basil Blackwell.

Muse, S. (2005). *Eternal sunshine of the scourgified mind*. Retrieved from http://www.fanfiction.net/s/2594688/1/

Normann, R., & Ramierez, R. (1993). From value chain to value constellation: Designing interactive strategy. *Harvard Business Review*, *71*(July–August), 65–77.

Prahalad, C. K. (2004). Invited commentaries on 'Evolving to a New Dominant Logic for Marketing'. *Journal of Marketing*, *68*(January), 18–27.

Prahalad, C. K., & Ramaswamy, V. (2000). Co-opting customer competence. *Harvard Business Review*, *78*(January–February), 79–87.

Prahalad, C. K., & Ramaswamy, V. (2004). Co-creation experiences: The next practice in value creation. *Journal of Interactive Marketing*, *18*(3), 5–14.

Rowling, J. K. (1997). *Harry Potter and the sorcerer's stone*. New York: Scholastic Press.

Rowling, J. K. (2003). *Harry Potter and the order of the phoenix*. New York: Scholastic Press.

Simmel, G. (1997). Fashion, adornment and style. In: D. Frisby & M. Featherstone (Eds), *Simmel on culture* (pp. 187–217). London: Sage.

Song, J. H., & Adams, C. R. (1993). Differentiation through customer involvement in production or delivery. *Journal of Consumer Marketing*, *10*(2), 4–12.

Surprenant, C. F., & Solomon, M. R. (1987). Predictability and personalization in the service encounter. *Journal of Marketing*, *51*(April), 86–96.

Vargo, S. L., & Lusch, R. F. (2004). Evolving to a new dominant logic for marketing. *Journal of Marketing*, *68*(January), 1–17.

Williams, R. (1983). *Keywords: A vocabulary of culture and society*. Oxford: Oxford University Press.

Wiseacre, M. (2004). *Harry Potter and The Veil of Darkness*. Retrieved from http://www.fanfiction.net/s/1590821/1/

Wonderr, The Brainless (2004). *The Pain Within*. Retrieved from http://www.fanfiction.net/s/1047228/1/

MULTIRACIAL IDENTITY AND ART CONSUMPTION

Mohammadali Zolfagharian and Ann T. Jordan

ABSTRACT

Compared to monoracials, multiracials appear (a) to be more concerned about acceptance within their select social groups and within society at large and (b) to have higher differentiation and uniqueness needs. Artworks help consumers successfully fulfill these needs, and multiracials are heavily dependent on artworks in their (racial) identity negotiations. In addition to these needs, familial background, school, and technical qualities of artworks serve as antecedents to artwork consumption. Multiracial identity influences artwork consumption both directly and indirectly. The indirect influence is mediated by social acceptability, group identification, and uniqueness needs. Artwork consumption serves multiracials in two ways: pleasure/escape and communication/identity negotiation.

INTRODUCTION

Thematically reviewing research on socio-cultural, experiential, symbolic, and ideological aspects of consumption, Arnould and Thompson (2005) assert that the key function of Consumer Culture Theory (CCT) is to

Consumer Culture Theory
Research in Consumer Behavior, Volume 11, 343–367

ISSN: 0885-2111/doi:10.1016/S0885-2111(06)11014-5

"explore the heterogeneous distribution of meanings and multiplicity of overlapping cultural groupings ..." (p. 869). They chart four research programs in CCT: consumer identity projects; marketplace cultures; sociohistoric patterning of consumption; and mass-mediated marketplace ideologies and consumers' interpretive strategies. They also call for further inquiry in the globalization of consumer culture and its manifestations. The present research examines a neglected segment of consumers, namely multiracials, and their identity negotiations. Since globalization has contributed to the emergence of the multiracial neotribe (Maffesoli, 1996), this study adds to our understanding of the heterogeneous distribution of meanings and multiplicity of overlapping cultural grouping as partial manifestations of globalization.

Consumer identity is an intricate combination of numerous cultural dimensions such as language, race, and religion (Burke, 1980), each of which influences his/her worldviews and values (Aaker, 2000; Peñaloza, 1994; Peñaloza & Gilly, 1999). What amplifies this intricacy is the interaction between the many possible combinations under each cultural dimension. For instance, consumers born with more than one language, race, and/or religion portray particular dispositions and behaviors that are not typical of other groups (Bowles, 1993; Hong, Morris, Chiu, & Benet-Martinez, 2000). These consumers draw upon multiple, sometimes conflicting, value systems and multicultural repertoire (Berry, 1986; Cardona, 2000). In response to Maheswaran and Shavitt's (2000) call for research in multicultural marketing, this chapter focuses on multiracial identity and defines a "multiracial" as an individual who perceives his/her parents to have distinct racial backgrounds (e.g., Hispanic father and Asian mother), and a "monoracial" as an individual who perceives his/her parents to have the same racial backgrounds (e.g., Asian father and Asian mother).

Our use of the term multiracial is warranted because the quest for recognizing multiracial people in the census and elsewhere was initiated and supported by multiracials themselves. As such, our analysis is an attempt to give voice to an asserted, not assigned, social meaning. In line with this goal, we ask the participants to describe their identity in their own terms. Moreover, no one denies the common use of such terms as biracial and multiracial in our language and the dramatic increase in interracial marriages in recent decades, causing the so-called "multiracial baby boom," (Perlmann, 1997).[1]

The chapter first provides a brief interdisciplinary review of research on two main aspects of multiracials' identity negotiation: identification need and uniqueness need, and explains how material objects (i.e., artworks) are used to negotiate identity. It then presents the findings from an ethnographic study to substantiate and add to the reviewed research. Lastly, a discussion of the findings and limitations will point to directions for further research.

CONCEPTUAL BACKGROUND AND A PRIORI THEMES

Identity and Race

Burke (1980) defines identity as a set of meanings that one attributes to oneself or another as an object in a socio-cultural situation. One of the major pivots in the structure of identity is race. The concept of race is difficult to define, mainly because it was traditionally used to signify biologically different groups of humans; yet no such groups ever existed (Goodman, 1997). Today, it is widely recognized that race is a social construct. We define race as a socially constructed, rather than genetically based, human category that conveys a variety of meanings to members and non-members. "Race is a group of human beings socially defined on the basis of physical characteristics" (Cornell & Hartmann, 1988). Racial identities are "created, inhabited, transformed, and destroyed" by human actions and are, therefore, preeminently social products (Omi & Winant, 1994, p. 55). This chapter uses race as a social construct, not a biological demarcation.

Race can limit or enhance one's life chances and social mobility (Rockquemore & Brunsma, 2002). Cornell and Hartmann (1998) view race as one of the most common categories that contemporary humans use to describe their identities. Racial identity undergirds many consumer needs (Nwankwo, Aiyeku, & Ogbuehi, 1997). Two needs that have attracted much attention across several fields including social psychology, sociology, anthropology, and marketing are identification and uniqueness (Bearden & Etzel, 1982).

Person–Person Negotiation of Identity: Identification and Uniqueness Needs

Two dominant theories have guided research on multiracial identity: Identity formation and symbolic interactionism. Both theories explain how people develop their identities in person–person relationships. Identity formation builds on Erikson's (1968) developmental framework and regards racial identity formation as similar to ego-identity formation. It assumes that the bulk of racial identity emerges in adolescence; a life-stage with the central function of forming a stable global self-identity; that is, a sense of personal sameness and historical continuity (Gibbs, 1997). Symbolic interactionism treats the self as the moving center of social formations (Bloomer, 1969). Thus, society is produced through a myriad of constantly varying exchanges (Du Gay, 1996). This theory focuses on multiracial identity from a micro-level analysis and assumes that people know things by their (symbolic) meanings, which emerge and change through social interaction (Bloomer, 1969). It holds that no social situation can be understood without reference to the actions and beliefs of those in it (Joas, 1987).

Multiracials and Identification Need

Relying on identity formation theory, researchers find that multiracials, responding to contextual factors such as familial and peer groups, often develop a contingent sense of self in relation to, and interaction with, the environment (Bowles, 1993; Herring, 1995). They further suggest that multiracials possess high levels of need for conformity with certain reference groups, resulting in increased anxiety and stress (Gibbs, 1997; Herring, 1992). Using symbolic interactionism, Gordon (1964) and Piskacek and Golub (1973) find that multiracials have self-esteem quandary, racial identity confusion, and psychological and behavioral problems. Furthermore, Gibbs (1973) states that multiracials might actually adopt the symbolic attitudes and behaviors (e.g., dress, speech, or décor) of one or multiple of their races in an exaggerated manner. Faulkner and Kich (1983) observe that the exaggerated behavior exists especially when multiracials perceive problems with their minority identities. Finally, Omi and Winant (1994) propose that multiracials face a momentary crisis of racial meaning whenever they are asked questions like, "What are you?"

Multiracials and Uniqueness Need

The reviewed literature offers mixed insight into multiracials' uniqueness need. On the one hand, as implied by Gibbs (1973), Piskacek and Golub (1973), and Rockquemore and Brunsma (2002), multiracials are expected to have lower levels of uniqueness need, since they are more likely to align their attitudes and behaviors with their select race references than are monoracials. Put differently, uniqueness need is expected to be stronger in consumers who have not had to cope with major (racial) identity dilemmas. Such dilemmas can easily inhibit the desire to think and act inimitably. On the other hand, Cauce et al. (1992), Fields (1996), Gay (1987), and Gibbs and Hines (1992) report that multiracials enjoy equal, if not higher, levels of positive qualities such as creativity, adaptability, resiliency, competence, and leadership. These studies dispute the notion that consumers born to monoracial families will be more likely to enjoy distinctive personal image or individual (unique) style. They imply that monoracials are at best equal to multiracials in terms of individuality and uniqueness.

Person–Object–Person Negotiation of Identity: The Role of Artworks

Researchers concur that consumers often work with market-generated materials to forge a coherent sense of self (Belk, 1988; McCracken, 1986). More specifically, postassimilationist consumer research suggests that racial groups assert an anchoring for identity by socially reconstructing their culture of origin as consumable works of art such as costumes, crafts, and music (Askegaard, Arnould, & Kjeldgaard, 2005; Oswald, 1999). By so doing, postassimilationism provides a dynamic and agentic alternative to more mechanistic structural models of acculturation (Peñaloza, 1994).

Since art is not a phenomenon but a concept (i.e., it has no objective referent), one cannot say what an artwork is or is not, but only what its artist or consumer means by it (Hatcher, 1999). For instance, graffiti creators and traders are position-creators, popularizing certain meanings; and graffiti consumers are position-takers, identifying with and occupying those meanings (Austin, 2001; Lachmann, 1988). Therefore, artworks may be an effective means of negotiating identity.

After facing and aesthetically responding to an artwork, consumers usually attempt to learn about its various meanings by asking where, how, who, why, and when questions. Asserted or assigned answers to these questions represent various aspects of consumers' identities. Although the visible (color, objects, etc.) and invisible (the past, taste, wealth, distinction, etc.) elements of an artwork are interrelated (Pomian, 1990), consumers respond less to the visible (intrinsic) attributes of cultural goods than to the invisible (including symbolic) meanings given to them (Dimaggio, 1987; Veblen, 1949). For instance, Lucie-Smith (1994) suggests that African American art, Chicano and Cuban art, and Maori art contain visible and invisible symbols that represent mythical bonds with ancestral beings and that offer social and moral injunctions.

How do multiracials compare to other racial groups in this respect? Hatcher (1999) suggests that art helps one to successfully carry out membership of a given community or society by reducing tension, anxiety, and frustration; by providing aesthetic pleasures; and by reflecting and reinforcing proper relationships. Accordingly, multiracials, who strive to identify with one or multiple racial identities, may find art consumption a convenient means of participating in their cultures. Further, Wallace (2001) observes that multiracials, when describing their identities, are very likely to refer to the material aspects of a community's culture such as food, customs, traditions, celebrations, holidays, and art. This might indicate that multiracials depend on artworks to a greater extent in identity negotiation.

RESEARCH ACTIVITY

The research project began in summer 2005 and ended in spring 2006. The analysis is informed by three sets of interviews, by observations in the form of home tours, and by pictures taken at the informants homes. The project commenced with 39 interviews with multiracial and monoracial consumers. After these interviews were in, however, a brief analysis of the data pointed to the ubiquitous nature of identification and uniqueness needs. Hence, more and different interviews were considered necessary to substantiate and augment the first data set with third-party narratives by multiracials' significant others (the second set of interviews), and with in-depth discussion of artworks (the third set of interviews; see Table 1). Almost all interviews took place at the informants' homes. In each of the three stages, data collection continued until new interviews produced only minor thematic variations from previous interviews (McQuarrie, 1993). Throughout the research activity, we sought an understanding of the phenomenon, not a representation of a population (McCracken, 1988). Appendices A and B provide summary and detail profiles of informants. To maintain informant privacy, pseudonyms will be used.

Semistructured Interviews with Multiracials and Monoracials

Eighteen monoracial and 21 multiracial residents in the southwestern United States were interviewed. In both groups, a large majority comprised professional adults in their 20s or 30s, identified themselves with middle social class, and were never-married singles. Multiracial informants were recruited with the aid of the Multicultural Center of a major public university. Monoracial informants were randomly selected and recruited

Table 1. Description and Rationale of Each Set of Interviews.

Interview	Interviewee	Type	No.	Duration (min)	Sampling	Purpose
First author	Multiracials	Semi-structured	21	40–80	Through multicultural center and by snowballing	To compare against monoracials
First author	Monoracials	Semi-structured	18	40–80	Randomly from phone listings	To compare against multiracials
Students	Monoracials, whose significant others were multiracial	Semi-structured	11	25–40	Through students	Triangulation by third-party narratives
First author	Multiracials	In-depth	7	100–180	By snowballing from multiracials above	To substantiate person–object–person relations

using telephone listings. Together, they represent a variety of educational fields and occupations. The first author conducted all of these interviews. The interview format was semistructured sc that consistency would be maintained across interviews. Interview probes individuated each interview (Price, Arnould, & Curasi, 2000). Interviews lasted between 40 and 80 min. No incidence of interview refusal or incompletion was encountered. In two cases, the interview was rescheduled and completed at a later time. The informants generally expressed interest in the study. One informant, for instance, remarked, "What a neat thing to research; someone finally cares what *I* think my race combination is … what *I* say I am" (Irene, 28, single, Asian-White-Hispanic).

Semistructured Interviews with Multiracials' Significant Others

The second set of interviews was completed by a fraction of the students in a consumer behavior class at a major public university. Eleven students volunteered to find one qualified informant each and interview him/her. A qualified informant was defined as a monoracial, whose significant other was multiracial. The first author trained and coached the interviewers. The profile of this group was generally similar to the previous pool of informants. These interviews lasted between 25 and 40 min. These interviews were undertaken to create third-party narratives about multiracials' lived experiences, and identification and uniqueness needs. It is hoped that combining the two data sets provides a means of triangulation and validation of self-reported data.

In-Depth Interviews

Seven nondirected, nonstructured, long, in-depth interviews with multiracials provided the third set of data. This practice is consistent with precedent research (see Fournier, 1998; McCracken, 1988; Price et al., 2000). Previous informants helped recruit these seven individuals, who were familiar with neither the research nor the interviewer. The first author conducted all of these interviews. Unlike the semistructured ones, the in-depth interviews lasted between 100 and 180 min, tapping the meanings and motivations behind artwork consumption among multiracials. The aim was to situate artworks and related meanings within the broader context of informants' homes and lives (i.e., in natural settings; Kvale, 1983). Most of the informants were professional adults, were married in their 30s, and identified with middle social class. In two cases, a follow-up interview was conducted because a preliminary analysis of the data revealed grave need for further illumination by informants. Both follow-up interviews lasted around 20 min. The informants were asked to give the researcher a tour of artworks in their homes. The interviewer took several pictures during each interview. These pictures partially inform the analysis. The interviews, probably due to their format and length, were characterized by stronger rapport and more affable conversation and narration.

Data Analysis

Data analysis followed a trajectory of identifying emerging themes by noting instances, patterns, and models. To keep with previous research (Curasi, Price, & Arnould, 2004; Price et al., 2000), the student interviewers had no input during the data analysis and reporting. All of the interviews were taped and transcribed by the first author. Atlas.ti 5.0 (a qualitative data analysis software) was used to organize, code, and sort the data. The combined database includes over 650 pages of transcripts and 140 pictures. The authors perused the transcripts and pictures several times and employed axial coding (Miles & Huberman, 1994) to identify and arrange emerging themes. Consistent with the bracketing practice (Denzin, 1989; Price et al., 2000; Thompson, Locander, & Pollio, 1989), the authors developed a thematic outline, created a separate computer file for each theme, reviewed the transcripts and pictures, and augmented each theme file with pertinent supporting or contrasting data. Additional themes emerged as the analysis progressed, signaling the increasing understanding of the phenomena and the data. A total of 54 theme files were identified. The largest theme was the "art-race relation" theme, contained over 200 data units (quotes and pictures), and excerpted from 56 of the 57 interviews. An iterative investigation and systematic coding over an extended period of time helped the authors reach a fairly comprehensive use and interpretation of the data (Spiggle, 1994). Note that, in the ensuing sections, informant racial combinations will begin with the race with which the informant identifies more strongly.

FINDINGS

Person–Person Identity Negotiation

The interview data suggest that (a) both identification and uniqueness needs are an integral part of identity negotiation among multiracials as well as monoracials; (b) identification need is stronger among multiracials; and (c) multiracials and monoracials are similar in terms of uniqueness need. Therefore, Deleuze's (1992) contention that identity engenders differentiation as well as dedifferentiation is confirmed. Identification need emerged as a two-dimensional construct. At one level, informants aspired to be a member of an in-group by complying with the group's values and norms. This can be referred to as "group identification" need. At the other level, informants aimed to be fit to, and desirable by, their society at large by respecting and practicing its broad cultural values and norms. This can be called "social acceptability" need.

Two factors discriminated between these two levels. First, the values and norms of an in-group are more lucid and concrete than those of society at large, making identification experiences with specific groups easier for the informant to explain than that with society at large. Second, whereas informants' identification with a group did not appear to interfere with their unique sense of self, general acceptability in society often conflicted with uniqueness need. Moreover, several informants seemed to be driven also by their uniqueness need when they were narrating how and why they sought membership in social/professional groups such as the Antique Collectors' Club or Ballet Austin. In contrast, a majority of informants indicated a trade-off between their unique sense of self and the sweeping, panoptic modes of conduct prescribed by society at large. The above findings are consistent with previous identity research: Consumer identity projects are goal-driven although the aims pursued are marked by points of conflict, internal contradiction, ambivalence, and even pathology (Hirschman, 1992; Mick & Buhl, 1992; Mick & Fournier, 1998; O'Guinn & Faber, 1989; Schau & Gilly, 2003).

Social Acceptability Need

Being a fitting member of society was a strong, recurring theme, and multiracials indicated a stronger concern for others' opinions and social values and norms than did monoracials. For instance, Stephanie (22, single, White-Hispanic) stated: "I think social image is more important to me than to my friends. They sometimes complain that I overemphasize people's opinions about me … but I don't agree. Most of my close friends are either White *or* Hispanic. They judge me from outside." Glynn (25, married, White) complained about his wife:

> She is mostly Armenian [White] with a little Cuban blood. I find her extremely worried about how people, even strangers, identify her; although she doesn't look Cuban at all, [n]either has she an accent. Our conversation always [centers] on what people think of her. This is much more than a woman's concern about how she looks or behaves.

In contrast, monoracials typically saw their opinions as important as, if not more important than, other's opinions and showed lesser concern for social values and norms. For example, Katy (29, married, Asian) stated, "I don't very much go with what society dictates … I know who I am and I usually resist the pressure. I usually see myself as an individual versus social institutions." Thus, the findings agree with identity formation theory (Bowles, 1993; Herring, 1995) that multiracials strongly conform to society's norms and values to reduce anxiety and stress.

To explain their strong concern with social-acceptability, multiracials reported numerous reasons, which are organized into two generic types. First, multiracials who strongly identify with a minority race feel much societal pressure towards the "Average American Lifestyle." In response, they diligently respect and comply with society's norms, aiming to portray a positive image of their minority cultures. Fred (31, single, Black-Hispanic-White) thinks he should "always go extra miles to be an 'American' because a lot of people still are too naive to understand the beauty in cultural differences." The extra miles here refers to behaviors such as driving American-brand cars, wearing trendy clothes, enjoying American sports, and engaging in community services. Cameron (21, single, Middle Eastern-White) remembers:

> I was on TV last year and they announced that I was Middle Eastern. It was kind of cool because people got to see that I am enjoying everything that is American and have American friends. So, I guess people with a stereotypical view of us got to see that we're not what they think ... Inside, I'm very Persian. But I always try to look, talk, act American. I even sometimes act up. I don't want to be a bad ambassador for my culture.

Second, most multiracials who play down their minority race exhibited an identity tension. On the one hand, they perceive themselves as "not really belong[ing] to the minority race." On the other hand, they are concerned that others easily identify them with their minority races. Although for different reasons, this group of multiracials also exhibits strong compliance with society's norms. Chris (36, divorced, White-Asian) thought, "Even though I am just like them, I am still less than 100% American ... All I can do, and I always try to do, is not remind them of my differences so I get closer to that 100%." Relying on the literature and findings here:

P 1. Compared to monoracials, multiracials have higher levels of social acceptability need.

Group Identification Need

The interview data, consistent with symbolic interactionism theory (Gordon, 1964; Gibbs, 1973), suggests that multiracials, compared to monoracials, possess stronger group identification need. Rochelle's (27, single, Hispanic-White) story puts it aptly:

> We used to get up late to go to school ... and my mom would let us go wrinkly, she could care less because she is white. But my dad [Hispanic] would never let us walk out of the house wrinkly. His whole reasoning was, "You are Mexican. You already have an underhand among your classmate. They are gonna judge you and say there's that Mexican kid. They didn't even care enough to iron their clothes." My parents [still] get in a fight over that. I think my father is right. My dad used to make me change into different clothes so he could iron them. He always says, "You should look your best to be accepted by everyone in your group of friends."

Monoracials, however, indicated lower levels of identification with various groups, of which they were members. For example, Matt (23, single, Black) said, "I look at it as a price, a price I have to pay to be accepted among my colleagues or friends or family. Beyond that price, which isn't very high, I have to say 'I am sorry ... I can't'."

Multiracials' high level of group identification was usually driven by one of the three factors below. Several multiracials perceived their minority race to be damaging their relationships with groups of people such as friends and peers, and thought portraying the image of "an otherwise perfect member" in those groups could minimize the damaging effect. Rochelle's story above is a case in point.

A second group of multiracials felt responsible to elevate the friends' and acquaintances' appreciation of cultural diversity. This group did not view minority races as a deficiency. They thought that educating others is impossible when one is not already accepted as a member in various social circles. Marcus (24, single, White-Middle Eastern) perceives the problem not in his mixed racial identity but in his friends' lack of exposure to other cultures. He contends, "… before I invite friends over to my house and expose them to our culture, I need to be accepted by them and by their standards."

The third group of multiracials related their high level of compliance to their ability to relate to others in their various social groups. For them, racial identity was irrelevant. They simply thought that their being multiracial enabled them to relate to all types of other people. Unlike the second group, this group did not seek to educate others. Eric (28, single, Hispanic-White) stated, "I've gotten to see differences and I've learned to quickly adapt to different ways"; and Courtney (31, single, Black-Hispanic) thought his mixed racial identity had taught him "how to respect boundaries and appreciate other modes of thinking." The findings, together with the reviewed literature, suggest:

P 2. Compared to monoracials, multiracials have higher levels of group identification need.

Uniqueness Need

As noted earlier, the literature is irresolute as to whether multiracials are characterized by high or low levels of uniqueness need. The interview data provides evidence in favor of Cauce et al. (1992), Fields (1996), Gay (1987), and Gibbs and Hines (1992) who argue for equal, if not higher, uniqueness need among multiracials. Both monoracials and multiracials repeatedly described themselves as different, unique, unlike, special, one of a kind, distinct; and avoided descriptors such as (just) like, alike, another, and no-different. For instance, Jasminra (38, married, Asian-Hispanic) reported, "Mixed identity has given me lots of uniqueness." Crystal (31, single, White), talking about her boyfriend (Asian-Hispanic), commented, "He has quite a few [racially] mixed friends and they all see themselves as very different from the rest of the world, just like he does." Finally, Ryan (30, married, White) reported, "I am different than anyone else ... My friends also are each unique in [their] own ways."

Among the extant works on uniqueness need, the scale developed by Tepper-Tian, Bearden, and Hunter (2001) is supported by the data. Specifically, their three-dimensional (creative, unpopular, and minority choice) nature of the construct is also implied by the interviews with multiracials. First, multiracials appear highly creative. For instance, Jackie (47, widowed and remarried) thought of her second husband, Daniel (Asian-White), as "the expanded family's problem solver and innovative brain. He usually saves the stuff we don't need anymore and makes new things with them." Second, despite their strong social acceptability and group identification needs, multiracials have a taste for unpopular choices, especially when it comes to artworks. The data suggests that the artworks collected and displayed by multiracials were considerably more esoteric and unpopular than those collected and displayed by monoracials. Third, as partly belonging to and identifying with racial minorities, a majority of multiracials never hesitated to consume and show off the elements of their minority races. Valerie (19, single, White-Asian) likes to wear the Sari her cousins have sent from India. She thinks, "The Sari strikes people as odd or out of ordinary and they come up and ask questions. I kind of enjoy this difference."

P 3. Multiracials do not differ from monoracials in terms of uniqueness need.

Person–Object–Person Identity Negotiation

The previous section concurred with Rockquemore and Brunsma (2002) and Cornell and Hartmann (1998) that racial identity undergirds much of consumer behavior, and illustrated the importance of identification and uniqueness needs in identity negotiation. This section explains how multiracials use tangible artworks to interact and negotiate identities (Bourdieu, 1984) and fulfill their identification and uniqueness needs. The data supports Wallace's (2001) contention that multiracials are very likely to refer to the material aspects, especially arts, of their minority races when they negotiate their racial identities.

Forms of Artwork Encountered

Although every product is, to some extent, representative of a certain culture, the focus here is on tangible artworks. The 57 informants collectively regarded the following as artwork: painting, drawing, statue, sculpture, toy, book, music, movie, bible, cross, crucifix, flag, tapestry, carpet, rug, quilt, patchwork, furniture, stamp, coin, bottled wine, firearm, medieval weapon, clock, jewelry, medallion, pottery, glass, poster, photograph, puzzle, car, musical instrument, costume, spice, food, kitchenware, home, and even trash. Some of these items might not be considered conventional works of art. However, the literature suggests that collectible and antique items such as musical instruments possess artistry and imaginative skill in arrangement and execution (Hatcher, 1999). Further, the aim was to capture consumer perception rather than expert opinions. The data suggest that, compared to monoracials, multiracials (a) possess more artworks and (b) more frequently refer to their artworks when asked about their identity and when probed about identification and uniqueness needs.

P 4. Compared to monoracials, multiracials consume more artworks.

P 5. Compared to monoracials, multiracials have higher dependence on artworks in identity negotiation.

Antecedents to Artwork Consumption

The data suggest that seven antecedents underlie the informants' artwork consumption: racial identity, family, school, technical qualities, social acceptability need, group identification need, and uniqueness need. Race seemed to directly relate to the magnitude and type of artwork consumption. A majority of informants viewed one of their races as more appreciative of and/or passionate about artworks. Literally all of the informants who identified with Asian or Hispanic races thought their appreciation for art is primarily due to their minority race. Rochelle (27, single, Hispanic-White) reported, "Although Caucasians also have a lot of arts, Mexican art has been a bigger influence on my art appreciation because Mexican art, like Mexicans themselves, is more passionate." It is possible that this perceived difference is a by-product of informants' subconscious empathy with and preference for their minority races. In fact, previous research (Gibbs, 1973; Faulkner & Kich, 1983) shows that multiracials might adopt the symbolic attitudes and behaviors (such as dress, speech, or décor) of one or multiple of their races in an exaggerated manner.

For many informants, a strong initial influence on art appreciation and consumption comes from a family member's (usually a parent's) interest in a type of art. The art interests of teachers and peers at school have a similar influence. The art interests of family and school members are sometimes driven by their racial identity and other times by their nonracial appreciation for specific forms of art. As the fourth antecedent, appreciation of the technical qualities in works of art includes the artist's creativity, expertise and identity; techniques used; style; and the time and effort invested.

Many informants discount others' influence and view their own identification and uniqueness needs and goals as the primary reasons. For example, Selena (28, single, Black-Native American-White) attributed her passion for Puerto Rican arts neither to the differential art appreciation across her three races nor to her family's or teachers' influence, but to her deliberate effort to maintain the bond with her heritage. Further, Karla (20, single, Black-Hispanic), who lost her family at an early age, never wants to forget her heritage and uses artworks to connect with her roots as well as to differentiate herself from the rest of the world.

An important concept within social acceptability need is "taste," which in part determines one's degree of fit in a socio-cultural context. Many informants find the existence and appropriateness of their artistic taste to influence their acceptability. For instance, Michael (27, single) thinks his Middle Eastern-Hispanic girlfriend is interested in and "uses African artworks because she wants others to appreciate her taste for alternative arts and [hopes] this will make her a more sociable person."

Group identification need, the sixth antecedent, was highly supported by the data. Multiracials generally complain that they cannot keep up with all of the cultural events and gatherings that take place within each of their racial cultures. As a result, they sometimes feel isolated and distanced from their heritage and resort to any artifact that can help them identify with their minority races. As such, they vicariously consume their culture through collecting and using artworks. For instance, Crystal (31, single, White) remembers that her half-Chinese boyfriend, having missed the Chinese New Year celebration, bought several Chinese artifacts and spent hours going through Chinese books and family pictures.

Some multiracials perceive their expertise about minority arts to serve as an advantage enhancing their membership in non-race related groups. In Neil's (25, single, Asian-White) words, "Many times my colleagues ask about Indian costumes, music, dance, and movies and I get the opportunity to educate them … [this] definitely affects my position and importance as a member of our work team." Nadia's (40, widowed) Hispanic-Black-White husband found a job in a furniture store because the employer valued his knowledge about Hispanic and Black aesthetics and preferences.

The link between uniqueness need and artworks is clearly implied by the data. The only caveat is that the source of uniqueness was twofold. An artwork is seen as unique because (1) it is "one of a kind" in that its creation is bound to a particular historical context (i.e., artist, time, place, style, etc.) and (2) the owner's first-hand experiences or post-purchase interactions with the theme or components of the artwork creates a unique personal history. Both of these sources were strongly supported. For instance, Alex (24, single, Hispanic-Asian), describing an idol he had bought from a Temple in India, said, "It is different from anything in the world because history is like a river ... You can't swim more than once in any river. I had the privilege to talk to the artist and hear that idol's story from a native philosopher." This is in line with Bloomer's (1969) observation that consumers know things by their symbolic meanings, which emerge and change through their interactions with those things.

Although racial identity is a direct antecedent of artwork consumption, it also indirectly affects artwork consumption as it is a key constituent of the other six antecedents.

P 6. Multiracial identity is associated with artwork consumption both directly and indirectly.

P 7. The indirect association between multiracial identity and artwork consumption is mediated through (a) social acceptability need; (b) group-identification need; and (c) uniqueness need.

P 8. Other antecedents of artwork consumption include (a) family; (b) school; and (c) technical qualities.

Uses of Artworks

The interview data suggest that artwork consumption serves multiracials in two ways. First, consuming artworks allows for aesthetic enjoyment and moments of escape from the immediate surroundings. The informants repeatedly used phrases similar to "for enjoyment and relaxation," "being at home but breathing Mediterranean air," "getting absorbed in all the beauty in it," "escaping into nature to calm down," "getting away from the typical," and "daydreaming while looking at it." Second, the informants had no doubt that artwork consumption conveyed meanings and comprised a sort of nonverbal communication. In Carly's (39, married, White-Asian) words, "artworks are conversational pieces."

Three factors emerged as pertinent to this. First, the meanings communicated might or might not be intended by the owner of the artwork. For instance, whereas Chris (36, divorced, White-Asian) wanted a certain message to be communicated when he displayed an artwork,

Kathryn (45, married, White-Hispanic) had never attempted to represent herself in her artworks. Second, artworks, and art in general, were repeatedly preferred over other verbal or nonverbal communication vehicles. For example, whenever Danielle (25, single, Hispanic-White) invites White friends to her home, she uses Mexican material culture (pots, costumes, etc.) instead of words to show her "minority pride." Courtney (31, single, Black-Hispanic) thinks, "Arts, especially music, are the best way to voice Mexican and African struggles and dreams ... which cannot really be explained in words." Third, first-hand experience with the themes or objects portrayed in an artwork enhances one's desire to display the artwork and ignite conversations about the stories behind it. Mick (30, married, Asian) described his Hispanic-White wife as "the kind to direct others' attention to the paintings of the rainforests and castles in Puerto Rico so she can *bore* them with all the little stories about her visits to Puerto Rico." Artwork consumption as communication comprises the most visible form of person–object–person negotiation of identity among multiracials. Hence:

P 9. Artwork consumption among multiracials serves as a nonverbal communication that can trigger other verbal or nonverbal communication.

P 10. Multiracials consume artworks in part for enjoyment and escape from the ordinary.

CONCLUSION

Both identity formation (Gibbs, 1997; Herring, 1992) and symbolic interactionism (Gibbs, 1973; Omi & Winant, 1994) theories imply that multiracials are highly concerned about their general acceptance within their select groups and within society at large. The three types of interviews confirm this implication by showing that multiracials do, in fact, have high social acceptability and group identification needs. The literature on multiracial identity is uncertain whether or not multiracials are characterized with lower levels of uniqueness need (see Cauce et al., 1992; Gay, 1987). The present research clarifies this issue and finds strong need for differentiation and uniqueness among multiracials.

The present research supports that artworks help consumers successfully (a) carry out their memberships in various societal groups (Hatcher, 1999) and (b) construct a personal social space in their pursuit of a unique identity

(Tepper-Tian et al., 2001). Multiracials, who possess high levels of identification and uniqueness needs, take contingent advantage of artworks in their negotiation of (racial) identity. In addition to these needs, familial background, school, and technical qualities of artworks are found as antecedents to artwork consumption. Race influences artwork consumption both directly and indirectly. The indirect influence is mediated by social-acceptability, group-identification, and uniqueness needs. Artwork consumption serves multiracials in two ways: pleasure/escape and communication/negotiation of identity.

LIMITATIONS AND DIRECTIONS FOR FUTURE RESEARCH

The heterogeneity across the many subgroups of multiracial populations (Funderburg, 1998) and inclusion of only two personality traits are two limitations of this research. Readers should note that interpretive research does not generalize to populations; rather, it can generalize to constructs or theories. Future research can extend this work in two ways. First, it can tap the differences among the subgroups of multiracial populations. As a corollary of this extension, other cultural dimensions of consumer identity such as religion and gender can be added. Second, a wider, or different, set of personality traits might be considered. Another limitation is the types of material objects included in this study. It is interesting to observe whether multiracials consume mundane products such as casual apparel and personal accessories in similar ways. Finally, as the research sought an understanding of the phenomenon, not a representation of a population (McCracken, 1988), more research is needed to verify the generality of the findings.

Race as a market-segmentation criterion has not received deserved attention (Lindridge & Dibb, 2002; Williams & Qualls, 1989). Multiracials satisfy the various tests of market segment viability: measurability, accessibility, substantiality, differentiability, and actionability (Kotler & Armstrong, 2003). Because positional advantage in the market is dependent upon effective market-segmentation and informed resource allocation (Day & Wensley, 1988), distinguishing multiracials from the general public can be essential, especially for marketers of cultural products. Differentiation, branding, advertising, and corporate sponsorship decisions are only a few examples of marketing strategies that need to be guided by such peculiarities.

Diffusion of innovation research can gainfully study multiracial identity. Specifically, we need to learn how multiracials compare to monoracials in terms of trait innovativeness, and what percentages of multiracials are innovators, early adopters, early majority, late majority, and laggards. Since need for uniqueness positively correlates with trait innovativeness (Rogers, 2003), multiracials and monoracials are expected to portray almost the same agency role in the process of innovation adoption. Such speculations shall await future research.

Last, but not least, use of symbolic interactionism in marketing research has been limited. One exception is Leigh and Gabel (1992) who suggest that consumers with strong desire to gain membership in a particular social group can be regarded as a segment. After its original notions are revisited and its contentions substantiated, symbolic interactionism can be useful, especially in the studies of personal and interpersonal marketing-related phenomena such as consumer behavior.

NOTE

1. In the year 2000, about seven million Americans (2.5% of the U.S. population) checked more than one racial category, indicating their identification as multiracial (U.S. Census Bureau; May 2005).

ACKNOWLEDGMENT

The authors thank Mariela Nunez-Janes and James D. Williams for their comments on an earlier version of this chapter.

REFERENCES

Aaker, J. L. (2000). Accessibility or diagnosticity? Disentangling the influence of culture on persuasion processes and attitudes. *Journal of Consumer Research*, *26*(4), 340–357.

Arnould, E. J., & Thompson, C. J. (2005). Consumer culture theory (CCT): Twenty years of research. *Journal of Consumer Research*, *31*(4), 868–882.

Askegaard, S., Arnould, E. J., & Kjeldgaard, D. (2005). Postassimilation ethnic consumer research: Qualifications and extensions. *Journal of Consumer Research*, *32*(1), 160–170.

Austin, J. (2001). *Taking the train: How graffiti art became an urban crisis in New York City*. New York: Columbia University Press.

Bearden, W. O., & Etzel, M. J. (1982). Reference group influence on product and brand purchase decisions. *Journal of Consumer Research*, *9*(2), 183–194.

Belk, R. W. (1988). Possessions and the extended self. *Journal of Consumer Research*, *15*(2), 139–168.

Berry, J. W. (1986). Multiculturalism and psychology in poor societies. In: L. H. Ekstrand (Ed.), *Ethnic minorities and immigrants in a cross-cultural perspective* (pp. 37–51). Lisse, The Netherlands: Swets & Zeitlinger.

Bloomer, H. (1969). *Symbolic interactionism: Perspective and method.* NJ: Prentice Hall.

Bourdieu, P. (1984). In: R. Nice (Trans.). [*Distinction: A social critique of the judgment of taste*] Cambridge: Harvard University Press.

Bowles, D. D. (1993). Bi-racial identity: Children born to African-American and white couples. *Clinical Social Work Journal*, *21*(4), 417–428.

Burke, P. (1980). The self: Measurement requirements from an interactionist perspective. *Social Psychology Quarterly*, *43*, 18–29.

Cardona, M. M. (2000). Multicultural marketing. *Advertising Age*, *65*(52), 16.

Cauce, A. M., Hiraga, Y., Mason, C., Aguilar, T., Ordonez, N., & Gonzales, N. (1992). Between a rock and a hard place: Social adjustment of biracial youth. In: M. P. P. Root (Ed.), *Radically mixed people in America* (pp. 207–222). CA: Sage Publications.

Cornell, S., & Hartmann, D. (1998). *Ethnicity and race: Making identities in a changing world.* CA: Sage.

Curasi, C. F., Price, L. L., & Arnould, E. J. (2004). How individuals' cherished possessions become families inalienable wealth. *Journal of Consumer Research*, *31*(3), 609–623.

Day, G. S., & Wensley, R. (1988). Assessing advantage: A framework for diagnosing competitive superiority. *Journal of Marketing*, *52*(2), 1–20.

Deleuze, G. (1992). *Postscript on the societies of control.* Cambridge: MIT Press.

Denzin, N. K. (1989). *Interpretive interactionism.* Newbury Park, CA: Sage.

Dimaggio, P. (1987). Classification in art. *American Sociological Review*, *53*(4), 440–455.

Du Gay, P. (1996). *Consumption and identity at work.* London: Sage.

Erikson, E. H. (1968). *Identity: Youth and crisis.* New York: W. W. Norton.

Faulkner, J., & Kich, G. (1983). Assessment and engagement stages in therapy with the interracial family. *Family Therapy Collections*, *6*, 78–90.

Fields, L. (1996). Piecing together the puzzle: Self-concept and group identity in biracial people in America: 1 black/white youth. In: M. P. P. Root (Ed.), *Multiracial experience: Racial borders as the new frontier* (pp. 211–226). CA: Sage.

Fournier, S. (1998). Consumers and their brands: Developing relationship theory in consumer research. *Journal of Consumer Research*, *24*(4), 343–373.

Funderburg, L. (1998). Crossing the demographic divide. *American Demographics*, *20*(10), 24–25.

Gay, K. (1987). *The rainbow effect: Interracial families.* New York: Franklin Watts.

Gibbs, J. T. (1973). Black students/white universities: Different expectations. *Personal and Guidance Journal*, *51*(7), 463–469.

Gibbs, J. T. (1997). Biracial adolescents. In: J. T. Gibbs & L. Huang (Eds), *Children of color: Psychological interventions with culturally diverse youth* (pp. 305–332). New York: Jossey-Bass.

Gibbs, J. T., & Hines, A. (1992). Negotiating ethnic identity: Issues for black-white biracial adolescents. In: M. P. P. Root (Ed.), *Radically mixed people in America* (pp. 223–238). CA: Sage.

Goodman, A. H. (1997). Problematics of "race" in contemporary biological anthropology. In: N. T. Boaz & L. D. Wolfe (Eds), *Biological anthropology: The state of the science* (pp. 221–243). Bend, OR: International Institute for Human Evolutionary Research.

Gordon, M. M. (1964). *Assimilation in American life: The role of race, religion and national origin*. Oxford: Oxford University Press.

Hatcher, E. P. (1999). *Art as culture: An introduction to the anthropology of art* (2nd ed.). CT: Bergin.

Herring, R. D. (1992). Biracial children: An increasing concern for elementary and middle school counselors. *Elementary School Guidance and Counseling*, *27*(2), 123–130.

Herring, R. D. (1995). Developing biracial ethnic identity: A review of the increasing dilemma. *Journal of Multicultural Counseling and Development*, *23*, 29–38.

Hirschman, E. C. (1992). The consciousness of addiction: Toward a general theory of compulsive consumption. *Journal of Consumer Research*, *19*(2), 155–179.

Hong, Y.-Y., Morris, M., Chiu, C.-Y., & Benet-Martinez, V. (2000). Multicultural minds: A dynamic constructivist approach to culture and cognition. *American Psychologist*, *55*(7), 709–720.

Joas, H. (1987). Symbolic interactionism. In: A. Giddens & J. H. Turner (Eds), *Social theory today* (pp. 82–115). Cambridge: Polity Press.

Kotler, P., & Armstrong, G. (2003). *Principles of marketing*. NJ: Prentice Hall.

Kvale, S. (1983). The qualitative research interview: A phenomenological and a hermeneutical mode of understanding. *Journal of Phenomenological Psychology*, *14*(2), 171–196.

Lachmann, R. (1988). Graffiti as career and ideology. *American Journal of Sociology*, *94*(2), 229–250.

Leigh, J. H., & Gabel, T. G. (1992). Symbolic interactionism: Its effects on consumer behavior and implications for marketing strategy. *Journal of Consumer Marketing*, *9*(1), 27–38.

Lindridge, A., & Dibb, S. (2002). Is culture a justifiable variable for market segmentation? A cross-cultural example. *Journal of Consumer Behavior*, *2*(3), 269–286.

Lucie-Smith, E. (1994). *Race, sex, and gender in contemporary art*. New York: Harry N Abrams.

Maffesoli, M. (1996). *The time of tribes*. Thousand Oaks, CA: Sage.

Maheswaran, D., & Shavitt, S. (2000). Issues and new directions in global consumer psychology. *Journal of Consumer Psychology*, *9*(2), 59–66.

McCracken, G. (1986). Culture and consumption: A theoretical account of the structure and movement of the cultural meaning of consumer goods. *Journal of Consumer Research*, *13*(1), 71–84.

McCracken, G. (1988). Lois roget: Curatorial consumer in a modern world. In: G. McCracken (Ed.), *Culture and consumption* (pp. 44–56). Bloomington: Indiana University Press.

McQuarrie, E. F. (1993). *Customer visits*. Newbury Park, CA: Sage.

Mick, D. G., & Buhl, C. (1992). A meaning-based model of advertising experiences. *Journal of Consumer Research*, *19*(3), 317–338.

Mick, D. G., & Fournier, S. (1998). Paradoxes of technology: Consumer cognizance, emotions, and coping strategies. *Journal of Consumer Research*, *25*(2), 123–143.

Miles, M. B., & Huberman, A. M. (1994). *Qualitative data analysis*. Thousand Oaks, CA: Sage.

Nwankwo, S., Aiyeku, J., & Ogbuehi, A. (1997). The marketing challenge of multiculturalism: An exploratory study. *Journal of International Marketing and Exporting*, *3*(1), 47–61.

O'Guinn, T. C., & Faber, R. J. (1989). Compulsive buying: A phenomenological exploration. *Journal of Consumer Research*, *16*(2), 147–157.

Omi, M., & Winant, H. (1994). *Racial formation in the United States: From the 1960s to the 1990s* (2nd ed.). New York: Routledge.

Oswald, L. R. (1999). Culture swapping: Consumption and the ethnogenesis of middle-class Haitian immigrants. *Journal of Consumer Research*, *25*(4), 303–318.

Peñaloza, L. (1994). Atravesando fronteras/border crossing: A critical ethnographic exploration of the consumer acculturation of Mexican immigrants. *Journal of Consumer Research*, *21*(1), 32–54.

Peñaloza, L., & Gilly, M. C. (1999). Marketer acculturation: The changer and the changed. *Journal of Marketing*, *63*(3), 84–104.

Perlmann, J. (1997). Multiracials, racial classification, and American intermarriage: The public's interest. *Macroeconomics 9712004*, Economics Working Paper Archive: WUSTL.

Piskacek, V., & Golub, M. (1973). Children of interracial marriage. In: I. Stewart & L. Abt (Eds), *Interracial marriage: Expectations and reality* (pp. 51–57). New York: Grossman.

Pomian, K. (1990). *Collectors and curiosities, Paris and Venice, 1500–1800*. Cambridge: Polity Press.

Price, L. L., Arnould, E. J., & Curasi, C. F. (2000). Older consumers' disposition of special possessions. *Journal of Consumer Research*, *27*(2), 179–201.

Rockquemore, K., & Brunsma, D. (2002). *Beyond black: Biracial identity in America*. CA: Sage.

Rogers, E. M. (2003). *Diffusion of innovations* (5th ed.). New York: Free Press.

Schau, H. J., & Gilly, M. C. (2003). We are what we post? Self-presentations in personal web spaces. *Journal of Consumer Research*, *30*(3), 385–404.

Spiggle, S. (1994). Analysis and interpretation of qualitative data in consumer research. *Journal of Consumer Research*, *21*(3), 491–503.

Tepper-Tian, K., Bearden, W. O., & Hunter, G. L. (2001). Consumers' need for uniqueness: Scale development and validation. *Journal of Consumer Research*, *28*(1), 50–66.

Thompson, C. J., Locander, W. B., & Pollio, H. R. (1989). Putting consumer experience back into consumer research: The philosophy and method of existential-phenomenology. *Journal of Consumer Research*, *16*(2), 133–146.

Veblen, T. (1949). *The theory of the leisure class*. London: George Allen and Unwin. (Originally published 1899 by Mcmillan, New York).

Wallace, K. R. (2001). *Relative/outsider: The art and politics of identity among mixed heritage students*. CT: Ablex.

Williams, J. D., & Qualls, W. J. (1989). Middle-class black consumers and intensity of ethnic identification. *Psychology & Marketing*, *6*(4), 263–286.

APPENDIX A. SUMMARY INFORMANT PROFILE

	Female (28)	Male (29)
Age:		
Age range	19–47	21–52
Average age	29.8	31.7
Education:		
Doctorate degree	1	1
Master's degree	2	3
Bachelor's degree	6	5
Some College	14	15
High School Diploma	4	4
Below high school	1	1
Marital status:		
Married	6	8
Widowed and remarried	1	1
Divorced and remarried	0	1
Widowed		
Divorced		
Single, never married	16	15
Social class:		
High	0	3
Upper-middle	6	4
Middle	14	11
Lower-Middle	6	8
Low	2	3
Income:		
Below $20,000	4	6
$20,000-$40,000	7	5
$40,000-$60,000	5	4
$60,000-$80,000	7	8
$80,000-$100,000	4	3
Above $100,000	1	3
Racial Mix:		
Asian-Hispanic	3	2
Asian-Middle Eastern	0	1
Asian-White	5	3
Black-Hispanic	2	1
Black-White	2	6
Hispanic-Middle Eastern	1	1
Hispanic-White	10	11
Middle Eastern-White	0	3
Asian-Hispanic-White	1	0
Asian-MiddleEastern-White	1	0
Black-AmericanIndian-White	1	0
Black-Hispanic-White	2	1
Current Occupation:		
Home-maker	3	0
Student	6	9
Professional Adult	18	20

APPENDIX B. DETAIL INFORMANT PROFILE

Pseudonym	Age	Gender	Education[a]	Marital Status[b]	Social Class	Income[c]	Race[d]
1. Semistructured Interviews with Multiracials							
Alex	24	m	sc	snm	h	5	Ha
Cameron	21	m	sc	snm	m	4	Mw
Carly	39	f	bd	m	lm	2	wa
Chris	36	m	sc	d	l	1	wa
Country	31	m	sc	snm	l	1	bh
Daniella	25	f	sc	snm	um	6	hw
Eric	28	m	md	snm	m	4	hw
Fred	31	m	hd	snm	lm	2	bhw
Irene	28	f	md	snm	m	3	awb
Jasminra	38	f	hd	m	m	4	ah
Joe	26	m	sc	snm	um	3	wh
Jonathan	37	m	dd	m	lm	4	wh
Kala	20	f	sc	snm	m	bh	bh
Kathryn	45	f	hd	m	lm	1	wh
Lindsay	26	f	sc	snm	m	4	hw
Marcus	24	m	sc	snm	m	5	wm
Neil	25	m	bd	snm	um	4	aw
Rochelle	27	f	bd	snm	m	4	hw
Selena	28	f	bd	snm	m	2	bnw
Stephanie	22	f	sc	snm	um	3	wh
Valeria	19	f	bh	snm	lm	2	wa
Range	19–45		bh–dd	–	l–h	1–6	–
Median	27	f	sc	–	m	3	–
2. Semistructured Interviews with Monoracials							
Aaron	22	m	sc	snm	h	6	h
Annette	29	f	hd	d	l	1	b
Becky	32	f	dd	m	m	5	w
Blake	24	m	sc	snm	m	3	a
Delia	25	f	sc	d	m	5	h
Derrick	34	M	bd	d	lm	2	w
Helen	26	f	bd	snm	um	4	b
Jeff	49	m	sc	w	um	5	w
Julie	24	F	Sc	snm	m	4	h
Katy	29	f	hd	m	um	4	a
Kendahl	36	F	md	d	um	5	w
Kevin	28	m	md	m	m	4	a
Linda	27	f	sc	snm	lm	3	n
Matt	23	m	sc	snm	m	4	b
Megan	38	f	sc	snm	m	1	w
Michael	27	m	bd	snm	l	1	m
Ryan	30	m	hd	snm	lm	4	w
Tony	34	m	hd	m	h	1	w
Range	22–49	–	bh–dd	–	l–h	1–6	–
Median	28.5	Equal	sc	–	m	4	–

APPENDIX B (*Continued*)

Pseudonym	Age	Gender	Education[a]	Marital Status[b]	Social Class	Income[c]	Race[d]
3. Semistructured Interviews with Multiracials' Significant Others							
Amanda	21	f	bd	snm	m	3	w
Crystal	31	f	sc	snm	lm	2	w
Dustin	44	m	sc	d	m	3	w
Gary	52	m	sc	wrm	h	6	h
Glynn	25	m	hd	m	lm	2	b
Jakie	47	f	sc	wrm	um	5	b
Joseph	25	m	sc	snm	m	2	a
Josh	37	m	md	snm	m	2	w
Mick	30	m	bd	m	lm	3	a
Nadia	40	f	sc	w	m	2	w
Tom	43	m	bh	drm	lm	1	h
Range	21–52	–	bh–md	–	Lm–h	1–6	–
Median	37	m	sc	–	m	2	–
4. Nonstructured, Depth Interviews with Multiracials							
Anthony	37	m	bd	m	lm	4	Mw
Bob	44	m	sc	m	um	6	Wh
Cindy	25	f	sc	snm	l	1	Ha
David	28	m	sc	snm	m	1	Aw
Lori	29	f	sc	m	lm	2	Bh
Natasha	26	f	sc	snm	m	4	Aw
Tracy	32	f	bd	d	m	3	Bw
Range	19–49	–	sc–bd	–	l–h	1–6	–
Median	29	f	sc	–	m	1	–

Racial combination begin with the race with which the information identifies more stronglyAsian includes citizens of the continent Asia except those from the Middle East.

[a]bh = Below high school; hd = High school diploma; sc = Some college; bd = Bachelor's degree; md = Master's degree; de = Doctorate degree

[b]m = Married; wrm = Widowed and remarried drm = Divorced and remarried; w = Widowed; d = Divorced; snm = Single, never married

[c]Annual household: 1) Below $20,000; 2) $20,000-$40,000; 3) $40,000-$60,000; 4) $60,000-$80,000; 5) $80,000-$100,000; 6) $100,000 +

[d]a = Asian; b = Black; h = Hispanic; m = Middle Eastern; n = Native American; W = White

COMMUNITY

DYNAMICS OF COMMUNITY ENGAGEMENT: THE ROLE OF INTERPERSONAL COMMUNICATIVE GENRES IN ONLINE COMMUNITY EVOLUTIONS

Anat Toder Alon and Frédéric F. Brunel

With close to three quarters of American adults using the Internet (Madden, 2006), the chatter from online consumer voices has been turned on high volume. The increasing participation has fueled the growth of a multitude of online communities in which geographically dispersed and otherwise unrelated consumers become participants. The role of these borderless and virtual communities extends well beyond basic informational or commercial exchanges. The Internet has become a space where people maintain and develop social ties, and toward which they turn for assistance during major life events (Boase, Horrigan, Wellman, & Rainie, 2006). It is also a place where a growing number of companies are flocking to in order to engage with consumers. Companies are discovering that there are compelling benefits to building online communities where they can facilitate and participate in consumer conversations. For example, a 2006 Communispace study

Consumer Culture Theory
Research in Consumer Behavior, Volume 11, 371–400

ISSN: 0885-2111/doi:10.1016/S0885-2111(06)11015-7

conducted with 2,196 members of company sponsored communities across diverse product categories and brands has revealed that, since joining the respective communities, 76 percent of respondents felt more positively about the company, 52 percent reported that they were more inclined to purchase products from the company, and 82 percent of respondents indicated that they were more likely to recommend the company's products (Lerman & Austin, 2006). Further, when consumers bond around common issues, their online conversations can be the source of more accurate and authentic information and can be used to generate critical business insights (Green, 2006). What remain unclear though are the processes and social dynamics that explain how such communities grow, how consumers develop these communal bonds and how one's community engagement changes throughout the life of a community.

Our analysis draws on insights from Consumer Culture Theory (Arnould & Thompson, 2005) in order to inform our understanding of the relationship dynamics in these networked social environments. As such, we acknowledge that contrary to traditional anthropological perspectives, we view participation in consumer communities as culture producing activities rather than culture bearing ones (Arnould & Thompson, 2005). As consumers participate in online communities, they don't just perform or play out the culture from which they come, but the act of participating in the community produces a culture of its own. This consumer culture production is directly traceable through the member-generated content which is encouraged and facilitated in online communities (Hagel & Armstrong, 1997). Thus, through systematic archiving and analysis of community conversations, we can observe manifestations of community actions and thereby develop a theoretical and practical understanding of members' engagement and relationship dynamics within consumer communities. Our analysis of conversations in online communities can be seen as an analysis of an emergent consumer culture that comes out of the community participation. Furthermore, a longitudinal perspective provides us with the means to look at cultural change in online consumer communities and develop an understanding of cultural identification/engagement over time.

In order to understand how community members forge bonds with others and orient themselves toward the community life, we study the micro-social interaction processes that take place inside online communities. More specifically, we seek to uncover how everyday communicative practices change throughout a community's different life phases. As part of this inquiry, we investigate how individual community members negotiate the tensions for belongingness and individualism, and how these opposing forces affect group communicative practices and overall community development. Our analysis is based on a netnographic analysis (Kozinets, 2002) of a group of consumers who are brought together through a shared event (pregnancy).

COMMUNICATIVE GENRE AND COMMUNITY DEVELOPMENT

In order to understand how specific communities might develop over time, it is important to take into account how the broader phenomenon of online consumer communities is itself situated in a bigger social context. As a whole, online communities can be seen as micro-social groups (Maffesoli, 1996) that exist at the "forgotten" level in consumer research (Bagozzi, 2000). This micro-social level, between individual and macro/cultural levels, is the level at which interactions and communications between people take place (Cova & Cova, 2002).

Online communities (or tribes) have emerged as a counteracting force to the isolation and individualistic pressures that are created in postmodern times (Maffesoli, 1996). It has therefore been suggested that instead of being connected to traditional notions of a neighborhood, village, or local club, people's social lives are now based on a new social arrangement: "networked individualism" (Wellman, 2001). As we observe the growth of e-tribes and the clustering of people around a wide array of affiliations (Kozinets, 1999), we need to consider the social and psychological forces that drive this emergent phenomenon. Whereas traditional perspectives on communities have typically implied that members share a well defined characteristic or interest and that one person typically belongs to one single and stable group, postmodern tribes are fluid and ephemeral and members can belong to multiple tribes and move across them (Maffesoli, 1996). As such, consumptions communities are often unified through shared emotions and passions and need not be defined by a specific common interest (Cova & Cova, 2002).

At the broad level, it has been suggested that the intentions of any community members need to be understood through efforts to "affiliate with others in the group and in general to 'fit in' and to achieve self-enhancement through group actions and achievement of group goals" (Bagozzi, 2000, p. 395). Specifically for the context of an online community, a consumer's affiliation with the community can represent a social benefit for reasons of identification and social integration (Hennig-Thurau, Gwinner, Walsh, &

Gremler, 2004). Indeed, consumer culture theorists have indicated that some of the strongest consumption communities are centered around marginalized or poorly integrated consumer groups (Muniz & Schau, 2005), and that in response to the feeling of alienation caused by a lack of integration or overall isolation, consumers seek to develop some type of collective identification by participating in ritualized and shared communal activities (Arnould & Thompson, 2005). We agree with this analysis, but we also believe that the basic community characteristics of consciousness of kind, presence of shared practices, and a sense of moral responsibility (Muniz & O'Guin, 2001) can be found across a wide array of non- or lesser-marginalized consumer groups. In post-modernity, consumers share a need to be free from traditional social constraints and also a demand for communal embeddedness (Cova & Cova, 2002). Online consumption communities are therefore social spaces where consumers can negotiate the tensions for individualism and belongingness to a group. We propose that these tensions reveal themselves through the nature of the interactions between community members and especially through their interpersonal communication practices. Community conversations contribute to the creation of social links, to the growth and development of the community, and to its overall identity formation.

Although consumer researchers have identified some central characteristics of consumer communities (Muniz & O'Guin, 2001) and have shown that specific events (e.g., shared experiences at Brandfests) might contribute to the strengthening of a community (McAlexander, Schouten, & Koenig, 2002), we do not have explicit models or frameworks that systematically identify consumer culture dynamics and sequential phases of community development and link these to the nature of consumers' engagement. Nonetheless, across social science disciplines, we can find various conceptual frameworks that have been proposed to capture the dynamic nature of community development and some of the reasons for growth and change. Most of these theories have adopted a life-cycle conceptualization or what Brent (1984) refers to as the levels-by-stages model. A variety of such models have been proposed in the interpersonal relationships literature (Levinger, 1983; Scanzoni, 1979) and in the organizational behavior literature (Lacoursiere, 1980; Tuckman, 1965). Although these models are appealing due to their parsimony and linear structures, one should keep in mind that communities are complex and dynamic systems. Even if groups may follow some of the same stages or periods, the exact composition, number, and ordering of stages require more particularity (Cissna, 1984; Poole, 1981). Indeed, "every group is like *all* groups in some respects, like *some* – or even *most* groups in some respects and like *no* groups in other respects" (Cissna, 1984, p. 25).

Furthermore, understanding relationship dynamics in online communities offers unique challenges. Even though, there is a general agreement that online communities can be conceptualized as having a "sufficient human feeling, to form webs of personal relationships in cyberspace" (Rheingold, 1993, p. 5), researchers and practitioners are "left in the dark as to when feelings will be sufficient to form webs of personal relationships and about the processes by which such communities will develop" (Wilbur, 1996, p. 7). Moreover, analyses have to be typically based on asynchronous text-based communications that lack many of the traditional community formation verbal and visual cues (Tepper, 1996).

Given the constraints and shortcomings of previous developmental models, and recognizing that any interpersonal communication "is not only representative of the relationship, but also constructs and performs the relationship" (Sahlstein & Duck, 2001, p. 373), we propose that a rhetorical analysis of the communicative genres might offer an appropriate analytical device that can uncover the nature and dynamics of community relationship development. A communicative genre can be defined as "typified rhetorical actions based in recurrent situations" (Miller, 1984, p. 159). As such, they may be perceived as a means to regulate and stabilize the life of a community. Therefore, by identifying a community's repertoire of communicative genres one can learn about the community's established communicative practices, and thus understand the nature of the relationships among its members (Orlikowski & Yates, 1994). Communicative genres do not simply restore social equilibrium, they are part of the ongoing process by which a community is continually redefining and renewing itself. As such, they provide a window on the dynamics by which members make and remake their interactions. Communicative genres might shift over time, and thus by tracking these shifts, one can uncover how the micro-social nature of community relationships evolves and thus provide insights into the dynamics of community development and the bases for members' engagement (Orlikowski & Yates, 1994). This type of approach has been successfully used in organizational and rhetorical research (Erickson, 1997, 2000; Miller, 1994; Orlikowski & Yates, 1994).

When looking to identify a repertoire of communicative genres, one has to be mindful that a classification of community communicative genres will be rhetorically sound if it contributes to an understanding of how communicative practices work – that is, if it reflects the experience of the people who create and interpret the communicative practices (Miller, 1984). It is important to note that a genre-oriented analysis also shifts the focus from issues such as the nature and degree of relationship among community members (typical concern in levels-by-stages models) to the communication purpose and its regularities of form and substance (Erickson, 1997). As Erickson (1997, p. 14) emphasizes: "online discourse may be useful and engaging to its participants even if the participants form no lasting relationships ... What is important, in many cases, is the communication itself – the shared informational artifact that is created by the participants." Thus, a genre-oriented analysis is useful because it shifts the focus from the participants and the relationships among them to their shared artifacts (that is, instances of the genre) and the way these artifacts are typically interpreted and used (Erickson, 1997).

METHODOLOGY

In this study, we employ the nethnography technique: a "qualitative research methodology that adapts ethnographic research techniques to study the cultures and communities that are emerging through computer-mediated communications" (Kozinets, 2002, p. 62). Text data was used from the discourse of bulletin boards hosted at babycenter.com. This is a website for new and expectant parents. The first author initially made her entrée in this milieu while pregnant herself. Following this initial experience, two data collection phases were undertaken. In the initial phase, messages were collected for a one-month period from five different bulletin boards (cross sectional) at two points in time (semi-longitudinal, September 1999 and November 2000). Across the five boards and two periods, these data reflected different community life stages (as communities are organized by due-dates). Data collection resulted in an archive of 12,830 messages. In the second phase of the data collection, a full longitudinal study was conducted. The complete text of all messages of one bulletin board was captured for a nine months period starting with the inception of the community. A total of 12,162 threads were captured and reviewed for that community, and 1,076 threads were archived for further analysis.

FINDINGS

Throughout the preliminary analysis of the data (initial period of data collection), for each conversation that appeared on the bulletin boards, we analyzed its regularities of content and form. Based on this analysis, we developed a typology of communicative genres. This typology served as an orienting device for the analysis of the longitudinal data collected in the second phase. This longitudinal inquiry uncovered new insights concerning the evolution of communication within the community, and allowed us to develop a new conceptualization of community development.

Toward a Typology of a Community's Communicative Genres

The tremendous variety of communicative genres observed in the data called for an attempt to organize them in some meaningful way. Based on our analysis of the communicative practices, we developed a two-dimensional typology (see Table 1). The two dimensions are: (1) identity orientation (i.e., the focus of the communicative genre); and (2) patterns of interaction (i.e., the functions that communicative genres serve). The main advantage of this typology is that it enables us to develop a deeper understanding of the sources of shifts in communicative genre, and of the ways in which these dynamics inspire communities' transformational processes. This emergent framework is consistent with previous theorizing on the communication practices inside e-tribes (Kozinets, 1999).

Communicative Genre Focus

Of special interest to our conceptual framework is social identity theory (Tajfel & Turner, 1986) and self-categorization theory (Turner, 1987). The central tenet of these theories is that belonging to a group is largely a psychological state, which is distinct from being a unique and separate individual. As such, a perception of belongingness confers social identity, a shared, collective representation of who one is and how one should behave (Turner, 1982). The notion that social identity and group belongingness are inextricably linked is based on the perception that one's identity is largely composed of self-descriptions in terms of the defining characteristics of

Table 1. A Typology of Communicative Genres.

Communicative Genre Function	Communicative Genre Focus	
	Personal Identity Salient	Social Identity Salient
Task-oriented Interaction	Self-centered Instrumental	Group-centered Instrumental
Socio-emotional Interaction	Self-centered Relational	Group-centered Relational

social groups to which one belongs (Hogg & Abrams, 1998). Social identity and self-categorization theories provide the foundations for the above typology of communicative genres in advocating that the self is not a fixed entity, but is instead contextually defined. Similarly, Belk (1988) uses the terms "sense of self" and "identity" as synonyms for how people subjectively make sense of who they are. Belk sees consumers as possessing a core self that is expanded to include items that then become part of the extended self. Hence, the self also includes various levels of group affiliations. Participants can assume different identities within the same interactive context. The ways in which people use identity during discourse in interaction show that identity is occasioned (i.e., the specific context shapes the way participants choose to negotiate their identity) and indexical (i.e., participants choose to give salience to specific aspects of the self based on their goals in that specific interactive moment) (Sacks, 1992).

Social identity and self-categorization theories assume that there are two types of self-regulation – as a group member (social identity salient) and as an individual (personal identity salient) (Reicher, 1987). The extent to which a categorization is applied at a particular level is referred to as its salience. Importantly, salience relates not only to the general relevance of a group membership, but also to selective changes in self-perception whereby people actually define themselves as unique individuals or as members of groups. When they define themselves as group members, they perceive themselves to be interchangeable with members of that group, and distinct from members of other groups. Further, the nature of behavior changes when different self-images become salient (Hogg & Abrams, 1998).

As already mentioned, the emergence of online community has created a "middle landscape" where individuals can exercise their impulses for both separation and connectedness (Healy, 1996). As such, online communities operate as sites where centrifugal and centripetal forces meet (Miller, 1994). Indeed, an important technical reality of the Internet is that although it connects people, it also isolates them physically. This duality has interesting and contradictory effects for our research. It has been suggested that de-individuation caused by immersion and anonymity in the group may not result in a loss of identity or reduced self-awareness (as proposed by classical de-individuation theory), but rather in a shift of self-focus from personal to group identity (Spears, Lea, & Postmes, 2000). In the same vein, we argue that the expression and nature of communicative genres in Internet communities change as a result of members' contrasting struggle between social identity and personal identity. In fact, conceptualizations of identity as derived from the continuous struggle between individuality and belongingness have been evidenced in other consumer behavior contexts (e.g., cosmopolitanism: Thompson & Tambyah, 1999; fashion: Thompson & Haytko, 1997). Similarly, we argue that online communities' communicative practices are co-determined by the simultaneous and dynamic forces of members' desires for involvement (i.e., social identity or commitment) and independence (i.e., personal identity or individualism). It is the dynamic characteristics of these contradictory desires that contribute to the dynamic nature of communicative genres, and consequently it is through these forces that communities develop and transform.

Communicative genres that focus on the individual (personal identity salient) are concentrated on the individual's emotions, needs, and goals. Examples of such communicative genres include confessions, sharing secrets or seeking advice. Typically, these communications will be initiated by some problem/report statement from one member, followed by responses by other participants. Individuals' intentions within these interactions may be viewed through efforts to achieve private goals (e.g., cleanse oneself or obtain some information/advice). By contrast, communicative genres that focus on the group (i.e., social identity salient) serve as a means for regulating group interactions. Similarly to themes discussed with respect to one's sense of communion with others (Arnould & Price, 1993), it is suggested here that when individuals define themselves as members of a group (i.e., social identity salient), they form a social entity and a world of meanings of and for themselves. Generally, communicative genres belong to this category when they demarcate a community's deepest values, assert particular norms, standards and values, and foster attachments to social groupings. These practices provide a sense of security and common understanding of their group belongingness to the members who act in line with this shared organization of meanings. Examples of these communicative genre practices include the establishment of certain signals and symbols that differentiate the community from others (e.g., creation of a community web page). These symbols aim to promote community pride, a sense of collectivity, and cohesiveness. Additional examples are interactions that are concerned with intra-community relations and with the formalization of rules, norms, and procedures.

Communicative Genre Functions

Although communications in Internet communities do not have formal scripts, we were able to observe evidence of emergent/implicit scripts. These reoccurring interactions tended to be posted with virtually the same content type and structure each time they appeared and served as symbolic community markers. As such, communicative genres can be conceptualized as social knowledge structures that are organized and stored in memory in the form of particular scripts. These communicative genre scripts may be viewed as "shared social schemas" that contain expected sequences of communicative practices in order to reach certain goals (e.g., a roll call may be conceptualized as a script for the creation of acquaintance between members of an Internet community). Since members of online communities may create or use communicative genres for specific functions, these genres reflect important social and personal needs and goals.

Drawing on Bales' (1951, 1970) seminal work on regularities in group interactions, we propose that communicative genres reflect two distinct interaction patterns: (1) an informational/instrumental/task-oriented communicative act; and (2) a symbolic/expressive/socio-emotional communicative act. Bales believed that groups have a natural tendency towards equilibrium and, therefore, tension reducing behaviors come into play, with groups moving through cycles of instrumental (e.g., give or ask for suggestions, opinions, or information) and expressive (e.g., show solidarity, friendliness, tensions, or antagonism) behaviors.

Following Bales' interaction process analysis (IPA), we suggest that communicative genres are instrumental or task-oriented to the extent that they attempt to accomplish something and serve as means for gaining information about the world (see also Katz, 1960). The information can be aimed either at individual needs (i.e., means for organizing individual's personal life) or at community needs (i.e., means for organizing community life). For example, instrumental communicative acts can be found in the first period of a community life cycle – the creation of the online community. In this period, we observed communicative genres, such as roll calls, that aim to generate and increase the acquaintance between members. Different types of roll calls are part of the genre, including generic roll calls (e.g., "Who's who?"), more detailed roll calls (e.g., "What kind of weather you are having?"), or even personal and intimate ones (e.g., "Where did you and your significant other meet?"). Roll call messages tend to be short and focused and can serve multiple instrumental purposes (e.g., getting to know each other, allowing members who lost track for a while to catch up, and giving newcomers an opportunity to become part of the community). Additional examples for instrumental communicative genres (e.g., joint-creation of a community web page or photo album) are concerned with the establishment of an organized community with its own differentiating signals and symbols. Although roll calls typically fit into the self-centered instrumental quadrant (personal identity salient), establishing a community's symbols typically fit into the group-centered instrumental quadrant (i.e., social identity salience).

Communicative genres are relational to the extent that they act to sustain or weaken interpersonal relationships within the group, or in other words "create the social fabric of a group by promoting relationships between and among group members" (Keyton, 1999, p. 192). These types of communicative genres include interactions that show solidarity, release tension, or indicate acceptance, or, alternatively, interactions that show disagreement, tension, and antagonism (see also Katz, 1960). For example, messages may invoke symbols of unity via implicitly increasing intimacy between members of the community (e.g., relating to other members as close friends or sharing personal secrets). Although this genre of messages serves to align oneself with other members of the community, the communicative genre here concentrates in the individuals' emotions, needs, and goals and not in the group's concerns per se. Hence, these communicative genres typically fit into the self-centered relational quadrant. Conversely, communicative genres that use symbols and symbolic actions to depict a group of people as a coherent and ordered community based on shared values and goals are examples from the group-centered relational quadrant. Examples include interactions that are concerned with intra-community relations and with formalization of rules, norms, and procedures. This genre of interactions consists of fairly long postings, typically in the form of short essays.

Summary

We confirmed that there are different communicative genres which have different foci (i.e., self-oriented versus group oriented) and support different functions (i.e., task oriented versus socio-emotional). These observations support the claim that individual conversations – even though carried out by the same group of people, in the same organizational context – can have very different structures, foci, purposes, and dynamics and, thus, be aptly characterized in terms of communicative genre (Erickson, 2000). Table 2 provides a summary of the major communicative genres that were observed in the various bulletin boards, illustrating the characteristics of each genre according to the typology that was presented in Table 1. We would like to emphasize that the purpose of employing the above typology is not for the sake of theorizing. Instead, this typology became a key orienting device for the analysis of the longitudinal data collected in the second period.

Table 2. Communicative Genre Expression.

Communicative Genres	Communicative Genre Focus	Communicative Genre Function	Overall Communicative Genre Characteristics
Getting Acquainted	Social Identity Salient	Task-oriented	Group-centered Instrumental
Joint Activities	Social Identity Salient	Task-oriented	Group-centered Instrumental
Getting Intimate	Personal Identity Salient	Socio-emotional	Self-centered Relational
Intra-group Relationship	Social Identity Salient	Socio-emotional	Group-centered Relational
Seeking/Generating Advice	Personal Identity Salient	Task-oriented	Self-centered Instrumental
Games, Polls	Social Identity Salient	Socio-emotional	Group-centered Relational

Nine Months with the November Bulletin Board

In this second period of data collection, the complete text of all messages on one bulletin board was captured for a nine-month period. Our analysis uncovered seven periods in this community lifespan. We showed that community's development is a continuous process of reciprocal social construction. As such, this novel perspective provides guidance on the interplay between a community's development and circumstantial events, on triggers of change, and on the mechanisms that cause a community to remain in any stable period. Table 3 provides an overview of the major periods that were observed, summarizing the focus and the pattern of interaction of the communicative genres, according to the typology that was presented earlier.

It is important to understand that although in the following netnographic investigation, we have separated genres of communicative practices into several periods; the actual process is fluid and undeterministic. At any moment, the group can reverse direction and move back into a previous communicative genre, or suddenly switch to a whole new communicative genre. Yet, for the purposes of simplicity and clarity, throughout this account, we concentrate on the sequence of major periods in the community's interaction processes. Periods emerge from the data, reflecting the dominant communicative genres at different times.

Table 3. Features of the Seven Major Periods.

Period	Participants' Communicative Focus	Interaction's Communicative Function	Examples of Communicative Genres
1. Joining	Personal Identity Salient	Task-oriented	Personal introductions (e.g., roll calls)
2. Coordination	Social Identity Salient	Task-oriented	Joint activities (e.g., photo album)
3. Prompting Intimacy	Personal Identity Salient	Socio-emotional	Intimate conversations (e.g., confessions)
4. Communal Sense	Social Identity Salient	Socio-emotional	Relationship building (e.g., defining norms)
5. Alienation and Splintering	Personal Identity Salient	Socio-emotional	Relationship reassessment (e.g., forming subgroups, debates)
6. Communal Again	Social Identity Salient	Socio-emotional	Relationship reaffirmation (e.g., praise, updating community mission)
7. Culmination	Personal Identity Salient	Socio-emotional	Sharing experiences (e.g., birthing stories)

Period 1 – Joining

March 200X was the inception date for the November 200X birth club bulletin board since this was the month when most members found out that they were pregnant and due in November 200X, thus, participants started to join the board. In the first period, which corresponds to approximately one month, there were around 30 members, and it was characterized by communicative genres that aimed at generating and increasing the acquaintance between community members. Specifically, roll calls were a dominant genre:

> [Getting to know the November 200X Board – 1] Name, Age, Dh [dear husband] Name, Age, were you live, Are you married, how long have you been married, hobbies, Pets, TTC# [number of times trying to conceive], do you work […] Family web-site, EDD [expected due date] or Test Date.

At this early period, members tended to write mainly about themselves with no evidence of being interested in or of even reading others' messages. In this first discontent period, members were still feeling alienated from the group, and centrifugal forces were dominant. Thus, although roll calls were initiated as a group activity, in fact, the communications were focused mostly on the individuals (i.e., personal identity salient). Further, since during the first two months of the community, members were finding out whether they were pregnant or not, many messages were initiated by new comers who "just discover that they are pregnant," or with current members who "have to say goodbye" because they are not pregnant. Hence, in the first month or two, the bulletin board seemed to be like a train, with people coming onboard and leaving regularly. Most of the messages at this period focused on individuals' needs and experiences (i.e., personal identity salient). This should be rather expected since during the first trimester of pregnancy, odds for miscarriages are quite high, thus, expecting mothers might be reluctant to forge deep attachments to the group. These concerns are evident in the next couple of threads which were concerned with the creation of a system of "secret mommies." Many members requested to postpone the activity for a few months, so that participants would feel more secure and confident with their pregnancies, and thus, would be more motivated to participate and commit to the board's joint activities:

> [Secret mommies sing up – 1] The idea is kind of like secret pals…You will have a secret Mommy for the next 7 or 8 months-During This time you need to […] be in contact with her at least weekly via email or cards etc. anniversary, Christmas […] you need to COMMIT to at least 3 a month […]

> [A secret mommies suggestion – 2] […] I am in no way ready to make a pregnancy-long commitment to someone at 7 weeks along, but I don't want to have to miss out on this altogether. My proposal is this: Those who are confident […] to go as Secret Mommies should take advantage of Maria's generosity in organizing right now. Then, in a couple of months when we're all in our second trimesters, those of us who are a little more hesitant and more concerned about m/c [miscarriage] can organize a second list […]

Period 2 – Coordination

As they advanced through the first trimester of pregnancy, participants organized joint activities which were aimed at creating a more organized community. As part of these organization and coordination activities, a board's website was created. The website included features such as a due date calendar, individual photo albums, biographies, ultrasound photos, gender guesses, and other games. Participants organized further with the nomination of a community's host and the creation of some daily routines.

[List of daily threads – 5] Here's a list of the November 200X Board daily threads:

- "Getting to Know the November Board" – a "getting to know everyone" thread
- "Roll Call," includes a QOTD [question of the day]
- "BFP [big fat positive] HPT [home pregnancy test]" – A list of BFPs sharing their testing info […]
- "Daily Tester" – a testing-buddy thread

During this period participants' communicative focus became group-centered; however, the communicative function remained at an instrumental level and focused mainly on organizational issues. Members still seemed to be reluctant to share intimate issues or forge deep attachments to each others. This might be due to the fairly high risk of miscarriage that is present during the first trimester.

Period 3 – Prompting Intimacy

Approaching their second trimester, the number of participating members was 120. Most members already knew their expected due dates and the number of participants joining or leaving the board had decreased significantly. Appropriately, the community's host acknowledged this landmark and leveraged it in order to initiate new ideas for joint activities:

> [Ideas for the board – 1] […] I promised I would get back to a few ideas for the board once the majority of us have EDD's [expected due dates] and know we are here to stay […] since we are there I am […] broaching this subject again. […] #1 please do not respond here … email me directly […] #4 Board Majority rules! […] Splitting into sub groups (based on EDD or # of children expected) […] Having email pals […] Having a mommy of the week […]

Feeling more assured and relaxed with their pregnancies, members started to feel more comfortable with being part of the community. Hence, besides task-oriented interactions (i.e., organization and coordination initiatives), this period was also characterized by interactions that were socio-emotional in nature. Particularly, members used the board for confessions and sharing personal secrets, thus demonstrating intimacy:

> [Telling my Baby's Father – 1] Hi, I just found out I'm 5 weeks pregnant. My dilemma is that my baby's father and I are not dating or anything (In fact we never have). I want to tell him ASAP, but I am worried that he will think it's not his child and reject us both. I don't know what to do […]

As previously emphasized, although this genre of messages serves to align oneself with other members of the community, communicative genres here concentrate on the individuals' emotions, needs, and goals (i.e., personal identity salient) and not on the group's concerns per se. Therefore, self-centered relational genres became more dominant over the course of Period 3.

Period 4 – Communal Sense

During the second trimester of pregnancy, participants started to organize several new joint activities, which were concerned with the creation of more profound and intimate relationships in the community. For instance, participants organized a MOTW (mother of the week) thread as "a great way to get to know all of the new mommies we have around here:"

> [Information on MOTW – 1] MOTW is a great way to get to know all of the new mommies we have around here. A new mommy will be featured each week, for an entire week (Mon–Fri). On Monday the MOTW will receive a standard list of questions and then anyone may post new questions throughout the week. [...]

The intimate interactions of the previous period had lead to initial signs of socio-emotional interactions that focused on the group, thus fitting into the group-centered relational quadrant. Interestingly, consistent with Arnould and Price's (1993) view, what drove this emergent sense of social identity was a shared recognition of common problems. Hence, the triggers for these group relational communicative genres were a few messages that had raised some questions and doubts with regards to the board's role as a support group:

> [Scared when reading posts – 1] I was just wondering if anyone felt like I do. I come on here a lot for support so i understand this IS a support board. However i see on this board a lot about m/cs [miscarriages] [...] is there anyway other board people can get support? [...] I do not mean to sound negative [...]

> [Signing off for a while – 1] [...] I sat here for the last few days really just getting depressed when I read this board. [...] So, I am signing off of here for a while [...]

These posts sparked off a number of threads that were focused on the community's intra-relationships, thereby allowing members to discuss the community's essence. This was accomplished through messages that showed solidarity, released tension, or indicated acceptance, or alternatively messages showing disagreement, tension, or even antagonism:

> [Scared when reading posts – 2] I can understand your concerns. However this IS a support board. Support is great when everything is going well, but even more important when things aren't [...] My advice to you is that if these things bother you, wait to read anything else until your u/s [ultrasound] [...]

> [Boards are for support – 1] I don't mean to be rude but when I came on these boards I loved all the support that every-one gave each other [...] I didn't expect there to be any

> problems but found out there are and I once again turned to my new found friends for support. Am I wrong or is what they are for? After a few comments that have been made about m/c posts, I am sick [...]

Despite their conflictual nature, these messages were essentially focused on the community, its importance, and its goals. In fact, it has been demonstrated that calling consumers' attention to their group identity can induce a group mind-set (Briley & Wyer, 2002). Accordingly, people who become aware of their membership in a group are likely to feel a sense of responsibility to its members, and this in turn, can bring to mind attitudes and behaviors consistent with the social identity (Briley & Wyer, 2002). Similarly, our findings suggest that even though awareness of their membership in this period resulted from conflicts and tensions, the group state of mind set out in motion a whole new atmosphere and resulted in a much more cohesive community. At this time, the centripetal forces were getting stronger and members' attention was focused on their relationships with the community:

> [You are all the best – 1] I just want to compliment my fellow posters (and lurkers!). I surfed over to a board I used to post on in my previous pregnancy. Those ladies there are vicious! One person asked for directions to a website that had instructions on how to make your own carseat. Not only did people point out that was a bad idea, they called her names like Troll and Moron. [...] So thank you all for creating such a warm and inviting place [...]

From that point, community-focused relational messages became habitual communicative practices. In the following months, participants discussed many of the community's intra-relationships issues (e.g., the appropriateness of certain conversation topics, procedures for participation in conversations, ways to prevent conflicts, community's hosts' role in monitoring conversations, and numerous reaffirming statements on the importance, value, and uniqueness of the board). Apart from transforming the community's atmosphere, these group-centered relational communications also affect individual members (see Keyton, 1999). Accordingly, when group members communicate about their relationships with one another, intragroup concerns are primed, providing relevancy for participants to identify where they fit within the network of intra-group relationships, and, ultimately, affecting participants' identity orientation and triggering social identity salience in other interactions.

Period 5 – Alienation and Splintering

During the second trimester, the number of members on the board grew significantly (120 members in June to 269 in July). In response, this period demonstrated cracks in the overall community cohesion, and witnessed the creation of several subgroups (e.g., the community was divided into subgroups based on members' due dates). The splintering initiatives revealed differences in viewpoints, disagreements, and tensions:

> [Idea for getting to know each other – 1] I saw on the May board they must have divided up into groups based on due date [...] I think it would be easier to know people if we did that, maybe 10–15 in a group so we could keep tabs on other mommies due around our due date [...] Feedback?

> [Idea for getting to know each other – 4] We voted on this awhile back and majority voted against it. I for one think it's better as a big group. I wouldn't change anything. But that's just my opinion.

> [Little punkins – 3] *I completely agree.* What is the big deal? [...] Why did there need to be a vote in the first place? I think this is just a way of getting to know a smaller group of ladies even better. I don't feel that it keeps us separated from the rest of the group [...] [our emphasis]

> [Little punkins – 4] *I agree*– I'd like to keep the group on this board as well I feel that this is a public forum and as such we should be allowed to post with as little or as much frequency as our group wishes. If people don't want to participate in the sub-group that's fine, but I don't think that should prevent those that do, from doing so. I also don't feel that having sub-groups takes away from the board as a whole. *Obviously, others disagree* [...] [our emphasis]

The fact that the board was divided into various subgroups resulted in many threads being aimed at different sub-communities. These circumstances lead many participants to complain that their messages went unnoticed, and to express feelings of alienation, disengagement, and disconnection. The following thread illustrates this pattern:

> [Leaving the board – 1] [...] I feel like I just can't connect to anyone here lately. I try to reply and post but hardly ever get any feedback or my threads just get hidden so fast [...]

> [Leaving the board – 2] I know how you feel. I only got one response to my thread about my ultrasound [...]

> [Leaving the board – 3] I can relate with you. Most of my threads go unnoticed. It makes me feel the same way. But, I can't complain because I don't respond to all the posts either

> [Leaving the board – 4] [...] As for the u/s [ultrasound] posts, I only got a couple of responses too, but I believe it's because there were so many around the same time. It's hard to post to them all!! ... This board is much slower than it used to be. Let's all stick together!! We've been through the hardest part [...]

> [Leaving the board – 5] [...] daytimes are not as busy now for a couple reasons: People are out doing things, or we just don't have any ??'s [questions] or concerns in the 2nd tri

[trimester]…….1st tri [trimester] m/c [miscarriage] threat is over and 3rd tri [trimester] aches and pains haven't kicked in full-on yet

Although some participants offered logical and rational reasons for the board's difficulties (e.g., members do not have as many concerns as earlier), it seems that the splintering lead to a general malaise. Outside of some specific subgroups, participant felt like they were "falling through the cracks", and reverted to a focus on personal identity. Feelings of disconnection were evident in conversations concerned with both community and intimate matter.

Interestingly, the events that brought the community to overcome these feelings of disconnection were a series of conversations on sensitive and controversial topics, which rekindled the community flame and dialogue. These topics triggered tensions and conflicts, and some even got "locked" by babycenter.com. The following messages about things that pregnant women should give up during the pregnancies (the full thread had 43 posts) capture the emotions, passions and conflicts in these conversations:

[Am I the only psycho? – 1] I have given up everything that could potentially be harmful to my unborn child. From eating all fish (mercury scare), to caffeine […] I figure, it is only for 9 months why not create the best environment for my child. It totally freaks me out that you guys all indulge in these things! *I am not telling you to stop*, I am just curious why you would do them […] *Am I alone here?!?!*

[Am I the only psycho? – 13] I AM LIVID! I tell you what, when you are ready to pay for this child in it's entirety, take care of it after it's born, all of that, then you can pass judgment on me. Until then, mind your own damn business! […] don't attack other people for not following the same psychotic routine you do […] I thought this board was all about not being judgmental? ARGH!

[Am I the only psycho? – 29] *This was my point about this medium being difficult to get your point across, if we were talking face to face we would probably see that we agree more than we disagree.* I certainly respect that you see most, if not all, of the things you listed as indulgences. My point is that not everybody does, and that by using the word indulge it **seems** like you are saying that moms that aren't avoiding those things are deliberately trying to hurt their children or just don't care […] [our emphasis]

[Am I the only psycho? – 36] I am going to forward this thread to the BabyCenter Community for consideration. I am not sure that any good is going to come out of this thread if it continues in this vein. It is one thing to share opinions on topics such as these, but it is entirely different to attack other board users […]

Soon after, a number of threads about circumcision caused the greatest conflicts the community had ever experienced, thus, dividing the community into opposing camps. This created high levels of discussion on that topic (59 posts in June, 13 in July, and 39 more in August) and elicited negative and hurtful comments from various members. It caused much tension and could have led to significant member defection, since in-group focus was reduced and members' individual opinions were made more salient:

> [Are you going to circumcise?- 39] […] I'm really trying to keep it nice here. Excuse any raging pregnancy hormones. I would strongly suggest that your dh [dear husband] read all the information you have read and do the research himself […] My dh tried this argument on me when I was expecting my ds [dear son]. Our baby is just that-ours. He doesn't exclusive rights to any decision, because he doesn't have exclusive rights to our child.

> [Are you going to circumcise? – 45] I've known I'm having a boy for over a week now and this hasn't even crossed my mind until now!! *No way* am I having my son circumcised […] As for the women saying it is hard to clean a boy's foreskin ??!?!?!! GIVE ME A BREAK! You obviously don't have a little girl to clean! […]

> [Please stop negativity – 1] I have noticed in a thread some negative comments about the original thread that I started about circumcision-I did NOT have a "bring it on attitude" […]. I find that comment rude and offensive-I have tried to apologize […] I am letting this go and wish others would do the same

> [Please stop negativity – 10] […]This board is not a free for all where anything can be said without repercussions. It's not acceptable to say "if you don't agree don't post" and then have people posting gross things that can and DO offend other posters […]

> [Please read – 6] […] Like a pp [previous poster] said *we're all individuals and are bound to have differing viewpoints*, the key is to accept each other and to be ok with our differences. [our emphasis]

> [Take care everyone – 1] I just wanted to say good luck to everyone with the rest of their pregnancies. I am not looking for sympathy or anything but my feelings are really hurt […] I felt like mean things were said to me as well […] I don't think I will be visiting this site any longer and wanted to thank all the nice people that have given me their opinions and support.

Nevertheless, despite triggering disagreements, the circumcision threads demonstrated an extremely connected and multidirectional interaction pattern. Participants were paying attention to others' posts and arguments, thus, forming their answers in relation to these comments. Interestingly, although the debates over circumcision emphasized individual opinions, views and values, at the same time they served as triggers for discussions on group values, norms, strategies for conflict resolution, and other group-oriented matters (i.e., social identity salience). Eventually, these conversations generated multidirectional socio-emotional conversations that were focused on the group (i.e., fit into the group-centered relational quadrant).

Period 6 – Communal Again

Although the community's cohesion became threatened by the conflicts of the previous period, it is the resulting discussion of this risk that held it together and arguably strengthened it. During this next period, communicative genres became very interactive, and connected. The centripetal forces became stronger and participants regularly demonstrated their attentiveness to other members' posts. Even confessions and other previously self-focused communicative practices became more interactive. The conflicts of the second trimester brought the community to reconsider some core aspects such as norms of interaction. In the current period, specifics around communal issues got defined and reaffirmed. Members proposed new protocols or rules, and a significant conversation ensued on the nature of these community processes.

> [Confused about purpose of this board – 1] I have always been under the impression that the purpose of this board was to get opinions and support. *When I respond to a poster, my response is to them alone. Obviously we can see each other's posts* and it's not uncommon to say we agree with a PP [previous poster] [...] What boggles my mind is why someone would quote a posters' response and try to pick a fight [our emphasis].

In the above example, the participant wished to advocate for a one to one communication style, as opposed to the multidirectional practices that we have discussed. Others however reiterated that multidirectional communications were part of the conversation practices in the community:

> [Confused about purpose of this board – 5] I agree, it is a support board [...] *in this kind of forum where you are not face to face, people are more likely to say exactly what they feel without thought of how it will make other posters feel* [...] [our emphasis]

The astute observation in the above message echoes research findings that have shown that participants in online communications are "isolated from social rules and feel less subject to criticism and control, ... [and] less inhibited in their relations with others" (Sproull & Kiesler, 1991, p. 48). Also, this freedom and lack of control allowed participants to make attempts at specifying rules or norms for discussions on the board. This is consistent with previous findings that have shown that most group norms are a result of in-situ communicative linkages among members (Festinger, Schachter, & Back, 1950). Conflict-handling norms tend to be developed "on the fly," typically through trial and error, and often, as a result of and through considerable turbulence (Arrow, McGrath, & Berdahl, 2000). These regulations "generally develop slowly, often implicitly, and typically unconsciously from social pressures exerted in group interaction" (Keyton, 1999,

p. 206). In the following messages, members were attempting to agree on group norms by specifying ways to present claims or views to the group:

> [Confused about purpose of this board – 5] [...] I usually try to be as supportive as possible, and *if I disagree with what another poster has written, I often try to tell them without attacking them.* It's hard to tell someone you don't agree without it coming across meaner then you meant it to be... because, again, these replies are in writing and tone of voice cannot be conveyed. With that said, I agree with Christine in that, *if you can't say something supportive, maybe you should just move on to the next topic* [...] [our emphasis]

> [Confused about purpose of this board – 4] There always will be and always have been ladies on every board that tend to be a little more aggressive with their posts then others [...] *I think baby center in general has done a pretty good job in keeping tabs and assigning hosts who they hope will do the same.* It's not easy ... sometimes it's very frustrating when you have to watch so closely [...] [our emphasis]

> [What is the mission of the group? – 1] [...] i do notice that at times though that we as a group can (perhaps this is something to do with our hormones) get wound up quickly [...] i am the only one who lives in a non democratic country and let me tell you ladies, it sucks! censorship is not perhaps the way to go on the board but instead having an agreed set of goals within our group may well be. for example: what is the mission of the november 200X babies club? [...] why don't we as a group come together and at least decide on what is our mission

Eventually, discussions on such matters as the boards' norms and mission prompted feelings of cohesiveness, thus, priming further social identity salience. Correspondingly, new messages reiterated the significant role that the board played in members' lives:

> [End of the day tribute – 1] [...] I have been off of my Paxil for over a week now, and even though I should hit a slump as I usually do, I haven't really [...] I think I finally realized why. Even though I popped onto this board abruptly, and don't get to chat or participate as much as I would like, you have all made me feel welcome [...] I don't know if you realize how much that means to someone like me, but it does mean quite a lot. I don't feel as scared or negative as I did before I joined this board.

> [This place rocks – 1] Just wanted to note that this board makes pregnancy so much better! I was laughing as I read through some of the threads about exhaustion, crap food days, moodiness, weight gain. As a few months ago it was more about when will m/c [miscarriage] end, how many more sleeps till my u/s [ultrasound], are you showing yet ... It's always nice to read that others are suffering/enjoying similar things at similar times[...] I predict that once the summer heat goes away, our threads will read more like "I'm not moving from this couch, I'm beyond huge, I live in a moomoo as no clothes fit and I'm not spending another penny of fat, I mean mat wear, and finally, WE HAD OUR BABY! The count down is on

> [Things we like about our board – 8] I like that every time I think I'm crazy or experiencing something strange, I can look on here and see 5 other women going through

> the same thing! whew!!!! i like that any questions i may have, whether silly or not, i can always find an answer on bc [babycenter]. i just like the feeling i get to know that i am not alone.
>
> [Things we like about our board – 9] I think that it is amazing that there are over 400 women who have posted to this board with babies due in November, and we are all from different walks of life, backgrounds, religions, political beliefs, education levels, geographical locations, etc., and for the most part, we get along and support each other. that is a really amazing feat. (yes, there are times when things get heated, but that would happen anywhere eventually, so it just needs to be looked at as a growing pain and moved through.). since i am more or less the first in my real life group to have a baby, i love that there is a place i can go to rejoice and complain about pregnancy. and all of its issues without boring my real life friends to death. i love that i've learned a lot about different parenting styles, diapering choices […]

This last message used dramatization as a means to create a common social reality for the group (see Bormann, 1996). Bormann's (1996) symbolic convergence theory posits that when members are releasing tensions, they also tend to remove themselves from the "here and now" through the mechanism of fantasy themes. As evidenced in the data above, these communicative genres (e.g., jokes, stories, imaginary situations, metaphors) might make references to the group's past, speculate on its future, or even comment on issues outside of the group (Bormann, 1996). For example, in the above messages some members project themselves and others into imaginary situations (e.g., "I predict that once the summer heat goes away, our threads will read more like "I'm not moving from this couch!"), others make jokes (e.g., "but if I didn't have you ladies, I would be making him miserable"), tell stories (e.g., "I have been off of my Paxil for over a week now, and even though I should hit a slump as I usually do, I haven't really"), and otherwise engage in acts of imagination. When members of a group exhibit common emotional responses to the imagery used, this creates a process of symbolic convergence that transforms a collection of people into a true community (Bormann, 1996). When symbolic convergence occurs, it creates a shared group consciousness, based on "a symbolic climate and culture that allow people to achieve emphatic communication as well as a 'meeting of the minds'" (Bormann, 1996, p. 89). Moreover, this also creates new relational dynamics for members' future interactions.

Period 7 – Culmination

By September all members were in their third trimester. This new period was characterized by a relative "quieting down", especially after the conflicts of the previous months:

[Board post slowing down – 1] Has anyone else noticed that as we have been getting closer to November there just aren't as many people posting anymore or answering threads? It seems like there's a whole batch of new people whose names I don't recognize-there are tons of people who I haven't seen in a while! [...]

[Board post slowing down – 4] Yeah, I've noticed too. I was going through the Nov. website (because I was bored from not much to read here!) and I noticed alot of names that haven't been around for awhile. I wonder what's happened to them. I was looking at the photo albums and it says when they became members, and so many from march and april have just disappeared. I guess when we went through the "miscarriage" time, maybe we forget? [...] We also had some pretty good debates...maybe some got pissed? As for the new people, I'm glad they are here. I love to see "old" regulars post though! I went through a period, second trimester, where I didn't post much, but still read everyday. I guess people are just really busy trying to get ready for baby, some are still working, and some chasing toddlers too. Hopefully everyone will come back to post pictures and stories about their precious little ones.

As participants' due dates were approaching, it seemed that members were more likely to identify with their salient sub-communities than with the community as a whole. This tendency might be a direct consequence of the conflicts of the previous months, as during periods of conflict and threat, which are often associated with group change, sub-groups membership become highly salient (Callan, 1993). The following message illustrates this process:

[What is the mission of the group? – 1] [...] me personally-i love the sub [...] we have fun and we have been developing some great friendships. for example, here is an overview of us: Lisa-she is luckily now having a nice holiday in aruba, [...] Mimi who have saved her ante-natal class notes in pdf format to send to us [...] now, if i don't post on the little blessings thread for a few days...i have twenty plus new friends wondering [...] i do believe the reason why our sub-thread has been working so well is that we do have mutual respect and we do really try to support each other [...] The advantage with the sub-threads is that they have a sort of small town feel to them [...] you pretty soon learn the rules of posting! the main board is something like being in the big city-with a big city attitude! people come and go, the posts move much more quickly and somehow everything switches a pace [...]

In the end of October and throughout November, most members gave birth to their babies. For obvious practical reasons (time availability, hospital stays, etc.), this period was marked with some distancing or absence from the board. Also, from a social perspective, the messages that dominated this period became more self-centered (dealing with delivery stories and members' personal experiences) but remained very intimate as a whole, and the overall interactions still served a social-emotional function. Thus, we observed that a self-centered and relational communicative genre became dominant. The following message illustrates this pattern:

> [Matt is here – 1] Matt as born on November 9 at 8:20 am. He was 7lbs. 8 ozs. and 21" long. They had to use the vacuum to get him out and I only got to hold him for a few seconds that day [...] The hospital staff was wonderful and gave me a room to stay in without charge. He is home and as healthy as can be [...] He has been eating and pooping so hopefully if its not all gone yet it will be soon. [...] Good luck to all the ladies still waiting.

Typically, a number of participants (usually 5–10) would reply to this type of messages by congratulating the mother or praising the pictures of the new baby. We have already emphasized that, although these self-centered relational messages serve to align oneself with other members of the community, they focus on the individuals' emotions, needs and goals (i.e., personal identity salience) and not in the group's concerns per se.

DISCUSSION

Our analysis conceptualized a community's life as a continually evolving entity, which is facilitated through and reflected in the dynamics of the communicative practices among members of the group. It is through the dynamics of these communicative practices that emotions are experienced and interpersonal relationships are formed and reformulated. Our research showed that communicative genre analysis is an appropriate analytical device that can allow researchers to probe the dynamic shifts that take place in online communities. As such, we showed that community communicative practices can reveal the characteristics of the community in which they are occurring, demarcate group membership and individuals' social identity orientation, and in general highlight participants' motivations in a particular community life stage. More specifically, through our observation and analysis of the communicative practices in the babycenter.com communities, we have been able to demonstrate how community conversation genres are linked to the fluid and often chaotic dynamics of community development and change. We also showed that throughout the different phases in the community life, the bases for individual engagement in the community shift between self and other-centered foci. This dynamic shift is important as it underscores that satisfying personal goals or supporting others are often non-contemporaneous and not always correlated motives, as thus we would advise against conceptualizing these two types of motives as indicators of a one-dimensional construct called community engagement (see Algesheimer, Dholakia, & Herrmann, 2005).

Consistent with Miller (1984), we have shown that communicative genres should be defined based on the actions they serve to accomplish rather than on the actual prima-facie substance of the conversation. Thus, a particular event (e.g., a debated topic), at different times, has different implications for group's communicative practices because the group and the context will have changed. This analysis calls attention to the fact that complex systems such as online communities never settle on a fixed state. On the contrary, these systems are subject to constant perturbation, which drives bursts of transient behavior (Arrow et al., 2000). Change events vary in how much and how directly they perturb a group's communicative genre. Accordingly, "groups do not respond to change as a generic event. Different kind of change has different meanings to group members and different implications for group coordination and development. The same event can evoke different responses from different groups or from the same group at different times" (Arrow et al., 2000, p. 195). In other words, although a particular event in the community life might lead to communicative practice shifts, the communication genres that are used by the community members are characteristics of that community period rather than representative of the actual particular event. Thus, as a whole, we should consider communicative genres as part of a community's cultural make-up and to some extent unique to that specific community.

This netnographic account has also demonstrated that change events encompass both macro-level forces such as periods in a community's life span (e.g., acquaintance period, first trimester of pregnancy, etc.) and immediate situations (e.g., a specific thread) that form the context for the community's interpersonal communication processes. It is important to acknowledge that group experiences occur in the context of the life course of its members (i.e., in the context of the life course of individuals; see Socha, 1999). Thus, developmentally speaking, communication in a birth club community will not only reflect evolutions in identification, belongingness, and cohesiveness, but also will be affected by changes in needs, tensions, and individuals' experiences related to the fact that pregnancy itself is a developmental process. It is therefore important to recognize that this has had a direct impact on our findings and therefore future research should attempt to investigate the role of communicative practices in other types of online (and off-line) communities.

Finally, through this study, it is hoped that consumer researchers will realize that there are many opportunities to leverage the unique assets of member-generated content, and that future research can advance our theoretical and practical understanding of this rich consumption arena. Also, we hope that future inquiries on how communities can be improved in order to serve and protect consumers' interests more efficiently will provide guidance for practitioners who create and manage these online communities. Understanding the detailed dynamics of a community's interactions can provide directions for better facilitation of consumer-to-consumer interactions in the community. Moreover, this analysis may provide marketers with tools to make the experience in an online community more compelling for members, and in particular realize the diversity and importance of the community communication genres. This is critical because different types of communication within social groups can have very distinct and often unintended impacts on a group's sense of satisfaction. It is assumed that the more satisfactory the experience, the less likely consumers are to switch to a competing community, and the more likely they are to spend more time on each visit. Also, marketers will be able to leverage member-generated content by becoming better listeners of consumers' issues. Through this increased understanding, we hope that companies become better relational partners and also have a more effective and open role in the conversations that take place in online communities. Through this increased consumer focus, online community hosts can foster a greater sense of belongingness and promote the salience of a given community by designing community features that incorporate and facilitate relevant psychological connections and provide social meanings which are appropriate to the consumer-to-consumer interactions within the community.

ACKNOWLEDGMENTS

This chapter was based on a doctoral dissertation written by the first author under the supervision of the second author. The authors wish to acknowledge the help and contribution from the other members of the doctoral committee: Professors George Psathas and Patrick J. Kaufmann (both from Boston University) and Professor Douglas B. Holt (Oxford University), as well as the advice from Esther González Martinez.

REFERENCES

Algesheimer, R., Dholakia, U. M., & Herrmann, A. (2005). The social influence of brand community: Evidence from European car clubs. *Journal of Marketing*, *69*(3), 19–34.

Arnould, E., & Price, L. L. (1993). River magic: Extraordinary experience and the extended service encounter. *Journal of Consumer Research*, *20*(June), 24–45.
Arnould, E., & Thompson, C. J. (2005). Consumer culture theory (CCT): Twenty years of research. *Journal of Consumer Research*, *31*(March), 868–882.
Arrow, H., McGrath, J. E., & Berdahl, J. L. (2000). *Small groups as complex systems: Formation, coordination, development, and adaptation*. Thousand Oaks, California: Sage Publications Inc..
Bagozzi, R. P. (2000). On the concept of intentional social action in consumer behavior. *Journal of Consumer Research*, *27*(3), 388–396.
Bales, R. F. (1951). *Interaction process analysis: A method for the study of small groups*. Cambridge: Addison-Wesley Press, Inc..
Bales, R. F. (1970). *Personality and interpersonal behavior*. New York: Holt, Rinehart and Winston.
Belk, R. W. (1988). Possessions and the extended self. *Journal of Consumer Research*, *15*(September), 139–168.
Boase, J., Horrigan, J. B., Wellman, B., & Rainie L. (2006). *The strength of Internet ties*. Washington, DC: Pew Internet & American life project.
Bormann, E. (1996). Symbolic convergence theory and communication in group decision making. In: R. Hirokawa & M. Poole (Eds), *Communication and group decision making*, (2nd ed.) (pp. 81–113). Thousand Oaks, CA: Sage.
Brent, S. (1984). *Psychological and social structures*. Hillsdale, NJ: Lawrence Erlbaum Associates.
Briley, D. A., & Wyer, R. S. (2002). The effects of group membership on the avoidance of negative outcomes: Implications for social and consumer decisions. *Journal of Consumer Research*, *29*(December), 400–415.
Callan, V. J. (1993). Individual and organizational strategies for coping with organizational change. *Work and Stress*, *7*(1), 63–75.
Cissna, K. (1984). Phases of group development. *Small Group Behavior*, *15*(1), 3–32.
Cova, B., & Cova, V. (2002). Tribal marketing – The tribalization of society and its impact on the conduct of marketing. *European Journal of Marketing*, *36*(5–6), 596–620.
Erickson, T. (1997). Social interaction on the net: Virtual community as participatory genre. In: R. H. Sprague Jr. (Ed.), *The proceedings of the thirtieth annual Hawaii international conference on systems sciences* (Vol. 6, pp. 13–21). CA: IEEE Press.
Erickson, T. (2000). Making sense of computer-mediated communication (CMC): Conversations as genres, CMC systems as genre ecologies. In: J. F. Nunamaker Jr. & R. H. Sprague Jr. (Eds.), *The proceedings of the thirty-third Hawaii international conference on systems science* (Vol. 2, pp., 1–10). CA: IEEE Press.
Festinger, L., Schachter, S., & Back, K. (1950). *Social pressures in informal groups: A study of human factors in housing*. Stanford, CA: Stanford University Press.
Green, H. (2006). It takes a web village: Private online communities are providing special insights into customers' needs. *Business Week*, Sep 4.
Hagel, J., III, & Armstrong, A. G. (1997). *Net gains: Expanding markets through virtual communities*. Boston: Harvard Business School Press.
Healy, D. (1996). Cyberspace and place: The Internet as middle landscape on the electronic frontier. In: D. Porter (Ed.), *Internet culture* (pp. 55–68). New York: Routledge Inc..
Hennig-Thurau, T., Gwinner, K. P., Walsh, G., & Gremler, D. D. (2004). Electronic word-of-mouth via consumers-opinion platforms: What motivates consumers to articulate themselves on the Internet? *Journal of Interactive Marketing*, *18*, 38–52.

Hogg, M. A., & Abrams, D. (1998). *Social identifications: A social psychology of intergroup relations and group processes*. London and New York: Routledge.

Katz, D. (1960). The functional approach to the study of attitudes. *Public Opinion Quarterly*, *24*, 163–204.

Keyton, J. (1999). Relational communication in groups. In: L. R. Frey, D. S. Gouran & M. S. Poole (Eds), *The handbook of group communication theory and research* (pp. 192–222). Thousand Oaks, CA: Sage.

Kozinets, R. V. (1999). E-tribalized marketing?: The strategic implications of virtual communities on consumption. *European Management Journal*, *17*(3), 252–264.

Kozinets, R. V. (2002). The field behind the screen: Using netnography for marketing research in online communities. *Journal of Marketing Research*, *39*(1), 61–73.

Lacoursiere, R. B. (1980). *The life cycle of groups: Group development stage theory*. NY: Human Science Press.

Lerman, K., & Austin, M. (2006). What companies gain from listening: The effect of community membership on member's attitudes and behavior in relation to the sponsoring company, White Paper, Communispace Corporation

Levinger, G. (1983). Development and change. In: H. H. Kelley, E. Berscheid, A. Christensen, J. Harvey, T. Huston, G. Levinger, E. McClintock, L. A. Peplau & D. Peterson (Eds), *Close relationships* (pp. 315–359). New York: Freeman.

Madden, K. M. (2006). Internet penetration and impact. *Pew Internet & American life project*, Washington, DC.

Maffesoli, M. (1996). *The time of the tribes: The decline of individualism in mass society*. London: Sage Publications.

McAlexander, J. H., Schouten, J. W., & Koenig, H. (2002). Building brand community. *Journal of Marketing*, *66*(1), 38–54.

Miller, C. R. (1984). Genre as social action. *Quarterly Journal of Speech*, 70, 151–167; A. Freedman, & P. Medway (Eds), *Genre and the new rhetoric* (pp. 23–42). London: Taylor and Francis.

Miller, C. R. (1994). Rhetorical community: The cultural basis of genre. In: A. Freedman & P. Medway (Eds), *Genre and the new rhetoric* (pp. 67–78). London: Taylor and Francis.

Muniz, A. M., & O'Guinn, T. C. (2001). Brand community. *Journal of Consumer Research*, *27*(March), 412–432.

Muniz, A. M., & Schau, H. J. (2005). Religiosity in the abandoned Apple Newton Brand community. *Journal of Consumer Research*, *31*(4, March), 737–747.

Orlikowski, W. J., & Yates, J. (1994). Genre repertoire: The structuring of communicative practices in organizations. *Administrative Science Quarterly*, *39*, 541–574.

Poole, M. S. (1981). Decision development in small groups I: A comparison of two models. *Communication Monographs*, *48*, 1–24.

Reicher, S. D. (1987). Crowd behavior as social action. In: J. C. Turner, M. A. Hogg, P. J. Oaks, S. D. Reicher & M. Wetherell (Eds), *Rediscovering the social group: A self-categorization theory* (pp. 171–202). Oxford and New York: Blackwell.

Rheingold, H. (1993). *The virtual community: Homesteading on the electronic frontier*. Reading, MA: Addison-Wesley.

Sacks, H. (1992). In: G. Jefferson (Ed.), *Lectures on conversation*. Oxford: Basil Blackwell.

Sahlstein, E., & Duck, S. W. (2001). How to do things with relationships. In: H. Giles & W. Robinson (Eds), *Handbook of language and social behavior* (pp. 371–382). Chichester, UK: Wiley.

Scanzoni, J. (1979). Social exchange and behavioral interdependence. In: R. L. Burgess & T. L. Huston (Eds), *Social exchange in developing relationships* (pp. 61–98). New York: Academic Press.

Socha, T. (1999). Communication in family units: Studying the first 'group'. In: L. Frey, D. Gouran & M. Poole (Eds), *The handbook of group communication theory and research* (pp. 475–492). Thousand Oaks: Sage.

Spears, R., Lea, M., & Postmes, T. (2000). Social psychological theories of computer-mediated communication: Social pain or social gain? In: P. Robinson & H. Giles (Eds), *The handbook of language and social psychology*. Chichester: Wiley.

Sproull, L., & Kiesler, S. (1991). *Connections: New ways of working in the networked organization*. Cambridge, MA: MIT Press.

Tajfel, H., & Turner, J. C. (1986). The social identity theory of intergroup behavior. In: S. Worchel & W. G. Austin (Eds), *Psychology of intergroup relations*. Chicago: Nelson-Hall.

Tepper, M. (1996). Usenet communities and the cultural politics of information. In: D. Porter (Ed.), *Internet culture* (pp. 39–54). New York: Routledge Inc.

Thompson, C. J., & Haytko, D. L. (1997). Speaking of fashion: Consumers' uses of fashion discourses and the appropriation of countervailing cultural meanings. *Journal of Consumer Research*, *24*(June), 15–42.

Thompson, C. J., & Tambyah, S. K. (1999). Trying to be cosmopolitan. *Journal of Consumer Research*, *26*(December), 214–241.

Tuckman, B. (1965). Developmental sequence in small groups. *Psychological Bulletin*, *63*, 384–399.

Turner, J. C. (1982). Towards a cognitive redefinition of the social group. In: H. Tajfel (Ed.), *Social identity and intergroup relations*. Cambridge: Cambridge University Press.

Turner, J. C. (1987). A self-categorisation theory. In: J. C. Turner, M. A. Hogg, P. J. Oakes, S. D. Reicher & M. S. Wetherell (Eds), *Rediscovering the social group: A self-categorization theory*. Oxford: Blackwell.

Wellman, B. (2001). Physical place and cyberspace: The rise of personalized networks. *International Urban and Regional Research*, *25*, 227–252.

Wilbur, S. P. (1996). An archaeology of cyberspaces: Virtuality, community, identity. In: D. Porter (Ed.), *Internet culture* (pp. 5–22). New York: Routledge Inc..

HOW BRAND COLLECTING SHAPES CONSUMERS' BRAND MEANINGS

Cele C. Otnes and Eliana N. Shapiro

ABSTRACT

This paper explores the phenomenon of collecting a plethora of memorabilia associated with a specific brand – in this case, the British Royal Family (BRF) brand. We explore the lifeworld of "Elizabeth," an über-collector of BRF memorabilia, and describe how her collection can be interpreted as extensions of three separate identities – Collector, Business Owner, and Media Expert. Within these three identities, Elizabeth expressed different emergent roles to the various social networks within whom she interacted (e.g., as a collector, she often acted as "Rescuer," taking in others' BRF collections in order to preserve them). We illuminate these different roles and offer suggestions for future research.

INTRODUCTION

The symbolic interactionist approach to consumers' relationships with brands argues that the shaping of meaning is a multifaceted process actively

Consumer Culture Theory
Research in Consumer Behavior, Volume 11, 401–419

ISSN: 0885-2111/doi:10.1016/S0885-2111(06)11016-9

negotiated by marketers and consumers within individual and social environments (Ligas & Cotte, 1999). More and more, consumers are recognized as vital components in meaning construction. For example, Muniz and O'Guinn (2001) and Schouten and McAlexander (1995) suggest consumer communities perform vital marketing functions in support of favored brands. Likewise, advocacy literature uncovers the notable impact consumer advocates have on brand growth and development, particularly through word-of-mouth action (e.g., Fullerton, 2005; Reichheld, 2003). This paper presents a case study to further explore the nature of a single consumer's influence on a brand, within the context of "brand collecting," which has become increasingly recognized as a salient means for consumers to build and maintain relationships with brands (e.g., Baker, Motley, & Henderson, 2004; Motley, Henderson, & Baker, 2003). Building upon Slater's (2001) analysis of "brand collectors," or consumers who amass memorabilia, merchandise, or collectibles associated with a particular brand, we address the following research question: What roles can a brand collector play in creating and modifying brand meaning for other consumers?

Our specific brand of interest is the British Royal Family (BRF) brand. Recently, Balmer, Greyser, and Urde (2004) have argued that rather than be relegated solely to the political sphere, the institution of the monarchy is conceptually comparable to a corporate brand. Specifically, the authors argue that the BRF can provide consumers with a respected and shared symbol of nationalism, help them engage in national "togetherness" and foster a sense of identity based on shared history, culture, and traditions.

Conceptualizing the monarchy as a brand seems especially appropriate for the British monarchy, which no longer retains real political power, but does shape a number of lucrative industries that foster the consumption of goods, services, and experiences related to the BRF within and outside the UK. We discuss the array of roles one specific collector of BRF memorabilia assumes, and how she shapes brand meaning for other consumers when expressing these roles. By doing so, we illuminate consumers' ability to nurture the construction of brand meaning on individual and social levels.

METHODS

This case study emerged from a larger data set that examines consumption of the BRF brand. "Elizabeth" (name disguised) emerged as a key informant throughout the data collection process. The first author interacted with Elizabeth in London, England during May 2004, April 2005, and July–August 2005. The 2004 and summer 2005 sessions yielded three in-depth interviews, which were audiotaped and transcribed, generating 131 pages of text. The seven-day April 2005 immersion was timed to coincide with a major historical event in the BRF: the marriage of Prince Charles and Camilla Parker-Bowles. This occasion presented the author a prime opportunity to conduct participant observation while a guest at Elizabeth's Bed and Breakfast (B&B). Specifically, the first author talked at length with Elizabeth every day, immersed herself in the BRF collection, accompanied her on BRF-related expeditions, spoke with members of Elizabeth's social network, and participated in a celebration commemorating the wedding ceremony. Although preliminary questions were compiled and used, the interviewer largely allowed informants to direct the flow of interactions. The first author generated 78 pages of notes from these interactions. Throughout the immersions, several different types of consumers and service providers were interviewed. These included key members of Elizabeth's social network such as BRF fans who attended her parties, friends who did not necessarily get to know Elizabeth through her collection but who assisted her in BRF-related events, retailers at stores selling BRF commemoratives, newspaper editors, and museum curators. The data set contains over 100 photographs as well. The appendix includes a detailed description of how Elizabeth's collecting began, and the nature of her collection.

The first and second author read the data many times, and were struck by the ways Elizabeth enabled other consumers to experience the BRF brand. We initially observed that others sought to interact with one or more of three emergent identities that together comprised Elizabeth's persona as a brand collector – Collector, Business Owner, and Media Expert. Related to this observation was the emergent finding that when occupying each aspect of these personas, Elizabeth tended to occupy and express different social roles when interacting with consumers. Social roles are identifiable and consistent sets of behaviors that emerge through interaction with others (Mead, 1934). Given that such distinct social roles emerged from our text and were not applied post hoc to the data, we employed Mead's role theory as our interpretation unfolded as a theoretical framework to enable us to analyze the specific ways Elizabeth shaped consumers' experiences with the BRF brand. We unpack these roles more thoroughly after providing a short biography of Elizabeth.

CASE STUDY: ELIZABETH

Elizabeth is a divorced, 60 year old retiree with four children and four grandchildren. Proud of her moniker as "Britain's Loyalist Royalist" (or the most fervent devotee of the BRF), she possesses what is probably the largest private collection of BRF memorabilia in the UK, and possibly the world. With over 7,000 pieces, it is insured for £40,000. Her collection began more than 25 years ago when she bought a small glass dish for 2.5 pence at a church jumble sale. Her objects range from traditional plates and mugs to novel oversized champagne bottles used at BRF parties, to actual-size concrete corgis and BRF cardboard cutouts (see Figs. 1 and 2). Her collection of ephemera alone includes hundreds of books, magazines, newspapers, videos, and scrapbooks.

Elizabeth's six-bedroom semi-detached home in a London suburb houses the entire collection, and in recent years she has converted it into a B&B. As her collection grew and grew, it increasingly drew media attention and sparked public interest: "What happened, people would see me on the television and then say, "Could they come and see it on a Saturday afternoon or something?" When they got here, they couldn't get through it all. So, it sort of evolved and they started staying and we would stay up and do quizzes and that sort of thing ...." She regards her home as a "mini-museum," with the collectibles occupying literally almost every nook and cranny, and rooms being renovated and added to support the constant growth. Consequently, Elizabeth has forfeited virtually all private space,

Fig. 1. Elizabeth's Dining Room.

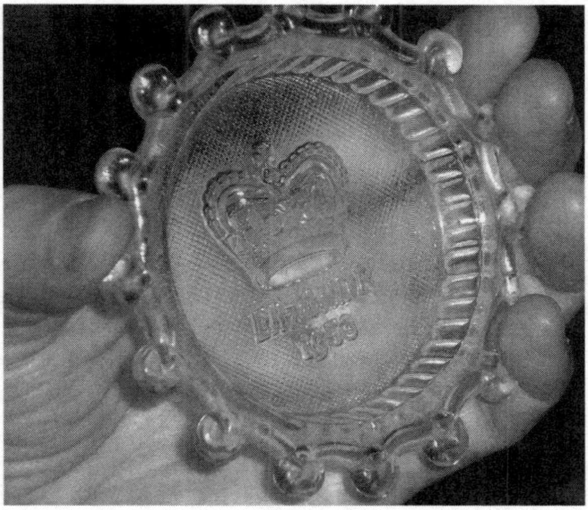

Fig. 2. The 2.5 Pence Dish that Started It All.

allotting herself merely a bedroom as well as "her" chair and a shelf of family photos in the living room. Although her house accommodates five overnight guests, she frequently hosts day visitors, including groups of 50 or more tourists. While guests pay a room fee, others may visit the collection free of charge.

Elizabeth's increased public visibility has paralleled her flourishing collection as the media continuously profile her activities. She is frequently showcased in both national and international media and across an array of outlets, including newspapers, television, books, and radio. Featured stories and appearances also span diverse formats such as documentaries, infotainment programming, morning talk-shows, collecting publications, and tourist guides. Various institutions have borrowed collection pieces to utilize for different purposes. For example, Kensington Palace filled four glass cases with her memorabilia during a recent major exhibit.

Originally conceived as a hobby, Elizabeth's collection has progressively transformed into "almost a way of life." She asserts, "Once it's in your blood, obviously you're hooked. Once you're hooked – it's all over." Her devotion to the collection is evident in her emphatic refusal to sell or dispose of any items and declarations like, "I would scrub floors if I had to" to finance the collection's growth. When asked how the word "happy" pertains to the collection, she replied, "Happy to have my facilities to have my collection. To have the facilities to share with other people." Her primary motive is not to drive profits, but to maximize exposure and share the collection with as many consumers as possible, thus further validating her passion.

FINDINGS

As stated earlier, we conceptualized Elizabeth's persona as a brand collector as containing three separate identities: Collector, Business Owner, and Media Expert. Within each identity, Elizabeth expresses distinct roles that shape consumers' interactions with the BRF brand. We interpret these roles below.

Roles Associated with the Collector Persona

Historian

As an historian, Elizabeth's role primarily entails narrating the BRF's modern history and educating others on aspects of that history. Elizabeth's pieces enable her to strand together the brand history in a creative and tangible manner, with myriad unique objects representing historical moments. Discussing any given piece, she offers narratives about key events in the BRF history. For example, Elizabeth's narrative about Prince Charles and his two marriages is told through reference to myriad Charles and Diana souvenirs, a Charles and Diana divorce plate, Charles and Camilla wedding tea towels, and so on. While discussing the breadth of Elizabeth's memorabilia, a Kensington Palace curator confirms, "The thing that was impressive … you just say any theme and she had things for it. Like 'kirby grips' [bobby pins] that were made for girls to decorate their hair for the Silver Jubilee and a makeup compact that was made for Queen Mary's coronation … you just can't find stuff like that any more." By tangibilizing these events, Elizabeth offers historical accounts of a more vivid or original nature than could any history book or documentary. Notably, she recognizes her duties as a public historian, stating: "I try to get a copy of everything you know, to me, so the people can weigh up whether they like it or whether they don't – because it *is* like a mini-museum."

As an historian, Elizabeth enhances the brand meaning for consumers in a number of ways. Collecting historical objects affords a brand collector extensive knowledge unmatched by the average consumer, or even many brand employees (Slater, 2001). Just as members of a brand community share information and perpetuate the brand's history (Muniz & O'Guinn, 2001), she in turn shares this knowledge and enriches the public's education. Also, with her collection's amassment rendering a "mini-museum," she blurs Belk's (1995) distinction between individual and institutional (i.e., museum) collectors. Typically, institutional collections are perceived as more objective, pedagogically-rooted, and "serious," while individual collections are "playful" and subject to the personal tastes of the owner (Belk, 1995, p. 125). At the same time, the scripted presentations and ubiquitous labels/signage accompanying museum pieces pose a threat of detracting from the collection's authenticity or diverting attention from the objects themselves (Belk, 1995). By actively treating her collection as a museum (and not discriminating against pieces deemed personally unappealing), she fulfills objective, educational aims. At the same time, she provides a more authentic environment that allows visitors to better connect with the pieces, and with the BRF brand itself.

Furthermore, as an historian Elizabeth connects consumers to the brand by personalizing, authenticating, and ritualizing their experiences with historical moments. The term "contagious magic" implies that sacred objects are empowered or fetishized, and the effect of contact with a sacred object continues even after contact has ended (Frazer, 1922). In addition, Belk (1995) observes that rituals associated with collecting (e.g., cleaning items; displaying them in special places) means seemingly ordinary items can become sacred, fulfilling consumers' needs for "something that is transcendent, numinous, or magical ..." (94). In Elizabeth's collection, some pieces may have come into physical contact with, or were in proximity to, BRF members. These include carpet from a hotel on which Princess Diana would have likely walked, or a chair used at Prince Charles' investiture ceremony. Consequentially, and with the assistance of narratives by Elizabeth, consumers might perceive these items as embodying magical or fetishistic properties that allow them to transcend time and space to connect with the brand on a more authentic, tangible level. For example, in discussing the addition of life-size cutouts to her breakfast area, Elizabeth notes, "So all of a sudden, it [the collection] went from plates and cups and mugs, to being more human. It humanized it. Because they became real people in a funny sort of way." Whereas the actual members of the BRF may be inaccessible to consumers, these tangible memorabilia adds a humanizing element that provides a space for consumers to forge a deeper personal connection to the brand, and to the historical moments these pieces represent.

Rescuer

As a rescuer, Elizabeth saves and protects memorabilia once belonging to private owners or public sites. Elizabeth's collection clearly serves as a safe haven for people wishing to preserve BRF brand memorabilia but are unable or unwilling to do so themselves. Sources of rescued items range from those who have moved and no longer have the necessary physical space, to others who find themselves owning objects once belonging to cherished family members. Both acquaintances and strangers actively seek out Elizabeth and ask her to shelter various items: "People track me down. They find me. They're determined they're going to do something with them, you know?" A handful of people have taken considerable measures to ensure their pieces reach Elizabeth's hands. One woman spent two years tracking down Elizabeth, ultimately with the help of the BBC, and asked her to take in 30 scrapbooks made by her deceased mother, stating, "You do remind me of my Mother. And I can't throw them away …" Another woman in Australia who saw Elizabeth on television sent her a tin inherited from her grandmother, explaining, "My Grandma loved this, and I'd like you to have it." In addition to rescuing memorabilia from other consumers, Elizabeth also eagerly tracks down and frequently rescues objects from public venues that might otherwise be discarded or destroyed. Such items range from store window displays to enormous museum-quality pieces from a longstanding public train station exhibit.

As a rescuer, Elizabeth occupies what Belk (1995) judges the extreme positive end of the collector continuum, where collectors are deemed passionately heroic. While some brand collectors employ the collecting-is-saving rationale to justify their excessive consumption habits, others like Elizabeth genuinely believe their mission is to preserve valuable items (Belk, 1995). Elizabeth's role as rescuer further serves a number of functions for other consumers, such as preserving relationships, mollifying guilt, and providing comfort: "I think I'm their conscience … because if they don't know what to do with something, or Grandma's died – if they're not all that interested – then if they pass it on to me, they know it will be looked after. They know it won't be sold." Material objects are conceptualized as extensions of the self, and even after death they retain and represent aspects of their owners' identities (Belk, 1988; Price, Arnould, & Curasi, 2000). By preserving memorabilia, individuals maintain not only their ties to loved ones, but also the deceased's interest in the BRF as expressed through the objects. People who ask Elizabeth to rescue possessions typically wish to preserve an emotional attachment or some aspect of the original owner that they believe the item retains. Thus, discarding valued possessions might symbolize the severing of a relationship or dismantling of a piece of the owner's identity. Thus, Elizabeth acts as a medium to uphold relations and preserve the emotions, memories, or interests associated with the memorabilia. At the same time, she alleviates the guilt that would inevitably accompany improper disposal: "Perhaps they feel while I'm looking after it, they don't have to worry about it." Some even exercise the option of revisiting the items that they send: "they very often come to stay. You see, because if they've got stuff then there's an interest there somewhere ...." As such, Elizabeth enables people to preserve the identities of deceased loved ones and alleviate their guilt over disposing items these loved ones once cherished.

Roles Associated with the Business Owner Persona

Social Facilitator

As a social facilitator, Elizabeth provides a social space in which she shapes interaction between consumers and the BRF brand. Specifically, her B&B allows individuals to wholly immerse themselves in the brand and to surround themselves with other brand loyalists. Discussing the evolution of her business, she recalls how she and visitors stayed up doing BRF quizzes and continues, "[we would] watch [BRF] videos, talk about [Princess Diana] non-stop. Well, talk about *all* the Royals non-stop!" Clearly, Elizabeth invites consumers to share their individual brand interests on a social level with others who can relate and reinforce one another's passions. As mentioned, she frequently entertains large groups of visitors, often tourists from various countries. But her venue allows intimate groups (e.g., local women's clubs) to connect with one another and the brand in a social, personable environment.

In conjunction with modern BRF events, Elizabeth organizes parties and gatherings to celebrate historical occasions. The first author participated in a party commemorating Prince Charles and Camilla's wedding, where close friends and media reporting on Elizabeth's activities met to socialize and watch the marriage proceedings on television. (Not surprisingly, that afternoon Elizabeth also braved the cold to mingle with the crowd in Windsor after the wedding). She also hosted parties for the 50th anniversary of the Queen's Coronation and her Golden Jubilee, which attracted 50 to 60 guests and a number of reporters. She opens the parties to "anyone who's interested in the Royal Family," including close friends, other Royalists in her network, and complete strangers who learn of the celebrations through TV and radio publicity. She draws together consumers sharing a common interest and allows them to celebrate the brand. As such, these attendees also become part of the brand's narrative through actively participating in its history.

Muniz and O'Guinn (2001) argue brand communities are characterized by three traditional markers of community: consciousness of kind, rituals and traditions, and moral responsibility. As a social facilitator, Elizabeth nurtures the first two markers. Consciousness of kind denotes a feeling of connectedness to not only the brand, but also to other brand consumers. Her B&B becomes a communal center where community members can gather, socialize, and relate to one another, subsequently cultivating connections. The enactment of rituals and traditions chiefly involves celebrating the brand history and sharing brand stories (Muniz & O'Guinn, 2001) that Elizabeth encourages through parties and everyday visits. These communities present an array of benefits for the brand, at the center of which is maintaining a core group of loyalists. Consumers also benefit by fulfilling social and psychological needs (e.g., affiliation).

The social nature of the celebrations at her B&B also bolsters consumer–consumer and consumer–brand relationships. Elizabeth's celebrations are comparable to the "brandfests" that McAlexander, Schouten, and Koenig (2002) discuss, because they promote brand usage among current and potential owners, nurture favorable brand impressions, and successfully foster strengthened connections between fellow consumers as well as consumers and the brand. However, because the events discussed in McAlexander et al. (2002) are sponsored and mediated by manufacturers and marketers of the brands, Elizabeth's lack of formal brand ties potentially lends additional benefits for both the brand and participants. Specifically, her celebrations provide positive reputation enhancement at no cost to the brand. For the consumer, the absence of corporate sponsorship and profit-driven motives affords the fests a more genuine character, hence heightening the significance of the relationships developed. In a closely related line of research, Schouten and McAlexander (1995) examine the Harley Davidson subculture of consumption, in which they explore the ways subculture members find meanings in the brand and incorporate the brand into their identity and lifestyle. Much of this meaning construction takes place in organized brand activities with other subculture members. The authors posit that marketers can also exert influence by taking an "active role in socializing new members and cultivating the commitment of current ones" (1995, p. 57). As a social facilitator, Elizabeth offers a space where BRF brand enthusiasts can negotiate brand meaning in relation to their identities, and she works tirelessly on behalf of the brand to welcome new members and strengthen the loyalties of existing ones.

Finally, Elizabeth establishes a social context in which brand meaning can be negotiated and established on a communal level. The symbolic interactionist perspective suggests that marketers attempt to assign specific meaning to a brand, but individual consumers decide what a particular brand means in their lives. However, a social environment containing multiple actors is required in order for the value of a brand to achieve some collectively recognized form of meaning (Ligas & Cotte, 1999). Through facilitating social interaction, Elizabeth encourages this meaning-making process. By nurturing a positive environment that celebrates the brand, she sets the stage for individuals to construct a favorable meaning. Not all social members will accept a construed meaning (Ligas & Cotte, 1999). In fact, currently in the UK, the majority of individuals reject the BRF brand's positive significance, consequentially threatening the brand's survival. Hence, the importance of Elizabeth's role escalates to aid in the construction of complementary meaning and likewise, its sustained existence.

Individual Facilitator

As an individual facilitator, Elizabeth customizes the brand experience and caters to the specialized needs of individual consumers. In particular, the B&B acts as an open outlet that permits consumers to take what they want from it. Elizabeth is attuned to what consumers seek from their visits and strives to best fulfill their varying personal interests. For example, realizing that German women tend to harbor strong sentiments for Princess Diana, she constructs a specific tour that purposefully plays to their emotions. While discussing an upcoming group of German tourists, she notes: "I'm just praying for nice weather so I can put them all out here [in the garden with the "Diana Rose"]. When I play 'Candle in the Wind' on my player, they start crying." She is also quick to fill personal requests that arise. A Parisian woman staying overnight wanted her two young daughters to experience the Charles and Diana wedding. Elizabeth located the video in her vast archive and stayed up until midnight watching it with her guests. Finally, she anticipates interests and tries to construct a personalized environment. For example, although most of her pieces fill the common areas of her house, when guests have an interest in a particular monarch, event, or period, she will fill their bedrooms with relevant objects.

As a flexible and accommodating business owner, Elizabeth hones the ability to develop personalized relationships between the brand and consumer. Although one-on-one relationships with consumers require large investments in money and time, brand community members can perform these duties in favor of the brand (Muniz & O'Guinn, 2001). Elizabeth helps consumers experience the BRF brand on a highly personal level and derive their own specialized meanings from them (Ligas & Cotte, 1999). For example, Elizabeth's guests each possess their own personalized meanings of the BRF brand and therefore carry different agendas for their stays at her B&B. She plays to their special interests and tailors visits to enrich the brand's relevance in their lives, ultimately aiding in the development of the kind of one-on-one brand relationships coveted by marketers. Again, these gestures come at no cost to the brand, yet they garner the benefits accompanying a strengthened relationship, such as brand loyalty. Similarly, consumers profit from the gains offered by a meaningful relationship (e.g., fulfillment of emotional and psychological needs).

Roles Associated with the Media Expert Persona

Opinion Leader

As an opinion leader, Elizabeth's insights regarding current BRF news and events are highly valued and constantly sought out. Slater (2001) notes many brand collectors become experts on the collectibles, and in turn, their opinions are respected by other collectors, the collecting industry, media, and the brand itself. Elizabeth carries this notion one step further through cultivating influential opinions on the brand at large. The combination of collecting and running a business puts Elizabeth on the map as an established brand expert. Indeed, she has become one of the initial sources reporters turn to following the announcement of major BRF news. The morning Princess Diana died, Fox TV was taping at her house by 6:30 a.m. Throughout Charles and Camilla's engagement and wedding, the media regularly reported her views:

> "When [they] announced their engagement, within three hours German television phoned here. But they were followed by Japanese ... I mean the man from Japanese television rang me up from New York! How did he get a hold of me? And Spanish television came twice. And a Spanish magazine, Norwegian, Danish, French ...."

She notes with astonishment that as an individual who lacks any official connections to the brand, she has become a respected source: "And so I'm taking calls. And I've got a lady in Norway who rings, and she wanted to know what I thought (about the engagement) ... Almost as I've got a sort of link with the Royals. And I've got nothing to do with the Royals!" Up until the day of Charles and Camilla's wedding, Elizabeth had several TV crews contacting her, wanting to observe her watching the ceremony and gauge her reaction.

Aside from the media, ordinary people frequently approach Elizabeth seeking her opinion: "Well they see me ... well, I don't know them. They feel they know me. They don't actually know me. But they feel they know me ... But I get people stopping me all the time." Individuals encountering her in everyday life recognize her and then wish to share thoughts, stories, and views. An editor at a major English newspaper recalls after he ran a story on Elizabeth's Charles and Camilla wedding party, "I got lots of letters. A lot of people wanted to be put in contact with her as well. Mostly it was just Royalists fascinated by her stories." The media help make her voice heard and instill respect for her collection, and as a result, she becomes a face familiar to the ordinary consumer and somewhat of a celebrity in her own right.

Research in consumer behavior literature argues that the "key characteristics of opinion leaders are enduring involvement, influence, expertise, and information sharing." Moreover, influence is related not to the status of the leader, but to the "knowledge and expertise ... opinion leaders acquire from being involved with the product" (Venkatraman, 1989, p. 55). Elizabeth certainly demonstrates a deep enduring involvement and pool of brand knowledge, and such expertise allows her to exert influence over others. Moreover, by vocalizing only favorable brand opinions, she potentially induces others to adopt positive views about the BRF as well.

International Ambassador

As an international ambassador, Elizabeth transports the brand across geographic borders as she is featured in a wealth of international media. Interest in Elizabeth's collection and opinions extends well beyond the British region and her media coverage now spans the globe. She comments, "I've had Australian [reporters], German, and I've been on South African TV ... that's when you know you've gone 'round the world.'" Countries frequently mentioned throughout conversations include: Australia, Denmark, France, Germany, Italy, Japan, Norway, South Africa, Spain, and the U.S. As evidenced in her quotes concerning media contacts following Charles and Camilla's engagement, international reporters are among the first requesting her opinion. She also mentions a Japanese tourism book that features her B&B as a worthy tourist destination. Often, brand community members work as "missionaries" to market the brand in outside communities (McAlexander et al., 2002). Elizabeth's international presence grants access to a number of new or unsaturated markets in which she can promote the brand. By default, the BRF's presence is more than predominant in the UK, but she can aid in sustaining its longevity through increasing interest abroad. And not only does she transport the brand into other cultures, but she also contributes to bringing people from abroad into England.

Advocate

Research on brand advocacy notes that affective brand commitment manifests itself beyond mere re-purchase intentions and is often channeled through advocacy, or the willingness to act as a referent on behalf of the brand (Fullerton, 2005). Advocacy is often conceptualized in terms of word-of-mouth behavior or the likelihood of referring the brand to others, and these word-of-mouth intentions are believed to serve as the strongest predictors of brand growth and development (Reichheld, 2003). Elizabeth's role as advocate of the brand consists of two dimensions. First, she relentlessly defends the BRF brand in the face of negative comments, thereby protecting the brand from detractors. She not only exercises great caution to "never say anything anti" about the BRF brand, but also publicly combats attacks on its reputation. She expresses great disdain towards the media's unfavorable treatment:

> "I wish people in this country wouldn't actually keep criticizing the Royal Family. I wish they would stand up and say, 'Look, we're very proud of our Royal Family!' You know, but they don't. They keep carping on them; they write reams of material in the newspapers about this or that ... why don't they leave them alone?"

When in the media spotlight herself, Elizabeth uses the opportunity to vocally guard the brand. She recalls being interviewed by a reporter who suggested distaste for the BRF brand: "I wasn't rude to him, but, you know, I really stood up for them." Although it seems the media sometimes hope to provoke an animated response or prompt her to "rant" in reaction to controversial issues, she maintains her composure and encourages a positive spin, even when privately she might express misgivings about events in the BRF. For example, because Elizabeth is such a fervent admirer of Princess Diana, she was initially very distressed about the marriage of Charles and Camilla. But a few months after their wedding, Elizabeth observed that Charles and Camilla have "got human failings same as the rest of us ... really now, [they] are role models in a way for divorced families who are making second marriages [work]." Community members tend to grant brands greater leeway in the wake of missteps (McAlexander et al., 2002). Similarly, Elizabeth looks past the BRF's mistakes, publicly speaks in their defense, and encourages others to follow her lead. Such reactions are antithetical to typical media responses that strive to keep the brand rooted in controversy. In short, she works to shift the public discourse away from controversy and instead, redirect it to one of pride.

In addition to staunchly defending the brand, as an advocate, Elizabeth also proactively makes favorable comments on behalf of the BRF brand in the hopes of shaping an overall positive image. Throughout conversations and interviews, she recurrently offers admiring comments: "I mean, I think they're the most wonderful family. I never tire of reading about them, I never tire of reading books, or doing my [newspaper] cuttings or whatever, I spend hours on it." As such, Elizabeth publicly paints the BRF in a favorable light, detracting from the scandalous stigma often attached to the brand. Obviously, her widely publicized collection and media activities in and of themselves suggest that the brand is worthy of lifelong devotion.

Notably, as her public presence has increased, Elizabeth's role has also expanded to that of an advocate trusted by those responsible for maintaining the reputation of the BRF brand itself. For example, representatives at Buckingham Palace referred Italian photographers to her: "I thought, 'My God, they're sending them around to me now.' I don't think it was the Queen or anything (laughs), but just to think that, you know, I was taking the weight off of them." She was also featured in a television special titled *Royalty A to Zed* that was produced by Prince Edward's company: "I was under "F," for Fan." Thus, the BRF brand's reliance upon Elizabeth indicates they clearly trust her intentions and abilities to consistently promote the brand.

In summary, in her persona as media expert, Elizabeth certainly generates a positive "buzz" around the brand, thus likely contributing to its health and expansion. Slater (2001, pp. 367–368) also notes that brand collectors effectively "advertise," "market," "increase visibility," and act as "good fodder for the press." Elizabeth accomplishes all of the above through her advocacy efforts, thus performing promotional work on behalf of the BRF brand.

DISCUSSION

This paper unpacks the various roles a brand collector can express when shaping brand meaning for other consumers. At the core of Elizabeth's persona lies a deep-seated brand loyalty that she expresses through collecting BRF brand memorabilia. From this principal collector identity, two new identities – business owner and media expert – emerged. Each identity increasingly builds on the other. For example, her collecting activities augment her ability as a business owner, as she becomes a tourist destination in her own right. Likewise, her subsequent authority as a business owner enables her to bolster her credibility such that she can confidently don a new identity of media expert. From these three identities, she expresses distinct roles that allow her to affect consumers' relationships with the BRF brand. As an historian and rescuer, Elizabeth mainly enhances consumers' brand knowledge and preserves individuals' relationships to one another and the brand. As a social and individual facilitator, she strengthens the brand community, cultivates consumer–consumer relationships, enables the social construction of BRF brand meaning, and personalizes consumer–brand relationships. Finally, as an opinion leader, international ambassador, and advocate, Elizabeth consistently acts as a favorable, influential voice for the BRF, heightens international consumers' interest, shields the brand from criticism, and provides the BRF with general, positive promotion.

As we have indicated in our analysis, a number of our findings validate Slater's (2001) analysis of brand collectors, support research on collecting behavior in general (Belk, 1995) and enhance brand community research (McAlexander et al., 2002; Muniz & O'Guinn, 2001). However, this case also expands upon previous research by honing in on the ways a specific individual can shape the brand experience of other consumers. Simply put, Elizabeth's case offers evidence that consumers can wield more power than is traditionally recognized by marketing scholars, in terms of affecting consumers' relationships with a brand, and with the visibility of the brand in the marketplace itself. Whether evoking personal brand-affiliated memories, preserving relationships expressed through brand objects, or creating a setting to enable consumers to experience emotion-laden brand interactions, Elizabeth guides people to recognize the distinct meanings the BRF brand holds for them. By both personalizing the meaning of the brand in consumers' lives, and offering social venues for interaction with the brand, meaning can be both personally understood and collectively negotiated – and the relationships between the individual consumer, other consumers in the social network, and the focal brand can be augmented. Thus, it is clear that meaning construction and relationship marketing are not solely the purview of marketers, but can in fact be strongly influenced by an empowered and visible consumer.

Furthermore, the data demonstrate how an ordinary consumer can evolve into what may be considered a major, valued brand ambassador. Although not formally linked to the BRF brand, Elizabeth voluntarily and single-handedly markets the brand on a broad level. Whether in an individual, social, or mass-mediated context, she carries a clear mission to sustain and enhance the brand's meaning in others' lives, and to also perpetually portray a positive image of the BRF brand. Increasingly, brands actively and purposefully employ "consumer ambassadors" to endorse a product within their communities or social spheres in exchange for goods or monetary compensation. However, few studies measure their effectiveness or examine the roles that unfold among these ambassadors. This case presents preliminary evidence of the functions an unofficial ambassador can fulfill, and their potential usefulness to the brand. That is, while promoting and heightening a brand's visibility, an ambassador can also help shape meaning and nurture relationships. In a similar vein, this work builds upon advocacy research that has thus far chiefly concentrated on the likelihood of referring the brand to others (e.g., Fullerton, 2005; Reichheld, 2003). Elizabeth essentially advocates brand usage by hosting celebrations and allowing consumers to learn about and immerse themselves in the BRF brand. Beyond simple brand referrals, she performs advocacy duties within several of her roles (e.g., offering favorable opinions and publicly speaking in the brand's defense). The combined effect of such activities aids in dismantling the brand's controversial reputation and deflecting consumers away from negative narratives associated with the brand and again assists the meaning-making and relationship-building processes.

Ultimately, a brand's longevity relies largely on its ability to remain relevant in consumers' lives. Our case study reveals not only the roles a brand collector can express, but also the ways these roles enable this collector to enrich a brand's relevance and meaning for others. Such power should not go unnoticed by consumer researchers. Rather, the ways empowered consumers can shape others' brand experiences – whether these consumers are paid by brands or whether they are passionately adhering to their own agendas with respect to cherished brands – is an area ripe for future research.

ACKNOWLEDGMENTS

The authors gratefully acknowledge the comments provided by attendees of the Consumer Culture Theory conference, as well as the editors of this volume and the two reviewers, in preparing the final version of this chapter. The authors thank the key informant and members of her social network for enabling us to study the lifeworld of collecting British Royal Family memorabilia.

REFERENCES

Baker, S. M., Motley, C., & Henderson, G. (2004). From despicable to collectible: The evolution of collective memories for and the value of black advertising memorabilia. *Journal of Advertising*, *33*(Fall), 37–50.

Balmer, J. M. T., Greyser, S. A., & Urde, M. (2004). Monarchies as Corporate Brands. Harvard Business School Working Papers Series, No. 05-002.

Belk, R. W. (1988). Possessions and the extended self. *Journal of Consumer Research*, *15*(September), 139–168.

Belk, R. W. (1995). *Collecting in a consumer society*. New York: Routledge.

Frazer, J. G. (1922). *The golden bough: A study in magic and religion*. New York: Macmillan Co.

Fullerton, G. (2005). The impact of brand commitment on loyalty to retail service brands. *Canadian Journal of Administrative Sciences*, *22*, 97–110.

Ligas, M., & Cotte, J. (1999). The process of negotiating brand meaning: A symbolic interactionist perspective. *Advances in Consumer Research*, *26*, 609–614.

McAlexander, J. H., Schouten, J. W., & Koenig, H. F. (2002). Building brand community. *Journal of Marketing*, *66*(January), 38–54.

Mead, G. H. (1934). *Mind, self, and society*. Chicago: University of Chicago Press.

Motley, C., Henderson, G., & Baker, S. M. (2003). Exploring collective memories associated with African-American Memorabilia: The good, the bad, and the ugly. *Journal of Advertising*, *32*(Spring), 47–58.

Muniz, A. M., & O'Guinn, T. C. (2001). Brand community. *Journal of Consumer Research*, *27*(March), 412–432.

Price, L. L., Arnould, E. J., & Curasi, C. F. (2000). Older Americans' disposition of special possessions. *Journal of Consumer Research*, *27*(September), 179–201.

Reichheld, F. F. (2003). The one number you need to grow. *Harvard Business Review*, *81*(December), 46–54.

Schouten, J. W., & McAlexander, J. H. (1995). Subcultures of consumption: An ethnography of the new bikers. *Journal of Consumer Research*, *22*(June), 43–61.

Slater, J. S. (2001). Collecting brand loyalty: A comparative analysis of how Coca-Cola and Hallmark use collecting behavior to enhance brand loyalty. *Advances in Consumer Research*, *28*, 362–369.

Venkatraman, M. P. (1989). Opinion leaders, adopters, and communicative adopters: A role analysis. *Psychology and Marketing*, *6*, 51–68.

APPENDIX: DESCRIPTION OF ELIZABETH'S COLLECTION

Elizabeth began collecting BRF memorabilia more than 25 years ago due to a serendipitous twist of fate. Although she has been a passionate admirer of the BRF her entire life (an interest she claims to have inherited from her parents), she did not express her devotion through collectibles. She purchased a small glass dish for 2.5 pence (depicted in Fig. 2) that she found aesthetically pleasing, and it triggered subsequent purchases. Her collection really "heated up" when she purchased numerous types of memorabilia marketed for the wedding of Prince Charles and Princess Diana in 1981. A number of her pieces are purchased in traditional retail settings and others are found at various markets and fairs. As Elizabeth has transformed into an avid collector, her acquisition techniques have grown more inventive and resourceful. For example, she will ask businesses such as bookstores for window displays after they are done utilizing them. She also relies on an extensive network of people who bring her foreign or rare items, such as a flight attendant who will bring her relevant publications from around the world and a toastmaster in charge of the Royal toast ceremonies at Buckingham Palace. Somewhat computer-phobic, she has yet to join the community of collectors who buy and sell online via Ebay or other auction sites.

In some respects, the collection's display mirrors that of a museum. She designates rooms and sectioned areas to particular monarchs, events, or time periods. But rather than enclosing these items in glass cases or behind ropes, all items are placed out in the open. The displays lack any labels or signage as Elizabeth orally narrates each item's origins and significance. Furthermore, Elizabeth has built and renovated rooms to support the collection's growth and frequently adds various shelving units and other display areas to better showcase the items. Nearly all items are positioned to be seen, except for a number of magazines and newspapers, which are stacked in various areas. Ceramics (plates, mugs, etc.), paintings, photographs, and posters line the walls ceiling to floor. Displays occupy literally every space so that individuals are immersed in the collection at all times. Nearly all items reside in the common areas of the house except for a few pieces in the bedrooms. The only personal spots Elizabeth assigns to herself include her bedroom, a single chair, and a shelf of family photographs. Maintenance is a continuous process and Elizabeth devotes much time to general upkeep and cleaning and enlists the help of her friend Daniel to aid her in the process.

Some of the collection's pieces were designed for the distinct purpose of collecting (i.e., commemorative ceramics used to mark various occasions). Others served a functional use at some point (i.e., a desk from where Diana attended school as a child). Other pieces were actually commissioned by Elizabeth (e.g., stained glass artwork representing Kensington Palace). While a number of pieces fit a more traditional mold, others are more original and even kitschy in nature. Examples include: Charles and Camilla scarecrows, a doll representing Prince William in his christening apparel, house slippers designed to look like Queen Elizabeth and Phillip lying in bed, a Fergie weight-loss book, and multiple concrete corgis (the Queen's favorite dog).

LIVING FOR "ETHICS": RESPONSIBLE CONSUMPTION IN EVERYDAY LIFE

Nil Ozcaglar-Toulouse

ABSTRACT

This research studies how current social and environmental concerns about consumption are reviving the topic of meaning in consumption practices. In a postmodern world characterized by symbolism in consumption and a global "crisis of meanings", ethical and responsible consumption behaviors are studied through their contribution to identity construction. A responsible consumption typology based on the meanings given by the narrators is suggested; it distinguishes the acts of "moral conformity" from the deep critical postures, the latter of which derive either from political essence or a desire for liberation from the consumption "system".

INTRODUCTION

In his "The Consequences of Modernity", Giddens (1990) undertakes an account of what the 20th century brought about: the Cold War, Hiroshima, Nazism, genocides, a growing gap between the rich and the poor, Chernobyl, etc. Humanity, having reached a certain disillusion with the

Consumer Culture Theory
Research in Consumer Behavior, Volume 11, 421–436

ISSN: 0885-2111/doi:10.1016/S0885-2111(06)11017-0

idea of progress, and developed a degree of shared mistrust, moves towards a "risk society" (Beck, 1992) characterized by growing difficulties in getting satisfaction in spite of a growing number of available goods and services, by undeniable evidence of environmental deterioration, and by increasing risks to future generations resulting from scarce natural resources, troubling economic instabilities and the persistence of famines and wars.

To this state of ill-being, one should add the contemporary profusion of signs and images, the growing hyper-communication in numerous societies (enabled by the diffusion of new information and communication technologies) and the end of the meta-narratives with which previous generations had identified themselves. These elements contribute to a superabundance of symbols that disables individuals from grasping the meanings of their lives. As a consequence, contemporary individualism poses above all, the question of meaning. The difficulty experienced by individuals in trying to give a meaning to their existence not only brings about "ontological insecurity" (Giddens, 1990), but also raises the question of the status of being in postmodern society. Consumption is a central facet of contemporary life. It can be seen as an active element in the construction of the meaning of life[1] (Belk, 1988).

Indeed, such diverse acts as deflating the tires of 4×4 s, daubing advertising posters, abandoning mountains of packaging in supermarkets, organizing rallies like Burning Man or Buy Nothing Day, or selling activities of fair-trade, ethical or organic products, represent conscious or unconscious ways of expressing and calling for ethics in consumption (Smith, 1990).

Moreover, the notion of responsibility in consumption is not restricted to the consumer's individual responsibility, but also indicates those of the producer and seller as being organic elements of the consumption chain. So to speak, this means to be able to respond to and justify one's acts (the words "respond" and "responsibility" have the same Latin origin "respondere"). In the consequentiality perspective (Barnett, Cafaro, & Newholm, 2005), the responsible consumer is seen as someone who reflects upon the consequences – in time and in space – of his/her acts related to consumption.

Responsible consumption has been studied in literature from different aspects and corresponds to a larger concept; however, the proposed definitions of the concept appear to be rather unsatisfactory, because they usually focus on a particular aspect of consumption (reflecting therefore varied approaches of researchers). In this context, I find it necessary to propose my own definition of responsible consumption as being

> the set of voluntary acts, situated in the sphere of consumption, achieved from the awareness of consequences judged as negatives of consumption on the outside world to

> oneself, these consequences raising therefore not from the functionality of the purchases nor from immediate personal interest (Ozcaglar-Toulouse, 2005, p. 52).

Most products, services, and firms are, in the perception of a responsible consumer, carriers of contradictory signs; the consumer is in a situation of conflict between the personal pleasure derived from the act of consuming and the suffering caused by its negative impact on the environment, on producers' living conditions, on social inequalities, etc. To solve this internal conflict, s/he can develop three strategies that I propose to study in the framework of Hirschmanian vocabulary (1970).

With the strategy of *exit*, the responsible consumer decides to renounce the act of consumption and the pleasure associated with it, with the objective of avoiding a possible complicity with its consequences. The strategy of *loyalty* allows a person to perform an act of consumption while trying to minimize its negative consequences and/or attempting to extract a maximum of benefit from the product/service. In this case, the consumer remains faithful to consumption and focuses on his/her ability to improve its functioning. Finally, the responsible consumer, with the strategy of *voice*, appears to feel no obligation to solve the conflict carried by his/her act of consumption, but rather, attempts to transform the whole system in an external way.

Many issues related to ethical consumerism have been studied along various dimensions (Belk, Devinney, & Eckhardt, 2005). Thus, *loyalty* (purchasing ethical products, recycling, etc.) and *voice* (boycott, etc.) are analyzed within numerous studies in literature (Anderson & Cunningham, 1972; Dickson, 2001; Friedman, 1996; Kinnear, Taylor, & Ahmed, 1974; Robert-Kréziak, 1998; Roberts, 1996; Sen & Bhattacharya, 2001; Sen, Gurhan-Canli, & Morwitz, 2001; Shaw, 2000; Smith, 1990; Webster, 1975; etc.). Such research has essentially focused on the study of the determinants of purchase decision-making and consumer segments. In addition, *exit* behaviors (for example, anti-consumption behavior or voluntary simplicity) seem to attract limited attention in market research (Leonard-Barton, 1981; Shaw & Newholm, 2002). Hence, it seems that the studies ignore that the same consumer can make use of all these three strategies depending on products and contexts, and can therefore display attitudes of simultaneous contradictory strategies.

Current research has focused on understanding the meaning and the strategies of responsible consumption and on how an individual makes the choices in his/her everyday life and consumption practices. Indeed, it seems difficult for a responsible consumer to develop and maintain a coherent sense of being in a consuming society. The consuming society has gradually turned out to be a constraint, a moral or an institution imposed upon the consumer (Baudrillard, 1970). In this societal model, individuals seem to be or feel uniformed. The search for uniqueness and "self" becomes difficult because of the anguish and awkwardness related to the risk of marginality (Fromm, 1976). In the consuming society, consumers express their extended self through their purchases (Belk, 1988). Paradoxically, some individuals criticize the consuming society through their consumption by using the moral beliefs that originate from their socio-political affiliations and from their ideal self.

By studying responsible consumption, this research tries to learn about the dynamics between identity construction and responsible consumption strategies and therefore to clarify the proximity of individual identity and consumption systems as well as the importance of consumption to identity.

METHOD

The relationship between responsible consumption and identity construction in everyday life, based on the propensity of people to talk about the social experiences in their daily lives and the significance of their consumption, suggests that a hermeneutic approach would be appropriate here (Arnold & Fischer, 1994; Thompson, 1997; Thompson, Pollio, &, Locander, 1994). In general, consumers are not in the habit of reflecting upon the meaning that they give to their consumption or the link that exists between their consuming acts and their life's trajectory. The narration method is used to provoke the consumers into speaking not only about their consumption, but also to enable them to assess their own consumption habits.

Authors of studies based on narratives have recommended that each narrator should be met several times to amplify the wealth of information (Atkinson, 2002; Thompson, 1997). Respecting this methodological advice, every narrator was interviewed three times. My aim was to elicit a range of responsible consumption practices rather than to attain a statistically representative sample. Forty interviews – corresponding to a total of 45 h with 14 consumers were transcribed on more than 500 pages and supplemented with various notes taken during and after the interviews. The data for this study was collected over a five-month period in 2005.

In order to increase the richness of the methodology and to reinforce data understanding (Yin, 1994), the stories of the narrators were supplemented with data from several other sources: immersion in the phenomenon studied, factual data on the narrators, "sneaky" information such as lifestyle indicators captured during the interviews that took place in their homes (Newholm, 1999), etc. During the interviews, questions covered the interviewees' life histories, their responsible consuming practices, their feelings about society, etc. I iteratively analyzed my data through continuous back and forth between individual transcripts and the emerging understanding of the entire set of textual data (Thompson, 1997).

The deliberation that I undertook with the experts was to pursue and present full detailed case studies. The two cases reported here were selected because they are representative of the whole analysis and provide good illustrations of major findings.

CASE STUDIES

Sabine

Sabine's Life Narrative

Sabine (33) is married, with two children, and works as an engineer on water issues in underdeveloped countries. As such, her interest in responsible behavior has a professional dimension as well as an ethical implication.

Except for the few years that she spent in Tunisia and in the south of France, Sabine has always lived in Paris. After a difficult and "not very happy childhood" marked by her mother's psychiatric problems and the divorce of her parents, Sabine became anorexic. She was able get better only after giving birth to her children. At present, she works on the uses of water. She thrives in her professional life since it perfectly meets two of her fundamental priorities: a good relationship with her colleagues and an ability to bestow a "meaning" to her work.

It was not easy to meet with Sabine simply because, during this period, she dedicated a lot of time to her children as well as to her professional and volunteer activities. The first interview took place at her home, where she was alone with the interviewer. Throughout the interview, Sabine was strongly involved in the telling of her story without requiring much probing. The first interview ended when Sabine's children returned home. This situation allowed the observation of a slight modification in her speech: Sabine became more anxious and worried. The other interviews took place at the researcher's home, in consideration of planning issues and of Sabine's own request; the presence of the children was also an important factor to take into account when scheduling the meetings. There was a meaningful moment when Sabine said that she had felt slightly depressed following the first interview:

> It is myself, I want to say in my head, but I don't know, because it is true that we spoke about fundamental things, about big questions, then maybe they moved something in myself. I don't really know why. I had a small stroke of the blues. But don't be worried, I finally ended the evening well!

This comment reveals how deeply involved Sabine felt in the construction of her narration (and also of her identity) and how profoundly and personally meaningful her consumption choices are.

Important Events in Sabine's Life

When speaking about her childhood, Sabine refers especially to her relation with her grandmother who incited a sort of hypersensitivity to "issues of injustice". The most prominent event in her narrative on consumption choices was her stay in Tunisia: it was a period of becoming aware of the stakes in the world. Back in France, she began to correspond with a Roman Catholic priest, living in Marseille, who would later baptize her. Sabine also speaks of her "civic" commitments in the community. She created an association within her apartment complex with the objective of establishing links among neighbors and to sensitize them to responsible consumption.

Sabine speaks for a long time about her involvement in an "Adbusters" event and about her actions against multinational retailers. The retail sales season is in general a difficult period for Sabine. She is "very proud to have known how to resist sales": she said to herself that "this year, I won't be taken for a ride by the (biannual retail) sales".

In a way, the majority of events that Sabine has detailed illustrate the complexity of her life given her consumption choices and her feeling of injustice about the economic "system".

Who Am I?

Sabine introduces herself at first as someone who "looks for consistency in her life". For Sabine, if she stops behaving as she does today, she will become "crazy" because she won't be "consistent with herself" anymore. She needs "to give a sense" to her life: that is her reason to live.

She also describes herself as an activist. Her membership in ATTAC[2] supports the financing of a counter-lobby. Whenever she sees an opportunity for "a small action", she "tries to take it". She also reflects this image to others: she is always seen as an activist in her job. Sabine is convinced that she acts as a role model to others.

She often oscillates between "pessimistic and optimistic feelings" about society and between "an ethical and environmental side and a practical side". In spite of her activism, she acknowledges having some "contradictions" since she is not and doesn't want to be an "extremist" or "stubborn" even though she notes that her behavior represents "normality" for her. Nonetheless, she is not so sure about the normality since her behavior begins to be exclusive and she is more and more preoccupied with it: "I am anguished", she says. She feels almost physically disgusted about consumption. She summarizes it by saying that "it nearly reaches a pathological attitude".

No matter how complex her consumption decisions are, Sabine is "proud of herself"; an expression that she uses rather often, but proud of what? Proud of having found a second-hand Barbie doll for her daughter and thus limiting her expense on such a "sweat shop product", of having managed to avoid being tight-fisted during an ethical purchase, of belonging to a "slightly marginal community" and especially proud of "resisting to a dominant model of easiness and comfort".

Why and How Consuming Responsibly?

Sabine grants a great deal of importance to "consistency" and she doesn't hesitate to comment on it on each occasion. It is the first argument of her narrative. She seeks consistency between discourse and action. Otherwise, she thinks that she would become either schizophrenic or crazy.

This quest for consistency has also been accompanied by a permanent effort to give sense to her life. She considers this concern as "a real condition to be able to give a sense to [her] life and thus not to be obsessed by possession". That is not only individual progress, but also a collective one. That means being "ethical". She considers her religious commitment as contributing to her quest for an ethical lifestyle and for personal evolution.

For this purpose, she adopts different strategies. First, her activism extends towards the volunteer social and political engagements that are not necessarily restricted merely by issues of consumption. She has adhered to ATTAC and to the Green Political Party. For Sabine, over-consumption has a particularly negative connotation. That is why she uses the strategy of extending the lifecycle of products. She recycles and buys regularly in second-hand markets in order to prolong the life of products.

Another strategy consists of buying mostly fair-trade or organic products and in privileging alternative or short shopping circuits or unknown brands. According to Sabine, nature also has the right to be respected. Being fair towards the environment is fundamental. In this sense, organic products are also fair-trade products, because they are fairer to nature as well as to the producers.

In spite of these different strategies, Sabine tries to avoid becoming an "extremist". At the same time, she considers herself as being a strong role model to others. Sabine is often in a flip-flop state between her ideal and its social representation. This is perhaps why she swings often between a particular pessimism and a resolute optimism. But the pessimism seems to be more distinct: "... That is not making a revolution, nor changing the world, because I am almost convinced that it is not possible". She hopes nevertheless that she will have an impact. Her pessimism originates particularly from a certain fatalism caused by the difficulty "to induce the authorities to act ... to transform the contemporary way of how things function, to influence decisions ...".

Sabine feels increasingly preoccupied with these issues to such an extent that it risks becoming "obsessive" or "psychiatric". But she cannot simply avoid it. It is difficult for her "to pay money for non-ethical purchases", "to profit from sales in retail", or "to buy a Barbie".

Sabine ascribes several explanations to her responsible consumption. Firstly, her grandmother's influence; secondly, her studies and what she had read, and finally, her stay in Tunisia where she discovered the cycle of agricultural production and the link between production and consumption. This last event represents a veritable turning point for Sabine.

But her responsible consumption is also related to her self-image: she believes that she "participate[s] in a generalized movement of consumption", she "influence[s] her entourage" and she "especially affirm[s] an identity different from others".

> Lately I asked of myself: if everybody were like me, would I then be otherwise? Is it just the pleasure of being different and to do things otherwise? I don't know!
>
> "But for as much I think that I would be delighted that everybody made the effort, but then, I would always find something else to go further".

Finally, Sabine likes to resist the dominant model of ease and comfort; a resistance that brings her a certain sense of pride: her ethical purchases should be also interpreted as acts of resistance; acts that seem to be the expression of her desire to control her life and the world that surrounds her. The fact that Sabine suffered from anorexia should be recalled. This eating disorder is interpreted by some specialists as a form of riposte to the ideal, socialized, body model promoted by society. It is internalized by the individual as self-control: to control herself and her body (Thompson & Hirschman, 1995; Peñaloza & Price, 1993).

Martin

Martin's Life Narrative

Martin is 23 years old. His father died of leukemia when Martin was 4 years old. As an educator, his father was involved in social action. For Martin, "that [professional and associative experience] influenced [his] activist attitude and [his] sensitivity vis-à-vis social problems". His mother remarried "a very kind person" whom he really loves. His stepfather is a "businessman, a senior executive". His mother is a psychotherapist working in palliative care. Martin describes his family's political stance as follows:

> On the political level, my mother is a woman of the left, my father was a man of the extreme left and my stepfather describes himself as in the center.

Martin, during the first interview, speaks for a long time about his childhood. Until the age of seven, he lived in the Parisian "ghetto". Then he moved to a rich district of Paris. He summarizes this situation as the passage from an economically disadvantaged neighborhood to a very bourgeois environment. For Martin, it is the source of his "bourgeois education mixed with popular surroundings, or with his wish to orient towards economically disadvantaged surroundings". "A mixture of the kinds", he summarizes. He explains later:

> When I was teenager, I was more inclined towards the idea of Gaullism … rightist ideas with a slight social blend. But, then I became intelligent … Quickly, I adopted leftist arguments, between the Socialist Party and the Green Party.

Later he enrolled in a business school outside Paris. After his master's degree in social economics, he started working as a consultant. During the first interview, he talked about his desire to change jobs:

> I don't feel at ease when working for a capitalistic system for which the aim is the maximization of shareholders' profit. I prefer the idea of getting paid to work, and not for capital. In most cases, capital is often an injustice. A simple proof of this phenomenon is myself!

This is why he expresses his wish to work in an "altruistic structure with a collective interest".

Who Am I?

Martin firstly describes himself through his political ideal: he is a leftist and he is progressively more present in "activist structures as well as in leftist and humanist environments aiming at the progress of humanity!" He then admits that he doesn't practice what he preaches; although he loves political debates:

> I am a guy who talks a lot but doesn't act necessarily as much as he talks … I am not necessarily disciplined enough with myself when compared to my discourses …. Yes, I can do much better. I talk a lot and act little.

He buys ethical products as much as he can. He is very sensitive to boycott. He is not an "extremist of the civic consumption": he is more inclined to responsible consumption if it is not more complicated than a classic purchase. He justifies his position on the one hand by the fact that he satiates his need of a "clear conscience" through his volunteer activities and on the other hand by the fact that he does not liken himself to a "Mother Teresa" type. He also defines himself as a "protester", but not "very extremist nor very aggressive nor systematic".

When he speaks about his actual purchases, Martin's discourse flirts a lot with "pride". For example he is proud to "show [his] bank card that supports the Medecins du Monde[3]" association, to "give a good self-image", to say that "[his] purchase allows three kids to attend school". Responsible purchases seem to participate fully in the construction of Martin's (personal and social) identity that he judges valorizing and flattering:

> In fact, it is extremely valorizing; it is arrogant. [Responsible consumption] flatters your ego. And I am very proud of myself, of my everyday purchasing acts. Maybe it's too much!

He says that even if he is proud of his consuming style, he does not know precisely why. After several probes, three possible explanations are apparent. First of all, he says that he is egotistical and for example, buying fair-trade products gives him on a personal level, "a superb image of himself": "I'm proud of this image that I give myself". He then believes that this self-image that is attained through responsible consumption would also be a sort of reflection of his father:

> I want to see myself as an altruist, activist a little, even sometimes slightly provocative etc. etc. It is the image that I want to give to myself … I think it is mainly influenced by my father's death, a wish to stretch towards my father's life … trying to be exactly how my family describes his character, what he created ….

Finally, he becomes a protagonist in others' lives; he would like to influence them:

> I have the role of a salesman … a salesman. Simply, I also have a sense of pedagogy; I explain why others should also be responsible consumers.

Why and How Consuming Responsibly?

Martin's narrative is organized in a binary logic between two big groups of arguments: visionary and practical. Firstly, he refers to his appeal for "civic consumption" as an adoption of simultaneously both a political and social vision of consumption on a conceptual level, and an egoistic satisfaction on a personal level. Secondly, he speaks of his day-to-day practices and explains why he cannot behave totally consistently.

About the practical dimension, he summarizes repeatedly: "I speak a lot but I act little", showing that his appeal for responsible consumption essentially remains theoretical. He nonetheless continues to prefer consuming fair-trade products simply because he doesn't mind spending a little more on an "ethical plus-value", and considers these products as a relatively simple means of acting positively upon the environment and of "remedying the problem of justice in the world". Conscious that he is not an "extremist", he does not fully develop this reasoning. He recognizes that even though he speaks about remedying the system, he looks first and foremost after his own well-being in consumption. Having actually set the quest for comfort as his main priority, he does not subsequently display a lot of effort. He considers therefore that there is still room for progress before reaching his ideal of being a responsible consumer.

When he evokes, on a more theoretical level, his appeals for responsible consumption, Martin shows that he has already reflected upon the issue and developed a more political analysis and vision: he sees consumption as an important and politically strong act leading to change in the world and to his becoming an activist. Martin distinguishes activism from protest. Activism is more associated to Martin's interior world. It is therefore "selfish behavior", because his activism is bound to a search for self-image valorization. While behaving as an activist to "save people's lives and to improve the well-being of humanity" Martin recognizes that he tries to valorize himself and that he enjoys feeling pride from his acts. By the same token, he tries to recover the activist image of his father. For Martin, protest is essentially related to the outside world: responsible consumption such as protest allows him to "materialize his ideas", to "concretize his discourse". Martin believes in the power of consumption as a means of controlling the economy. In the case of fair-trade, Martin uses it as a strategy to recover the link between production and consumption and to redefine the economy in more social terms.

Finally, Martin uses activism and protest at the same time, with the objective of influencing others. During each interview, the gap between his discourse and his arguments and his real consumption practices grew evident. Yet, in the last interview, three months after the first meeting, Martin announced that he had resigned from his job and had started working for a non-profit firm in the social economics field. This professional change can be interpreted as an effort to narrow the observed gap or as a sign of radicalization.

DISCUSSION

The Centrality of Events in Responsible Consumption

Each of the two narrators, in their narratives, grants an important place to the description of "founding" events (crisis in the professional life, moving to a new home, societal events, domestic crises, travels, etc.) that s/he considers as the origin of their inclination towards responsible consumption practices. These practices bring about an important transformation of their consumption experience. Later on, these responsible consumption practices enabled them, more extensively, to vitalize and reinforce a modification of their life trajectory and to start adopting (or enhancing) a more global new identity. This process then triggers new, and now deliberate, ruptures in life. This observation illustrates the strength of the symbolic nature of responsible consumption and its capacity to act as cement in a personal reconstruction after a rupture, and/or as an impulse for new ruptures in life.

Responsible Consumption as a Life Project

The analysis of narratives illustrates the way consumers make sense of the events in their lives, especially of the responsible consumption experience. Responsible consumption is seen as an "ongoing project" (it means that there is a personal evaluation process which never ends). Both Sabine and Martin's narratives as well as the other narratives not presented in this paper reveal that these consumers can improve, and often want to improve their consumption practices (in a more responsible way!).

Punctual and unexpected events (not provoked intentionally by the consumer) are frequently at the origin of both their awareness and the actions they undertake in the beginning. The process of adopting a new identity, thanks to responsible consumption, is like a "march of life": individuals have to assure the permanence and continuity because this new identity (and the perception of self that comes along with it) would be threatened if the process were suddenly interrupted. This "march of life" could become necessary to reorganize everyday life, with a sense of perpetual evolution (professional changes, a new job, membership in a political party, a sabbatical year in southern countries, etc.).

Some Binary Opposition About the Perception of Consumption

The way the narrators talk about their lives as well as their consumption practices and the development from plot to resolution, provide information about different actors. Narrators position these actors into two groups in binary opposition. The first group consists of those from whom the narrators differ: retailers, mass agricultural producers, the state, other consumers "obsessed with consumption". The second group represents those with whom narrators feel a similarity or proximity: smaller agricultural producers (e.g., in the south of France), responsible consumers, future generations, etc.

This binary opposition reveals the general consumption strategy of the narrators. The consequences of responsible consumption are valorized positively: the risks related to the actors of "similarity" are transferred to the actors of "differentiation". The consequences of mass consumption are perceived negatively: the generated risks of mass consumption are greater among the actors of "similarity" than among the actors of "differentiation". Consumption choices seem to be guided by a desire to minimize the negative consequences for "similarities" and to maximize them for "differences".

Towards a Theory of the Critical Consumption

In summary, the different stories told by these consumers highlight some similarities in their severe critiques of consumption and the consuming society: they feel oppressed by the economic system that they criticize for its "tyrannical nature".

Even if some similarities exist among all narrators, the nature and the aims of responsible consumption can be divided into two groups. The narrators do not share the same position on the way they should act: it is essentially on this dimension that I can distinguish their approaches and the way they articulate their responsible consumption practices within their everyday lifestyles. These two groups represent the dominant position founded upon responsible consumption. It does not mean that they are necessarily exclusive. An individual can shift from one to the other or can find him/herself in these two groups on different occasions.

The first group is composed of people that usually want to get out of the "system" of consumption, which they consider as imposed upon them. For them, responsible consumption represents an act of liberation. Narrators in this group argue that there are too many incentives to consume and that people are deprived of the freedom to think about the consequences of their acts. Consumption is a cultural system that imposes identities as well as alienations. Developing his/her proper "system of consumption" represents breaking free from this system. In this sense, it is an act of resistance, experienced both as simple (by buying less and consuming better) and complicated (because it requires a permanent arbitration) act.

The second group is characterized by a common will to use consumption in order to change the world. For this group, responsible consumption is a political act. From the perspective of their critics in the actual consumer society, this group exhibits similarities with the first group. However consumers who identify with this group do not interpret their position in the same way. For these narrators, an existence based only on the ability to consume leads to over- and "bad" consumption. But they believe that it is due to a social norm that should be modified. They seem to consider their individualities as a means of political critique. Besides, they claim to belong to a group of consumers who militate for and influence society.

The main difference between these two groups of people comes from the identities they present (a strong personal identity for the "act of liberation" group and a strong social identity for the "political critique" group). Apart from these two types of expressed identities, two of the narrators interviewed seemed not to belong to either of the two groups. Instead, they expressed responsible consumption as an act of "moral conformity", thus with a minor identity dimension. This research has led us to draw a typology of responsible consumption according to the sense given to it by the narrators: it distinguishes between acts of "moral conformity" and "critical acts", themselves divided between the acts of political essence and acts with a liberating aim.

The goal of this research has been to better understand responsible consumption, particularly through the meaning consumers give to their personal practices. It has also focused on the link between meaning and identity construction for these responsible consumers. The article shows that the responsible consumers who were interviewed in this study construct their lives around multiple realities and strategies, thus reminding us of the Consumer Culture Theory (Arnould & Thompson, 2005) in highlighting the nature of the ethical dilemmas lived by responsible consumers; these dilemmas differ according to their identity construction and the ways they criticize the consuming society. In this context, this study aims to bring a contribution to the identification of new frontiers within Consumer Culture Theory.

NOTES

1. By considering the role of consumption in providing meaning in life ... (Belk, 1988, p. 160).
2. Association for the Taxation of Financial Transactions for the Aid of Citizens.
3. Doctors of the world.

ACKNOWLEDGMENTS

The author would like to express her gratitude to Russell W. Belk for his advice, to Marie-Hélène Fosse-Gomez, Deirdre Shaw and Marie Taillard for commenting on the preliminary versions of this text.

REFERENCES

Anderson, W. T., Jr., & Cunningham, W. H. (1972). The socially conscious consumer. *Journal of Marketing*, *36*(July), 23–31.

Arnold, S., & Fischer, E. (1994). Hermeneutics and consumer research. *Journal of Consumer Research*, *21*(June), 55–70.

Arnould, E. J., & Thompson, C. J. (2005). Consumer Culture Theory (CCT): Twenty years of research. *Journal of Consumer Research*, *31*(March), 868–882.

Atkinson, R. (2002). The life story interview. In: J. F. Gubrium & J. A. Holstein (Eds), *Handbook of interview research: Context & method* (pp. 121–140). USA: Sage Publication.

Barnett, C., Cafaro, P., & Newholm, T. (2005). Philosophy and ethical consumption. In: R. Harrison, T. Newholm & D. Shaw (Eds), *The ethical consumer* (pp. 11–24). UK: Sage Publications.

Baudrillard, J. (1970). *La Société de Consommation*. Paris Denoël.

Beck, U. (1992). *Risk society: Towards a new modernity*. London: Sage.

Belk, R. W. (1988). Possessions and the extended self. *Journal of Consumer Research*, *15*(September), 139–168.

Belk, R. W., Devinney, T., & Eckhardt, G. (2005). Consumer ethics across cultures. *Consumption, Markets and Culture*, *8*(September), 275–289.

Dickson, M. A. (2001). Utility of no sweat labels for apparel consumers: Profiling label users and predicting their purchases. *Journal of Consumer Affairs*, *35*(June), 96–119.

Friedman, M. (1996). A positive approach to organized consumer action: The "Buycott" as an alternative to the boycott. *Journal of Consumer Policy*, *19*(December), 439–451.

Fromm, E. (1976). *To have or to be?* NY: Harper & Row Publishers.

Giddens, A. (1990). *The consequences of modernity*. Stanford: Stanford University Press.

Hirschman, A. O. (1970). *Exit, voice and loyalty: Response to decline in firms, organisations, and states*. Cambridge/Massachusetts: Harvard University Press.

Kinnear, T. C., Taylor, J. C., & Ahmed, S. A. (1974). Ecologically concerned consumers: Who are they? *Journal of Marketing*, *38*(April), 20–24.

Leonard-Barton, D. (1981). Voluntary simplicity lifestyles and energy conservation. *Journal of Consumer Research*, *8*(December), 243–252.

Newholm, T. (1999). *Understanding the ethical consumer: Employing a frame of bounded rationality*. Doctoral Thesis, Open University, UK.

Ozcaglar-Toulouse, N. (2005). *Apport du Concept d'Identité à la Compréhension du Comportement du Consommateur Responsable : une Application à la Consommation des Produits issus du Commerce Equitable*, Doctoral Thesis, Université de Lille 2, France.

Peñaloza, L., & Price, L. L. (1993). Consumer resistance: A conceptual overview. In: L. McAlister & M. L. Rothschild (Eds), *Advances in consumer research*, (Vol. 20, pp. 123–128). Provo, Utah: Association for Consumer Research.

Roberts, J. A. (1996). Will the real socially responsible consumer please step forward? *Business Horizons*, *39*(January/February), 79–83.

Robert-Kréziak, D. (1998). *Les Motivations de la Consommation Verte : une Approche par les Chaînages Cognitifs*, Doctoral Thesis, Ecole Supérieure des Affaires de Grenoble, France.

Sen, S., & Bhattacharya, C. B. (2001). Does doing good always lead to doing better? Consumer reactions to corporate social responsibility. *Journal of Marketing Research*, *38*(May), 225–243.

Sen, S., Gurhan-Canli, Z., & Morwitz, V. G. (2001). Withholding consumption: A social dilemma perspective on consumer boycotts. *Journal of Consumer Research*, *28*(December), 399–417.

Shaw, D. (2000). *Consumed by ethics? A model building approach to ethical consumer decision-making*. Doctoral thesis, Glasgow Caledonian University, UK.

Shaw, D., & Newholm, T. (2002). Voluntary simplicity and the ethics of consumption. *Psychology & Marketing*, *19*(February), 167–185.

Smith, N. C. (1990). *Morality and the market: Consumer pressure for corporate accountability*. London and New York: Routledge.

Thompson, C. J. (1997). Interpreting consumers: A hermeneutical framework for deriving marketing insights from the texts of consumers' consumption stories. *Journal of Marketing Research*, *34*(November), 438–456.

Thompson, C. J., & Hirschman, E. C. (1995). Understanding the socialized body: A post-structuralist analysis of consumers' self-conceptions, body image, and self-care practices. *Journal of Consumer Research*, *22*(September), 139–153.

Thompson, C. J., Pollio, H. R., & Locander, W. B. (1994). The spoken and unspoken: A hermeneutic approach to understanding the cultural viewpoints that underlie consumers' expressed meanings. *Journal of Consumer Research*, *21*(December), 432–452.

Webster, F. E., Jr. (1975). Determining the characteristics of the socially conscious consumer. *Journal of Consumer Research*, *2*(December), 188–196.

Yin, R. K. (1994). *Case study research: Design and methods* (2nd ed.). Thousand Oaks, CA: Sage.

POETRY

YOU ARE GETTING SLEEPY

you wish to become more aware
you watch the news
you are getting sleepy
    very, very sleepy
sleepy pill seductions…

you see the Lunesta butterfly cartoon
    and you are getting sleepy
floating back to your cartoon childhood
you watch a little news
sandwiched between the drug ads
sandwich!

blood to stomach… cartoon to brain…
aware of the news
the politician is…
very, very sleepy

you dream Ambien dreams
    drowsy dreams of
    unaware
trademarked winds
    the storm has…
    no survivors were…
sleepy dopey couchy potatoey
    grouchy

you are…
dreaming Tinkerbell butterflies
    floating in the violence
drive-by butterflies
    sleepy in your stomach
warding off the day

warding off the night
like news of nothing

you feel…
very sleepy
no rest for the living dead
      wary of your weary

Dormatil, Restoril,
Melloril, whooperwill,
the night-fix
      Peter Panned

eye prod
urge to yawn
sleep to dawn
dimming down
tv pill…

you are getting…
electro-chemical brain rinsed
      all wired tapped
      sleepy anxiety
      of wish-world fantasia

perchance to…
      buy the drug
      sleep on it
awakening
      very, very sleepy
drugged with unaware

take me
O Lunecstatic Ambulance
      alleviate Bolivia
      obliviate Namibia
      enumerate amphibia
when sleep is twinned to death.

Eugene Halton

SFO

Signs on the baggage carts say "Welcome
to San Francisco," but this is not
San Francisco.
At the table next to mine a woman
with rust-colored hair and baggy pants
rummages in her purse then lights
a cigarette, which she angles
toward the mirrored ceiling.
There I believe she verifies
her presence in this place.

The chair I have taken urges me
to settle, to round my lower back.
Whether by design or by the mode
of countless other travelers
that have slouched here before me,
it steers me to intimacy
with wood-grained Formica
and dust gathering on silk camellias.
I tend my senses in a whiskey glass
and let my thoughts go elsewhere.

They choose to follow this woman
who waits my table with black
hair and big, orbiting hips.
They accompany her to a house,
white with an open porch,
where she lives with her mother,
her children, and a sister,
sixteen and full of fire.
In a room with floral wallpaper,
doilies, and a crucifix

she sheds her tight skirt
for the forgiving folds of a robe.
Then she counts her tips.

I project the blond girl in the corner
to a faux Tudor on a cul-de-sac.
She is twenty-two and drives a BMW.
No.
Place her instead on a gravel drive
walking toward a barn.
Savor the crunching sound of her footsteps.

The bartender wears a "Santa's helper" hat,
and his laughter lands heavily on the bar.
I imagine him on the way home stopping
for drinks at a bar where another man pours.
At home in his flat there are dishes in the sink.
His lover, having found only
the energy to bathe and shave his face,
enters a painful sleep.

A flight attendant strides by with luggage in tow.
Her African cheekbones
cut through the air like a prism.
Mentally I undress her and gasp
at the fluid pride of muscle and bone.
A sign by the exit says "Happy Landings."
My thoughts fly home.
The images are palpable, heavy, familiar.
I gather my bags and coat
and fish in my pocket for a tip.

John Schouten

PHILOSOPHER'S THWART BAG

Imagine
Mainstream
Consumer research,
A boulder dumped along a glacial lake,
Cloaked in lichens, fouled by forest fauna,
Immovable, enduring and immense.
Now conjure up interpretive research,
A blue spruce rooted on that awesome rock,
Inexorably fracturing its perch,
A sentinel condemned to leave its post.
Assume the field of marketing research,
The lake that laps the stone and laves the tree,
Coaxing rock to crack and spruce to topple,
Its mirrored face a cue for loons to laugh.
The weathered boulder cracks along its crown,
The evergreen surrenders to the wind,
The lake receives the conifer and shards.
The splash is heard by no one everywhere.
I've seen the tableaux play from my canoe
Three days before I reach the mindful space
Where theory ends and measurement suspends,
And all is
dammed
By beavers,
Panned
By mink.

John Sherry

"ON THE CIRCLE OF CONSUMPTION..."

George M. Zinkhan

University of Georgia

PRODUCTION:

"of human bondage, an hour before daylight ..."

at one with the earth, the simple farmer's life – undeniably
uncertain, never-ending, irrepressible, ceaseless, oppressive,
under the unswerving influence of our father's father's father's
father ...

Behold the postmodern, urban farmer, bound to the soil,
in servitude, as are all serfs, planters & animal tenders
throughout the long, dusty history of human struggles & experience

Amsterdam

July 2006

ACQUISITION

"turns of the wheel"

In the 19th century, monks would gather in the wide
hall to worship their God, exhibiting
humility, piety, penance, and other earthly virtues

In the 20th century, following a precipitous
decline in the number of active monks,
the monastery closes its doors

In the 21st century, the same space
is filled up with bright-faced, business students,
eager to acquire – to learn the ways & wiles of post-modern commerce:

communications, blogging, brand extensions, spam
strategies, physhing, insider trading, brand equity, survival of the fittest,
relationship marketing, corporate espionage, day trading, & naïve
psychology

spokes groan, and the wheel
lurches, turning round
again

University of Maastricht, The Netherlands

June 2006

CONSUMPTION:

"… who were boys"

Three brothers who were boys together
wrestling on the lawn with balls
trying to forget that they are forty and beyond

huffing and puffing
erupting into an ice cream fight
with chocolate and vanilla mixed
melting on their balding heads and
rolling down their graying beards

The young children of three brothers who were boys together
stare and wonder:
"What's got into them?"

Sparks, MD

July 1991

DISPOSAL

(Voluntary):

"Dead Rat Tomorrow"

"Son, get the shovel.
There's a dead rat stinking in the backyard."

"Why do we have to now, Dad?
It was out there yesterday.
It'll be there tomorrow."

"Let's go now.
Turn off the TV."

"It's raining, Dad
And the rat is shrinking.
It used to be more of a rat."

"More of a rat?"

"Tomorrow, Dad."

"Tomorrow?"

Houston, TX

October 1989

Involuntary disposal:

"The Old Man and His Garage"

"You might as well get some kerosene
and put that whole garage

To the torch," the old man told his
daughter over breakfast.

Later that afternoon the old man
looked out his bathroom window

To see sixty-five years of accumulated
papers and memories

Blowing here and there across the yard
and out into the street.

"What the hell do you think you're
doing?"

Shouted the old man to his daughter,
cleaning out the garage.

Detroit, Michigan

April 1988